AMERICA
AS A
WORLD
POWER

Other Books by the Author

Empire on the Pacific: A Study in American Continental Expansion (1955, 1983).
The New Isolationism: A Study in Politics and Foreign Policy Since 1950 (1956).
Cold War Diplomacy: American Foreign Policy, 1945–1975 (1962, 1977).
A History of the United States, 2 vols. (1970). With Gilbert C. Fite and Philip L. White.
A History of the American People (1970, 1975). With Gilbert C. Fite and Philip L. White.
Recent United States History (1972). With Gilbert C. Fite.
The Age of Global Power: The United States Since 1939 (1979). American Republic Series.

Books Edited

The Enduring Lincoln (1959).
Politics and the Crisis of 1860 (1961).
An Uncertain Tradition: American Secretaries of State in the Twentieth Century (1961).
The Cold War: A Conflict of Ideology and Power (1963, 1976).
Ideas and Diplomacy: Readings in the Intellectual Tradition of American Foreign Policy (1964).
Manifest Destiny (1968).
Nationalism and Communism in Asia: The American Response (1977).
Freedom in America: A 200-Year Perspective (1977).
American Diplomatic History to 1900 (1978). Goldentree Bibliographies in American History.
Traditions and Values: American Diplomacy, 1776–1865 (1984).
Traditions and Values: American Diplomacy, 1865–1945 (1984).

AMERICA AS A WORLD POWER

A Realist Appraisal from Wilson to Reagan

Essays by
Norman A. Graebner

 Scholarly Resources Inc.
Wilmington, Delaware

First published 1984
Second printing 1986
Printed and bound in the United States of America

Scholarly Resources Inc.
104 Greenhill Avenue
Wilmington, Delaware 19805

Library of Congress Cataloging in Publication Data

Graebner, Norman A.
  America as a world power.

  Includes index.
  1. United States—Foreign relations—20th century—
Addresses, essays, lectures. I. Title.
E744.G684 1984   327.73   84–10706
ISBN 0–8420–2230–9
ISBN 0–8420–2232–5 (pbk.)

Contents

Foreword

NORMAN A. GRAEBNER was born in Kingman, Kansas, on October 19, 1915. Upon graduation from Washington High School, Milwaukee, Wisconsin, he pursued his post-high school education at Milwaukee State Teachers College (now the University of Wisconsin–Milwaukee), from which he graduated in 1939. His studies continued at the University of Oklahoma where he received his master's degree in 1940. After teaching for two years, one in a small Oklahoma high school and the other at Oklahoma College for Women, he entered the U.S. Army. His active service included fourteen months as a lieutenant in the Pacific Theater, initially in the Philippines and then in Japan for the first ten months of the occupation. In Yokohama he established Japan's first school for American soldiers, and for that accomplishment General Robert Eichelberger, Eighth Army Commander, awarded him a special citation. Returning home in the summer of 1946, he taught another year at Oklahoma College for Women.

Entering the University of Chicago in 1947, he studied primarily under the direction of a trio of American historians—Avery Craven, Thomas Hutchinson, and Walter Johnson—and received his Ph.D. in 1949. Having focused on American history, he was exposed only later to the developing theories of Chicago's noted political scientist, Hans J. Morgenthau. Meanwhile, in 1948, he had undertaken his teaching duties at Iowa State College, Ames, where he spent the next eight years, broken only by one year at Stanford University. In 1956 he moved to the University of Illinois as professor of history; there he remained for eleven years, serving that department as chairman in 1961–63. In 1967 the University of Virginia invited him to accept a chair as Edward R. Stettinius, Jr., Professor of Modern American History, and in 1982 he became the Randolph P. Compton Professor of History and Public Affairs at the University of Virginia where he presently teaches.

Throughout his career Professor Graebner has devoted consuming energy to his teaching. Encouraged by the responsiveness of students at Iowa State, he developed special lecturing skills at the outset. At the University of Illinois, as his reputation spread across the campus, his classes grew to such size that both his survey course in American history and his upper division and graduate courses in diplomatic history were moved in order to accommodate the demand for enrollment. Teaching assistants assigned to his classes still remember vividly the dynamism that flowed from the lecturn and the incredible response from the undergraduates. Invariably the last lecture of the semester brought forth a standing ovation from the class. Fifteen years after he left the University of Illinois, Jim Vermette, a former student and now president of that university's Alumni Association, introduced an appeal to the alumni with these words:

> Did you know Norman Graebner?
>
> Lean, dark, and dynamic. His eyes fixed your attention and his fast-moving words fastened your mind to his thoughts. His subjects were American history and international diplomacy, his real love was teaching, and how I and other students appreciated him! He made us see the forces that shaped this country and how it relates to the world in a way that I had never realized.

While he was at Illinois, one of the greatest compliments to Professor Graebner's pedagogic and speaking abilities came from the Speech Department where graduate students were encouraged to attend his diplomacy courses in order to study his lecturing style. As a teacher, his reputation preceded him to the University of Virginia where his classes were large from the beginning.

Further testimony to Norman Graebner's teaching skills rests on the fact that he has received distinguished teaching awards wherever he has been, including the first Outstanding Teacher Award given at the University of Illinois, the Z Society and IMP Society awards, and the Alumni Association Distinguished Professor Award at Virginia. Not only has he been a distinguished lecturer to undergraduate students but also his seminars have been model laboratories for the training of more than thirty graduate students he has guided to receiving their Ph.D. degrees at Illinois and Virginia. Together with his wife Laura, a historian in her own right, Professor Graebner has been both friend and mentor to these men and women who recently established the Norman and Laura Graebner Distinguished Service Award through the Society for Historians of American Foreign Relations. This award will be given for the first time after Professor Graebner's retirement from teaching in 1986.

Norman Graebner has reached one of the widest audiences of any American historian of modern times. He has lectured at some two hundred colleges and universities in the United States, Western Europe, and the Far East. In thirty-eight years of college teaching his under-graduate enrollments have reached approximately 30,000, as his classes in all but seminars have exceeded 250 students since the early 1950s and often have reached 500. His perspectives have gained an even wider audience through his writings on politics and diplomatic history. Since 1951 he has published seven books, eleven edited volumes, and over one hundred articles, essays, and booklets. In 1958–59, and again in 1966, his University of Illinois course in U.S. diplomatic history was broadcast from the classroom to an estimated regular listening audience of 75,000. From 1958 to 1960 he had a weekly radio program over WBBM, Chicago, entitled "Background of the News."

If Professor Graebner's prowess as a teacher recommended him to an expansive lectureship around the world, his many writings on the history of American foreign relations established his reputation as a scholar. Possessing ideas and the ability to communciate them, he has received many special invitations to visit other institutions. He was the Commonwealth Fund Lecturer, University College, London, in 1958; he delivered the Walter Linwood Fleming Lectures at Louisiana State University in 1962; he was a Fulbright Lecturer at the University of Queensland, Brisbane, Australia, in 1963; and served again as a Fulbright Lecturer at the University of Sydney in the summer of 1983. He was the Distinguished Visiting Professor of History, Pennsyl-vania State University, 1975–76, where he directed that university's award-winning bicentennial program, "Freedom: Then, Now, and Tomorrow." He also was selected for the prestigious Harold Vyvyan Harmsworth Professorship of American History at Oxford University, 1978–79. Most recently he was the Pettyjohn Distinguished Lecturer at Washington State University in 1980 and Visiting Professor of His-tory at the U.S. Military Academy, West Point, in 1981–82, for the purpose of directing the special year-long symposium on "The Theory and Practice of National Security, 1945–1960." For this he received the Outstanding Civilian Service Medal from West Point after his return to Virginia.

Among the numerous expressions of esteem that have come to Norman Graebner are several that reflect his stature in the academic community. In 1972 he was elected as one of the earliest presidents of the Society for Historians of American Foreign Relations. Also he was awarded the Litt.D. degree by Albright College in 1976 and the Doctor of Humane Letters degree by the University of Pittsburgh and Val-paraiso University in 1981. That spring the University of Virginia chapter of Phi Beta Kappa made him an honorary member of that fraternity. During the 1981–82 academic year he served as a Phi Beta

Kappa Visiting Scholar, traveling to nine colleges and universities. In 1983 he was elected to membership in the highly respected Massachusetts Historical Society. Professor Graebner has been very active in professional affairs. He has appeared on more than two dozen sessions of the annual meetings of major historical societies and has sat on a number of permanent and ad hoc committees of these societies. He has served as chairman of the Program and Nominating committees as well as a member of the Executive Board of the Organization of American Historians. For a period of six years each, he represented the Organization of American Historians on the Joint Committee on Historians and Archivists and the American Historical Association on the National Archives Advisory Council. He was also a member of the Advisory Committee for American Studies Abroad for almost a decade.

Perhaps more than any other historian in the United States Professor Graebner has expostulated a realist evaluation of American diplomatic history. Having studied political rather than diplomatic history as a graduate student, he entered the study of international affairs largely through the writings of Hans Morgenthau, Walter Lippmann, and George F. Kennan. To further the efforts of these men to analyze the external expertise of the United States in terms of the historical principles of international politics, Graebner extended his intellectual foundations to include the works of such writers on the European state system as Callières, Fénelon, Bolingbroke, Vattel, Metternich, and Clausewitz, as well as this nation's Founding Fathers who sought to embody the best European thought on international affairs in the early foreign policies of the United States.

Through all the years in which he developed his perspective on effective foreign policy, although he has refined and honed his original conceptual framework, Norman Graebner has been consistent in his insistence that a successful foreign policy rests on balancing ends and means, on preserving a clear understanding of the difference between defensible national interests and national ideals, and on the capacity of leaders to perceive the differences between broadly defined personal ambitions for the nation and precisely defined national needs. He also has lived by the rule that effective assessment of the foreign policy process requires evaluation of a broad range of causes for national behavior which transcend the mere accumulation of empirical data, believed by some to make decision making predictable. Behavioralism, at least in its extreme form, he has argued, assigns far too much rationality to the human species. In the introduction to his text, *Ideas and Diplomacy* (Oxford, 1964), Professor Graebner summed up his advice to both practitioners and students of foreign policy:

National greatness is determined as much by wisdom as by power. . . . To employ its power wisely a nation must learn from experience. And that experience, if it is to be helpful (for precise situations seldom recur), must lie in the general concepts of diplomacy, power, national interest, and world society which determined the actual decisions and against which their results must then be measured.

It is within this framework that the material in the subsequent pages should be read and absorbed.

Edward M. Bennett
Richard Dean Burns

Introduction

WHEN THE GUNS fell silent on the western front in November 1918, American power, actual and potential, dominated the European scene. At the Versailles Conference, for the first time in history, an American diplomatist—President Woodrow Wilson—became a major arbiter in the affairs of the world. Historically, nations that dictated a peace carried the responsibility for its preservation. Because power and interests shift through time, the great treaties of history seldom survived the generations that created them. To perpetuate what they had wrought at Versailles, the victorious democracies had no choice but to integrate American power and leadership permanently into European politics. This challenge to national performance had not escaped American scholars and statesmen as they contemplated a proper role for the United States in world affairs. Viewing the world from a pinnacle, they had agreed long before 1914 that the nation's favored position required above all a high degree of international stability, for instability either would cause some possible retrogression in the American position or at least would require a heavy price to maintain the established position. During the war's final months, they averred, the United States, as the world's leading power, could not avoid commitments to preserve the essential elements in the postwar treaty structure.

If Americans could agree on the need of an orderly world, they could not agree on the basic ingredients of the desired stability or the policies that would best assure the United States its favored position. Some looked to the framework of the international order—the traditional balance of power. The institution of the balance of power recognized war both as an evil to be restrained and as an instrument for protecting the essential interests of international society. Unable to effect change peacefully, nations accepted war as the one available means of achieving it. If at times ambitious rulers, in their pursuit of change, revealed little concern for the international equilibrium, they soon faced the preponderant power of those who favored the status quo. Indeed, it was the assured threat of counterviolence that held national ambitions in check and rendered the ultimate costs of unreasonable aggressions prohibitive.[1] Whereas the balance of power had not prevented wars, it had limited their consequences and thereby preserved that order of power which had served the interests of the United States so admirably. For American proponents of the balancing system, the nation would best perpetuate its advantages and maximize world stability by underwriting the international equilibrium, and that largely in conjunction with British policy and power.

Unfortunately, that British power in the Atlantic and elsewhere which had maintained American security throughout the nineteenth century no longer existed. Wielding limited power in a stable Europe and against a fundamentally weak and backward Afro-Asian world, Britain had gained its nineteenth-century military triumphs and its imperial structure in the absence of any direct confrontation with a major power. For that reason it required no more than the rise of Germany to a major position in world affairs to expose the overextension of the British Empire and the British overcommitment to European and world stability. By 1900 it was clear that Britain's responsibilities had outstripped its resources. As Sir Henry Campbell-Bannerman wrote in 1903, "the truth is we cannot provide for a fighting empire, and nothing will give us that power."[2] London had no choice but to compromise its devotion to the nineteenth-century order of power or rely on the strength of other countries to maintain it. In part, Britain found the needed support against Germany in its Triple Entente with France and Russia.

When the British simultaneously attempted to push much of the burden of the status quo onto the United States, they uncovered a remarkable mutuality of interest, for any decline in British authority would confront the American people with the necessity of either contributing heavily to the maintenance of the old order or accepting potentially massive changes in that order. Senator Henry Cabot Lodge recognized this inescapable choice when he declared that "the downfall of the British Empire is something which no rational American could regard as anything but a misfortune to the United States."[3] By 1914 the United States, with British encouragement, had undertaken the task of preserving much of the nineteenth-century order with special

---

[1] For superb evaluations of the balance of power system see Hans J. Morgenthau, *Politics Among Nations* (New York, 1949), pp. 125–66; and Hedley Bull, *The Anarchical Society: A Study of Order in World Politics* (London, 1977), pp. 101–26.

[2] Campbell-Bannerman quoted in Bradford Perkins, *The Great Rapprochement: England and the United States, 1895–1914* (New York, 1968), p. 156.

[3] Lodge to Roosevelt, February 2, 1900, in Henry Cabot Lodge, ed., *Selections from the Correspondence of Theodore Roosevelt and Henry Cabot Lodge* (New York, 1925), 1:446.

commitments to Latin America and the western Pacific, two regions where British interests had simply outrun British capabilities. So preponderant was American power in the Caribbean that it monopolized the use of force in the management of regional affairs and overthrew Caribbean governments with such astonishing ease that the element of coercion was scarcely visible at all.[4] In time, Britain would desert its 1902 alliance with Japan and cast its lot in the Far East completely with the United States. Thus the two leading Western democracies entered the twentieth century as conservative partners in pursuit of the status quo. For many in Washington and London, the twentieth century promised to be the Anglo-American century, stable and secure.[5]

For the country's dominant foreign policy elite, however, it was not an Anglo-American alliance built on power and joined by other status quo nations that would sustain the peace. Rather, the century's new leadership attached its hopes for a stable and improving future to the general acceptance of a more rational behavior among the major governments of the world. Nineteenth-century rationalism had denied the essentially evil nature of society and had anticipated a world free of conflict, oppression, tyranny, and other irrational uses of power. American progress during that century, gained amid limitless opportunities and a minimum of conflict and coercion, substantiated the illusion that force was giving way to consensus in the resolution of human problems. World opinion, the expression of that consensus on the international scene, would soon replace power politics as the major force in affairs among nations. Of all human activity none appeared more irrational and appalling than war. The elimination of war, finally, would solidify the existing international order. This fundamental relationship between peace and the status quo encouraged American leaders to place the nation's interests in world stability on the altar of human reason.

Desiring nothing after 1900 except the perpetuation of their favored position, the American foreign policy elite, amply supported by much of the public, began to think less of precise, tangible interests to be sustained through diplomacy and force and to seek the defense of the nation's special status with appeals to abstract, reasoned objectives

[4]What characterized U.S. involvement in the politics of the Caribbean countries was the almost total absence of resistance to American actions. Nowhere was this more true than in the Nicaraguan revolution of 1909. The nations of Central America were simply too weak and too dependent on the United States to defy the will of the government in Washington.

[5]Roosevelt expressed this view repeatedly. See, for example, Roosevelt to Cecil Spring Rice, March 16, 1901, in Elting E. Morison, ed., *The Letters of Theodore Roosevelt* (Cambridge, MA, 1951), 3:16.

such as peace and peaceful change, order, justice, and self-determination. A world environment in which such purposes emerged triumphant would indeed serve the American interest admirably, for against such bulwarks of stability and the status quo nations could alter very little, if at all, the established order of power, or even the world's territorial arrangements. Peace became the country's primary concern, not because Americans shared any special abhorrence of war but because peace would demonstrate that the world in reality had accepted the territorial and political conditions which then prevailed. Because the nation after the Philippine annexation of 1899 would enter every crisis without asking anything for itself, it could reasonably demand that other nations attach the same sanctity to established treaties and other international arrangements and change them through general agreement alone.

It was logical that the United States, as the world's major satisfied nation, would assume the lead in the twentieth-century advocacy of nonpower devices, such as arbitration and conciliation, as the only legitimate means for settling international disputes. President William Howard Taft emphasized his commitment to peaceful procedures in his inaugural of March 1909: "Our international policy is always to promote peace. . . . We favor every instrumentality, like that of the Hague Tribunal and arbitration treaties made with a view to its use in all international controversies, in order to maintain peace and to avoid war."[6] The Taft administration negotiated sweeping arbitration treaties with Britain and France. For such noted jurists as Taft and Elihu Root, the final guarantee of world peace lay in a world court of such dignity and astuteness that the entire world would have absolute confidence in its judgments. Such an institution, if universally accepted, would guarantee the nation its international advantages without the necessity of war or extensive military preparations.

Those Americans who identified the nation's interests with international stability had thus two policy concepts before them. One would seek to preserve the framework of the international order, employing force if necessary to prevent major changes in the established hierarchy of power while permitting a myriad of minor changes to occur under the assumption that not all change challenged the security or welfare of the United States. The concept of balance was political; it assumed the role of force in affairs among nations. Nowhere did that tradition outlaw war. Its concern was the maintenance of stability at the core

---

[6]Taft's inaugural address, March 4, 1909, in James D. Richardson, ed., *A Compilation of the Messages and Papers of the Presidents* (New York, 1917), 15:7372.

of world politics, not the elimination of international conflict. A balanced order did not prevent war; it only limited the consequences of war. The second approach to international order, one that had no foundation in history, would attempt to prevent all change except that which resulted from mutual agreement. It ruled that peace was indivisible and insisted that affairs among nations should be governed by law, not by force which allegedly endangered peace and international stability everywhere. A structure of peace based on law is judicial, not political, in nature. Its purpose is not the management but the elimination of war, for every resort to force is an infraction of the law. Power might serve the cause of peace legally if it assumed the form of an imperium that would suppress every assault on the status quo.

Were these two approaches to an American role compatible? Could the country pursue simultaneously the balance of power and a world order based on an effective system of international law, to be enforced by predictable sanctions? In practice, the United States would use force, more indeed than any country in history, but always in pursuit of a peaceful international order in which force would have no role.

II

For Wilson the choice between power and law was clear and inescapable. Long before the United States entered the Great War as an active participant, he had rejected the institution of the balance of power simply because it had failed to eliminate war. Obviously the world could not endure conflicts of such magnitude. Europe's rulers had neglected their obligations to govern with wisdom; instead, they had plunged much of the globe into the most catastrophic of wars. Europe's long record of war and repression had demonstrated its perennial ineptitude in creating an international order that would advance the cause of peace and answer the needs of a distraught and exploited humanity. Wilson developed a profound contempt for the political and diplomatic traditions that seemed to serve mankind so badly. He conceived of the United States as a nation uniquely endowed to lead the world out of the jungle of war into a new era of peace in which law and reason would govern the behavior of nations.

Wilson's conviction that the country's special character gave it a transcendant mission to serve humanity came easily enough. To him the United States alone possessed the idealism, integrity, and disinterestedness necessary for designing a new international community. America was born, he once declared, that men might be free. In accepting the Democratic nomination in 1912, he expressed the hope that the nation had "awakened to the knowledge that she has certain cherished liberties and . . . priceless resources . . . to hold in trust for posterity and for all mankind."[7] On Independence Day 1914, Wilson again staked out an American claim to world leadership: "My dream is that as . . . the world knows more and more of America, it . . . will turn to America for those moral inspirations which lie at the basis of all freedom, . . . and that America will come into the full light of day when all shall know that she puts human rights above all other rights, and that her flag is the flag not only of America, but of humanity."[8] Earlier William James, the American philosopher, had condemned the belief that the United States possessed virtue beyond that generally shared by status quo powers. "Angelic impulses and predatory lusts," he wrote, "divide our heart exactly as they divide the heart of other countries." In the wake of the Great War such admonitions were scarcely audible. Americans agreed readily with the president that the United States was peculiarly constituted to accept the mission that he assigned it.

Wilson required a postwar international structure that would translate his preferences for a peaceful, humane order into specific programs of action. In this quest the president was not alone. The Great War, with its attendant horrors, had convinced thoughtful Americans and Englishmen alike that civilization could not easily survive another such tragedy. One group of distinguished Americans launched the League to Enforce Peace in 1915. At Independence Hall, Philadelphia, in June of that year, the league elected former President Taft as its president. The heart of the league's proposal was a system of collective security whereby all nations would assume the obligation to enforce conciliation and, if necessary, to combine their forces to punish an aggressor. "The delinquent who contemplates a break in the peace," declared Harvard President A. Lawrence Lowell, "must know that retribution will be certain, instant, and irresistible."[9]

Wilson's public endorsement of the collective security principle

---

[7]Wilson's acceptance speech, August 7, 1912, in Ray Stannard Baker and William E. Dodd, eds., *The Public Papers of Woodrow Wilson: College and State* (New York, 1925), 2:453.

[8]Wilson's address at Independence Hall, Philadelphia, July 4, 1914, Baker and Dodd, *The Public Papers of Woodrow Wilson: The New Democracy* (New York, 1927), 1:147.

[9]A. Lawrence Lowell wrote on the League to Enforce Peace in the following: *Independent* 82 (June 28, 1915): 523; *Atlantic Monthly* 116 (September 1915): 393–97; *World's Work* 30 (October 1915): 720; and *North American Review* 205 (January 1917): 29–30. "What is needed," wrote Lowell, "is the certainty of collision with an overwhelming force. Such a force, if it could really be created by a league to enforce peace, would probably never be used. The very fact of its existence would be enough."

came slowly, in part because it anchored peace ultimately to the contemplated use of force. Much of the internationalist pressure on the president came from London where Sir Edward Grey, the British foreign minister, had become convinced by 1915 that a stable and permanent postwar settlement would require a direct and continuous U.S. involvement in European affairs. Grey seized the league idea as an indirect method of bringing American influence to bear on world politics after the conclusion of the war. At last in November 1915, Wilson informed Grey that he favored a concert of nations organized to prevent war.[10] Then on May 27, 1916 in Washington the president addressed a mammoth assembly of the League to Enforce Peace and proclaimed his interest in an association of nations "to prevent any war begun either contrary to treaty covenants or without warning and full submission of the causes to the opinion of the world, a virtual guarantee of territorial integrity and political independence."[11] Under this new association, governments would summon coercion, not to selfish ambition but to the service of peace, order, and justice.

For Wilson the war itself quickly emerged as the agency for creating the humane and peaceful civilization that he contemplated. In his noted speech before the Senate on January 22, 1917, the president made known his concern that the treaties and agreements which terminated the war "create a peace that is worth guaranteeing and preserving, a peace that will win the approval of mankind, not merely a peace that will serve the several interests and immediate aims of the nations engaged." Agreements alone, however, whatever their quality, would not make the peace secure. To assure the permanence of the postwar settlement, the world would require an international power so dominant that "no nation, no probable combination of nations could face or withstand it." If peace would endure, declared Wilson, it must be made secure "by the organized major force of mankind." The president pointedly eliminated from his postwar peace structure all appurtenances of power politics. Europe's future stability, he believed, simply demanded a tranquility that the balance of power could never achieve. "There must be," he averred, "not a balance of power, but a community of power; not organized rivalries, but an organized common peace." Wilson did not inform the American people of their deep historic interest in the European equilibrium; instead, he made himself the prophet of a world free of power politics, one in which the old balance of power

[10]George M. Trevelyan, *Grey of Fallodon* (Boston, 1937), pp. 356–59.
[11]Wilson's address to the League to Enforce Peace, Washington, May 27, 1916, in Baker and Dodd, *The New Democracy*, 2:184–88. Quotation on p. 188.

would recede before a new community of power. Thus the president admonished the European states to avoid entangling alliances "which would draw them into competitions of power, catch them in a net of intrigue and selfish rivalry, and disturb their own affairs with influences intruded from without."[12] The concert of nations he envisioned would not require alliances and other trappings of power.

America's entry into the war merely assured the gains for humanity which President Wilson anticipated from the war. During his peace efforts of 1916, the president had seemed to believe that there was little to choose between Germany and the Allies. After April 1917, however, the war became one between democracy and autocracy. Now the kaiser's Germany alone stood between the military necessities of the moment and the promised triumph of international peace, order, and justice. If war comprised temporary and irrational resorts to violence, perpetrated by wicked, undemocratic governments, then, believed Wilson, permanent peace and justice required a concert of purpose and action among "the really free and self-governed people of the world." Only free peoples, he added, "can hold their purposes and their honor steady to a common end and prefer the interests of mankind to any interest of their own." In his war message, Wilson placed his war aims in their final form: "[W]e shall fight for the things which we have always carried nearest our hearts—for democracy, for the right of those who submit to authority to have a voice in their own Governments, for the rights and liberties of small nations, for a universal dominion of right by such a concert of free peoples as shall bring peace and safety to all nations and make the world itself at last free."[13]

III

Wilson's wartime planning was concerned less with victory in Europe than with the task of strengthening his role as the spokesman of peace. The president understood clearly that the European allies did not share his vision of the postwar world. That understanding, added to his private conviction that the war was a critical episode in mankind's search for peace, forced him to establish his leadership.[14] In January

---

[12]Wilson's address to the Senate, January 22, 1917, ibid., pp. 408–14.

[13]Wilson's war message, April 2, 1917, in Baker and Dodd, *The Public Papers of Woodrow Wilson: War and Peace* (New York, 1927), 1:16.

[14]In his Mount Vernon address of July 4, 1918, Wilson explained why the United States must have its way: "The Past and the Present are in deadly grapple and the peoples of the world are being done to death between them. . . . The settlement must be final. There can be no compromise. No halfway decision would be tolerable." Ibid., p. 233.

1918, in a major bid for popular support, both in the United States and in Europe, Wilson presented his famed Fourteen Point peace program to the joint session of Congress. Again he sought to erase the historic notion that world stability rested on superior power committed to its defense by assigning the postwar status quo to "a great association of nations . . . [that would offer] mutual guarantees of political independence and territorial integrity to great and small states alike."[15] By the summer of 1918, Wilson's towering prestige seemed to assure him a dominant role in the peace settlement. During the closing weeks of the war, the president made his final preparations to dictate the peace terms not only to the Central Powers but also to Britain and France. As late as the armistice of November 1918, his leadership appeared unchallengeable. He had refused to enter into any wartime agreements with the Allies which might infringe on his Fourteen Points. By fighting on their own front in France, U.S. forces had made a measurable contribution to the Allied victory. Britain and France had accepted the Fourteen Points, at least in principle, in the prearmistice agreement and, with that acceptance, Wilson's essential purpose of creating a peace system based on collective security and self-determination of peoples.

At Versailles, Wilson's Fourteen Points faced their initial challenge in the Allied secret treaties of the war years. The president's refusal to recognize these treaties in no measure undermined their effectiveness. Such European realists as David Lloyd George and Georges Clemenceau, representing Britain and France at the conference, were determined from the beginning to fulfill their obligations under the treaties. These men spoke for nations that had paid a horrendous price in death and destruction to send them to the victors' table. Wilson's open disapprobation, anchored to an attitude and rhetoric which insisted that the United States stood on a higher moral plane of international conduct, both puzzled and angered the European leaders. In his reliance on abstract principles such as self-determination, Wilson sought to substitute for individual national interests a new order in which all nations, the United States included, would cease to pursue their interests at all. Unwilling to assert the national interest of the United States in his design for the postwar world, Wilson could not prevent the other members of the wartime alliance from asserting their own concrete interests. For them there were no other guides to effective national action.

Wilson's great victory for self-determination at Versailles came

---

[15]Wilson's address to Congress, January 8, 1918, ibid., p. 161.

with the creation of the new states across East-Central Europe. Later the president characterized the Versailles settlement not merely as a postwar arrangement with Germany but as "a readjustment of those great injustices which underlie the whole structure of European and Asian society. . . . It is a people's treaty that accomplishes by a great sweep of practical justice the liberation of men who never could have liberated themselves, and the power of the most powerful nations has been devoted not to their aggrandizement but to the liberation of people whom they could have put under their control if they had chosen to do so."[16] Unfortunately, the gains for self-determination had been far more limited than the president acknowledged. At Versailles that principle became the means of breaking up the empires of the defeated powers. The new nations of East-Central Europe rose on the ashes of the German, Austrian, and Turkish empires. The Versailles settlement did not touch the vast holdings of the victors—Britain, France, Belgium, Holland, and the United States. This massive failure of self-determination left the entire Afro-Asian world awash with anti-Western, anti-Wilson sentiment.

Far more promising for postwar international stability was the apparent success of the Western democracies in reforging the old nineteenth-century hierarchy of power. To defend their favored position, the makers of the Versailles Treaty either could sustain the alliance that had defeated Germany and subsequently dictated the peace, or they could attempt to institutionalize the peace through the creation of a league of nations. Wilson's known rejection of power politics and preference for a concert of democratic states narrowed the choices at Versailles; it did not eliminate them. However, following Wilson's lead the democracies readily embarked on the second course, one which rested on the two fundamental assumptions that a new rationality had gained control of international affairs and that all major powers, even the defeated, had accepted the hierarchy of power and prestige embodied in the postwar order. There was no evidence at Versailles that either assumption had validity.

After the Versailles Conference voted in January 1919 to establish the League of Nations, British and American representatives prepared a basic draft which satisfied their preferences for a league based on moral sanctions alone. Wilson regarded Article X of the League Covenant fundamental to the defense of the postwar treaty structure. Under

---

[16]Wilson quoted in David F. Trask, "Woodrow Wilson and International Statecraft: A Modern Assessment," *Naval War College Review* 36 (March–April 1983): 66. Because this theme was central to Wilson's defense of the Versailles Treaty, he repeated it on many occasions. See, for example, Wilson's address at Columbus, Ohio, September 4, 1919, in Baker and Dodd, *War and Peace*, 1:594–95, 597.

this article, League members agreed to "preserve as against external aggression the territorial integrity and existing political independence of all Members of the League." France had accepted the treaty provisions for Germany on the promise of a guaranty treaty with Britain and the United States; it remained uncertain whether either country would accept any postwar guarantees of French security.[17] For the French the League was the only immediate defense against the possible rebirth of German power and ambition. The French delegation, therefore, demanded a specific provision for a strong League Council and a permanent military staff capable of implementing Article X effectively. Power alone, argued the French, would deter aggression; for them a league without force was scarcely a league at all. Wilson, however, informed the conference that a league of his design would not rest on a system of force. He agreed with the French delegation that military action might become necessary, but he rejected any precise formula for its employment. Repeatedly at Paris the president recognized the need for economic and military sanctions to compel nations to accept peaceful settlements, but he refused to make them automatic.

On July 10, 1919, Wilson presented the Versailles Treaty to the Senate for its approval, saying that to reject the League of Nations would break the heart of the world. The president opened the great debate over the League issue by declaring his uncompromising adherence to Article X as the heart of the Versailles peace structure. That article, he said, "means every great fighting power in the world . . . solemnly engages to respect and preserve . . . the territorial integrity . . . of the other members of the League. If you do that, you have absolutely stopped ambitious and aggressive war."[18] In the event of aggression, actual or threatened, the League Council would advise the members as to the means required to fulfill the obligations to peace. What, asked the critics, was the relationship between collective security

---

[17]Wilson's defense of a guaranty treaty, July 29, 1919, in Baker and Dodd, *War and Peace*, pp. 555–57. For a superb evaluation of the French view of security, see Stéphane Lauzanne, "France and the Treaty," *North American Review* 210 (November 1919): 604–12.

[18]Quotation from Wilson's speech at Reno, Nevada, September 22, 1919, in Baker and Dodd, *War and Peace*, 2:332–33. Wilson explained the need for Article X and the obligations it posed for the United States in his statement to members of the Senate Foreign Relations Committee, August 19, 1919, ibid., 1:578–80. Wilson's faith in the power of Article X was unbounded. He declared at Indianapolis on September 4, 1919: "A nation that is boycotted is a nation that is in sight of surrender. Apply this economic, peaceful, silent, deadly remedy and there will be no need for force. It is a terrible remedy. It does not cost a life outside the nation boycotted, but it brings a pressure upon that nation which, in my judgment, no modern nation could resist." Ibid., p. 612. At Seattle on September 13, Wilson declared that Article X will "cut the heart of war out of civilization." Ibid., 2:186.

and national sovereignty? Could the League compel a member nation to commit its armed forces to collective action? No country would necessarily vindicate Article X unless the aggressor endangered its own economic or security interests. Moreover, there were arrangements in the Versailles Treaty for which few, if any, nations would fight.

Senator Lodge, Republican chairman of the Senate Foreign Relations Committee, had posed the collective security dilemma facing Wilson before the debate began. The League, he declared, must be either an assemblage of phrases or a practical and effective organization based on force. Only if it possessed the authority to issue decrees and enforce them could it be effective. "Are you ready," he asked the nation, "to put your sailors at the disposition of other nations? If you are not, there will be no power of enforcing the decrees." Any reliable league, warned Lodge, would require such infringements on national sovereignty that no one, not even the president, would favor it.[19] "What will your league amount to," asked Senator William E. Borah, Idaho's noted isolationist, "if it does not contain powers that no one dreams of giving it?" This question required an answer, but Wilson no more than other proponents of collective security could resolve the central conflict between obligation and sovereignty. Clearly collective security, to be automatic and instantaneous, required national sacrifice as well as machinery capable of mobilizing preponderant force against one or more aggressor nations. The president's strenuous effort to dispose of the question of international obligation under the League by attempting to distinguish between its moral and legal implications was as incomprehensible as it was heroic. It was no less Wilson's failure to satisfy his critics than the partisanship of those who demanded an explanation of collective security that undermined the seriousness of the great debate of 1919.

IV

Throughout the war years and the great debate that followed, President Wilson waged his public war on traditional diplomacy, the balance of power, and the concept of national interest—the three fundamental accouterments of power politics—with sufficient success to weaken, if not terminate, the country's historic identification with the modern state system and reliance on national interest and the balance of power.

---

[19]Lodge's speech before the Senate, *Congressional Record*, 64th Cong., 2d sess., February 1, 1917, p. 2367; Lodge's speech in the Senate against the League of Nations, August 12, 1919, *Congressional Record*, 66th Cong., 1st sess., pp. 3779–84. Quotation taken from Lodge's speech of December 21, 1918, *Congressional Record*, 65th Cong., 3d sess., pp. 727–28.

The great debate over the League membership in 1919 ignored almost totally the concepts of national interest, equilibrium, and alliance. As one result of that debate, the United States withdrew its power and obligation from the European scene in the conviction either that the decisions made at Versailles, including the establishment of the League of Nations, would maintain world stability, or that any future breakdown of the peace need not concern the government and people of the United States. Whether the Senate rejected U.S. membership in the League or not, countless American writers, scholars, journalists, and politicians agreed that peace was the country's paramount interest and that the Wilsonian peace program was the surest guarantee of its permanence.

Determined to avoid a recurrence of the recent European catastrophe, Wilsonian internationalists, no less than the president himself, simply ignored the persistence of power politics in history and in the world around them. It was not strange that wishing and generalization soon prevailed over any analysis of the ongoing realities of international life. The end of lasting and universal peace overwhelmed the problem of means. Wilson once quieted the doubts of his adversaries who questioned the effectiveness of the League of Nations by assuring them that "if it won't work, it must be made to work."[20] Schemes for rendering the League effective did not require explanations of how they would work; the consequences of failure were too disastrous to contemplate. This propensity of laudable purposes to cloud the importance of means led the economist Alfred Marshall, in another context, to compare utopian programs—those which lacked the means for their achievement—to the "bold facility of the weak player who will speedily solve the most difficult chess problem by taking on himself to move the black men as well as the white."[21]

To those who argued that the fundamentally anarchic state system could not provide the peace and stability that the world required, the realists—a tiny minority in that euphoric age—offered two observations. First, perhaps it was true that the balance of power system before 1914 had not always defended the highest interests of civilization, but, they argued, a world of sovereign nations would never find a substitute. The United States had the choice between the balance of power system or no system at all. Second, realists insisted that the failure of the European equilibrium to prevent the disaster of 1914 was

---

[20]Wilson quoted in Edward Hallett Carr, *The Twenty Years' Crisis, 1919–1939* (London, 1956), p. 8.
[21]Alfred Marshall, "The Social Possibilities of Economic Chivalry," *Economic Journal* 17 (March 1907): 16n.

no evidence that the traditional state system was hopeless. When properly managed it had provided the world with a high degree of international stability, one measurable by the progress, complexity, and triumphs of modern national and international society. Clearly world stability had never required the rule of law. Governments had often maintained peace over long periods of time without the benefit of any international law. In a political world, moreover, peace would always require arrangements among nations, reflecting interest and power, that no law could guarantee. What would limit aggression in the future as in the past was the threat of counterforce, not the presence of law. Thus the realist's approach to world order after Versailles demanded that the United States, in alliance with Britain and France, maintain the preponderance of power that had triumphed over Germany. At the war's end American diplomatist Lewis Einstein reminded the nation: "At no time even unknown to us, were European politics a matter of indifference to our vital interests, but if hitherto we were impotent to alter their march, a fortunate destiny preserved the existing balance independently of us. . . . [W]e have today a distinct and legitimate duty in the family of great nations in contributing to preserve those elements which compose the balance of power, and to which we can only be blind at our later cost."[22]

Wilson's answer to the challenge of postwar international stability and aggression was simple and reassuring. For him peace required not the existence of preponderant power wielded in defense of the status quo, as some realists advocated, but a world opinion pervasive enough either to limit change to mutual agreement or to eliminate it altogether. The notion that only peaceful change was morally acceptable denied the need, even the legitimacy, of dealing with aggressors. In a world allegedly governed by principle and law, no country had the right to bargain with aggressors over changes in established treaties, especially since such bargaining would merely stimulate the appetite for gain. The pleasant assumption that the United States could avoid the necessity of confronting aggressors directly absolved the government of the need to define the country's interests precisely or prepare a strategy for their defense. Wilson's formula for preventing aggression abjured the use of both force and diplomacy; it consisted rather of a strong reliance on moral and legal principles that left no room for change resulting from force.

Wilson thus anchored the nation's new stabilizing role in world affairs to the defense of the status quo. So acceptable was this purpose

[22]Lewis Einstein, *A Prophecy of War* (New York, 1918), pp. 45-46.

and so thoroughly did it satisfy the conservative interests and idealism of the American people that only with difficulty would the country, despite its remarkable strength, ever accept the traditional obligations of great power. For such leadership demanded above all that the United States recognize the essentially political character of international life—that power and interests, not morality and law, determined the behavior of nations. In such a world successful leadership would necessitate the willingness and capacity to deal forthrightly with the policies, even the aggressive policies, of other powers, accepting, opposing, or ignoring them as interests might require.

Clinging to the dream of a fundamentally unchanging world order, in the name of democracy, morality, and peace, would turn out to be folly, not because such universalism failed to square with America's special interest in international stability but because it was unworkable in the real world of power politics. Neither Wilson nor his successors could devise a peace structure that would prevent nations from seeking the enlargement of their influence, prestige, or security with resort to force. For such direct assaults on the status quo, Wilson had provided no answer. The Versailles system created no mechanism for achieving change peacefully. To the extent that any treaty structure embodied some injustices—and that created at Versailles was no exception—future change emanating from force would not necessarily be unjust, reprehensible, or dangerous. Peace had always been divisible; throughout modern times most resorts to violence had been exceedingly limited in scope. The forces upholding the status quo, whether in possession of the great democracies or the League of Nations, would never be sufficient to prevent all unwanted defiance of the status quo. Turmoil and aggression would continue to torment international relations. The assumption that change, to be legitimate, also needed to be peaceful would be costly indeed, often placing the United States at odds with the century's revolutionary movements and with peoples who in no way endangered its interests or regarded themselves as its enemies. Whatever its preference for a stable, unchanging international order, the United States could not escape the necessity of coming to terms with change that did not challenge its interests.

Similarly, the country's post-Versailles tendency to assign a special morality to the status quo would not eliminate the obligation to deal with major aggressors on the basis of competing interests, not principles of self-determination and peaceful change. Nations devoted to the existing treaty structure could curtail the aggressiveness of the dissatisfied only through direct diplomacy aimed at accommodation or through force. Even on issues that lay outside the country's economic and security interests, American diplomatists might find concessions to aggressors personally repugnant and publicly injurious, but the mere refusal to negotiate with expansionist states would not control their behavior. At the end, Washington's determination to avoid accommodation would permit the unfortunate choice between the acceptance of unwanted change, unmodified by mutual agreement, or war. In short, the neglect of diplomacy in the name of principle would simply eliminate the considerable power and influence of the United States from decisions affecting its own and the world's future.

CHAPTER
ONE

The Retreat to Utopia*

FOR THE UNITED STATES the Great War provided two essential lessons.
The unwanted involvement against Germany demonstrated that policies at once passive and legalistic would not deter other countries from
pursuing their interests as they perceived them. Again at Versailles
President Wilson could no more control the victorious powers with
appeals to principle than he could determine German behavior on the
high seas before April 1917. None of the victors at Versailles shared
the president's wartime vision of a new world order based primarily
on the substitution of democratic and judicial procedures for force in
international life. Despite the destructiveness of the Great War, Europe's
statesmen could detect no changes in the international environment
that would permit a diminished reliance on force in the defense of
national interests. For them there could be no new international
order. What provided Wilson his fleeting moment of leadership in European affairs was not his appealing design for a peaceful future but
the fact that he led a country with a remarkable capacity to wage
total war—indeed, the country that had made the defeat of Germany
possible.

If the country's supreme venture into European politics revealed
its limited capacity to exorcise traditional modes of behavior from
international affairs, it predicted as well that the American people
would not escape any future war on the European continent that endangered their interests in the Atlantic. The United States, in the future

*Address delivered at the Center for the Study of the Recent History of the
United States, University of Iowa, Iowa City, April 2, 1980. Published as "Between
the Wars: The Intellectual Climate of American Foreign Relations," in John N. Schacht,
ed., *Three Faces of Midwestern Isolationism* (Iowa City, 1981), pp. 45–70. Reprinted by
permission.

1

as in the recent past, would exercise its influence in a world of power politics, facing challenges which it could neither escape nor control. Thus of necessity sound national policy would avoid the extreme goals of shunning world responsibilities entirely and of rescuing, with appeals to self-determination and peaceful change, oppressed and endangered humanity everywhere. It instead would be directed toward the recognition and pursuit of a variety of specific national interests in competition with nations which could discover in the international system no effective substitute for the established rules of power politics.

That the American people drew precisely the wrong conclusions from their wartime experience was a tribute to Wilson's influence over their thoughts and emotions. Indeed, so profound yet so divisive was his impact on the Republic, that it drove American behavior toward the extremes against which the recent diplomatic past had warned. Wilson had promised the transformation of world politics in accordance with his principles. Much of the American populace chose to measure his success by the goals that he had set for himself and the nation; by those standards he had failed. If few Americans asked themselves what influence a German victory might have had on United States security, it was because the president and members of his administration consistently refused to formulate national purposes in terms of preserving the traditional balance of power, the only real emolument of victory available to the American people. Indeed, Wilson succeeded in eliminating altogether the concept of international equilibrium from the main currents of the nation's thought. In veiling the nation's considerable contribution to the defense of the old order, he managed to convert a successful national effort into a lost crusade.

In proclaiming goals whose achievement always eluded him, Wilson laid the foundation for a pervading postwar isolationism. For countless Americans nothing in the country's experience dictated the necessity of a permanent or continuous American involvement in European politics. The widespread disillusionment with the war merely reinforced that conviction. Not without reason they concluded that the United States had gained little more for its trans-Atlantic experience than Prohibition and the flu, or, as H. L. Mencken suggested, American Legion parades and the new Soviet colossus. The disillusionment quickly focused on the country's wartime associates, Britain and France, whose leaders had warred so effectively on American neutrality and now refused to pay their countries' wartime debts to the United States. The powerful newspaper publisher, William Randolph Hearst, reminded his readers that Britain had often been the target of American patriotism.[1] Unable to discern any demonstrable gain from their European venture, millions of Americans entered the 1920s determined to prevent its repetition. "We ask only to live our own life in our own way," declared California's Hiram W. Johnson in March 1922, "in friendship and sympathy with all, in alliance with none."[2] For Indiana's Albert J. Beveridge the country's "divinely ordained mission [was] to develop and exercise, by friendship to all and partnership with none, a moral influence circling the globe."[3]

Isolationists recognized no danger to the nation's interests in political and military detachment from European affairs. Europe's peace, they charged, was not the responsibility of the United States. Isolationism would not prevent another European war, but it would enable the United States to avoid such a struggle. Indeed, argued Beveridge, the European powers would carefully skirt any action that might involve the United States in their future conflicts. "After the incredible blunder of the German High Command in attacking us and thus forcing us into war," he asked, "does anybody imagine that any other nation hereafter at war with another nation will repeat that tragic folly?"[4] Isolationists admitted that the United States was not isolated from Europe commercially or intellectually; they insisted simply that the country could avoid the quarrels, intrigues, politics, ambitions, and animosities that had driven other countries to war for centuries.

Isolationists centered their attack on the League of Nations, a program for peace at once too ambitious and too threatening to national sovereignty. If the United States entered the League, declared Senator Johnson, "I must abandon the lessons of my youth, which until this moment have been the creed of my manhood, of American ideals, American principles, and American patriotism." Senator Borah's distrust of the League was equally profound. To submit a vital issue to the decision of foreign powers, he complained, was nothing less than moral treason. As the Senate's leading proponent of isolationism, Borah insisted that he did not oppose cooperation with other nations. "What I have opposed from the beginning," he declared, "is any commitment of this nation to a given line of procedure in a future exigency, the facts as to which could not be known before the event." Congressman

---

[1]On William Randolph Hearst see Selig Adler, *The Isolationist Impulse: Its Twentieth-Century Reaction* (New York, 1957), p. 79.

[2]Johnson quoted in Alexander DeConde, ed., *Isolation and Security* (Durham, NC, 1957), pp. 10–11.

[3]Albert J. Beveridge, "George Washington and Present American Problems," *American Monthly* 13 (April 1921): 46.

[4]Beveridge, *The State of the Nation* (Indianapolis, 1924), pp. 8–9.

Ogden L. Mills of New York agreed that effective cooperation did not require prior commitments. "We believe," he said, "that the United States can better serve by maintaining her independence of action than by pooling her influence in advance."[5] These isolationists never explained how the country could prepare for an emergency unless it had ordered its affairs with such possible exigencies in mind. Borah denied that cooperation and independence were incompatible. By setting a good example and limiting cooperation to voluntary behavior, the United States could exercise effective world leadership. For Borah, however, the United States could exert that leadership only if it stayed out of European affairs. "I do not think we can have here a great, powerful, independent, self-governing republic and do anything else," he remarked. "I do not think it is possible for us to continue to be the leading intellectual and moral power in the world and do anything else."[6]

Anti-League sentiments controlled President Warren G. Harding's policies toward Europe. At a celebration of his election at Marion, Ohio, Harding delivered an obituary to the League. "You didn't want a surrender of the U.S.A.," he reminded his fellow townsmen, "you wanted America to go on under American ideals. That's why you didn't care for the League *which is now deceased*."[7] In his inaugural, Harding declared that the United States was "ready to associate with the nations of the world, great and small, for conference and counsel . . . [and] to participate in suggesting plans for mediation, conciliation, and arbitration." For Borah, Harding's commitment to associate was unnecessarily dangerous to the country's freedom of action. Such doubts conformed to the nation's mood; thereafter, the Republican administration exercised greater care. Until 1923 it refused to answer League communications. Shortly before his death that year, Harding remarked: "I have no unseemly comment to offer on the League. If it is serving the world helpfully, more power to it. But it is not for us. The Senate has so declared, the Executive has so declared, the people have so declared. Nothing could be more decisively stamped with finality."[8] Apparently the anti-League forces had triumphed.

[5]Johnson quoted in Adler, *The Isolationist Impulse*, p. 104. For Borah's views see Charles W. Toth, "Isolationism and the Emergence of Borah: An Appeal to American Tradition," *Western Political Quarterly* 14 (June 1961): 555–56. Mills quoted in *New York Times*, October 29, 1924, p. 6.

[6]Borah quoted in Karl Schriftgiesser, *This Was Normalcy* (Boston, 1948), p. 132.

[7]Harding quoted in ibid., p. 131 (emphasis in original).

[8]Harding's inaugural address, *Congressional Record*, 67th Cong., special sess., March 4, 1921, p. 5; Toth, "Isolationism and Borah," p. 557; Schriftgiesser, *This Was Normalcy*, p. 133.

II

For other Americans—often intellectuals and academicians—Wilson's vision of a new world order free of all reliance on force was too essential for the world's future to be discarded in deference to isolationism. If postwar Wilsonians ignored the persistent role of power in affairs among nations, it was because they regarded the end of lasting and universal peace sufficiently overwhelming to negate the problem of means.[9] Thus Wilsonian internationalism denied, as did isolationism, that the United States need be concerned with any specific configuration of political or military power in Europe or Asia. Both were equally antagonistic to the conservative tradition of American diplomacy. Whereas isolationism insisted that the nation had no external interests that merited the use of force (although it never recognized any necessity for curtailing the country's commitments in the Far East), internationalism declared that American interests existed wherever governments challenged peace or human rights. Isolationism preached that events outside the hemisphere were inconsequential; internationalism insisted not only that they mattered but also that the universal acceptance of democratically inspired principles of peaceful change would control them. Every program fostered by American internationalists during the 1920s—membership in the League of Nations or the World Court, the employment of arbitration conventions, the resort to consultation in the event of crises, collective security, naval disarmament, or the outlawry of war—denied the need of any precise definition of ends and means in American foreign policy and anchored the effectiveness of policy to the power of world opinion to bring aggressors before the bar of justice.

Internationalists in the 1920s comprised largely the pro-League forces which insisted that the United States redeem its pledges to the past and the future. League proponents, unlike isolationists, argued that the United States would not avoid a future European war. The country, therefore, would fulfill its obligation to its own and the world's peace by preventing, not merely by trying to escape, a breakdown of the peace. For many internationalists the League of Nations wielded the necessary authority to prevent war. The central issue before the American people, pro-League editors argued, was whether or not they would play their part in eliminating dangerous competition from international life by joining the League.[10] John Eugene Harley, professor of

---

[9]The almost total neglect of means as an essential element in international relations characterized the nation's thought during the 1920s. It affected the followers of Wilson everywhere—in the successive presidential administrations, Congress, the press, and the country's leading universities.

[10]Hamilton Holt, "The Successful League of Nations," *Independent* 104 (October 23, 1920): 124.

political science at the University of Southern California, explained that the League would maintain international order by making international law the rule of conduct. To achieve this purpose the League might require sanctions but not war. "The desire for order as expressed by the public opinion of the world," he wrote, "is the true and ultimate force which will sustain the League in the effort to maintain order through international law."[11] Raymond B. Fosdick, briefly undersecretary general of the League and thereafter a New York lawyer, noted that the League would prevent war by making compulsory all the forces for peace that were absent in 1914—delay, discourse, arbitration, and law.[12] He, no less than others, assumed that all countries would follow League rules, that argument would dictate behavior, and that governments, having argued the issues, would ultimately prefer any settlement to war. Should a crisis demand League intervention to prevent aggression, the council, as a last resort, would recommend military force, but membership would not obligate any country to enter military or naval action.[13]

If League membership carried no military obligations, then its power to prevent aggression was moral or nonexistent. Indeed, it was the League's reliance on moral force that made American adherence so essential. Specifically, internationalists agreed, U.S. membership would guarantee the League its needed effectiveness by increasing its prestige and its command of world opinion, the only genuine foundation of peace. "The League lives by and through public opinion," the noted author G. Lowes Dickinson reminded his readers. "It has practically no other power. To refuse to mobilize this opinion, to damp it down, to pretend that it does not exist, is in effect to destroy it."[14] Yale economist Irving Fisher argued that American adherence to the League would give the organization the moral influence it required to sustain international order. This country, he explained, was the world's "greatest reserve of moral power, with ideals . . . more unselfish than those of other countries and therefore [able to] exert a special moral influence against the ill-conceived and little restrained European scramble for spoils."[15]

Internationalists attributed the apparent successes of the League

[11]John Eugene Harley, *The League of Nations and the New International Order* (New York, 1921), p. 7.

[12]Raymond B. Fosdick, "Will the League Stop Wars?" *New York Times Book Review and Magazine*, October 17, 1920, p. 1.

[13]Irving Fisher, *America's Interest in World Peace* (New York, 1924), p. 61.

[14]G. Lowes Dickinson, "Can These Bones Live?" *New Republic* 36 (October 24, 1923): 229–30.

[15]Irving Fisher, *League or War* (New York, 1923), p. 159.

in the early 1920s to the growing force of world opinion. Fosdick in August 1922 noted that the League had settled the boundary dispute between Yugoslavia and Albania. "The method was effective," he wrote, "not because it represented force, but because it had behind it the moral judgment of civilization." Again Fosdick attributed Italy's retreat from Corfu in 1923 to the opinion of mankind, given cohesion and force by the League of Nations. Fisher arrived at the same conclusion. The small states, he observed, "made their protests vociferously in the Assembly of the League, and public opinion throughout the world was quickly mobilized against Italy."[16] Internationalists pondered the additional triumphs that the moral leadership of the United States might have brought to the League. Franklin D. Roosevelt had observed as early as August 1920 that, except for the American rejection of League membership, Poland would not be fighting the Russians with its back to the wall. Had the United States entered the League, Fisher argued in 1924, "war would be outlawed, universal disarmament would be no longer a dream, and reparations and debts and balanced budgets and currency stabilization and gigantic standing armies would be problems solved or on their way to solution."[17]

Still Republican leaders, following Harding's death, remained adamantly opposed to League membership. On October 23, 1923, President Calvin Coolidge explained his party's foreign policy: "We have a well defined foreign policy, known to all men who will give it candid consideration. It has as its foundation peace with independence. We have abstained from joining the League of Nations mainly for the purpose of avoiding political entanglements and committing ourselves to the assumption of the obligations of others, which have been created without our authority and in which we have no direct interest."[18] By 1924 the Coolidge administration had inaugurated a policy of cooperation with the League's humanitarian ventures. The president acknowledged the role of the United States in formulating the Dawes Plan of 1924 on German reparations. Under Republican leadership, observed Secretary of State Charles Evans Hughes, the United States had achieved much for peace and humanity without entangling or

---

[16]Raymond B. Fosdick, "The League of Nations After Two Years," *Atlantic Monthly* 130 (August 1922): 262. In the Yugoslav-Albanian conflict, financial pressure and the threat of a blockade contributed to the settlement. On the Corfu question see Fosdick, "Mussolini and the League of Nations," *Review of Reviews* 67 (November 1923): 482; and Fisher, *America's Interest*, p. 57. Actually the Council of Ambassadors in Paris arranged the return of Corfu to Greece in exchange for a payment of damages to Italy.

[17]Roosevelt in *New York Times*, August 13, 1920, p. 3; Fisher, *America's Interest*, p. 27.

[18]*New York Times*, October 24, 1924, p. 4.

injurious commitments. At its 1924 convention the Republican party reaffirmed Coolidge's decision to avoid League membership. "The Government," declared its platform, "has definitely refused membership in the League of Nations, and to assume any obligation under the Covenant of the League. On this we stand." The United States would maintain both its independence and its concern for other nations "through cooperation without entangling alliances."[19] So thoroughly did Coolidge's victory reflect public approval of Republican foreign policy that the Democratic party dropped the League issue completely. The Republican conquest of the nation's mind on matters of external affairs was complete.

III

Consigned by adverse opinion to failure on the League issue, internationalists seized upon World Court membership as an alternate approach to effective international cooperation. Eventually the court battle comprised the most determined internationalist counterattack of the decade. When in May 1922 the court officially opened for business, the noted American international law expert, John Bassett Moore, was among its eleven judges. Many anti-League Republicans like Elihu Root shared the confidence of pro-League leaders in the World Court. Secretary of State Hughes pressed Harding to submit the question of court membership to the Senate. To satisfy congressional isolationists, he suggested four reservations that would absolve the United States of all commitments to the League but would demand for the country all powers on the court enjoyed by League members. Harding proposed membership to Congress on these terms as early as February 1923, but Borah, as chairman of the Senate Foreign Relations Committee, opposed the plan as an overcommitment of American power and prestige to the League cause.[20] Both major parties endorsed court membership in their 1924 platforms.

Still anti-League isolationists in the Senate continued to stall, convinced that adherence to the World Court, a creation of the League, would gradually entrap the United States in the League itself. Coolidge argued for court membership in his March 1925 inaugural: "The weight of our enormous influence must be cast upon the side of a reign not of

---

[19]George D. Ellis, ed., *Platforms of the Two Great Political Parties* (Washington, 1932), pp. 278–79.
[20]Denna F. Fleming, *The United States and the World Court* (Garden City, NY, 1945), pp. 40–41.

force, but of law and trial, not by battle, but by reason."[21] Finally, in December, when the issue of membership had won the support of peace societies, women's clubs, pro-League forces, countless mass meetings, and much of the press, the Senate agreed to act. Early in 1926 it approved membership by a vote of 76 to 17. To forestall an assault on the question of advisory opinions, Senator Claude A. Swanson of Virginia introduced a fifth reservation that denied the court the right to render an advisory opinion on any question touching the interests of the United States.[22] In response, the court demanded the right to impose reservations of its own. Coolidge acknowledged the impasse and in November 1926 announced that U.S. membership in the World Court had become a dead issue.

Unfortunately, the World Court, without compulsory jurisdiction or means of enforcement, was scarcely the agency to settle issues on which hinged the future of peace and war. Thus the great debate over court membership which raged across the nation during the mid-1920s had little relationship to the realities of world politics and the limited role reserved for the court on questions of importance. Court proponents viewed membership simply as a matter of moral obligation, the obligation of the country to support any movement or institution that contributed to peace. The New York *World* voiced the convictions of many leading editors when it declared: "President Harding's recommendation represents the shortest step forward that could be taken in the way of meeting the nation's moral obligation to sustain the peace of the world." During the final Senate debates over membership, Swanson argued characteristically: "I am strongly persuaded from every moral consideration . . . that we should adhere to this World Court."[23] United States membership, argued Fisher, would strengthen the court's influence; "the Court has no sheriff except public opinion. America's adhesion would double its authority in the minds of men."[24]

What made U.S. membership so appealing was the court's alleged capacity, magnified by American support, to assert the primacy of law over force. The Federal Council of Churches of Christ in America appealed to its member congregations: "Pray and speak for the extension of the sway of law over force and for the wholehearted readiness on the part of our nation to play its part in bringing this about." By

---

[21]Ibid., p. 48; Adler, *The Isolationist Impulse,* pp. 204–05.

[22]Fleming, *The United States and the World Court,* p. 56.

[23]On the World Court's limited jurisdiction see Edward Hallett Carr, *The Twenty Years' Crisis, 1919–1939* (London, 1956), pp. 193, 206. Swanson quoted in *Congressional Digest,* February 1926, p. 71.

[24]Fisher, *America's Interest,* p. 117.

joining the World Court, Harding had assured a St. Louis audience in July 1923, the United States would promote the substitution of "reason for prejudice, law for obduracy, and justice for passion."[25] Fisher reminded Americans that courts had displaced conflict in every field where they had been instituted. "It only remains," he added, "to apply this great principle between nations . . . to abolish war as an institution wholly and forever." Students of international law took the lead in urging the American people to accept their responsibility for promoting international justice through court membership. Manley O. Hudson of Harvard University asked the nation to throw "the full weight of [its] moral influence [behind] a movement for the substitution of law for force in international affairs." Not even the absence of enforcement machinery seemed detrimental to the court's effectiveness. "It is not unreasonable to believe," asserted Professor Harley, "that civilized nations will honor the awards of a tribunal which they have solemnly created to make such awards."[26] World opinion would enforce the court's decrees.

Court membership, finally, would solidify the world's peace structure without any specific American obligation to a system of force. Herbert Hoover, secretary of commerce, reminded a Des Moines audience in April 1923 that in joining the court the United States would "enter into no obligations to use arms or take no commitment that limits our freedom of action."[27] Indeed, the United States, through court membership, would undertake only two commitments: to participate in the selection of judges and to pay its share of the court's expenses, estimated at forty thousand dollars per year. Whatever the annual cost of maintaining the court, however, Congress would reserve the right to determine what the nation's share would be. During the final Senate debate, spokesmen for the court insisted repeatedly that membership carried no national obligation except to the court itself. As Senator Thomas J. Walsh of Montana declared, "we enter into no covenant to do or refrain from doing anything."[28] The battle over court membership, like that over the League, revealed the nature of American internationalism in the 1920s. The United States would support world peace, not through specific commitments to the defense of the Versailles

[25]"A Prayer for the World Court," *Literary Digest*, June 23, 1923, p. 34; James W. Murphy, ed., *Speeches and Addresses of Warren G. Harding, President of the United States* (Washington, 1923), pp. 37–38.

[26]Fisher, *America's Interest*, p. 36; Manley O. Hudson, "The Permanent Court of International Justice—An Indispensable First Step," *Annals of the American Academy* 108 (July 1923): 188–90; John Eugene Harley, "The World Court of Justice," *Journal of Applied Sociology* 7 (May–June 1923): 245.

[27]*Congressional Digest*, May 1923, p. 239.

[28]*Congressional Record*, 69th Cong., 1st sess., December 18, 1925, p. 1085.

settlement but through the encouragement of any organization or procedure that promised to limit change in international life to peaceful processes.

Internationalists agreed that neither the League nor the World Court had confronted any major political issues, nor had they demonstrated any capacity to restrain a major power. "The League," noted the *Independent,* "is discreetly keeping its hands off crucial matters, and the 'balance of power,' which had been held up as a devilish thing, still goes on."[29] The cooperative effort was new, Fosdick reminded the skeptics. In time, he predicted, the League could become a "central rallying-point around which the forces of law and peace may gather and slowly develop new approaches to common dangers and new methods of common action." Similarly, journalist and historian Francis Hackett observed in July 1924 that the League, given time, would grow into an effective organization. "The more complex the creature," he wrote, "the more helpless its youth. When the League's members recognize the full value of their creation, it will become incredibly strong."[30]

Realists, that tiny minority which challenged the decade's euphoria, saw no future in either the League or the World Court as guarantors of peace. Their reasoning was clear. Such international agencies, whatever their devotion to peaceful change, would always serve the status quo; they would never find a standard equally acceptable to all countries. No state dissatisfied with the distribution of power, resources, or territory would entrust its future to an international agency. The fallacy in the concept of peaceful change lay essentially in the fact that international disputes were overwhelmingly political, not judicial, in nature; their resolution would reflect power and not the judgments of deliberative bodies. For that reason the satisfied peoples would protect their world, not with law and peaceful procedures but with superior force. "The League conception," warned H. H. Powers, an economist and student of European affairs, "is that world order, as regards the nations, is static. The nations are finalities. They are to stay at home, avoid trespass, and maintain neighborly relations. . . . Mussolini and his like regard the world order as still dynamic. The nations are not finalities. The forces of aggression and absorption are perilously active, and the nation that assumes a passive attitude is doomed."[31] The impulse toward self-assertion would keep the world dynamic and sorely troubled. Those who dominated the public's education during the 1920s did not prepare

---

[29]"The League on Its Merits," *Independent* 109 (April 14, 1923): 242.
[30]Francis Hackett, "The League at the Calf Stage," *Survey* 52 (July 1, 1924): 388.
[31]H. H. Powers, "After Five Years," *Atlantic Monthly* 133 (May 1924): 694–95. Powers expected little of the League but believed that the United States should enter it. See p. 696.

the country to recognize this central warning. Little in their teaching challenged the notion that the United States could fulfill its obligations to international stability without power, commitments, or alliances. Seldom did the instruction of the decade propose any strategic concept capable of guaranteeing the country's minimal security requirements.

IV

American power contributed substantially to the shape of the Versailles settlement. If that treaty defined generally the interests of the United States in its distribution of power and territory, then of necessity any major threat to the postwar treaty structure would be a matter of national concern. Any forthright American response might contribute either to the defense of the Versailles decisions or to their modification as interests might dictate. Except for Washington's preparedness to make such decisions, the United States would possess no foreign policy at all. France above all other European countries understood the necessity of an American role in maintaining the stability of Europe. From the moment of its establishment in 1870–71, the German Empire had outdistanced France militarily. For that reason French supremacy on the Continent required nothing less than the dismemberment of Germany. Having failed to achieve this objective at Versailles, French negotiators extracted from Wilson a guaranty treaty whereby the United States would assure France protection against future aggression. Britain offered the French government similar guarantees contingent upon the ratification of a Franco-American treaty. At Versailles these pacts were the means whereby President Wilson and British Prime Minister David Lloyd George encouraged France to give up its extreme demands on Germany. The subsequent failure of the U.S. Senate to accept either a guaranty treaty or the Versailles Treaty threw France on its own resources and contributed to that country's postwar bitterness and insecurity.[32]

At the heart of the Versailles settlement was not only French military primacy on the Continent but also the independence of the new states of Eastern Europe. In actuality, self-determination in Eastern Europe would not long survive a lapse of France's military dominance of Europe. By the mid-1920s both the Soviet Union and Germany had made clear their ultimate intentions toward these countries. The

---

[32]For the French problem see Stéphane Lauzanne, "France and the Treaty," *North American Review* 210 (November 1919): 604–12; Robert H. Ferrell, *Peace in Their Time: The Origins of the Kellogg-Briand Pact* (New Haven, CT, 1952), pp. 52–62; and Hajo Holborn, *The Political Collapse of Europe* (New York, 1951), pp. 125–27.

Soviet assault on the Eastern European settlement began as early as 1920 when the new Bolshevik regime, recoiling from the unsuccessful invasion of White armies into Soviet territory during the previous year, dispatched the Red Army into Poland. Immediately Jay Pierrepont Moffat, a member of the American embassy staff in Warsaw, warned Washington that a Soviet triumph over Poland would ignite revolutions in Germany, Austria, and perhaps even Italy. Hugh R. Wilson, another distinguished American diplomat, responded to the Soviet siege of Warsaw by observing that "we have to go back to the defense of Vienna against the Turks and other crucial battles in the world's history to find one of equal significance."[33] France sent token aid to the Polish government; the United States and England sent none. American Secretary of State Bainbridge Colby placed his reliance on another Soviet revolution. Poland held by a narrow margin and the crisis passed, but the lessons were clear for all to observe. Having only recently created at Versailles the political structure of Eastern Europe as a great democratic achievement, the Western democracies revealed no intention to fight for its preservation. The dilemma, if largely unrecognized, was not unlike that which confronted Secretary of State John Hay and Theodore Roosevelt earlier in the century when they attempted to maintain the principle of the Open Door policy in China—recently heralded as a great diplomatic achievement—in the face of Russian aggressiveness.[34]

German resentment and ambition after Versailles also focused on Eastern Europe. The treaty's eastern provisions, especially those regarding Austria, Czechoslovakia, Danzig, and the Polish Corridor, had the effect of directing German attention toward Eastern Europe where the obviously minimal interests of the Western powers, added to the internal confusion of the new states, created opportunities for unlimited political and military gains. Beyond the new states, it is true, loomed the Soviet Union, but Germany came to terms with the Soviet colossus in the 1922 Treaty of Rapallo. Perhaps no one stated with greater precision Germany's long-term interest in destroying the Versailles arrangement in Eastern Europe than did Adolf Hitler in his book

[33]Nancy H. Hooker, ed., *The Moffat Papers: Selections from the Diplomatic Journals of Jay Pierrepont Moffat, 1919–1943* (Cambridge, MA, 1956), pp. 20–21; Hugh R. Wilson, *Diplomat Between Wars* (New York, 1941), p. 18.

[34]For example, Roosevelt wrote to Hay on May 22, 1903: "As for China, I do not see that there is anything we can say, even by way of suggestion. The mendacity of the Russians is something appalling. The bad feature of the situation from our standpoint is that as yet it seems that we cannot fight to keep Manchuria open. I hate being in the position of seeming to bluster without backing it up." In Elting E. Morison, ed., *The Letters of Theodore Roosevelt* (Cambridge, MA, 1951), 3:478.

Mein Kampf (1924). In his ideal world, Britain would exist as a great nation but would abandon its balance of power policies on the Continent and maintain only its traditional maritime and imperial interests. France would retain its national integrity and colonial empire but would return to the status of a secondary power in European affairs. These changes, coming with time, would permit Germany the freedom to pursue its real interests—the occupation and colonization of Eastern Europe.[35]

Such unhidden threats to the Versailles structure, emanating from both the Soviet Union and Germany, would eventually demand of the United States and Britain a willingness either to employ force to maintain the political integrity of Eastern Europe or to accept diplomatically whatever political and territorial changes in the Versailles settlement appeared consonant with their interests and security.[36] Such inescapable questions regarding Europe's future were far too precise and potentially troublesome for the vagaries of American thought. For British leaders they were equally unwelcome. In February 1925, Sir James Headlam-Morley, historical adviser of the British Foreign Office, warned his government that the Vistula, not the Rhine, was the real danger point in Europe and thus of vital concern to the Western powers. In a prophetic memorandum to Foreign Minister Sir Austen Chamberlain, he posed a critical question:

> Has anyone attempted to realize what would happen if there were to be a new partition of Poland, or if the Czechoslovak state were to be so curtailed and dismembered that in fact it disappeared from the map of Europe? The whole of Europe would at once be in chaos. There would no longer be any principle, meaning, or sense in the territorial arrangements of the continent. Imagine, for instance, that under some improbable condition, Austria rejoined Germany; that Germany using the discontented minority in Bohemia, demanded a new frontier far over the mountains, including Carlsbad and Pilsen, and that at the same time, in alliance with Germany, the Hungarians recovered the southern slope of the Carpathians. This would be catastrophic, and, even if we neglected to interfere in time to prevent it, we should afterwards be driven to interfere, probably too late.[37]

In the Far East the United States possessed a long record of involvement. Unfortunately, the guiding principle of the Open Door

---

[35]Adolf Hitler, *Mein Kampf* (New York, 1940), pp. 894–932, 944–49, 957–63.
[36]For postwar British policy see Holborn, *Political Collapse of Europe*, pp. 127–30.
[37]Sir James Headlam-Morley, *Studies in Diplomatic History* (London, 1930), pp. 182, 184.

for China was scarcely helpful in determining a diplomatic course that measured the country's genuine interests in that critical region of the world. Nor was it probable that in the utopian atmosphere of the 1920s American policies vis-à-vis China and Japan would assume any greater realism. American and Japanese writers stressed repeatedly in the early 1920s the inescapable factors in the Chinese-Japanese confrontation that would plague American Far Eastern policy.[38] They elaborated in detail the nature and motivation of possible Japanese expansionism.

Three objectives, largely self-contradictory, determined the nature of U.S. policy toward Japan and China after the Great War. First and foremost, American officials desired additional guarantees of the Open Door principle in China to counter Japan's dominant postwar position in the western Pacific. However, this fundamental purpose of neutralizing Japan's gains of the war years and preventing their extension faced the second American objective: the negotiation of a worldwide program of naval reduction. Many Americans, including Secretary of State Hughes and Senator Borah, were convinced that armaments had caused the world war and that naval expansion, continuing unabated into the postwar years, would eventually undermine world peace again. Naval reduction would satisfy another pervading American interest, that of tax reduction. If the United States preferred to spend less on naval armaments, it could still maintain its naval leadership in the Pacific by imposing naval limitations on Japan through general agreement.[39]

Third, U.S. officials, in their determination to resolve the quarrel with Japan without expenditure or compromise, favored the annulment of the Anglo-Japanese Treaty of 1902. That treaty had neutralized British opposition to Japanese expansion during the war at China's expense and thus appeared to Washington as an encouraging element in Japan's continuing encroachment on Chinese territorial integrity. British officials differed among themselves as to the value of the alliance. Some had no interest in the Open Door principle and believed that Japan had the right to pursue its destiny as a Far Eastern power, even at the expense of China. The denial of Japanese interests on the mainland might require another major war. The British understood, moreover, that for many Japanese leaders the Anglo-Japanese Treaty was an essential element in their nation's prestige and security. Secretary Hughes, however, transformed the issue of the alliance into a simple one of moral and political choice. Britain, he declared, must support

---

[38]The Japanese writer K. K. Kawakami analyzed Japan's view of the Far East in "A Japanese Liberal's View," *Nation* 113 (November 1, 1921): 530–31.
[39]See William E. Borah, "Disarmament," *Nation's Business* 9 (September 1921): 7–8.

either the United States or Japan; it could not do both. Such pressure brought the British government, along with Australia and Canada, into line.[40]

To achieve such conflicting purposes as naval and tax reduction, the abrogation of the Anglo-Japanese Treaty, and the leashing of Japan was diplomatically impossible. On the surface, Hughes had gained all of these objectives at the Washington Conference of 1921–22. Through the Five Power Naval Limitation Treaty he forced on Japan, with his famous 5–5–3 ratio, the acceptance of a permanently inferior naval position, as compared with Britain and the United States. At the same time, the Five Power Treaty (signed by the United States, Britain, Japan, France, and Italy) denied the Western powers the right to fortify those islands in the western Pacific from which they might launch an effective campaign against the Japanese homeland.[41] In the Nine Power Treaty, Hughes secured another formal Japanese acceptance of the principle of the commercial and territorial integrity of China. Then in the Four Power Pact the secretary managed to replace the older Anglo-Japanese alliance with a vague agreement among the United States, Britain, France, and Japan to consult in case any question of aggression should arise in the Orient.[42]

As a parchment arrangement the Washington treaties were magnificent. That there was little relationship between the actual treaty provisions and the realities of international politics in the Far East was clear to naval and press observers even before the pacts were signed. The Senate refused to approve the Four Power Pact before it had attached an amendment which declared that the pact was understood to contain "no commitment to armed force, no alliance, no obligation to join in any defense." The Five Power Treaty granted Japan unlimited freedom to increase the number of its naval vessels in several important categories. Indeed, the treaty restrictions applied only to large battleships. Nor did the pact prevent any nation from increasing the range

[40]For an analysis of Hughes's pressures on the British government see J. Chal Vinson, "The Imperial Conference of 1921 and the Anglo-Japanese Alliance," *Pacific Historical Review* 31 (August 1962): 258. Prime Minister Jan Smuts of South Africa responded to Hughes's request with the remark that "the only path of safety for the British Empire is the path which can be trodden with America." Ibid., p. 261.

[41]Diplomatic exchanges on Hughes's naval limitation proposal can be found in *Papers Relating to the Foreign Relations of the United States, 1922* (Washington, 1938), 1:53–253 (hereafter cited as *FRUS*, followed by year); nonfortification agreement, ibid., pp. 252–53.

[42]For the diplomatic exchanges on the Four Power Pact see ibid., pp. 2–50. The State Department assured Senator Medill McCormick of Illinois on March 13, 1922 that the United States undertook no obligations except to communicate in case of aggression. Ibid., p. 51.

and firepower of its existing warships. The agreement on the nonfortification of the central and western Pacific denied the United States
the right to maintain naval bases on Guam or in the Philippines. For
the United States this was no sacrifice because Congress had no interest
in such distant fortifications. For some naval analysts the Five Power
Treaty comprised an unprecedented diplomatic victory for Japan.[43]
Elmer Davis, the well-known journalist and critic, observed in the *New
York Times* of February 6, 1922:

> An estimate of the success or failure of the conference can hardly
> be made until some decades have passed. . . . As the score stands
> at present, it seems hardly too much to say that this conference
> has been the greatest success in Japanese diplomatic history. Japan
> has won more at other conferences, but always at the expense of
> hard feelings left behind. Her triumphs have usually been con-
> ditioned by the certainty that the defeated nation was only waiting
> its chance to start a fight. . . . Japan retains her strategic suprem-
> acy, military and political, on the continent of Asia, and is rea-
> sonably sure that if ever this supremacy should be challenged by
> Russia or China, Russia or China would have to fight alone. . . .
> Japan has Asia to herself.

Certainly the United States gained nothing from the dissolution
of the Anglo-Japanese alliance. Years later Winston Churchill was to
write: "The annulment caused a profound impression in Japan, and
was viewed as the spurning of an Asiatic Power by the Western World.
Many links were sundered which might afterwards have proved of
decisive value to peace."[44] The Japanese at Washington gave up their
claims to Shandong (Shantung) as they had agreed in advance. What
remained after 1922 to guarantee the status quo in the Pacific was the
Nine Power Treaty whereby Japan agreed to uphold the Open Door.
For the fulfillment of this ultimate American objective in the Far East,
the nation could only rely on the moderation of future Japanese policy
on the Asian mainland.

V

This American reliance on paper—stocks and bonds at home and treaty
arrangements abroad—culminated in the late 1920s with the Kellogg-
Briand Pact. Aristide Briand, the French foreign minister, created an

---

[43]For one example of this view see William Howard Gardiner, "A Naval View of
the Conference," *Atlantic Monthly* 129 (April 1922): 522–39.

[44]Winston Churchill, *The Second World War: The Gathering Storm* (Boston, 1948),
p. 14.

unprecedented stir in American peace circles when in April 1927 he proposed a pact between the United States and France for the bilateral renunciation of force in any future conflict in which the two nations might become involved. By the mid-1920s the concept of outlawry, as the ultimate means of applying rationality to international affairs, had caught the national mood. Senator Borah quickly emerged as a leading champion of the idea, arguing that as all human evils were vulnerable to an outraged public sentiment, supported by law, so war could be banished from the earth by educating the peoples of the world that it was immoral.[45]

Secretary of State Frank B. Kellogg resisted the pressures within the nation that the government of the United States accept the opportunity to eliminate war as a legitimate exercise of national power. To him, as he explained to a number of senators, the Briand proposal was nothing less than a bilateral alliance. Suddenly, during the spring of 1928, the idea of a general outlawry pact to include all nations began to push all opposition aside, for a multilateral treaty would eliminate the danger of war everywhere and at the same time would universalize the American commitment to peace so completely that it would destroy all sense of specific national obligation to any country or region threatened by aggression. So popular was this new approach to outlawry that Kellogg eventually claimed it as his own.[46] Some Washington realists, however, found the trend disheartening. William R. Castle, a State Department official, visited his office one Sunday in late May 1928 and discovered the secretary in an adjoining office involved in a discussion of multilateral treaties. Castle confided his dismay to his diary:

> They think that they are remaking the world and actually it is nothing but a beautiful gesture while the Jugoslavs tear down Italian consular flags and the Chinese fight and the Japanese stand at attention. The gesture is worth while if it is made just right and with a little guidance in wording the Secretary would make it right. . . . [But otherwise it] may seriously tie our hands, as the originators of the plan, if the time comes when as honorable people we must step in with force . . . words can never take the place of actions . . . the only way to achieve peace is by quietly and steadily standing for the right and the fair thing. We could change the whole sentiment of Latin America toward the United States by getting other nations to cooperate with us in our police measures.

[45]William E. Borah, "Public Opinion Outlaws War," *Independent* 113 (September 13, 1924): 147–49.
[46]See Ferrell, *Peace in Their Time*, pp. 140–41.

We have stood for moderation in China and we can be careful not to suspect and offend the Japanese. We can learn courtesy in our dealings without losing any of our firmness. We cannot remake humanity in a day. We cannot abolish war with a pen but we can take the lead in making war unnecessary.[47]

Eventually the proponents of outlawry achieved their triumph in the Kellogg-Briand Pact, signed with appropriate pomp in Paris on August 27, 1928. President Coolidge's observations on the pact carried the utopian spirit of the decade to a new high. "Had an agreement of this kind been in existence in 1914," he informed a Wausau, Wisconsin, throng, "there is every reason to suppose that it would have saved the situation and delivered the world from all the misery which was inflicted by the great war. . . . It holds a greater hope for peaceful relations than was ever before given to the world. . . . It is a fitting consummation of the first decade of peace."[48] With varying degrees of enthusiasm, the Senate ratified the treaty in January 1929 by a vote of 85 to 1.

For most Americans the Pact of Paris comprised a successful assault of a democratically led world on the institution of war. The fact that Japan had signed the treaty was further assurance that Tokyo had accepted the status quo in the Far East or, at any rate, had abjured the use of force in changing it. Still the pact was not without its critics. Some regarded it merely worthless; others viewed it as a positive danger to peace because, like all utopian proposals, it eliminated the need of either diplomatic precision or military commitment. As the well-known philosopher and critic Salvador de Madariaga observed with remarkable perception, the outlawry-of-war scheme enabled the United States to "bridge over the gap between its two favorite tendencies: the tendency to isolation (from Europe, at any rate), and the tendency to see itself as a leading nation in moral as well as in material progress."[49] Frank H. Simonds, the noted American journalist, feared that U.S. involvement in the pact would mistakenly encourage Europeans to believe that the United States had deserted its isolationism. The ultimate impact of the Kellogg-Briand treaty on the foreign policies of the United States was negligible.

What made the Kellogg-Briand Pact attractive to American isolationists and internationalists alike was the absence of enforcement machinery and Secretary of State Kellogg's firm denial that the United States assumed any obligations under the pact. Many lauded the treaty's

[47]Castle quoted in ibid., p. 185n.
[48]Coolidge's Wausau speech quoted in ibid., p. 208.
[49]Salvador de Madariaga, "Disarmament—American Plan," *Atlantic Monthly* 143 (April 1929): 537–38.

reliance on international morality. Such a reliance seemed to assure success with a minimum of risk, but Roland S. Morris, professor of international law at the University of Pennsylvania, wondered how a pact based on moral force alone could protect the peace. Speaking before the American Society of International Law in April 1929, Morris questioned the pact's importance: "I am not unmindful of the *moral* obligations which are implied in such a strong statement of intention to avoid all war and to seek pacific means. But let us never forget that the legal import of a national or an international document is no measure whatever of its social or political potentialities."[50] For the more resolute internationalists, however, the pact opened new possibilities for binding the United States more closely to the European security system through active consultation with the League. David Hunter Miller, a drafter of the League Covenant, declared that the treaty "links the United States to the League of Nations as a guardian of peace; it makes the aim of that institution and the aims of our foreign policy in the largest sense identical. It is not too much to say that the Treaty in fact, though not in form, is a Treaty between the United States and the League."[51]

For other internationalists the Kellogg-Briand Pact's essential contribution to peace lay in its challenge to neutrality. Columbia University's Joseph P. Chamberlain reminded the American Society of International Law in 1929 that the pact gave nations both the opportunity and the right to stall aggression by pledging not to aid any treaty-breaking power. Similarly, Quincy Wright, professor of international law at the University of Chicago, argued in 1930 that aggression against any state was an aggression against all, including the United States. If the pact imposed no obligation to act, it did not deny any country the right to help the victims of aggression. "[B]y ratifying the Kellogg Pact," he concluded, "the United States gave up the rights of neutral trade with violators of the Pact and was relieved of the duties of neutrality for the benefit of such states."[52] Clyde Eagleton, professor of government at New York University, insisted again that the United States would strengthen the Kellogg-Briand Pact most effectively by rejecting the rights of neutrality and threatening sanctions against would-be aggressors. "The world," he wrote, "stands waiting for us to translate

[50]Roland S. Morris in *Proceedings of the American Society of International Law* (1930), p. 90.

[51]James T. Shotwell, "The Pact of Paris: With Historical Commentary," *International Conciliation* 243 (October 1928): 453, 458; David Hunter Miller, *The Pact of Paris: A Study of the Briand-Kellogg Treaty* (New York, 1928), p. 132.

[52]Chamberlain in *Proceedings of the American Society of International Law* (1929), p. 93; Wright in ibid., 1930, p. 84.

our frequent words in behalf of peace into some form of actual support for peace. . . . If we want peace, as we have said in the Pact of Paris, we must support peace when the Pact is broken. We must consult and cooperate with other states to that end."[53] Eventually those who favored peace enforcement advocated consultation, nonrecognition, and neutrality revision. These responses to aggression did not imply any commitment to the direct use of force, nor did they receive the support of the American public or congressional isolationists.[54]

Hoover, who became president in March 1929, was one American official who regarded the new worldwide peace structure with profound seriousness. For him the U.S. naval establishment was quite adequate, and, since the Kellogg-Briand treaty had indeed eliminated war except for defense, the continued drain of naval expenditures from more useful and humane projects had lost its rationality. Armaments not only comprised an unconscionable burden for mankind but also generated illwill and rivalries among nations. During his first month in office, Hoover initiated discussions with British officials on the question of further naval reduction. In his Armistice Day address he recounted the progress in disarmament achieved since the war and assured the American people that the key to world peace lay not in preparedness or diplomacy but in the existence of a spirit of goodwill among nations.[55]

Hoover's actual negotiations with British Prime Minister Ramsay MacDonald in August and September 1929 illustrated fully the extent to which American naval power was divorced from policy. For the prime minister, England possessed an empire that required nothing less than a global defense effort. For Britain, moreover, the U.S. fleet was a source of security, not a threat of war. Thus MacDonald had little interest in either British or American naval reduction.[56] Eventually at Hoover's prodding the London government called the famous London Naval Conference of 1930. Its five delegations represented the United States, Britain, France, Italy, and Japan. From the outset the conference ran into insurmountable difficulties. All the nations present, except the United States, pointed to specific interests and potential

[53]Eagleton in ibid., pp. 90, 94, 113.

[54]For a more extensive analysis of the Kellogg-Briand Pact in American internationalist thought see Harold Josephson, "Outlawing War: Internationalism and the Pact of Paris, *Diplomatic History* 3 (Fall 1939): 377–90. See also Richard N. Current, "The United States and 'Collective Security': Notes on the History of an Idea," DeConde, *Isolation and Security*, pp. 39–44.

[55]Hoover's Armistice Day address, Washington, November 11, 1929, in William Starr Myers, ed., *The State Papers and Other Public Writings of Herbert Hoover* (Garden City, NY, 1934), 1:125–32.

[56]MacDonald to Charles G. Dawes, August 9, and September 24, 1929, *FRUS, 1929* (Washington, 1943), 1:186–88, 254–56.

rivals that necessitated either adequate naval power or other security guarantees. The Japanese, for example, made it painfully clear that they had interests and ambitions in the Pacific which demanded a higher naval ratio than that imposed on them by the Washington treaties. The United States, too, had its distant and vulnerable commitments. It simply refused to recognize any relationship between those outposts and the power required to defend them, and it alone among the great nations declined to be burdened by obligations of empire.

At length the United States, Britain, and Japan signed a new naval agreement imposing tonnage on lesser naval craft, but it failed to limit. Indeed, the United States required a major naval-building program if it would reach its quota. France held the key to genuine naval reduction, but French officials established early one immutable condition to any naval agreement: a security pact with the United States. The American delegation, headed by Secretary of State Henry L. Stimson, hoped to coerce France by arousing public sentiment against the French demands. They discovered, as did Woodrow Wilson eleven years earlier, that the French government, whatever its views on naval reduction, had the full support of French public opinion. Eventually Stimson had to choose between the collapse of the conference and a consultative pact for France. He chose the latter course, only to be repudiated in Washington. Thereafter a five-power agreement became impossible, and, at the end of the conference, France and Italy refused to sign any treaty at all. Simonds, writing in the *Review of Reviews* of May 1930, summarized the security dilemma at London: "The British and Americans were always seeking formulae which would give the French the semblance of security without the reality, the French were always demanding the reality and rejecting the semblance."

From Versailles to the London Conference the predominant foreign policy mood of the United States had gradually conformed to the pattern of utopian internationalism which found its ultimate expression in the Kellogg-Briand Pact. According to Lewis Einstein, the outbreak of another war in Europe would find the United States as unprepared physically and emotionally as it had been in 1914. For him, in that depression year, American foreign policy was nonexistent: "Beyond current platitudes of peace and good-will, beyond a predilection for forms of legal remedy which we are only ready to accept for questions of secondary interest, beyond pushing our dwindling exports on an impoverished Europe, what more has been our recent foreign policy?"[57]

Even the internationalists who believed that the United States

[57]Lewis Einstein, "Our Still Dubious Foreign Policy," *North American Review* 232 (September 1931): 210–18.

should play a leading role in world affairs seldom acknowledged the obligation that the country act responsibly, that it measure events carefully to judge how and where its interests were involved, and that it be prepared to engage in the immediate defense of positions of vital concern and to negotiate on matters of secondary importance. At times the attention that American officials gave to international bodies and conferences created a semblance of genuine world leadership, whereas the utopian methods employed permitted the country to escape its responsibilities totally. The perennial avoidance of hard political settlements turned the concepts of conciliation, cooperation, consultation, and peaceful adjustment into ends in themselves. For a leadership that had led a nation to expect perfection in diplomacy at little expense to itself, it was easier and cheaper to allow potentially costly issues to drift. The peace of the 1920s was no demonstration of either a general acceptance of the Versailles settlement (symbolic of the status quo) or even the universal rejection of force. What sustained the assumption that all wars had been fought and all issues resolved was the predominance of Western power which permitted the spokesmen of the democracies to manage the game of international politics so effortlessly that they were quite unconscious of the role which power had played in their success. Thus peace rested primarily on the weakness of those countries—the Soviet Union, Germany, and Japan especially—whose governments had already made clear their dissatisfaction with the Versailles settlement. Any collapse of the Western monopoly of power would witness the almost immediate return of force to international life.

Americans, however, experiencing perennial peace without demonstrable risks or heavy costs, assumed that the world of the 1920s had responded to American principles of peaceful change rather than the West's near monopoly of power based largely on the potential might of the United States. No one saw the error in such assumptions more clearly than did Edwin L. James of the *New York Times*. He argued that America's world position resulted not from moral leadership but from the country's wealth and material resources, and that, if the United States were a poor and weak nation, the world would care no more about what it thought than it did before the Great War.

> Now those who still believe that 'the moral sense' of America is a real factor in international affairs will surely cite the Kellogg pact as an example of how we do good and do it altruistically. But no one who has lived in Europe in recent years can believe in the dominant moral effect of the Kellogg pact as an active factor in world affairs. Almost the only attraction Europe ever saw in it was

the line the United States signed on. No European nation promised anything in the anti-war pact that it had not already agreed to in the covenant of the League of Nations. But there was the signature of the United States, which seemed to promise the co-operation of our great material power in curbing the aggressor in another war. And that made a powerful appeal. . . . Does any one believe seriously that the deference and respect Britain has shown for us in the past decade represent a belief in our moral superiority, a realization of a superior civilization on this side of the Atlantic or a better system of government and social order? Not at all. Britain is extremely practical in foreign affairs. There is no new approval of America and Americans, but there is a realization of our material power as something to be reckoned with seriously, and Britain does just that.[58]

VI

Events in Europe and Asia after the mid-1930s challenged profoundly the entire spectrum of utopian assumptions on which postwar American foreign policy had been erected. In its various confrontations of the 1920s, the United States had abjured involvement completely or accepted the limited obligation to confer; it accepted no commitment to defend its privileged position. So favorable was the international environment throughout the Republican years that the perennial defiance of the traditional rules of diplomacy scarcely impinged on the country's complacency at all. Much of the phraseology of the 1920s attributed the continuing stability of the international order to the power of world opinion and the universal preference for peace and not to a variety of special circumstances soon to pass away.

Suddenly in 1935 the Versailles structure in Europe began to crumble under the impact of aggression and war. Nowhere could the democracies respond. Whether they suffered from paralysis or mistaken concepts matters little. In Europe the two guardians of the status quo, Britain and France, gave Europe's two aggressive dictators, Italy's Benito Mussolini and Germany's Adolf Hitler, the green light to attack the provisions of the Versailles Treaty without any real intention of doing so. In March 1935, Hitler announced the reinstitution of universal military conscription and the establishment of a new German army of thirty-six divisions with over five hundred thousand men. Shortly thereafter Hermann Göeing, the high Nazi official, apprised the world that Germany would create an air force. Thus Germany,

[58]Edwin L. James, "Our World Power and Moral Influence," *International Digest* 1 (October 1930): 21–24.

without facing any threat of big-power retaliation, subverted the vital military clauses of the Versailles Treaty.[59] Almost at once Germany threatened French military superiority on the European continent.

To mollify Hitler, Britain in June 1935 scrapped the naval clauses of the Versailles settlement, permitting Germany a navy 35 percent the tonnage of Britain's. This decision, in large measure, condoned Germany's entire armament program. France, isolated by these events, had turned in May of that year to the Soviet Union and Czechoslovakia for mutual assistance pacts. Unwilling to antagonize Italy, France approved Mussolini's decision of October to dispatch his black-shirted legions into Ethiopia in another open assault on the Versailles system. In further defiance of the Versailles arrangements, Nazi troops occupied the Rhineland in March 1936, but again there was no Western response. Churchill saw the significance of this failure and warned the House of Commons that "when there is a line of fortifications . . . it *will be a barrier across Germany's front door which will leave her free to sally out eastwards and southwards by the other doors.*"[60] Ultimately, all the diplomatic concessions did not prevent Mussolini from joining Hitler. During 1936 the two dictators formed what was to become the Rome-Berlin Axis and openly entered the Spanish civil war as partisans of Francisco Franco and his rebel forces.

These world events pushed American isolationism toward a new militancy. Tinged with Anglophobia, isolationism in the 1930s took its chief strength from the broad conviction that a genuinely neutral United States could have avoided involvement in the Great War. During 1934, Senator Gerald P. Nye of North Dakota had launched his investigation of the munitions industry.[61] His conclusions seemed to prove what most Americans wanted to hear: Woodrow Wilson had committed the nation to the Allied cause, not to defend the nation's interests but to underwrite the private ambitions of the industrialists who had enjoyed such unprecedented profits during the early war years. To prevent Wall Street from driving the United States into another European war, Nye in April 1935 introduced a series of resolutions in the Senate designed to prevent a repetition of those events which had dragged the country into the Great War of 1914. During August, Congress passed the first Neutrality Act which authorized the president, in the event of a foreign war, to embargo munitions to all belligerents and warn Americans traveling

[59]For the German rearmament program see William L. Shirer, *Berlin Diary: The Journal of a Foreign Correspondent, 1934–1941* (London, 1941), pp. 31–34; and Cordell Hull, *The Memoirs of Cordell Hull* (New York, 1948), 1:243.

[60]Churchill, *The Gathering Storm*, p. 204 (emphasis in original).

[61]Adler, *The Isolationist Impulse*, pp. 256–57; Wayne S. Cole, *Senator Gerald P. Nye and American Foreign Relations* (Minneapolis, 1962), pp. 71–96.

on the vessels of warring nations that they did so at their own risk. In supporting the measure, Nye repeated what became the standard liberal argument in defense of future American neutrality:

> Our experience of twenty years ago is, or should be, a ready reminder of the power of the forces that would drag a great nation into wars not of its own making. We witnessed in our last effort to remain neutral how munitions sales, bankers' loans to the Allies, and Americans sailing upon the vessels of nations at war, such as the *Lusitania*, tended to bring us into a conflict which was in its inception of no relation to us. Had America had a well-defined and strong neutrality policy at the beginning of the World War, she might have escaped participation in that war, and escaped, too, the penalties which we have been bearing and paying ever since, with the end not yet in sight.[62]

Confronted at home with the pressures of American isolationism and abroad with the burgeoning aggressions of the dictators, the administration of Franklin D. Roosevelt faced the inescapable obligation, too seldom acknowledged, to bring some semblance of balance between the interests of the United States and its capacity to act in their defense. Eventually Roosevelt and his secretary of state, Cordell Hull, in an effort to satisfy the incompatible demands of domestic and international politics, formulated a national response that appeared to meet the requirements of the times but which in reality perpetuated the utopianism inherited from the Republican years. That utopianism found its most perfect expression in the words and actions of Secretary Hull. When Hitler announced the expansion of the German military machine in March 1935, Hull defined the official American response before a press conference: "Everybody knows that the United States has always believed that treaties must constitute the foundation on which any stable peace structure must rest. . . . I believe that the moral influence of the United States and its people must always encourage living up to treaties."[63] What the United States would do if other governments ignored such preachments he did not say. Nor did Hull, in upholding the entire international treaty structure, define specific interests that the United States would defend.

Roosevelt's noted address at Chautauqua, New York, in August 1936 contained all the fundamental ingredients of an acceptable response to the disturbing events of that year. After inviting all the countries of

---

[62]For the key issues in the congressional debate on wartime trade, see *Congressional Record*, 74th Cong., 1st sess., August 20, 21, 23, 24, 1935, pp. 13,776–93, 13,951–56, 14,282–84, 14,430–38.

[63]Hull, *Memoirs*, 1:243.

the world to accept the American principle of the good neighbor, the president acknowledged with regret that some aggressor nations had rejected such standards of behavior. "It is a bitter experience to us," he said, "when the spirit of agreements to which we are a party is not lived up to. It is an even more bitter experience for the whole company of nations to witness not only the spirit but the letter of international agreements violated with impunity and without regard to the simple principles of honor. Permanent friendships between nations as between men can be sustained only by scrupulous respect for the pledged word." Having noted that some nations were challenging the world's treaty arrangements through force, Roosevelt disposed of the American obligation to international order by reminding his listeners that the United States had participated in its share of conferences. Thereafter he reaffirmed the administration's isolationist intentions. "I hate war," he assured the doubters. "I have passed unnumbered hours, I shall pass unnumbered hours thinking and planning how war may be kept from this nation. I wish I could keep war from all nations, but that is beyond my power."[64] The president's diplomatic thought, encompassing both internationalism and isolationism, was characterized by a profound escapism.

Writers on world affairs, no less than national leaders, examined the critical problems of peace, stability, and change in international society. Scholars agreed that peace assigned no special merit to the status quo. James T. Shotwell, the noted historian of Columbia University, observed accurately that the central problem confronting international relations was "the need for a more flexible structure than that which identifies justice with the *status quo*." It was better to permit change even through force, echoed Yale's Edwin M. Borchard, than to "endow the existing *status quo* with moral sanctity." To uphold a decaying status quo, he noted, might be "anything but constructive."[65] Edwin DeWitt Dickinson, professor of international law at the University of California, warned that the organization of effective sanctions dared not take precedence over "the development of procedures for orderly modification of the *status quo*." In emphasizing the need for peaceful change, Dickinson added: "If security for the society of nations implies an assurance of orderly progress, collective security may be

---

[64]Roosevelt's address at Chautauqua, New York, August 14, 1936, in Samuel I. Rosenman, ed., *The Public Papers and Addresses of Franklin D. Roosevelt, 1936: The People Approve* (New York, 1938), 5:288–89.
[65]Shotwell quoted in Current, "The United States and 'Collective Security,' " p. 46; Edwin M. Borchard, "Neutrality," in Frank P. Davidson and George S. Viereck, Jr., eds., *Before America Decides: Foresight in Foreign Affairs* (Cambridge, MA, 1938), pp. 222, 226.

defined as co-operation in the attainment of such an assurance." Professor Eagleton, who observed that the community of nations would never prevent war until it provided individual states with peaceful procedures to remedy injustices, predicted: "[I]f force is used merely to maintain the *status quo*, to preserve for the *beati possidentes* their happy situation, the system is bound to fail."[66]

If American and European students of international affairs rarely advocated force to uphold the status quo in the 1930s, they could not ignore the immediate challenge to the peace embodied in the policies of Italy, Germany, and Japan. Quite logically they responded to the threat of aggression with Wilsonian appeals to collective security. In 1934 and 1935 the Collective Security Committee of the League-sponsored International Studies Conference met in London. The committee sought some formula that would enable the United States to discard neutrality in favor of collaboration. In August 1935, C. A. W. Manning of the University of London delivered a lecture on collective security at the Geneva Institute of International Relations: "I suspect [the term collective security] was invented, quite recently, as a sly means of suggesting to the more 'soft-boiled' Americans that somehow their country, in signing the Kellogg Pact, has inadvertently and against its desires assumed a quasi-membership in the League."[67]

Strangely those who advocated collective security almost invariably regarded it as a substitute for power politics. They assumed that the preponderance of nations, dedicated to preserving the status quo, could prevent aggression without war. Sir Alfred Zimmern, the noted British publicist and professor of international relations at Oxford, defined collective security as "*the safety of all by all.*" Fortunately for him the free, constitutional, and democratic states which he trusted controlled the bulk of the world's resources; through cooperative economic policies they could defend their universe against aggression without compromise or war. Denna Frank Fleming of Vanderbilt University, writing in November 1937, insisted that the United States take its place at the center of a collective security system, whether the commitment be to the League or to an alliance, but he denied that collective security would lead to war. "No collective action taken by a preponderance of the nations against an aggressor can hereafter be legally called war, nor be morally considered as war." He agreed with Zimmern that preponderant economic power, if used effectively, would prevent

[66]Edwin DeWitt Dickinson, "The United States and Collective Security," in Quincy Wright, ed., *Neutrality and Collective Security* (Chicago, 1936), pp. 158, 163; Clyde Eagleton, "Collective Security," in Davidson and Viereck, *Before America Decides*, pp. 212–13.
    [67]Manning quoted in Current, "The United States and 'Collective Security,' " p. 44.

aggression without the danger of war.[68] Eagleton, in a speech at Harvard in December 1937, agreed that collective action did not mean war: "Collective security," he explained, "means the combination *omnium contra unum*—of the community against the lawbreaker, whoever he may be." Such a combination of all countries would render aggression futile; thereafter, Eagleton wrote, "no state would have to demand the blood of its mothers' sons. . . . [A]n international police force recruited by volunteer efforts would be sufficient."[69]

Those who advocated collective security through the League generally denied that League action need involve the United States in the politics of Europe or Asia. Shotwell had insisted in 1936 that the world could sustain the peace no better "than by maintaining an international organ of cooperative pacification. The League is that one body." For Shotwell, typically, collective defense under the League would require only a regional commitment. Dickinson argued that League sanctions, if organized regionally, would eliminate the United States from a European or Asian security system. He presented his formula for global security at the University of Chicago in June 1936:

> Collective security may encompass the globe without universalizing every sanctioning device. In our time the universal league of nations will be a league of consultation and co-operation . . . fortified by a sanctioning procedure which supplements universal commitments with regional undertakings graduated with due regard for the geographical position of members of the international community. As regards the assurance of collective security, this probably means that we shall have a league of nations for Europe within the universal league.

For Fleming also the League's collective security system would not commit the United States or even the European powers to the protection of peace everywhere. Geographic safety permitted a graduated responsibility. Those most directly endangered by aggression would carry the major responsibility for opposing it. More distant countries would fulfill their obligations by applying economic sanctions. It was not strange that critics of collective security, such as Borchard, predicted that the system would always fail. "In practice," he wrote, "the collectivists do not remain collected and . . . the divergence of their interests is disclosed

---

[68]Alfred Zimmern, "The Problem of Collective Security," in Wright, *Neutrality and Collective Security*, pp. 4, 23, 55, 72–73 (emphasis in original); Denna F. Fleming, *The United States and World Organization, 1920–1933* (New York, 1938), pp. 536–37.

[69]Eagleton, "Collective Security," in Davidson and Viereck, *Before America Decides*, pp. 191–92, 204–05, 211.

as soon as they are asked to act." Nations, he suggested, would never defend interests other than their own.[70]

Unfortunately, collective security designed to avoid the necessity of force offered no defense against aggression, nor did it present any solution for the problem of peaceful change. In practice, any system of collective security would seek order rather than change. For British historian Edward Hallett Carr, collective security was merely a device of the status quo powers to prevent unwanted change in the international system.

> Just as the ruling class in a community prays for domestic peace, which guarantees its own security and predominance, . . . so international peace becomes a special vested interest of predominant Powers. In the past, Roman and British imperialism were commended to the world in the guise of *pax Romana* and the *pax Britannica*. Today, when no single Power is strong enough to dominate the world, and supremacy is vested in a group of nations, slogans like 'collective security' and 'resistance to aggression' serve the same purpose of proclaiming an identity of interest between the dominant group and the world as a whole in the maintenance of peace.[71]

The Western preference for the status quo, in the absence of any program to change it peacefully, never recommended the means for preserving it except the resort to war.

---

[70]James T. Shotwell, *On the Rim of the Abyss* (New York, 1936), p. 353; Dickinson, "The United States and Collective Security," in Wright, *Neutrality and Collective Security*, pp. 179–80, 182; Fleming, *World Organization*, p. 543; Borchard, "Neutrality," in Davidson and Viereck, *Before America Decides*, p. 225.

[71]Carr, *The Twenty Years' Crisis*, p. 82.

CHAPTER TWO

Roosevelt, Chamberlain, and the Coming of War*

By 1937 Adolf Hitler's challenge to Europe had become overt and threatening. Through two years of unrestrained defiance of the Versailles Treaty's military provisions, German rearmament had become the dominant factor in European politics. Why Germany's military effort had emerged as a special danger to Europe's security was explained by American diplomat Hugh Wilson from Switzerland: "The ability of a dictator to devote practically the entire resources of his country to armament cannot be matched by democratic countries in time of peace." From Berlin, Ambassador William E. Dodd warned Washington that "the development of the [German] army and the recent throwing off of restraints of these past 17 years have brought matters back to a place where Germany is even more dangerous to the world than in 1914."[1] Foreign correspondent William L. Shirer recorded Europe's declining confidence in his diary notation of April 20, 1937:

> Hitler's birthday. He gets more and more like a Caesar. Today a public holiday . . . and a great military parade. The Reichswehr revealed a little of what it has: heavy artillery, tanks, and magnificently trained men. Hitler stood on the reviewing stand in front of the Technishe Hochschule, as happy as a child with tin soldiers, standing there more than two hours and saluting every tank and gun. The military attachés of France, Britain, and Russia, I hear, were impressed. So were ours.

*The Harmsworth Inaugural Lecture delivered at the University of Oxford, May 21, 1979. Published as *Roosevelt and the Search for a European Policy, 1937–1939* (Oxford, 1980). Reprinted by permission.

[1]Wilson to Hull, January 27, 1936, and Dodd to Hull, February 8, 1936, *FRUS, 1936* (Washington, 1953), 1:186, 195.

In May, French Premier Léon Blum admitted to American Ambassador William C. Bullitt that "Hitler had the political initiative on the continent of Europe."[2]

Hitler's ambitions were no secret. German officials acknowledged freely the intention of the Reich not only to dominate Central and Eastern Europe but also to secure the return of Germany's prewar colonies, or their equivalent. No longer, they added, would Germany condone the vindictive clauses in the Versailles Treaty. Nazi aggressiveness had a quality of its own. Internally, Hitler, divorced from the German past, operated in a moral void, accepting no limits on his determination to dismantle the German state machine and substitute organized chaos with himself in absolute command. Still Hitler's external challenge was not unlike those which ambitious rulers had posed for neighboring states in previous generations. Essentially he gave Europe the choice of accepting massive changes in its treaty structure or facing the probability of war. He warned Britain's Lord Halifax in November 1937 that Europe's leaders must approach him directly, prepared to negotiate on specific issues, or not at all. "The League system," he argued, "means the perpetuation of the *status quo*. It is useless to evade the issue by saying that Article 19 of the Covenant provides for peaceful revision. . . . It is impossible to imagine peaceful revision with the consent of all. . . . It is a fact, perhaps an inconvenient fact, that Germany is now a great and powerful nation, pulsating with energy and determined to realize what she believes to be her legitimate aspirations."[3] For the United States as well as for Europe, the threatened destruction of the Versailles order carried a heavy penalty, presaging the decline of Britain and France as great powers, with consequences damaging to Western security. Beyond the decline of Western primacy lay the predictable conflict between Germany and the Soviet Union— the ultimate issue in Europe's faltering stability. How the European balance of power could survive that clash was nowhere apparent. Nor was it clear how the creators of Versailles intended to protect their world from such disaster.

II

This impending collapse of Europe's Versailles order troubled Washington, but it did not create the foundations of an adequate American response. Except for the Philippine Islands, the United States possessed

---

[2]William L. Shirer, *Berlin Diary: The Journal of a Foreign Correspondent, 1934–1941* (London, 1941), p. 63; Bullitt to Hull, May 20, 1937, *FRUS, 1937* (Washington, 1954), 1:94.

[3]Hitler quoted in the Earl of Birkenhead, *Halifax* (London, 1965), p. 371.

no specific political or military commitments in the Eastern Hemisphere. With American interests outside the Western Hemisphere remote and ill-defined, politicians, journalists, and scholars sustained the illusion that diplomatic and military isolation from Europe's strife could guarantee the nation's peace with a minimum of risk. What separated Americans in their response to the Nazi challenge was not their desire to avoid war but their varying perceptions of the price that such avoidance would demand. Isolationists assumed that continued peace would require its price in diminished trade and a changing international order. Many agreed that Versailles had imposed unfair restrictions on Germany; the democracies, therefore, could serve their interests more effectively through treaty revision than through sanctions against Germany which would save neither the treaty nor the peace. Isolationist Senator Nye insisted that the American people would not "consciously endorse a war which had no other object than to maintain the particular status quo which was established at Versailles." Similarly, the *Alexandria* (VA) *Gazette* argued that the Fascist nations making trouble in Europe would not remain at peace unless they had better access to new territory and raw materials.[4] Although convinced that the United States was safe from European attack, isolationists after 1935 had voted overwhelmingly for military appropriations in their desire to strengthen the country's hemispheric defenses. Such preparedness would keep order in the Western Hemisphere. There the Republic could flourish without regard to what happened in the outside world.

Like many isolationists, the internationalists who dominated the Roosevelt administration did not regard every territorial arrangement embodied in the Versailles Treaty as sacred or even just. Nevertheless, the admittedly arbitrary boundaries now defined the international legal structure; any effort to alter them by force would provoke legitimate resistance and thereby threaten the peace. Sharing the Wilsonian belief that the breakdown of peace anywhere endangered the peace everywhere, internationalists insisted that U.S. security required the rejection of every armed assault on the world's treaty system. They found the means to uphold the status quo in international law and the principles of peaceful change and self-determination, the moral bulwarks of the established order. As operating forces in international life, these constraints eliminated the legitimacy, even the necessity, of accepting the consequences of aggression.

[4]Wayne S. Cole, *Senator Gerald P. Nye and American Foreign Relations* (Minneapolis, 1962), pp. 164, 168–69; Manfred Jonas, *Isolationism in America, 1935–1941* (Ithaca, NY, 1966), pp. 107–08; *Alexandria* (VA) *Gazette*, October 14, 1937, p. 4, and October 23, 1937, p. 4. The neutrality legislation after 1935 assumed that the United States in order to avoid war would pay a heavy price in lost commerce.

Roosevelt and Hull required a formula that would convey the administration's deep concern for Europe's stability, even while it permitted the United States to escape all responsibility for its preservation. Hull perfected a uniquely American tactic for upholding the status quo (without any American commitment to it) by urging aggressors to follow the treaty-abiding examples of the United States. He called on all countries to observe faithfully their international agreements and to modify them, if necessary, "by orderly processes carried out in a spirit of mutual helpfulness and accommodation." In October 1937, Hull assured the Soviet ambassador that effective resistance to aggression required not military force or economic coercion but "a combination of all possible moral and other influences to outlaw war." How appeals to international law and the precepts of the Kellogg-Briand Pact, which avoided both commitments and risk, could be effective in preventing aggression was not clear. In the past, nonrecognition and the enunciation of principles had served only as a device to escape responsibility for what occurred. Roosevelt's occasional references in private to sanctions, blockades, international cooperation, and the need for relaxation of the neutrality laws suggested that he doubted the power of principles in world affairs. Publicly, however, the president never acknowledged the essential roles of power and diplomacy in dealing with an unstable international order. His refusal to confront the dictators with choices that defined the country's interests partly reflected his acceptance of the internationalist creed and partly his conviction that he would lose an open political battle with the isolationists. Skilled politician that he was, Roosevelt would balance what was desirable with what was practicable.

Nothing in the post-Versailles American experience had prepared Roosevelt or the country to accept the need for either the negotiation of settlements or the preparation of war. As president, Roosevelt could not ignore Europe's drift toward disaster, and, with his advisers pressing him to act, he concluded from time to time that he might display world leadership by calling an international conference, without accepting any unwanted commitments. Such a conference, conforming to Hull's emphasis on orderly and peaceful procedures, would search for the principles whereby nations might resolve their differences through mutual agreement. Unfortunately, this reliance on rules of conduct, with its concomitant burden of eliminating Hitler's demands totally without the necessity of war, rendered U.S. diplomacy irrelevant. Ambassador to Poland John Cudahy reminded Roosevelt that a conference would settle nothing, and in a note to the president he acknowledged the difficulty of dealing with Hitler when no one could anticipate his actions. He advised Roosevelt, however, that any intervention "without some specific remedy for the difficulties over here would not only be unavailing but would be a mistake from the viewpoint of American prestige. . . . I do not like to clutter your very much over-cluttered desk with letters, but I do want to impress upon you the futility of attempting any gesture toward Europe at this time unless this be based upon realistic remedies for the relief of existing troubles."[5] Only if Roosevelt were prepared to face Germany's demands directly, Cudahy concluded, would the effort achieve any purpose.

Whatever his limited expectations for European cooperation, Roosevelt refused to discard the conference idea. In January 1937 he suggested to Dodd in Berlin that "if five or six heads of the important governments could meet together for a week with complete inaccessibility to press or cables or radio, a definite, useful agreement might result."[6] Limited to the contemplation of conference proposals Roosevelt reacted impatiently to assertions that he alone could terminate Europe's difficulties. When Secretary of the Treasury Henry Morgenthau suggested in March that Europe looked to him, Roosevelt retorted: "I feel like throwing either a cup and saucer at you or the coffee pot. Well, I had Hull [and] Norman Davis to lunch and Davis said, the only person who can save the situation is Roosevelt and then I said to Davis how, and Davis said by sending an envoy to Europe."[7]

Morgenthau, deeply concerned over Europe's drift toward bankruptcy, recommended a disarmament conference. Roosevelt favored a meeting of a half dozen countries. "He would tell their delegates," Morgenthau recorded, "that the problem was theirs, and send them to some other building to work out a solution and come back with it." Those who defied the agreements would face an economic boycott. On March 26, Neville Chamberlain, Britain's chancellor of the exchequer, argued against such a conference, reminding Washington that armaments were Europe's only deterrent to German aggression. "No other country, he wrote, not Italy, since she has her hands full with the task of consolidating her Abyssinia conquest, not Russia with all her military preparations, certainly not France, England, or any of the smaller

[5]Cudahy to Roosevelt, January 7, 1937, in Edgar B. Nixon, ed., *Franklin D. Roosevelt and Foreign Affairs* (Cambridge, MA, 1969), 3:572–73. See also Cudahy to Roosevelt, December 26, 1936, *FRUS, 1937*, 1:24.

[6]Roosevelt to Dodd, January 9, 1937, in Elliott Roosevelt, ed., *F.D.R.: His Personal Letters, 1928–1945* (New York, 1950), 1:649.

[7]John Morton Blum, *From the Morgenthau Diaries*, vol. 1, *Years of Crisis, 1928–1938* (Boston, 1959), p. 458.

Powers, is for a moment credited with any aggressive designs." Germany would resist any military arrangements that defeated its aggressive purposes. "The only consideration which would influence her to a contrary decision," Chamberlain concluded, "would be the conviction that the efforts to secure superior force were doomed to failure by reason of the superior force which would meet her if she attempted aggression."[8]

European leaders joined the quest for a Rooseveltian peace initiative. The president's dismissive reply came in July 1937 when he told newsmen that people were looking "for somebody outside Europe to come forward with a hat and a rabbit in it. Well, . . . I haven't got a hat and I haven't got a rabbit in it."[9] What Europeans wanted of Roosevelt was not a call for a world conference but some positive display of America's intention to support the forces opposing Hitler. For British and French leaders living under the immediate threat of German expansionism, the economic and military power of the United States was indeed relevant to Europe's stability. Chamberlain had reminded Morgenthau in May that "the greatest single contribution which the United States could make at the present moment to the preservation of world peace would be the amendment of the existing neutrality legislation. . . . The legislation in its present form constitutes an indirect but potent encouragement to aggression, and it is earnestly hoped that some way may be found of leaving sufficient discretion with the Executive to deal with each case on its merits."[10]

For the moment Roosevelt avoided that challenge, but in September he toyed with a proposal designed to establish a system of economic sanctions. That month he informed Secretary of the Interior Harold L. Ickes of his plan to write to all nations of the world (except possibly Germany, Italy, and Japan), suggesting that the peace-loving states, by denying trade and raw materials, should isolate any country that threatened the liberties of another. This program, the president hoped, would be "a warning to the nations that are today running amuck."[11] Roosevelt was not alone in this private advocacy of force. Assistant Secretary of State George W. Messersmith, deeply distrustful of the Reich, reminded Hull in October that the United States either

[8]Ibid., pp. 459, 463–64.

[9]Quoted in Robert Dallek, *Franklin D. Roosevelt and American Foreign Policy, 1932–1945* (New York, 1979), p. 144.

[10]Chamberlain memorandum, May 1937, *FRUS, 1937*, 1:99. Denying the importance of power, the State Department replied that the U.S. government "firmly believes that the opportunity exists today for directing national policies into a channel of political and economic cooperation, based upon a common-sense harmonization of national interests and upon a spirit of mutual friendliness and fair-dealing." Ibid., pp. 105–06.

[11]Harold L. Ickes, *The Secret Diary of Harold L. Ickes*, vol. 2, *The Inside Struggle, 1936–1939* (London, 1955), p. 213.

would continue the temporizing of the past, predictably leading to war, or would accept a course that offered some chance of maintaining international order.[12] What this concern for power, whether economic or military, had in common with the administration's fundamental reliance on principle was the assumption that this country could preserve the status quo without coming to terms with its aggressors. Unfortunately, actions that emphasized power, rather than principle, would be effective only in direct proportion to their defiance of official American neutrality.

Roosevelt's famed "quarantine" speech delivered in Chicago on October 5, 1937 inaugurated his halting effort to increase the weight of American influence in world affairs. He warned his listeners that terror and lawlessness were endangering the foundations of their civilization. From such international anarchy and instability, there was "no escape through mere isolation and neutrality." It was essential that the United States play a role in leading the world to a "triumph of law and moral principles in order that peace, justice, and confidence may prevail in the world." To achieve this internationalist goal, he proposed a quarantine of the aggressors, suggesting that, "when an epidemic of physical disease starts to spread, the community approves and joins in a quarantine of the patients in order to protect the health of the community against the spread of the disease." In his moral defense of the status quo, Roosevelt spoke not of interests to be defended or compromised according to circumstances but of those abstract principles which, if triumphant, would eliminate all unwanted change from the world. In subsequent conversations with members of the press, Roosevelt admitted only that he sought some new concept of preserving peace; he did not contemplate, he told George William Cardinal Mundelein of Chicago, the use of military or naval force against aggressor nations. Foreign newspapers, one correspondent informed Roosevelt, described his speech as "an attitude without a program," to which the president replied: "It is an attitude and it does not outline a program but it says we are looking for a program."[13]

On October 6—the day following the "quarantine" speech— Undersecretary of State Sumner Welles, convinced that the solution of Europe's problems required the worldwide adoption of a framework of principles, suggested that on November 11 (Armistice Day) the

---

[12]Messersmith to Hull, October 11, 1937, *FRUS, 1937*, 1:140–41.
[13]For Roosevelt's efforts to explain the meaning of his "quarantine" speech, see Dorothy Borg, *The United States and the Far Eastern Crisis of 1933–1938* (Cambridge, MA, 1964), pp. 381–86.

president call a spectacular White House meeting of all diplomatic representatives in Washington. There he would invite the nations of the world to gather at the conference table and arrive at agreements on principles of international conduct, disarmament, and trade. Roosevelt accepted the idea, but Hull, arguing against the proposal as a drastic assault on American isolationist opinion, reminded him that Germany, Italy, and Japan and already taken the offensive and would disregard any treaties or agreements that an international conference might produce. Moreover, to announce a conference without prior consultation with Britain and France would be unfair and unwise. Early in January 1938, Hull withdrew his opposition to a White House meeting and subsequent conference but insisted that Roosevelt first consult Chamberlain, since June 1937 the prime minister of Britain. Only after securing Chamberlain's approval should Roosevelt then turn to France, Germany, and Italy.

Roosevelt now agreed to send a revised version of Welles's original proposal to Chamberlain. At the contemplated White House meeting, the president would suggest that all governments strive to reach a unanimous agreement on the essential principles that would govern future international relations. Because inequities existed in the postwar settlements, Roosevelt acknowledged that lasting peace required international adjustments of various kinds aimed at the removal of those injustices. Under no circumstance, the president added, would he compromise traditional American freedom from European politics.[14] Should the governments support his plan, Roosevelt would not summon a world conference but would invite Sweden, the Netherlands, Belgium, Switzerland, Hungary, Yugoslavia, Turkey, and three Latin American states to send representatives to Washington and there work out general principles on the questions listed in the draft. Those principles would give Hitler the choice of accepting the limitations imposed on Germany by the treaty system or defying that system through force and accepting the risks of that decision. Welles delivered the message to British Ambassador Sir Ronald Lindsay on January 11, 1938 and reminded him that American opinion would not permit a stronger U.S. commitment to Europe's peace. The president would proceed if by January 17 he received the assurance that the British government supported the proposal. British opposition, Lindsay warned London, would annul all progress made in Anglo-American cooperation during the two previous years.

---

[14]Cabinet notes, January 1938, CAB 27/626/5887, Public Record Office (PRO), London. For Hull's reaction to the Welles's proposal, see *The Memoirs of Cordell Hull* (London, 1948), 1:546–48.

III

For Chamberlain, Roosevelt's proposal was less than helpful. Unlike the United States, Britain could not escape the immediate threat of German power and ambition. Britain's commitments were global and vastly exceeded the country's capabilities. In the Pacific especially the British position rested on tradition and bluff. London, no more than Washington, desired to involve itself in the specific problems on East-Central Europe. The British lived under no illusion that they could escape a European war, and a continental struggle against Germany would endanger a rich and vulnerable empire. Unable to renounce its worldwide obligations, London could protect its interests in Europe and elsewhere either by organizing a permanent balance against the Axis or by composing the ambitions of the aggressors through direct diplomacy. British attempts to reach an understanding with Germany were inevitable. Unless the London government made such an effort and demonstrably failed, few in Britain, either inside or outside the government, would accept the probability of war that resistance to Germany entailed.

Behind Britain's refusal to meet the German military challenge with a broad and vigorous rearmament program of its own were the terrifying memories of the Great War and the consequent longing for peace. Predictably another war, reflecting the gains in aircraft technology, would rain destruction from the skies. After 1935 British leaders acknowledged the speed of German rearmament, but they assumed, perhaps correctly, that the British public preferred to discount the German threat. Britain's economy and public finances remained weak; British rearmament, therefore, never exceeded what the Treasury would sanction. Heavy arms expenditures would drain Britain's limited resources, needed for recovery, into wasteful production and eliminate the possibility of financial solvency. When chancellor of the exchequer in 1936, Chamberlain had sought above all to protect Britain's needed export trade. "If we were now to . . . sacrifice our commerce to the manufacture of arms," he warned late that year, "we should inflict a certain injury on our trade from which it would take generations to recover, . . . and we should cripple our revenue." The British defense program focused on the expansion of the air force and the rebuilding of the battle fleet. As prime minister, Chamberlain restricted British rearmament to what seemed essential for home defense and the protection of British commitments outside Europe.[15]

---

[15]Keith Feiling discusses the problems and nature of British rearmament in *The Life of Neville Chamberlain* (London, 1946), pp. 312–19.

Whatever the limitations of British preparedness, the future of collective security seemed promising enough. Every country of Europe, including Italy, opposed German expansion. In 1935 France had negotiated anti-German alliances with the Soviet Union and Czechoslovakia. With the exception of France and Czechoslovakia, however, every European nation balked at Soviet inclusion in a system of collective security. Chamberlain distrusted Soviet purpose and discounted Soviet power. British cooperation or alliance with the USSR, or even with France, moreover, seemed likely to make understandings with Germany more difficult to attain. On the other hand, U.S. support would be welcome; it would strengthen British diplomacy without restricting British freedom. Unfortunately, experience suggested to British officials that the United States, despite its great potential power, remained unpredictable and unreliable. "The U.S.A.," Chamberlain wrote, "has drawn close to us, but the isolationists there are so strong and so vocal that she cannot be depended on for help if we get into trouble." Upon reading Roosevelt's "quarantine" speech, Chamberlain concluded narrowly that it was "always best and safest to count on nothing from the Americans but words."[16]

This unpredictability of the United States reinforced Chamberlain's sense of British weakness and provided further argument for a conciliatory policy. The fact that the Germans and Italians were difficult did not eliminate the possibility of dealing with them effectively. Indeed, he believed Britain to be uniquely situated to lead Europe through a period of crisis without permitting the impending disruption of the postwar order to terminate in war. As he assured a Birmingham audience, "there must be something in common between us if only we can find it, and perhaps by our very aloofness from the rest of Europe we may have some special part to play as conciliator and mediator."[17] The prime minister regarded himself as sufficiently unprejudiced against Hitler and Mussolini to offer Europe disinterested leadership. Above all, Chamberlain recognized the importance of avoiding a direct confrontation with Germany over Central Europe. By establishing a framework for negotiation, the prime minister hoped to limit Hitler's assaults on the Eastern European settlement sufficiently to preserve the peace.

Negotiation comprised the necessary means for determining the extent of German ambition. Direct pressure on Hitler, argued Sir Alexander Cadogan, deputy undersecretary of state, would compel him to

---

[16]Chamberlain diary, February 19, 1938, NC 2/24A, Neville Chamberlain Papers, University of Birmingham; Chamberlain to Hilda Chamberlain, October 9, 1937, NC 18/1/1023, Chamberlain Papers.

[17]Quoted in Feiling, *Life of Neville Chamberlain*, pp. 321, 324.

announce a reasonable program or put himself in the wrong. "If everyone in Germany is mad, and if all are bent on our destruction," he wrote in April 1937, "disaster *must* come. . . . Therefore we *must* try and talk with some of them and encourage some of them. It's no use shutting our eyes and hiding our heads in the sand and doing nothing. If our rearmament is backward, we must have time. We must *do* something."[18] Chamberlain shared that conviction, writing in July: "If only I could get on terms with the Germans, I would not care a rap for Musso." Still Italy's aggressiveness in the Mediterranean comprised the immediate danger to peace. Chamberlain, moreover, had defined a reasonable formula for settling British differences with Italy. If Mussolini would renounce any territorial designs toward Spain and French North Africa and withdraw some Italian "volunteers" from Spain, Britain would recognize the Italian conquest of Abyssinia. "We can't go on for ever refusing recognition in the Abyssinian affair," he wrote to his sister, "and it seems to me that we had better give it while we can still get something in return for it."[19] Through direct bilateral diplomacy, Chamberlain hoped as well to satisfy Hitler's demands: "I don't see why we shouldn't say to Germany, 'Give us satisfactory assurances that you won't use force to deal with the Austrians and the Czechoslovakians and we will give similar assurances that we won't use force to prevent the changes you want if you can get them by peaceful means.'"[20]

Chamberlain inaugurated his personal search for a settlement with Germany in November 1937 when he urged Lord Halifax, lord president of the council, to accept the invitation to attend an international sporting exhibition in Berlin and to visit Hitler in Berchtesgaden. The prime minister sought no specific German terms but hoped to reassure Hitler of British sincerity and to determine in general what Hitler desired to gain in Europe and elsewhere. Chamberlain intended to avoid territorial concessions to Germany except as part of a general settlement in which Germany would accept peaceful means as the method of securing reasonable justice for its claims. Any general settlement, in all probability, would require a series of bilateral treaties. Still British Ambassador Nevile Henderson warned the government in London that Hitler had no interest in bargains and in particular would not exchange a colonial settlement for one in Europe. For Henderson

---

[18]David Dilks, ed., *The Diaries of Sir Alexander Cadogan, 1938–1945* (London, 1971), p. 14.
[19]Chamberlain to Hilda Chamberlain, August 29, 1937, NC 18/1/1018, Chamberlain Papers.
[20]Chamberlain to Ida Chamberlain, November 26, 1937, NC 18/1/1030, Chamberlain Papers.

the Austrian question was no longer open for discussion; any Czech settlement that satisfied Hitler would render Czechoslovakia dependent on Germany rather than on France or the Soviet Union.[21]

Clearly the challenges facing Europe could find no solution in Roosevelt's January 1938 proposal, and Chamberlain rejected it. In his diary the prime minister wrote that "the plan appears to me fantastic & likely to excite the derision of Germany & Italy. They might even use it to postpone conversations with us & if we were associated with it they would see in it another attempt on the part of the democratic bloc to put the dictators in the wrong."[22] Negotiations with Germany and Italy, ran the fundamental theme of his reply, required some concrete bases of agreement. Britain, therefore, would recognize the de jure Italian conquest of Abyssinia and in time would propose similar measures to satisfy German aspirations. Cadogan, permanent undersecretary since early January, like Chamberlain, accused Roosevelt of harboring "wild ideas about formulating a world settlement." The president's proposal, he agreed, presented difficulties; still, Cadogan advised the cabinet to avoid a break with Roosevelt: "Whatever else may be decided *we must not turn him down.*"[23] Chamberlain compromised his response by suggesting that Roosevelt delay his conference call while the London government tackled some of the specific questions in European politics.

Roosevelt's second message, withdrawing his project, clarified the depth of his tactical disagreement with Chamberlain and demonstrated his concern for American opinion. He reminded the prime minister that the de jure recognition of Italy's claim to Abyssinia would undermine the efforts of other countries to defend their territories against aggression. Specifically, noted Roosevelt, it might have a harmful effect "upon the nature of the peace terms which Japan might demand from China." He warned, moreover, that a surrender of the principles of nonrecognition would seriously damage public opinion in the United States. The American people would support measures of international cooperation only if they were "destined to re-establish and maintain the principles of international law and morality."[24] In Washington, Hull reminded Ambassador Lindsay that U.S. policy rested primarily

[21]Henderson to Anthony Eden, December 15, 1937, annex to cabinet notes, January 1938, CAB 27/626/5887, PRO.

[22]Chamberlain diary, February 19, 1938, NC 2/24A, Chamberlain Papers.

[23]Chamberlain to Roosevelt, January 14, 1938, *FRUS, 1938* (Washington, 1955), 1:118–19; cabinet notes, January 24, 1938, CAB 23/92/6455, PRO; Dilks, *Diaries of Sir Alexander Cadogan*, p. 39 (emphasis in original).

[24]Roosevelt to Chamberlain, January 17, 1938, *FRUS, 1938*, 1:120–22.

on moral precepts and "the sanctity of agreements and the preservation of international law, both of which rest on this moral foundation."[25] The desperado nations, he cautioned, would herald British recognition of the Italian conquest as a virtual ratification of their treaty-breaking policies. The secretary admitted that the decision for nonrecognition as one of indefinite duration, presented difficulties. He insisted, however, that a policy so central to the maintenance of international order could be modified only by general agreement among the nations of the world.

Washington's obvious dissatisfaction with British policy placed the London government in a dilemma. The cabinet's Foreign Policy Committee wanted to strengthen British relations with the United States, but Chamberlain and the committee found Roosevelt's principles unimaginative and unrealistic. The purpose of British policy was to rid Europe of its immediate perils, whereas the American initiative would both antagonize the dictators and place responsibility for a settlement on small states unsuited for a major international role. By the time that Roosevelt's second message reached London, Foreign Minister Anthony Eden had returned from his vacation in the south of France. Eden fully accepted Lindsay's advice that Britain should encourage the president's interest in European affairs even at the cost of inconvenience to British diplomacy. Chamberlain's next communication to Roosevelt, which reflected Eden's wishes, informed him that the prime minister did not now feel justified in asking the president to postpone his White House meeting and assured him that the British government would do all in its power to guarantee the success of the effort. Britain, Chamberlain insisted, would seek de jure recognition but only as part of a general Mediterranean settlement. Privately, Chamberlain explained to Lindsay why the British government could not offer more enthusiastic support for Roosevelt's proposals: "In case they received a bad reception after they had been launched, we were anxious neither, on the one hand, to share the responsibility with the President for them, nor, on the other, for the President to be able to say that we had given him no warning but unqualified encouragement."[26]

Despite Chamberlain's assurances that he would support the conference call, Roosevelt never renewed his proposal. Opponents of

[25]Memorandum of Hull's conversation with Lindsay, January 17, 1938, ibid., pp. 133–34.

[26]Cabinet notes, January 24, 1938, CAB 23/92/6455, PRO. Eden's reaction to Roosevelt's proposal can be found in detail in the Earl of Avon, *The Eden Memoirs: Facing the Dictators* (London, 1962), pp. 548–68. To the end Eden believed that a comparable opportunity to avoid catastrophe never recurred.

Chamberlain argued that his attitude had angered the president. Possibly Roosevelt had merely come to share the prime minister's skepticism. From Paris, Ambassador Bullitt offered the president little encouragement when he wrote: "I remember talking over with you the idea that you might call a world conference. . . . I feel now that, while such an appeal would be acceptable to American public opinion, it would seem an escape from reality to the rest of the world. It would be as if in the palmiest days of Al Capone you had summoned a national conference of psychoanalysts to Washington to discuss the psychological causes of crime."[27] Still as late as March 8, Welles informed Lindsay that the United States opposed any direct approach to the German and Italian governments. Editorials as well as personal letters, he informed the ambassador, accused the British government of denying the principle of peaceful change and lending support to the dictators. "It is not," Lindsay replied, "that we like dictators nor that we want to associate ourselves with them, but since we are confronted with a world in which there are dictators, we have reached the conclusion that the only thing to do in order to prevent war is to try to find a basis for peaceful understanding with them."[28] Confronted with the rapid deterioration of European stability, Britain had no choice but to pursue direct negotiations.

To Eden and much of the Foreign Office, Chamberlain's handling of Roosevelt had been unsubtle and potentially disastrous. Oliver Harvey, his official private secretary, reminded Eden that "the only fatal risk for us is to antagonize Roosevelt and America: without his backing we might be overwhelmed in a war. . . . We may try and persuade Roosevelt to delay or modify [his] scheme, but if he persists we should heartily concur and co-operate for all we are worth. We should not be forgiven if we turned it down."[29] Eden concluded that Britain should drop the idea of Abyssinia's de jure recognition. Certainly, he argued, Roosevelt's initiative was more important to Britain than an agreement with Mussolini. Ambassador Dino Grandi's assurances that Rome wanted a settlement with Britain merely aggravated Eden's suspicions; the fact that Mussolini wanted conversations was sufficient reason to avoid them. Even when Grandi informed Eden and Chamberlain in February 1938 that Mussolini accepted the British

[27]Bullitt to Roosevelt, January 20, 1938, in Orville H. Bullitt, ed., *For the President Personal and Secret: Correspondence Between Franklin D. Roosevelt and William C. Bullitt* (Boston, 1972), p. 252.
    [28]Welles's memorandum of conversation with Lindsay, March 8, 1938, *FRUS, 1938*, 1:127.
    [29]John Harvey, ed., *The Diplomatic Diaries of Oliver Harvey, 1937–1940* (London, 1970), pp. 69–70.

formula for a Mediterranean settlement, Eden refused to budge. For Chamberlain his break with Eden was now complete. Late in February he accepted Eden's resignation and replaced him with Halifax. The prime minister's quarrel with Eden "was not whether we should have conversations now but whether we should have them at all. I have gradually arrived at the conclusion that at bottom Anthony did not want to talk either with Hitler or Mussolini and, as I did, he was right to go." Cadogan had supported Eden on the matter of Roosevelt's conference proposal, but he agreed with Chamberlain on the need to push the Italian negotiations.[30]

IV

Hitler, unlike Roosevelt and Chamberlain, knew that in world politics significant change could not be peaceful. For him the choice lay between admitting the superior morality of the status quo or defying it with force. As he explained to his military chiefs in November 1937, "there had never . . . been spaces without a master, and there were none today: the attacker always comes up against a possessor. The question for Germany was: where could she achieve the greatest gain at the lowest cost."[31] Ready to gamble Germany's future for high stakes, Hitler stripped his ministry and officer corps of their cautious elements and by January 1938 was prepared to test the commitment of the Western democracies to the Versailles settlement. Already he had eliminated the question of Austria's future from European diplomacy. Hull responded to Hitler's seizure of Austria in March with a characteristic appeal to principle: "It is our profound conviction that the most effective contribution we, as a nation sincerely devoted to peace, can make . . . is to have this country respected throughout the world for integrity, justice, goodwill, strength, and unswerving loyalty to principles."

Chamberlain, powerless to act, accepted the *Anschluss* as gracefully as he could. He objected only to Hitler's methods which he claimed "were extremely distasteful to His Majesty's Government." The momentary failure of Chamberlain's appeasement policy in Berlin merely spurred the prime minister to reach a settlement with Rome. In the Anglo-Italian agreement of April 16, 1938, Italy pledged to evacuate

[30]Chamberlain to Hilda Chamberlain, February 27, 1938, NC 18/1/1040, Chamberlain Papers; Dilks, *Diaries of Sir Alexander Cadogan*, p. 54.

[31]Minutes of the conference in the Reich chancellery, Berlin, November 5, 1937, printed in Francis L. Loewenheim, ed., *Peace or Appeasement? Hitler, Chamberlain, and the Munich Crisis* (Boston, 1965), pp. xv, 3. See also Alan Bullock, *Hitler—A Study in Tyranny* (New York, 1963), p. 368. Hermann Göring warned Bullitt in November 1937 that Germany would annex the German populations of Austria and Czechoslovakia. Bullitt's report, *FRUS, 1937*, 1:171–72.

volunteers from Spain and to seek no permanent advantages in that country. London agreed, in exchange, to bring the issue of de jure recognition of Abyssinia before the League of Nations but added that the treaty would take effect only when Italy complied with the Spanish provisions. Surprisingly, Roosevelt viewed the Anglo-Italian pact sympathetically, stating that the United States advocated the maintenance of international law and order; therefore, it favored the promotion of peace through friendly settlements of controversies between states. He made clear that Washington would not recognize the Italian conquest. Understandably, Assistant Secretary of State Jay Pierrepont Moffat complained of Roosevelt's inconsistency: "In one breath we praise the British for getting together with the Italians; in the next breath we imply that the Italians are treaty breakers and unworthy to be dealt with on a footing of equality."[32]

Hitler's annexation of Austria marked Czechoslovakia's Sudetenland, with its large discontented German majority, as Germany's next target. Heavily fortified and industrialized, this borderland was a natural frontier that separated Germany from Czechoslovakia's predominantly Slavic populations. While Nazi puppet Konrad Henlein churned the German nationalism of some 3 million Sudeten Germans, Eduard Beneš's Czech government, backed by a good army and a strong Czech nationalism, prepared to fight. European and American diplomats, who had scarcely reacted to the Austrian *Anschluss*, recognized the international significance of the mounting Czech crisis, for Czechoslovakia was allied both to France and to the Soviet Union. Germany's threat to annex the Sudetenland gave Hitler's opponents the choice of standing together in defense of peaceful procedures or witnessing the further disintegration of the Versailles structure.

Chamberlain understood why Britain would reject the first alternative. It was evident "that force is the only argument Germany understands and that 'collective security' cannot offer any prospect of preventing such events until it can show a visible force of overwhelming strength backed by determination to use it."[33] In the absence of such strength, the prime minister regarded resistance to Germany through combined action a desperate course. In March, Chamberlain confided to his sister:

---

[32]Halifax to State Department, March 11, 1938, *FRUS, 1938*, 1:132; Roosevelt's press statement on the Anglo-Italian pact, April 19, 1938, ibid., pp. 147–48. For Moffat's observation see Dallek, *Franklin D. Roosevelt and American Foreign Policy*, p. 158.

[33]Chamberlain to Hilda Chamberlain, March 13, 1938, NC 18/1/1041, Chamberlain Papers. Later Chamberlain wrote that "the Germans who are bullies by nature are too conscious of their strength and our weakness and until we are as strong as they we shall always be kept in this state of chronic anxiety." Chamberlain to Hilda Chamberlain, May 22, 1938, NC 18/1/1053, Chamberlain Papers.

It is a very attractive idea . . . until you come to examine its practicability. From that moment its attraction vanishes. You have only to look at the map to see that nothing that France or we could do could possibly save Czecho-Slovakia from being over run by the Germans if they wanted to do it. . . . [S]he would simply be the pretext for going to war with Germany. That we could not think of unless we had a reasonable prospect of being able to beat her . . . and of that I see no sign. I have therefore abandoned any idea of giving guarantees to Czechoslovakia or to France in connection with her obligations to that country.[34]

Those in the British Foreign Office who discounted the German threat and thus opposed any direct approach to Hitler favored the "guessing position" which Eden had outlined in a Leamington speech of November 1936. Its theory was simple: as long as Germany was never sure that Britain would not fight and France was never sure that it would, both countries would be discouraged from adopting forward policies. Under the assumption that Germany would avoid a European war at all costs, British policy need only assure Germany that aggression against Czechoslovakia might set off a conflict in which Britain would support France. On March 24, 1938, Chamberlain adopted this formula in his speech before the House of Commons in which he listed the specific British obligations that might demand the use of force. These comprised the defense of Britain, the British Commonwealth, Western Europe, and the Middle East. London would accept no obligation to Czechoslovakia under the January 1924 Franco-Czech treaty; to do so would deny London full control of British policy. As a warning to Germany and as an assurance to France, Chamberlain added: "Where peace and war are concerned, legal obligations are not alone involved, and, if war broke out, it would be unlikely to be confined to those who have assumed such obligations. It would be quite impossible to say where it would end and what Governments might become involved. The inexorable pressure of facts might well prove more powerful than formal pronouncements."[35] Countries such as Britain and France could hardly escape a European war. This admonition carried the burden of British policy in the Czech crisis. Unfortunately, it assured no resolution of the Sudeten question. Chamberlain promised to enlist the resources of diplomacy in the search for a peaceful settlement.

Without explicit British support, French policy could not survive;

[34]Chamberlain to Ida Chamberlain, March 20, 1938, NC 18/1/1042, Chamberlain Papers.

[35]Joseph P. Kennedy to Hull, March 23, 1938, *FRUS, 1938*, 1:40; Monica Curtis, ed., *Documents on International Affairs, 1938* (London, 1943), 2:121–23.

Bullitt recorded its predictable demise. Late in April 1938, French Premier Édouard Daladier and French Foreign Minister Georges Bonnet traveled to London to secure the essential British commitment to the defense of Czechoslovakia. Chamberlain refused to compromise his statement of March 24; Britain's frontier was the Rhine. Isolated in the west and unable to penetrate Germany's western defenses, France required effective help in the east. Poland, despite its alliance with France, denied that it had any obligation to Czechoslovakia. Moreover, it warned that it would meet with force any Soviet attempt to aid Czechoslovakia by crossing Polish territory. Troubled by Europe's heavy stake in Czechoslovakia, Robert Coulondre, French ambassador in Moscow, urged his government to perfect the Franco-Russian alliance by negotiating a military agreement with the Soviets. Paris rejected the advice.[36] For the moment it mattered little. Maxim Litvinov, Soviet commissar of Foreign Affairs, reminded the French government that his country, under any circumstances, would await French action in any war over Czechoslovakia. How the Soviet Union could aid Czechoslovakia without defying Poland no one could explain. The French alliance system was dead.

With the collapse of German encirclement, Daladier could only endorse Britain's effort to appease Hitler. Early in August, Chamberlain sent Viscount Runciman to Prague to negotiate a settlement of the Sudeten question. Through five weeks of conferring, Runciman failed to secure minimum concessions from either Germany or Czechoslovakia. Convinced that a war would destroy what remained of French prestige, French officials turned on Czechoslovakia. Any French effort to protect that country, Bonnet complained to Bullitt, "would mean the defeat and dismemberment of France." Daladier observed bitterly, in conversation with Bullitt, that France was on the verge "of reaping one of the wars the seeds of which had been sown in the [Versailles] treaty." Daladier and Bonnet had wrecked their careers temporarily by fighting the Versailles settlement. "Both are convinced," Bullitt informed Hull, "that the treaty must be revised and at bottom regard an alteration in the Czechoslovak State as a necessary revision—the necessity for which they pointed out nearly 20 years ago." Paris advised Prague that it expected the Czech government to carry the Sudeten negotiations to a successful conclusion. As the crisis deepened, French leaders insisted that their commitment to Czechoslovakia's defense

---

[36]London meeting reported in *FRUS, 1938*, 1:47–50. Franklin L. Ford and Carl E. Schorske discuss Coulondre in "The Voice in the Wilderness: Robert Coulondre," in Gordon A. Craig and Felix Gilbert, eds., *The Diplomats, 1919–1939* (New York, 1963), 2:561, 574. On Poland and the Soviet Union see Bullitt to Hull, May 16, 1938, *FRUS, 1938*, 1:502.

carried the right to guide the Prague government in its pursuit of a settlement. On September 14, Bonnet told Bullitt that, if Czechoslovakia did not grant autonomy to the Sudeten Germans, France would desert its obligations to that country.[37]

Washington remained diplomatically, if not emotionally, detached from the Czech crisis. Occasionally Roosevelt and Hull implored Europeans to subscribe to American principles. They both denied, however, that the United States had any interest in the specific issues of the Sudeten controversy. As German preparations and maneuvering became more threatening, Roosevelt and Hull, on August 16 and 18, made public speeches to reaffirm American disapproval of aggression. "I give you assurance," the president told a Canadian audience, "that the people of the United States will not stand idly if domination of Canadian soil is threatened by any other Empire."[38] That commitment to the defense of North America was sufficiently traditional to excite no response. Roosevelt himself admitted that any president could have announced it fifty years earlier. Later that month Morgenthau and Roosevelt formulated a plan to impede German expansion with economic sanctions. To secure Hull's approval, the president phoned the secretary and explained that the plan would enable the government to purchase earmarked British and French gold in the United States for one year at $35 per ounce. Next, Roosevelt declared his intention to inform the German ambassador in Washington that the United States would apply countervailing duties against his country if it entered Czechoslovakia. Hull believed the scheme unsound and unnecessarily threatening to American isolationism. His objection reaffirmed the president's own doubts and terminated the project.

State Department officials who had some understanding of the role of force in international affairs wondered how the United States could sustain the treaty structure of Europe without undertaking some commitments which both isolationists and internationalists believed avoidable. Moffat confided to his diary on August 12 that the best American contribution to Europe's peace "would be to create a doubt in the minds of Germany and company that we would under all circumstances stay out and at the same time to create a doubt in the mind of England and company that they could count on us for direct assistance no matter what transpired."[39] Earlier Bullitt adopted a similar formula in a recommendation to Roosevelt. After asserting that the

---

[37]Wilson to Hull, May 6, 1938, *FRUS, 1938*, 1:492–93; Bullitt to Hull, May 16, and September 8, 14, 15, 1938, ibid., pp. 501, 581, 595–96, 600–01.

[38]Quoted in Dallek, *Franklin D. Roosevelt and American Foreign Policy*, p. 163.

[39]Nancy Harvison Hooker, ed., *The Moffat Papers: Selections from the Diplomatic Journal of Jay Pierrepont Moffat, 1919–1943* (Cambridge, MA, 1956), p. 194.

real danger to peace lay in the French commitment to Czechoslovakia and not in the German demands on Prague, he advised the president to warn the French ambassador that his country's resistance to Hitler would reduce all Europe to ruins. At the same time, continued Bullitt, Roosevelt might inform the German ambassador "that France will fight and England will fight, that war in Europe today can end only in the establishment of Bolshevism from one end of the Continent to the other."[40] That warning would remind Hitler of the price that Germany would pay for a European war. Such formulations, like those of British leaders, assumed invariably that threats of possible British and American involvement in a wider conflict would check German aggression.

V

Even as Chamberlain moved to stop the drift toward disaster with personal diplomacy, he believed that successful appeasement would not nullify his quest for peaceful change. On September 13, 1938 he addressed a note to Hitler, offering to fly to Germany and there seek a solution to the Sudeten problem. Two days later he conferred with Hitler at Berchtesgaden. Six days later the British and French governments agreed that peace, as well as Czechoslovakia's future, required the transfer of the Sudeten region to the Reich, either by plebiscite or by simple cession. The two countries promised to guarantee the new boundaries but warned the Czech government that it alone would carry responsibility for any breakdown of the peace. Bonnet was confident that Prague would accept the Anglo-French proposal. "We will not," he informed Bullitt, "let Benes . . . drive 40 million French people to their deaths and he knows it."[41] Chamberlain met Hitler at Godesberg on September 22, with the Czech acceptance in hand. Hitler angrily rejected the British formula and demanded the right to occupy the Sudetenland immediately. Later he agreed to delay the occupation until October 1. Again the burden of peace fell on Prague.

Roosevelt's State Department advisers urged him to ignore these dramatic events publicly. Any statement that emphasized the importance of peace, Moffat noted, would appear to endorse Chamberlain's appeasement of Hitler. Any statement that stressed the importance of a just settlement and encouraged Britain to resist German demands would burden the United States with moral responsibility for any war that ensued. At issue in America's leadership crisis was Roosevelt's

[40]Bullitt to Roosevelt, May 20, 1938, in Bullitt, *For the President Personal and Secret*, p. 263.
[41]Bullitt to Hull, September 19, 1938, *FRUS, 1938*, 1:621.

determination to escape the pressures of revisionism. Assistant Secretary of State Adolf A. Berle argued in a memorandum to the president that Hitler, whatever his methods, was putting a logical end to the mistakes at Versailles, especially the decision to break up the Austro-Hungarian Empire. American emotions, he wrote, should not be permitted to lead the United States into a general war "to try to maintain a situation which was untenable from the time it was created." On September 20, Roosevelt informed Lindsay in Washington that he favored a world conference to resolve rationally all boundary disputes. In no direct communication with London or Berlin, however, did he hint at treaty revision. Others could carry the responsibility for the collapse of Europe's treaty structure. Privately, the president was torn between the remorseless sacrifice being demanded of Czechoslovakia and the prospect that Prague would not acquiesce. On September 25, while London, Paris, and Prague pondered Hitler's latest demands, Beneš asked Roosevelt to defend Czechoslovakia against a British and French sellout.[42] As predicted, the president refused to intercede in the Sudeten affair.

Roosevelt followed the more expedient route, placing the burden on Hitler. The next day he reminded Hitler that no country, including the United States, could escape the consequences of a European conflict: "The traditional policy of the United States has been the furtherance of the settlement of international disputes by pacific means." On behalf of humanity everywhere, the president declared, "I most earnestly appeal to you not to break off negotiations looking to a peaceful, fair, and constructive settlement of the questions at issue." The United States, Roosevelt assured Hitler, had no political entanglements in Europe. Berlin remained intransigent, attributing the crisis solely to Czech mistreatment of German and other minorities. On September 27, Roosevelt again urged Hitler to accept a peaceful solution of the Sudeten problem. "The Government of the United States," he wrote, "has no political involvements in Europe, and will assume no obligation in the conduct of the present negotiations. Yet in our own right we recognize our responsibilities as a part of a world of neighbors."[43] Roosevelt's veiled warnings and appeals to principle combined his own and the

[42]Hooker, *The Moffat Papers*, p. 205; Berle's memorandum, September 1, 1938, in Beatrice Bishop Berle and Travis Beal Jacobs, eds., *Navigating the Rapids, 1918–1971: From the Papers of Adolf A. Berle* (New York, 1973), pp. 183–84; Lindsay to Halifax, September 20, 1938, in E. L. Woodward and Rohan Butler, eds., *Documents on British Foreign Policy, 1919–1939*, 3d ser. (London, 1954), 3:627–29; Wilbur J. Carr to Hull, September 25, 1938, *FRUS, 1938* 1:649–50.

[43]Roosevelt to Hitler, September 26, 27, 1938, *FRUS, 1938*, 1:657–58, 684–85; Hitler to Roosevelt, September 27, 1938, ibid., pp. 669–72; Hull to Kennedy, September 28, 1938, ibid., p. 688.

State Department's thought on a proper U.S. response to Hitler's Godesberg demands. When a day later Chamberlain's efforts culminated in the invitation to Munich, Roosevelt sent a simple congratulation. Chamberlain, joined by Daladier, met Hitler and Mussolini at Munich on September 30. There he accepted, in essence, what the British cabinet had rejected. Czechoslovakia's final capitulation under pressure sustained the illusion of peaceful change, especially since Hitler agreed to consult London on all future international problems.

Chamberlain's decisions at Munich were a clear measure of both British opinion and tradition. The British public, both at home and in the Dominions, feared another war and recognized the limits that Britain's military weakness imposed on the country's diplomacy. No more than the people were the leaders and editors of Britain and the Dominions ready to endorse a rejection of the Munich terms. The exclusion of the victim, Czechoslovakia, and a major interested power, the Soviet Union, from the negotiations was consistent with Britain's historic attitudes toward Central and Eastern Europe. True, Britain had generally refrained in the past from helping other powers annex territory in that region without compensation. The issue at Munich, however, was not treaty revision but war, and Britain had often sought to escape any conflicts that might prove to be inconclusive or counterproductive. As Chamberlain had explained in his radio broadcast of September 27, "however much we may sympathize with a small nation confronted by a big and powerful neighbour, we cannot in all circumstances undertake to involve the whole British Empire in war simply on her account. If we have to fight it must be on larger issues than that. . . . [I]f I were convinced that any nation had made up its mind to dominate the world by fear of its forces, I should feel that it must be resisted."[44]

Throughout the Czech crisis, Chamberlain exploited, rather than confronted, his country's lack of preparedness and its apparent preference for peace at any price. In the process he gained time needed for rearmament but no more than did Hitler. Meanwhile, he lost thirty-five well-trained Czech divisions and the entire Czech arsenal, Soviet and French confidence, and Europe's moral leadership. Chamberlain's assumption that German expansion into Central Europe would not endanger British interests in the West was no longer true. Whether a firmer stand would have prevented these security losses and still preserved the peace is doubtful. Hitler confronted Chamberlain at Munich

---

[44]Radio broadcast, September 27, 1938, in *Times* (London), September 28, 1938, p. 10; *New York Times*, September 28, 1938, p. 24. Paul W. Schroeder analyzes British policy at Munich in terms of British tradition, noting the changed conditions in Eastern Europe which assured failure rather than success for the policy, in "Munich and the British Tradition," *Historical Journal* 19 (1976): 223–43.

with the disastrous choice of an ignominious peace or war. The prime minister ignored the choice by proclaiming the settlement a victory. He wrote to the archbishop of Canterbury on October 2: "I am sure that someday the Czechs will see that what we did was to save them for a happier future. And I sincerely believe that we have at last opened the way to that general appeasement which alone can save the world from chaos."[45] At the end, Chamberlain recognized no failure in his performance and thereby denied himself the freedom to instruct. Therein, lay the tragedy of Munich.

Munich destroyed the illusion of American isolation from the political affairs of Europe. The news of Hitler's dramatic annexations, especially in overseas radio reports, stirred the nation's consciousness. Historian Selig Adler described the phenomenon:

> . . . Americans . . . could hardly shut their ears to the blow-by-blow description of events. As *putsches*, invasions, threats, surrenders, dramatic airplane flights of prime ministers followed one another *seriatim*, the dispensation of foreign news became increasingly efficient. Gifted on-the-spot radio correspondents broadcast round-ups that could be heard from four countries in one program. Never before had the Old World seemed so close.[46]

American writers and editors agreed overwhelmingly that the Munich settlement comprised a massive and dangerous collapse of Western leadership. Much of the press attributed this costly failure of collective security, not to the force of German aggression but to the unnecessary weakness and vacillation in British and French diplomacy. Other editors, however, tellingly reminded the critics of Munich that their rebukes were totally illogical, if not dishonest. "No one who approves the course this country has pursued since 1920," cautioned the *Richmond* (VA) *Times Dispatch*, "has a right to criticize those democracies for the course they have pursued. The United States has followed policies in the past 18 years which have not only helped to make the rise of the dictators inevitable, but which have made resistance by Britain and France to the dictators much more difficult." The *New York Times* challenged those who would condemn the British and French nations:

> Let no man say that too high a price has been paid for peace in Europe until he has searched his soul and found himself willing

[45]Chamberlain's letter quoted in Feiling, *Life of Neville Chamberlain*, p. 375.
[46]Selig Adler, *The Isolationist Impulse: Its Twentieth-Century Reaction* (London, 1957), p. 269.

to risk in war the lives of those who are nearest and dearest to him. Let no man say that it would have been better to resist, and to fight it out, 'now rather than later,' unless he himself would have sent young men marching into the dreary hell of war. Let no man say that the statesmen of Britain and France were out-traded in the bargain they have struck, until he has attempted to add the total of the price they might have to pay for any other settlement than the one which they have taken.

Ultimately, the press defended American isolationism by accepting the logic that the peace achieved at Munich, whatever the cost to others, was preferable to war. For his immediate achievement of a settlement, the *New York Times* praised Chamberlain unstintingly: "Whatever happens in Europe—and what happens now depends on how much sanity still prevails in the councils of Berlin—Mr. Chamberlain will emerge from the momentous events of the past fortnight as a heroic figure, with the respect and admiration of men of good-will the whole world over."[47]

Both Roosevelt and Hull saw in the Munich agreement not only a costly and fragile peace but also the possibilities for a more principled future. The president confided to Ambassador William Phillips in Rome that "I want you to know that I am not a bit upset over the final result." Hull, ignoring the role which threats had played in the settlement, declared that "the forces which stand for the principles governing peaceful and orderly international relations . . . should not relax, but redouble, their efforts to maintain these principles of order under law." Similarly, Welles informed a nationwide radio audience that from the crisis had emerged the best opportunity in twenty years to establish "a new world order based upon justice and law." Roosevelt wired Chamberlain that "I fully share your hope and belief that there exists today the greatest opportunity in years for the establishment of a new order based on justice and law. Now that you have established personal contact with Chancellor Hitler, I know that you will be taking up with him from time to time many of the problems which must be resolved in order to bring about that new and better order."[48]

It was not long, however, before Roosevelt realized that the hopes of Munich were illusory. In his message to Congress on January 4, 1939, he admitted that he was again searching for an American answer to aggression but had not found it. "Words may be futile but war is not the only means of commanding a decent respect for the opinions

[47]*Richmond* (VA) *Times Dispatch*, September 26, 1938, p. 8; *New York Times*, September 28, 1938, p. 24, and September 30, 1938, p. 20.
[48]Roosevelt to Phillips, October 17, 1938, in Elliott Roosevelt, *F.D.R.: His Personal Letters*, 2:817, 818; *Memoirs of Cordell Hull*, 1:595; Department of State, *Press Releases* 19 (1938): 240.

of mankind. There are many methods short of war, but stronger and more effective than mere words, of bringing home to aggressor governments the aggregate sentiments of our own people." At least, he continued, the United States should not engage in any policy that would strengthen an aggressor. America's answer to treaty breaking, in short, lay in a modification of the neutrality legislation to enable the country to aid the victims of aggression.

VI

Hitler's seizure of Czechoslovakia in March 1939 opened a new chapter in European history, for the German annexation of a Slav population terminated whatever legitimacy Hitler's earlier aggressions had sustained in Western eyes. No longer did the universally recognized principle of self-determination set limits to German ambition. Soon reports spread across Europe that Germany had designs on Poland. Britain possessed no power to save that country, nor did Danzig, Hitler's immediate objective in Poland, represent any historic British interest. To preserve what remained of European stability, Chamberlain resolved to deny Hitler another easy triumph. On March 31 he announced in the House of Commons that Britain would come to the assistance of Poland with all the power at its command "in the event of any action which clearly threatened Polish independence, and which the Polish Government accordingly considered it vital to resist with their national forces." This clear effort at deterrence could threaten Germany with an economic blockade and a long war of attrition. Unfortunately, Hitler was concerned with immediate advantages, not the ultimate consequences, of his actions.[49] In April, following Italy's occupation of Albania, Britain promised to defend the independence of Greece and Romania. The Anglo-Turkish declaration of May 1939 committed both countries to joint resistance in the event of aggression in the eastern Mediterranean.

Hitler's annexation of Czechoslovakia troubled Washington deeply. "No one here," observed Berle, "has any illusions that the German Napoleonic machine will not extend itself almost indefinitely; and I suppose this is the year. It looks to me like a hot summer ahead." Berle predicted war in four months. If American reaction was violent, it was also impersonal; the United States had no traditional interests in Czechoslovakia. "It is a reaction to something horrifying and shocking," Welles reported to Bullitt, "but not personally connected." Before the

---

[49]For an evaluation of Chamberlain's March 31 statement as a futile effort at deterrence see Alan Alexandroff and Richard Rosecrance, "Deterrence in 1939," *World Politics* 29 (1977): 404–24.

United States became concerned over the future of Poland and Eastern Europe, Berle observed, it should have some notion of how the countries opposed to Hitler intended to reconstruct the area. The Soviet Union, he noted, would capitalize on any war that involved Britain, France, and Germany. "Not much would be gained," he recorded, "if central Europe were saved from efficient Nazi tyranny and cruelty . . . and were turned over to an equally cruel Russian tyranny."[50]

Europe's predictable destabilization under the dual assault of German and Soviet power failed to diminish the administration's peculiar reliance on the principle of peaceful change. The State Department's official pronouncement on Hitler's annihilation of the Czech state differed only in language from Hull's response to the Austrian *Anschluss*:

> This government . . . cannot refrain from making known this country's condemnation of the acts which have resulted in the temporary extinguishment of the liberties of a free and independent people. . . . The position of the government of the United States has been made consistently clear. It has emphasized the need for respect for the sanctity of treaties and the pledged word, and for non-intervention by any nation in the domestic affairs of other nations; and it has . . . expressed its condemnation of a policy of military aggression.

Several days later Hull reminded the press of America's role in European affairs when he stated that "we in this country have striven, particularly in recent years, and we shall continue to strive, to strengthen the threatened structure of world peace by fostering in every possible way the rule of law."[51] For an isolationist nation the merit of such internationalism lay in its total irrelevance to the existing conditions in international affairs.

Roosevelt could not ignore Hitler's recurrent threats to Europe's peace. In a carefully planned letter which ultimately reflected his own views, he reminded Hitler and Mussolini on April 14, 1939 that they were, through their open aggressions, subjecting the world to the constant fear of another war. "The existence of this fear—and the possibility of such a conflict," he wrote, "is of definite concern to the people of the United States for whom I speak. . . . All of them know that any major war, even if it were to be confined to other continents, must bear

---

[50]Berle and Jacobs, *Navigating the Rapids*, pp. 201–08; memorandum of conversation between Welles and Bullitt, March 15, 1939, *FRUS, 1939* (Washington, 1956), 1:41.

[51]Department of State, *Press Releases* 20 (1939): 199–200; *FRUS, 1939*, 1:49–50; Hull's statement of March 24, 1939, ibid., p. 60.

heavily on them during its continuance and also for generations to come." With the two Axis powers rejecting American appeals to settle their problems through peaceful means, the president reflected that "the world is moving toward the moment when the situation must end in catastrophe unless a more rational way of guiding events is found." Committed to American noninvolvement in European affairs, he again attempted to bind Germany and Italy to the European status quo by asking them to enter reciprocal guarantees against aggression with all the countries of Europe. Such reciprocal reassurances would bring to the world a newborn sense of security. Thereafter the United States would join any discussions leading to relief from armaments and restrictive international trade barriers. Chamberlain lauded Roosevelt's message to the dictators: "I think the appeal is very skillfully framed and has put H. and M. into a tight corner. I have no doubt they will refuse to play, though I cannot say whether it will be a polite, an evasive, or a rude refusal. But world opinion and particularly American opinion will have been further consolidated against them." Hitler answered Roosevelt in the Reichstag on April 28, challenging him to name one country that believed itself threatened by Germany.[52] Mussolini responded with a scathing personal attack on the president.

European leaders, supported by many American internationalists, had long argued that the United States could influence events in Europe only at the price of American neutrality. Former Secretary of State Henry L. Stimson had observed in a letter to the *New York Times* dated March 6 that the United States could do nothing for the potential victims of aggression until it dropped all semblance of impartiality.[53] Congressional isolationists had anchored their antiwar program to the neutrality acts and were determined to keep the policy of enforced neutrality in operation. During May, Senator Key Pittman, who served as the administration's spokesman in Congress, prepared a modified neutrality bill that would extend the principle of cash-and-carry beyond the May 1, 1939 deadline and make no distinction in its application between arms and raw materials such as steel, copper, oil, and scrap metal. So strong was the opposition that Pittman would not bring his measure out of committee. Roosevelt turned to the House with no greater success.

Still Roosevelt refused to retreat on the neutrality issue. On May 19 he explained to Democratic leaders at the White House that with the

[52]Roosevelt to Hitler, April 14, 1939, *FRUS, 1939*, 1:130–33; Chamberlain to Hilda Chamberlain, April 15, 1939, NC 18/1/1094, Chamberlain Papers; Geist to Hull, April 28, 1939, *FRUS, 1939*, 1:159.

[53]Henry L. Stimson and McGeorge Bundy, *On Active Service in Peace and War* (New York, 1948), p. 140.

expiration of cash-and-carry the United States could make none of its industrial potential available to Britain and France in the event of war, but his arguments failed to move the isolationists. On July 11, Pittman's Foreign Relations Committee finally rejected the new neutrality measure. The president retorted bitterly that the administration should "introduce a bill for statues of [Senators] Austin, Vandenberg, Lodge and Taft . . . to be erected in Berlin and put the swastika on them."[54] Roosevelt sent another appeal to Congress three days later, and on July 15 he called leading senators to the White House to remind them of the probability of a European war. Isolationist Senator Borah insisted that his information was more reliable than that received at the State Department; it assured him that Europe was in no danger of war. At last the administration gave in. Vice-President John Nance Garner informed the president that "you haven't got the votes, and that's all there is to it."

Meanwhile, Roosevelt urged a more vigorous British policy in Europe. On March 26 he asked distinguished British journalist Sir Arthur Willert: "Why did we [the British] not have conscription? Why did we let Germany have a monopoly of intimidation? Why did we not build more bombers or at least say that we were building more? Why did we not let stories leak out about the tremendous preparation on foot to bomb Germany? He believed the German home front was pretty weak anyhow. Such stories (even if they were not true) would weaken it still more." That most Americans in 1939 desired Britain to pursue a more determined policy of confrontation in Europe implied not an American readiness to follow the British lead but the hope that British firmness would eliminate the need for U.S. intervention. With Britain carrying the risk, the British guarantee to Poland evoked a favorable response in the United States. The Washington correspondent of the *Times* observed: "When the American people see European nations— and especially those nations, Britain and France—which have their sympathy—courageously taking the leadership which they strongly feel must not be American, their disquiet gives way to unstinted approval."[55]

VII

After March 1939 the only possible short-term deterrent against further Nazi aggression lay in a firm alliance among Britain, France, and the Soviet Union. American observers doubted from the beginning that the

---

[54]Quoted in Dallek, *Franklin D. Roosevelt and American Foreign Policy*, p. 191.

[55]For the reference to the *Times* (London) and to the Willert letter, the original of which is in the Public Record Office, I am indebted to Alexander E. Campbell.

mutual fear of Germany would overcome the suspicions and conflicting purposes of the three powers. Chamberlain hoped to limit Britain's obligations in Eastern Europe to Poland and Romania, avoiding an alliance with the Soviet Union. He intended, however, to strengthen Britain's eastern defenses by finding some formula that would enable the Kremlin to aid Poland and Romania despite the refusal of the two countries to tolerate Soviet forces within their borders.[56] Chamberlain's critics reminded him that Soviet cooperation alone could save Britain from disaster. Allied with Germany in war, the Soviet Union would assure an Anglo-French defeat; neutral, it would emerge from war as Europe's dominant power. In a minute prepared for the Foreign Office on May 22, Robert Vansittart, chief foreign policy adviser to the British government, recalled the warning of French General Maxime Weygand that "it was essential, if there must be war, to try to involve the Soviet Union in it, otherwise at the end of the war the Soviet Union, with her army intact and England and Germany in ruins, would dominate Europe."[57] Such predictions did not govern British policy.

Soviet intentions emerged with equal clarity. Lindsay informed Secretary Welles that the Soviet government, like its czarist predecessors, desired to keep the rest of Europe at a distance, under the assumption that the USSR was invulnerable as long as it fought defensively and limited its commitments to bordering regions. The Soviet Union would avoid obligations outside Eastern Europe while it attempted to strengthen its borderland defenses against Germany. The basic Soviet proposal of April 18 demanded a three-power agreement covering both mutual assistance and the protection of all states lying along the Soviet western frontier between the Baltic and the Black seas. During subsequent weeks the Kremlin demanded, in addition, the right to occupy the Baltic states without their consent should these countries refuse to resist German encroachments. Finally, the Kremlin requested a convention to arrange matters of military cooperation. Following a month of diplomatic maneuvering, U.S. Ambassador Joseph P. Kennedy could send Hull the draft of a British counterproposal. If Britain, France, or the Soviet Union became involved in war directly, or as the result of aggression against another European state that offered resistance, the

[56]Kennedy to Hull, March 22, 1939, *FRUS, 1939*, 1:92–93; Bullitt to Hull, April 15, 1939, ibid., p. 233. In his letters to his sisters, Chamberlain expressed freely his opposition to the Kremlin. See, for example, Chamberlain to Ida Chamberlain, March 26, 1939, NC 18/1/1091; Chamberlain to Hilda Chamberlain, April 29, 1939, NC 18/1/1096; Chamberlain to Ida Chamberlain, May 21, 1939, NC 18/1/1100; and Chamberlain to Hilda Chamberlain, May 28, 1939, NC 18/1/1101, Chamberlain Papers.

[57]Woodward and Butler, *Documents on British Foreign Policy, 1919–1939*, 3d ser. (London, 1952), 5:646.

three countries would enter into consultation under the League Covenant. This arrangement would remove the appearance of a Soviet threat to Poland and Romania while it avoided reciprocal guarantees to the Kremlin.[58] British purpose remained consistent.

Clearly Anglo-Soviet differences were profound. Nevertheless, on May 27, 1939 the British and French governments, under intense public pressure, opened political discussions through their ambassadors in Moscow. From the outset the two Western powers refused to accept the Kremlin's demands for boundary adjustments and military occupations in areas belonging to the Soviet Union's western neighbors. In Washington the Soviet price for agreement seemed excessive. "The latest terms that Russia has demanded," Ickes recorded in his diary on June 17, "would give her the right to go into any of the Baltic States on the Russian frontier, not only to meet a military invasion but to meet an economic or propaganda invasion, and France and Great Britain would have to stand by even though the decision as to whether Russia should go in would be Russia's alone. Bill [Bullitt] said that such terms were absurd and that even the French would not agree to them." In Paris, Bonnet complained to Bullitt that the Soviet right to counter Germany's "indirect aggression" was no more than a pretext for annexing the Baltic states. During June, Chamberlain informed Kennedy that, except for the psychological importance which many Londoners attached to a Soviet pact, the cabinet would terminate the conversations in Moscow.[59]

As the political discussions continued aimlessly, the British government on July 27 agreed to send a military mission to Moscow. The mission left London on August 5 and after a slow trip by boat arrived there on August 11 without authority to negotiate. As late as August 18, Poland refused to accept any aid from Moscow unless Britain and France guaranteed the subsequent Soviet evacuation of Polish territory. A week later the Soviet-Western quest for political and military agreement came to an end, for Germany had entered the bidding. In the Nazi-Soviet Pact signed on August 23, the German government granted the Kremlin the freedom to refashion its relations with its small European neighbors, including Poland. Thereafter no Western action could prevent Central and Eastern Europe from slipping totally into Soviet

---

[58]Welles's memorandum of June 23, 1939, *FRUS, 1939*, 1:274; Kennedy to Hull, April 18, and May 25, 1939, ibid., pp. 235, 262–63; Bullitt to Hull, April 18, and May 30, 1939, ibid., pp. 237, 265; Wilson to Hull, June 24, 1939, ibid., pp. 274–75. Cadogan's observations on the Soviet proposal of April 18 appear in Dilks, *Diaries of Sir Alexander Cadogan*, p. 175.

[59]Ickes, *Secret Diary of Harold L. Ickes*, 2:652; Kennedy to Hull, June 27, 1939, *FRUS, 1939*, 1:276.

and German hands. Unable to trust the West to save him from Hitler, Joseph Stalin bought time to improve his defenses. Hitler, having neutralized the Soviet Union, was free to venture elsewhere. The failure of the Moscow alliance negotiations and the Nazi-Soviet Pact heralded another crisis.

In anticipation of this new threat to peace, Daladier appealed to Roosevelt, asking him to summon "all the nations of the earth to send delegates immediately to Washington to try to work out a pacific solution of the present situation." If Germany did not attend, the president at least would have clarified the moral issue. Instead, Roosevelt on August 23 addressed a message to King Victor Emmanuel III of Italy. After referring to his April 14 appeal to Hitler and Mussolini, Roosevelt invited the Italian government to frame specific proposals for a solution of the crisis. The United States, he added, would happily enter any peaceful discussions. That day Chamberlain warned Hitler that Britain would come to the defense of Poland but expressed the hope that Germany and Poland could avert a general European war. Unlike Munich, Britain would not urge Poland to give up Danzig in the interest of a peaceful settlement. However, Kennedy reported that London hoped Washington might exert pressure on Poland to negotiate a solution with Hitler. "If the President is contemplating any action for peace," wrote the ambassador, "it seems to me that the place to work is on [Foreign Minister Jozef] Beck in Poland. . . . I see no other possibility."[60] Berle wondered how Washington might word a strong message to Poland, for the Nazi-Soviet Pact granted western Poland to Germany and eastern Poland to the Soviet Union, along with Estonia and Bessarabia as well. According to Berle, the message would need to begin: "In view of the fact that your suicide is required, kindly oblige etc." Britain, Washington assumed, wanted the United States to do what it could not do. "As we saw it here," Moffat noted, "it merely meant that they wanted us to assume the responsibility of a new Munich and to do their dirty work for them."[61] Roosevelt refused to arrange what might have led to the sellout of another country.

On August 24, Roosevelt responded to the accumulating pressures by addressing messages to Hitler and President Ignacy Moscicki of Poland, urging them to settle their differences through negotiation, arbitration, or conciliation. To avoid responsibility for any specific settlement, Roosevelt denied that any country had the right to achieve its end through force when it could achieve just and reasonable purposes

[60]Bullitt to Hull, August 22, 1939, *FRUS, 1939*, 1:350; Welles to Phillips, August 23, 1939, ibid., p. 352; Kennedy to Hull, August 23, 1939, ibid., pp. 355–56.
[61]Berle and Jacobs, *Navigating the Rapids*, p. 243; Hooker, *The Moffat Papers*, p. 253.

peacefully. For unreasonable objectives he had no answer, and Berle discounted the president's effort. Two days later Moscicki expressed to Hitler his hope for direct negotiations; Berlin never responded. As the situation in Europe disintegrated, Washington focused its attention on London, hoping that Britain might still avert war by negotiating a Danzig settlement. "There really is not much for us to do other than wait," Moffat observed on August 28; "what trumps we had were long since played."[62] Chamberlain, Kennedy reported, doubted that Danzig was worth a war and hoped that Poland might compromise, but no Polish officials would follow the footsteps of Czech leaders to their destruction. For too long, some American officials and editors complained, Britain had haggled with the Soviets under the assumption that it might secure a more desirable agreement from Germany.[63] Hitler's invasion of Poland on September 1 dragged the West into war with no support in the East at all.

Throughout the crisis months of 1938 and 1939, Roosevelt and his advisers assumed that in a rational environment the highest interests of nations would automatically converge on the question of peace. In rejecting war, however, governments had no choice but to accept the limits imposed on them by the world's treaty structure. It was logical, therefore, that Roosevelt and Secretary Hull would direct their major diplomatic effort toward the goal of impressing on all governments their obligations to honor their international agreements. Tragically, the status quo that Washington sought to preserve did not serve the interests of all countries equally. Its approach to the problem of conflict, which in practice was designed to eliminate all but the most insignificant change in the Versailles order, served the interests of the United States and the Western democracies quite as admirably as the destruction of that order would serve the interests of other less satisfied countries. The administration's rigid principles based world politics not on the rights conveyed by strength and efficiency but on the rights of possession. This would-be utopia formed the bulwark of an unchanging order.

National leaders, no less than students of international relations, defined proper American policies, not in terms of the world that existed but in terms of the world that they thought should exist, one that

---

[62]Roosevelt to Hitler, August 24, 1939, *FRUS, 1939*, 1:360–61; Roosevelt to Moscicki, August 24, 1939, ibid., pp. 361–62; Moscicki to Roosevelt, August 25, 1939, ibid., p. 368; Hooker, *The Moffat Papers*, p. 257.

[63]Ickes argued this view in *Secret Diary of Harold L. Ickes*, p. 705. In a long analysis of the three-power negotiations, Alice Teichova concluded that the British government never wanted a treaty with the Soviet Union, hoping rather to achieve one with Germany. See Teichova, "Great Britain in European Affairs, March 15 to August 21, 1939," *Historica* 3 (Prague, 1961): 239–311.

through rules of proper international conduct could resolve peacefully and without change the conflicting purposes between the satisfied and dissatisfied powers. The difficulty with such reasoning was that the realities of European politics were different; the choices confronting the democracies were limited, immediate, and uncomfortable. Europe's arbitrary boundaries, as well as Europe's peace, rested on the strength of arms. As time passed, the makers of the Versailles Treaty had either to revise those boundaries, through diplomatic procedures, or to keep potential aggressors weak by force. They did neither, preferring instead to assume that they could protect their privileged positions without sacrificing their freedom in binding defensive guarantees or accepting a new European order of power. Having abjured the historic courses available to them, they would now defend what remained of their universe through the very alliances and destruction they sought to avoid.

CHAPTER THREE

Japan: Unanswered Challenge*

JAPAN'S CHALLENGE to U.S. foreign policy during the decade before Pearl Harbor was unique only in matters of time and place. In nature and quality that challenge, no less than the response it produced in Washington, created tensions not unlike those that nonstatus quo powers traditionally exert on the international order, especially on that country which regards itself as the special guarantor of that order. What rendered the Japanese assault on established international relationships embarrassingly troublesome for the United States, however, was the total lack of symmetry between Japanese and American interests in the Far East. For the United States, the status of that region was of marginal concern; for Japan, it raised questions not only of national self-esteem but also of national survival. Thus, to Japan, the pursuit of a new order in East Asia never excluded the use of force; to the United States, the maintenance of the old order was scarcely worth the price of war. Still Washington officials, for reasons of their own, refused to the end to compromise the old order in the interest of peace. It was not strange, therefore, that war came to the United States in December 1941 by inadvertence. Because of the absence of any clear American interest in China worth defending, it could hardly have been otherwise.

Tokyo's rejection of the post-Versailles order in the Far East was profound. Japanese expansionism was bound up in Japan's history, geographical position, food supply, population problems in relation to

*Walter Prescott Webb Lecture, University of Texas, Arlington, March 22, 1973. Published as "Japan: Unanswered Challenge, 1931–1941," in Margaret F. Morris and Sandra L. Myres, eds., *Essays on American Foreign Policy* (Austin, 1974). Reprinted by permission.

its land areas, and the availability of raw materials for industrial expansion. Japan's scarcely concealed ambitions toward China reflected both insecurity and economic necessity. What disturbed Tokyo especially was the perennial danger that the Western powers would enlarge their presence in China at the expense of Chinese integrity and Japanese security. "Japan is an island nation," admitted Viscount Ishii Kikujiro, Japan's noted statesman, "but her distance from the continent of Asia is so small that she cannot be indifferent to what happens in Korea, Manchuria and Siberia."[1]

Japan's direct designs for China reflected fundamentally the needs of the Japanese population. American writer Arthur Bullard described the essence of Japanese expansionism toward the mainland when he wrote that "however threatening Japanese ambitions may be to us, they have to face a worse menace at home. They have a baby-peril, more dangerous than Oriental immigration ever was to us. Each new child born to them means the desperate pressure of over-population."[2] Japan faced three choices: famine, emigration, or industrial expansion; there were no others. It was certain that the Japanese government would never accept the first alternative and that no Western country would willingly eliminate its policies of exclusion aimed at the Asian peoples. Japan, therefore, could sustain its growing population only with expanding industry and commerce.

Japanese industrialization raised the fundamental question of the distribution of the world's land and natural resources, for Japan lacked the three essentials of oil, iron, and coal. Ultimately, Asian stability would require a more equitable distribution of territory and resources throughout the Far East. To satisfy its immediate industrial needs, Japan demanded the opportunity to share in the development of China's natural resources, especially those in Manchuria, whether China consented or not. General Sadao Araki, Japanese minister of war in the early 1930s, declared that, since mankind had "the right to live upon the earth," no country with abundant resources had the right to deny them to another country insufficiently endowed by nature.[3] Japan's special economic ambitions in China carried with them the self-assigned responsibility for leading China into a new age of economic efficiency and political stability.[4]

[1]Viscount Ishii Kikujiro, "The Permanent Bases of Japanese Foreign Policy," *Foreign Affairs* 11 (January 1933): 224.
[2]Arthur Bullard, "Expanding Japan," *Harper's Magazine* 139 (November 1919): 857–58.
[3]Quoted in George H. Blakeslee, "The Japanese Monroe Doctrine," *Foreign Affairs* 11 (July 1933): 676.
[4]Ibid., p. 673.

In large measure the concept of a "Japanese Monroe Doctrine" embodied Tokyo's claims to special or paramount interests in the Far East. It explained both Japan's objectives in China and its attitudes toward the Western powers in the Far East. Japan's Monroe Doctrine, like that of the United States, asserted Tokyo's special claims to regional leadership. "From our point of view," observed Ishii, "Japan possesses interests superior to other Powers in China as a whole, especially in the contiguous regions, much as the position of [the United States] in the Western Hemisphere."[5] Japan demanded recognition of its superior rights and its dominant power in the western Pacific as well as the international courtesy and the advantages that accrued generally to the world's modern, progressive, and efficient countries. Japan viewed itself, moreover, as the one country that, by reducing Western influence in East Asia, could establish the principle of "Asia for the Asiatics."

Nowhere, however, could Japan alter the status quo in East and Southeast Asia without challenging a wide spectrum of Western possessions and treaty rights, which the non-Asian powers would never willingly surrender. The Great War had eliminated Russia and Germany from the main currents of Asian affairs; it had weakened Britain and France beyond recall. Thus, after Versailles, the United States alone possessed sufficient power in the Pacific to curtail Japanese expansion. Japan confronted the United States with two inescapable alternatives in the Far East: either this country would accept a dominant economic and political role for Japan in East Asia or it would fight to prevent it. Bullard defined the American choice in such terms as early as 1919. "Unless we want to 'smash' Japan," he warned, "we must facilitate her commercial access to China."[6] Either response to Japanese expansion—and there was really no third—exceeded the military and political limits of an acceptable American policy. Still, as early as the Manchurian crisis of 1931, Washington officials searched for the means of escape from the cruel dilemmas posed by Japanese behavior.

Manchuria emerged as the key to Japanese industrial expansion. Under Japanese control that region served as a minimal barrier to Soviet encroachment along the Asian littoral. Beyond that, Manchuria possessed the natural riches that Formosa and Korea had failed to supply. With time, it promised to furnish much of the food and raw materials necessary for Japan's economic existence. So successful had been Japanese investments and industrial leadership in developing the Manchurian economy that by 1931 almost 30 million people, overwhelmingly Chinese, lived in the three Japanese-controlled provinces.

[5]Ibid., p. 671.
[6]Bullard, "Expanding Japan," pp. 865–66.

However, it was becoming increasingly clear that the Chinese migration was evolving into a massive effort to drive the Japanese out of the region. Convinced that Chinese nationalism and antiforeignism endangered Japan's privileged position in Manchuria, Japanese officials in the province determined to exploit the Mukden incident of September 1931, occasioned by the alleged destruction of track along the Japanese-controlled South Manchurian Railway, to convert Manchuria into a Japanese dependency.

II

When news of the Mukden clash reached Washington, President Herbert Hoover and his advisers revealed no inclination to escape responsibility for what occurred. Their response to Manchuria established the post-Versailles pattern of American behavior toward unwanted changes in international life. What disturbed Washington in the Japanese assault on Manchuria was not the violation of this nation's vital interests. No major U.S. official, either in Washington or in the Far East, ever defined any American interest in Asia sufficiently important to justify war. What the Japanese assault endangered was the credibility of the entire post-Versailles international treaty structure that supposedly had eliminated the employment of force in relations among states. The United States had not entered the League of Nations, but it had assumed the lead in negotiating both the Nine Power Treaty of 1922 and the Kellogg-Briand Pact of 1928. For Washington, these two treaties safeguarded the world's peace, not by the exercise of power but by the promise of each signatory to refrain from activities that would infringe on the rights of other countries. Japan, in signing them, had agreed to share the responsibility for maintaining the peace of Asia. At stake in Manchuria, therefore, was the stability of the post-Versailles international order. Clearly the United States, as the most powerful country with interests in China, would not ignore the events in Manchuria.

This American devotion to the treaty system reduced U.S. purpose in the Manchurian crisis to the simplistic quest of obtaining Japan's compliance with its international obligations. Such an approach, if successful, would enable Washington to bridge the gap between its determination to uphold the status quo in the Far East and its determination to avoid a war over the future of China. Stanley K. Hornbeck, chief of the Division of Far Eastern Affairs, advised the Hoover administration to base any protests to Tokyo, not on the principle of the Open Door and U.S. interests in China but on the question of international peace. Nelson T. Johnson, U.S. minister to China, admitted his indifference to Manchuria's future but not to the future of world peace, which, he wrote, demanded that all nations accept their commitments under the Kellogg-Briand Pact and the League of Nations. "The fate of Manchuria," he warned the State Department in November 1931, "is of secondary importance compared to the fate of the League."[7] League proponents found immense satisfaction in Hoover's initial decision of October to cooperate with the League.

Secretary Stimson readily agreed with Hornbeck and Johnson that U.S. interests in China were insignificant when contrasted to the American stake in the world's peace structure. On October 9 at a cabinet meeting, Stimson cautioned President Hoover against placing the United States in a humiliating position should Japan refuse to honor its signatures on the Nine Power and Kellogg-Briand treaties. Then in his diary he recorded the essential role of the peace treaties in the assumptions and purposes of U.S. foreign policy:

> The question of the 'scraps of paper' is a pretty crucial one. We have nothing but 'scraps of paper.' This fight has come on in the worst part of the world for peace treaties. The peace treaties of modern Europe made out by the Western nations of the world do no more fit the three great races of Russia, Japan, and China, who are meeting in Manchuria, than, as I put it to the Cabinet, a stovepipe hat would fit an African savage. Nevertheless they are parties to these treaties and the whole world looks on to see whether the treaties are good for anything or not, and if we lie down and treat them like scraps of paper nothing will happen, and in the future the peace movement will receive a blow that it will not recover from for a long time.[8]

For Stimson peace had become indivisible. Japanese aggression, if unchallenged, would destroy the credibility of the entire system of collective security built essentially on the single force of world opinion. Stimson therefore would demand that Japan, as a signatory of the Nine Power and Kellogg-Briand pacts, sacrifice its interests and ambitions to the higher good of world peace which underlay the interests of the United States. Hoover confirmed this American response to the Manchurian crisis in a memorandum presented to his cabinet in mid-October. Japanese behavior, he said, was outrageous, a moral affront to the United States. He reminded the cabinet that this nation carried no obligation to maintain peace among other states by force. Both the Nine Power and Kellogg-Briand pacts were "solely moral instruments

---

[7]Johnson to Peck, November 3, 1931, in Roland N. Stromberg, *Collective Security and American Foreign Policy* (New York, 1963), p. 68.

[8]Henry L. Stimson and McGeorge Bundy, *On Active Service in Peace and War* (New York, 1948), p. 233.

based upon the hope that peace in the world can be held by the rectitude of nations and enforced solely by the moral reprobation of the world."[9] If Japan imperiled no fundamental American interests, the United States still had the "moral obligation to use every influence short of war to have the treaties upheld or limited by mutual agreement." Again, in his December 1931 message to Congress, the president acknowledged U.S. responsibility for the integrity of China under the Nine Power and Kellogg-Briand treaties.[10] For Hoover and Stimson it appeared essential that the United States make its will effective in Japanese-Chinese relations without resorting to either economic or military sanctions.

How then could they achieve their purpose? Japan, it was clear, was preparing to establish permanent control over Manchuria. As early as November, Stimson contemplated a resort to moral sanctions. He concluded that month that it might be wise "to outlaw Japan and let her sizzle [under a Chinese boycott] and all the moral pressure of the world."[11] Early in December, Hoover suggested to the cabinet that the United States propose to the League that its members refuse to recognize any changes in Manchuria that resulted from violations of the Kellogg-Briand Pact. Stimson himself resurrected the Wilsonian doctrine of nonrecognition when he wrote to Charles G. Dawes, the U.S. observer at the League: "We do not see how we can do anything more ourselves . . . than to announce our disapproval and to announce that we will not recognize any treaties which may be forced by Japan under the pressure of military occupation."[12] Stimson realized both the need and the limitations of nonrecognition as the means for reinforcing the treaty system. "If the fruits of aggression should be recognized," he admitted, "the whole theory of the Kellogg Pact would be repudiated, and the world would be at once returned to the point of recognizing war as a legitimate instrument of national policy. Nonrecognition might not prevent aggression, but recognition would give it outright approval."[13]

On January 7, 1932, Stimson, in his first effort to terminate Japanese expansion through moral sanctions, sent identical notes to Japan and China, declaring that this nation could not "admit the legality of

[9]For the text of Hoover's cabinet memorandum see William Starr Myers, *The Foreign Policies of Herbert Hoover, 1929–1933* (New York, 1940), pp. 156–59.

[10]Ray Lyman Wilbur and Arthur Mastick Hyde, eds., *The Hoover Policies* (New York, 1937), pp. 601–02.

[11]Quoted in Stromberg, *Collective Security*, p. 77.

[12]Ibid.

[13]Stimson and Bundy, *On Active Service*, p. 235.

any situation *de facto* nor does it intend to recognize any treaty or agreement entered into between those Governments" that might impair either the treaty rights of the United States or the territorial and administrative integrity of the Republic of China.[14] Both Hoover and Stimson believed that the note would be effective. Furthermore, the president declared that it had mobilized world opinion against Japan and would stand as one of the country's great state papers. Much of the American press agreed. The *Providence Journal* lauded the note as one of "clear and far-reaching importance in the history of twentieth-century diplomacy."[15] Only a minority warned that the note would not serve the cause of peace at all. The *Chicago Daily News* admitted that the reassertion of American principles might appear harmless enough, "but pin-prick notes," ran its conclusion, "irritate the sensitive and proud Japanese, and stiffen the attitude of the dominant military clique. China's ultimate interests may be served better by a policy of patience and discretion, by overlooking Japan's inconsistencies, and letting it restore order and security throughout Manchuria."[16] Even the U.S. ambassador to Tokyo, W. Cameron Forbes, found little in Stimson's verbal toughness that would stop Japan or serve the interests of the United States. To Forbes, the paper treaties of the 1920s had lost their relevance; rhetorical recriminations based on such documents would only aggravate tensions in the Pacific.

Japan, undaunted by Stimson's moral strictures, continued to exert pressure on China. Finally, on January 28, 1932 the Japanese invaded Shanghai. Again Stimson was outraged. He hoped, he confided to his diary, that the Japanese would not withdraw until the United States could pass firm judgment against the new aggression.[17] "As I reflected upon it," he recalled later, "it seemed to me that in future years I should not like to face a verdict of history to the effect that a government to which I belonged had failed to express itself adequately upon such a situation."[18] On February 16 the League Council supported the nonrecognition doctrine and called upon Japan to fulfill its obligations under the Nine Power Treaty. Thereupon, in the form of an open letter dated February 23 to Senator Borah, Stimson leveled his second moral blast at Japan. Nothing, he declared, had occurred to

[14]Ibid., pp. 235–36.
[15]Quoted in *Literary Digest*, January 23, 1932, p. 5.
[16]Ibid., p. 6.
[17]See Richard N. Current, "The Stimson Doctrine and the Hoover Doctrine," *American Historical Review* 59 (April 1954): 529.
[18]Henry L. Stimson, *The Far Eastern Crisis: Recollections and Observations* (New York, 1939), p. 157.

challenge the validity of either the Nine Power or the Kellogg-Briand pact. These two documents, he reminded Japan, "represent independent but harmonious steps taken for the purpose of aligning the conscience and public opinion of the world in favor of a system of orderly development by the law of nations, including a settlement of all controversies by methods of justice and peace instead of by arbitrary force." Stimson warned Tokyo that nonrecognition, if adopted by the other powers, "will eventually lead to the restoration to China of rights and titles of which she may have been deprived."[19] Never before had Stimson made such extravagant claims for the coercive power of nonrecognition. Still Japan continued to move. During March the Japanese smuggled Henry Pu Yi, former emperor of China, into Manchuria and installed him as head of the new Japanese-controlled puppet state of Manchukuo.

Nonrecognition, an an ineffective sanction, gave the administration the remaining choice of resorting to arms or acknowledging the failure of its moral rhetoric. Stimson again escaped the first alternative with a further attempt at moral pressure. Addressing the New York Council on Foreign Relations in August, he implored the nations to join the United States in strengthening the Kellogg-Briand Pact by adding their voices of condemnation to that expressed by this country in January. "Moral disapproval," he said, "when it becomes the disapproval of the whole world, takes on a significance hitherto unknown in international law. For never before has international opinion been so organized and mobilized."[20] Stimson received the customary adulation for his peaceful disposition of the Japanese problem. The *New York World Telegram* praised the Hoover-Stimson doctrine of nonrecognition as "the most important international step taken by the United States since the World War."[21] Stimson asserted that the Hoover administration, in supporting the Kellogg-Briand Pact, had made it "a living force of law in the world."[22]

Thus Washington managed in 1932 both to avoid war in the Pacific and to escape any admission of failure in the Manchurian crisis. For that reason the Hoover-Stimson doctrine emerged as an astonishingly attractive formula domestically, but the doctrine was scarcely promising abroad. It had not stopped Japan, and it had nailed the American preference for the status quo in the Far East, not to American

[19]*FRUS: Japan, 1931–1941* (Washington, 1943), 1:87.

[20]Stimson and Bundy, *On Active Service*, p. 259; *Literary Digest*, August 20, 1932, p. 6.

[21]Ibid.

[22]Henry L. Stimson, "Bases of American Foreign Policy during the Past Four Years," *Foreign Affairs* 11 (April 1933): 394, 396.

power but to the sanctity of an outmoded treaty structure. Washington's military abstention from the Manchurian affair illustrated clearly that Japan had not challenged any immediate U.S. interest. However, the Hoover administration, by defining Japanese aggression as a threat to world peace, permitted the United States only a temporary escape from the continuing Far Eastern crisis. By preventing Japan from solidifying its gains through universally recognized agreements, the United States would one day emerge as Japan's enemy and the major source of its ultimate frustration. The Hoover-Stimson doctrine, designed to avoid a Japanese-American confrontation in Asia, rendered war inevitable.

III

Still the Hoover-Stimson doctrine appeared so laudable in precept and so promising in action that President Roosevelt accepted it without modification as the essence of his Far Eastern policy. Following a long conversation with Stimson at Hyde Park, Roosevelt agreed on January 17, 1933 that "American foreign policy must *uphold* the *sanctity* of international treaties. This is the cornerstone on which all relations between nations must rest."[23] Throughout Roosevelt's first term, the Japanese continued to make clear their rejection of the Far Eastern treaty structure. Tokyo officials warned repeatedly that Japan alone carried the responsibility for peace and order in East Asia. In April 1934, Amau Eiji, a Japanese Foreign Ministry spokesman, declared that no country could share that responsibility but China. "We oppose, therefore," he warned, "any attempt on the part of China to avail herself of the influence of any other country to resist Japan."[24] Whatever the level of their conflicting interests in the Orient, the United States and Japan were clearly on a collision course.

Roosevelt and Secretary Hull adopted the Republican formula of nonrecognition with little regard for its consequences. Their automatic rejection of Japanese gains eliminated the need for either an understanding of Japanese expansionism or an accurate measurement of U.S. interests in the Far East. In practice, Hull would avoid direct military

[23]Edgar B. Nixon, ed., *Franklin D. Roosevelt and Foreign Affairs* (Cambridge, MA, 1969), 1:4. Roosevelt's advisers, Raymond Moley and Rexford G. Tugwell, warned Roosevelt that his January 17, 1933 statement ran the risk of placing the United States in an impossible position in the Far East. The president answered that he sympathized with the Chinese people and therefore had no choice but to go along with Stimson on the Japanese question. Moley observed: "That was all. It was so simple, so incredible, there could be no answer." See Moley, *After Seven Years* (New York, 1939), pp. 94–95; and Bernard Sternsher, "The Stimson Doctrine: F.D.R. *versus* Moley and Tugwell," *Pacific Historical Review* 31 (August 1962): 281–89.

[24]*New York Times*, April 21, 1934.

involvement in the Pacific even while he sought, through the constant reiteration of American principles of peaceful change, the total capitulation of Japan to Chinese will. To close the gap between these two fundamentally incongruous objectives, he would exhort Japan to live peacefully by limiting its demands to what all parties in China would accept through negotiation alone.

Meanwhile, China carried the burden of protecting what remained of the Open Door. It was better that China suffer, observed Hornbeck in February 1934, for any settlement would compel China to recognize Japanese-imposed change in direct defiance of the Nine Power Treaty.[25] Scrapping the Open Door in China, moreover, would compel the United States to give up its treaty rights. "If we did this without making an announcement," ran a State Department memorandum, "we would produce all sorts of misunderstanding and confusion. If we did it with an announcement, such announcement would be tantamount to a declaration that, so far as we are concerned, Japan may do as she pleases in and with regard to China."[26] Compromise would demonstrate a lack of moral firmness and thus become an invitation to disaster. Even while the Roosevelt administration revealed no intention of fighting Japan, it viewed the United States as the special guarantor of the status quo in the Far East.

War returned to the Orient on July 7, 1937 when a regiment of Japanese troops on maneuvers near the Marco Polo Bridge outside Beijing (Peking) exchanged shots with local Chinese soldiers. Tokyo seized this armed clash, much as it had the Mukden incident five years earlier, to wrest another body of special concessions from the Chinese government. Hull's response to this crisis was almost identical to that of Stimson. On July 16 he released a statement to the press that reaffirmed this country's devotion to the treaty structure: "We advocate adjustment of problems in international relations by processes of peaceful negotiation and agreement. We advocate faithful observance of international agreements. Upholding the principle of the sanctity of treaties, we believe in modification of provisions of treaties . . . by orderly processes carried out in a spirit of mutual helpfulness and accommodation."[27] These principles again eliminated every possibility that Washington might come to terms with Japan over the future of China.

[25]Hornbeck memorandum, May 9, 1933, President's Secretary's File (hereafter cited as PSF): China, 1933–1936, Box 3, Franklin D. Roosevelt Library, Hyde Park, New York (hereafter cited as FDRL).
[26]Memorandum of January 3, 1935, PSF: Diplomatic Correspondence, Japan, Box 13, FDRL.
[27]FRUS, 1937 (Washington, 1954), 1:699–700.

Roosevelt's famed "quarantine" speech bespoke a stronger response to Japanese aggression, including a suggestion of collective security. Still that speech scarcely altered the quality of American policy in the Far East. The president's open partisanship aroused the nation's isolationists; never again would they trust him. His speech had failed to create the foundation for a national policy; it did not define U.S. interests anywhere except in terms of the status quo. Peace-loving nations, he said, "must work together for the triumph of law and moral principles in order that peace, justice, and confidence may prevail in the world." Nor did the president suggest any body of means that might be effective. He favored, he told newsmen, a program that might create a stronger neutrality. Two weeks after the speech he handed foreign policy adviser Norman H. Davis, later selected by the president to head the American delegation at Brussels, a statement that suggested "the possibility of a constructive program in which a group of neutrals, acting together, but without threat of force, might make their influence felt."[28]

On October 6 the League of Nations invited its members, who were also signatories of the Nine Power Treaty, to call an international conference to settle the Sino-Japanese dispute. Roosevelt suggested Brussels but refused to permit the Belgian government to send out invitations in his name. Brussels confronted Washington with another policy crisis in that Roosevelt's goal of halting Japan had no relationship to the means available to him. Unable to act, yet required to do so, Roosevelt retreated to the Hoover-Stimson formula of resorting to moral sanctions that had permitted Washington to escape a similar dilemma in 1932. The president instructed Davis to reject either joint action with the League or a British-led quest for collective security. Instead, said Roosevelt, the delegates should pose questions to Japan "which would become increasingly embarrassing and which would continue to mobilize public opinion and moral force."[29] For Hull the conference would become the agency "for educating public opinion and bringing to bear upon Japan all possible moral pressure."[30]

Even before the Brussels Conference opened on November 3, 1937, the delegates were seeking an excuse to terminate the discussions. Davis stood alone. The smaller European powers with interests in the Far East were too powerless to take any stand against Japan. Britain, France, the Soviet Union, and China had no interest in condemnatory resolutions that they knew would be ineffective. The Japanese made it

[28]Dorothy Borg, *The United States and the Far Eastern Crisis of 1933–1938* (Cambridge, MA, 1964), pp. 381–86. This is a superb account of Roosevelt and the "quarantine" speech.

[29]Memorandum in PSF: State Department, 1937, Box 32, FDRL.

[30]Cordell Hull, *Memoirs of Cordell Hull* (New York, 1948), 1:552.

clear that they would not attend the conference at all. Following the opening statements at Brussels, Western leaders generally, as well as much of the press, found the American program of stopping Japan with an aroused world opinion untenable. Davis's reports dwelt on the almost universal rejection of U.S. policy. Still Washington would not be dissuaded. Welles reminded Davis of American objectives. "Every effort," he instructed him, "is to be made to rally moral opinion in every other country of the world in favor of the principles embodied in the Nine Power Treaty. . . . The whole premise of the government in going to the Brussels Conference was the keeping alive . . . of international law and morality."[31]

Despite his efforts to impose the U.S. formula on the conference, Davis could stem neither the cynicism of the press nor the resentment of the other delegations. The British, he informed Hull, demanded strong action or the immediate termination of the conference. For the London delegation there was no merit or dignity in a mere statement of principles. Hull countered by informing Davis that he could best relieve the criticism of American leadership with "a strong reaffirmation of the principles which should underlie international relationships," but time had run out and Hull agreed to an adjournment.[32] On November 24, three weeks after it opened, the Brussels Conference adopted its resolutions and disbanded. Davis reminded the disillusioned Chinese that the powers "had rendered a real service to China, particularly in reaffirming their adherence to the principles of the Nine Power Treaty."[33] For Stimson the Brussels Conference comprised a grave and inescapable challenge to American leadership. It was essential, he reminded Roosevelt, that the United States both uphold its principles at Brussels and find a genuine solution to the Far Eastern problem. Nothing less than universal peace and freedom was at stake in China.[34] Roosevelt and Hull admitted the gravity of the crisis as well as their inability to offer a solution.

IV

Following the failure at Brussels, Japan continued to confront Washington with only two realistic alternatives: to accept a larger role for Japan in the affairs of the Orient or to terminate Japan's expanding

---

[31]*FRUS, 1937*, 4:154–55.
[32]Ibid., pp. 184–85, 194–96, 225–26.
[33]Ibid., pp. 231–33.
[34]Stimson to Roosevelt, November 15, 1937, Roosevelt to Hull, November 22, 1937, Roosevelt to Stimson, November 24, 1937, President's Personal File 20 (hereafter cited as PPF), FDRL.

war in China with force. For Roosevelt neither alternative was acceptable. To stop Japan would require a military price far out of proportion to American interests in China. To abjure the traditional guardianship of the Open Door and the treaty system in China would demand a political price equally unacceptable. Hull explained simply in January 1938 that "the Government of the United States . . . has asked and is asking that the rights of the United States . . . be respected, and at the same time it has sought and is seeking to avoid involvement of this country in the disputes of other countries."[35] Even while the administration attempted to escape any military involvement in the Far East, it remained, by choice, the final arbiter in Chinese affairs. As long as Roosevelt could tolerate the Japanese assault on American citizens and property in China, he could extend his formula of moral involvement without military commitment into an indefinite future.

On November 3, 1938 the Japanese government promulgated its ultimate design for a "New Order in East Asia." In a radio broadcast that day, Premier Konoe Fumimaro explained: "Japan desires to build up a stabilized Far East by cooperating with the Chinese people who have awakened to the needs of self-determination as an Oriental race. . . . History shows that Japan, Manchukuo and China are so related to each other that they must bind themselves closely together in a common mission for the establishment of peace and order in the Far East."[36] For the United States the choices in the Far East were narrowing perceptibly. Still Roosevelt refused to confront the Japanese with either threatened sanctions or a willingness to acknowledge Japan's economic and psychological dilemmas which drove that country along its expansionist course. Instead, U.S. Ambassador to Tokyo Joseph C. Grew complained to the Japanese Foreign Office that Japan attempted to create its new order, not in accordance with its treaty obligations but "by methods of its own selection, regardless of treaty pledges and the established rights of other powers concerned." Changing conditions in the Orient demanded new agreements, Grew admitted, but these required "orderly processes of negotiation and agreement among the parties thereto."[37] Opposed by a treaty structure changeable only by general agreement, Japan faced the simple choice of limiting its status in China to its treaty rights or extending its war across China into an unknown future.

[35]Hull's statement of January 15, 1938, quoted in William Crane Johnstone, *The United States and Japan's New Order* (New York, 1941), p. 254.
[36]Quoted in Chihiro Hosoya, "Miscalculations in Deterrent Policy: Japanese-U.S. Relations, 1938–1941," *Journal of Peace Research* (Oslo), no. 2 (1968): 113.
[37]Grew to Arita, December 30, 1938, in Department of State, *Peace and War: United States Foreign Policy, 1931–1941* (Washington, 1943), pp. 441–47.

To stop the drift in U.S. policy, which refused either to undo or to accept Japan's struggle for a new order in East Asia, Roosevelt's friends and advisers urged him to consider some form of coercion against Japan. This group agreed overwhelmingly that economic sanctions would be the surest and safest means of forcing Japan to capitulate. In November 1938, Admiral William D. Leahy reminded Roosevelt that Japan depended on open sea lanes for its vital commerce. "Any threat against these lines of communication," Leahy predicted, "will have a profound effect on her attitude of mind regarding the settlement of the present controversy."[38] Writing from China, a Roosevelt correspondent, Marine Captain Evans F. Carlson, commented that "if the flow of oil and munitions to Japan was stopped she could not continue this conflict for another six months."[39] Hornbeck urged the administration to exert economic pressure on Tokyo by terminating the U.S.-Japanese commercial treaty of 1911, thereby placing American trade with Japan on a day-to-day basis. He insisted that U.S. economic retaliation against Japan would produce rapid and significant revisions in Japan's new order.[40]

Still convinced that no American interest in China was worth a war in the Pacific, Roosevelt hesitated to antagonize Tokyo with either financial aid to China or commercial restrictions against Japan. Finally, in December he responded to Henry Morgenthau's arguments favoring financial aid to China with a $25 million loan. Then during January 1939 the president initiated a "moral embargo" on airplanes and parts to Japan and the next month ordered a cessation of credits. Responding to the mounting domestic pressure now centering in the Congress, the State Department on July 26, 1939 formally notified Tokyo of the abrogation of the 1911 treaty. Six months later—January 26, 1940—the treaty would cease to be effective. Friends of the administration were delighted. "Warm congratulations on your notice," former Senator William G. McAdoo wired the president; "this ought to have a great and beneficial effect."[41] Admiral Richard E. Byrd commended the president: "History will, without a doubt, show the great effectiveness of the very firm stand you have taken in the direction of international law and order."[42] Even the threat of economic sanctions, prophesied Carlson, would halt Japan without war.

Roosevelt's preparations for economic sanctions began to separate

---

[38]For a similar view see Irving Fisher to Roosevelt, August 20, 1937, PPF 431, FDRL.

[39]Carlson to Miss LeHand, November 15, 1938, PPF 4951, FDRL.

[40]*FRUS, 1938* (Washington, 1955), 3:425–27.

[41]McAdoo to Roosevelt, July 27, 1939, Roosevelt to McAdoo, August 3, 1939, PPF 308, FDRL.

[42]Byrd to Roosevelt, July 31, 1939, Roosevelt to Byrd, August 2, 1939, PPF 201, FDRL.

those advisers who believed that such sanctions would terminate Japanese aggression from those who warned that such policies would drive Japan into new forms of expansion and probably into war with the United States. In January 1940, Stimson urged an embargo on war materials against Japan. This, he said, would entail no risk inasmuch as Japan would avoid war with the United States. Frank Knox, publisher of the *Chicago Daily News*, assured the president that Japan's position was weakening: "The tendency is a healthy one which will continue if Uncle Sam stays tough and the Chinese remain uncooperative. The only hope for a return to peace and sanity in the Far East is the continuance of this trend."[43] Within the administration, those who most notably favored the hard line were Morgenthau, Hornbeck, and Interior Secretary Ickes. The president strengthened this group when in 1940 he appointed Stimson and Knox to the cabinet as the new secretaries of war and the navy, respectively. Stimson wrote shortly after assuming his new office that "the only way to treat Japan is not to give her anything."[44]

Others were not convinced. Grew had warned Roosevelt in November 1939 that an embargo against Japan would produce a total disintegration in U.S.-Japanese relations. From Tokyo, Assistant Secretary of State Francis Sayre warned Washington that an embargo would inflame Japanese opinion and render a Far Eastern settlement almost impossible. It would compel Tokyo to pursue its new order with greater determination.[45] Those in the State Department who shared the conviction that economic pressure on Japan would produce war rather than capitulation were Hull, Welles, and Maxwell Hamilton of the Far East Division. If these men did not favor extensive concessions to Japan, they agreed generally that U.S. interests in the Far East were too negligible to necessitate a drastic response to Japan's encroachments on the mainland.

As late as 1940 the United States had offered little tangible aid to China. The American conception of national interest had been bound less to Chinese integrity than to the integrity of the treaty system, a broader but more abstract concern that had demanded no real response to Japanese aggression. Until mid-1940, U.S. officials assumed that Chinese resistance, added to the threat of economic sanctions, would ultimately place limits on Japanese ambitions. Suddenly, Washington discovered too late that Japanese expansion had entered a new and more threatening phase. The German offensive in Europe during May

[43]Knox to Roosevelt, January 23, 1940, PSF: Frank Knox, Box 28, FDRL.

[44]Quoted in Hosoya, "Miscalculations in Deterrent Policy," p. 106.

[45]Grew to Roosevelt, November 6, 1939, PSF: Diplomatic Correspondence, Japan, Box 13, FDRL; Sayre memorandum, May 1, 1940, ibid.

and June 1940 rendered the Dutch, French, and British empires in Southeast Asia vulnerable to Japanese encroachments. Unable to negotiate a settlement with China, the Japanese moved to consolidate their position by controlling the southern approaches to that country. The threatened embargo on oil, moreover, focused Japanese attention on the oil resources of the Dutch East Indies. With France's defeat, Tokyo demanded that Britain stop all shipments to China. At the same time, Tokyo extracted the promise of 1 million tons of oil from the Dutch and pressed France for the right to occupy northern Indochina.

Japan's burgeoning assault on the European empires in Southeast Asia broadened the American interest from concern for the treaty system in China to the defense of the East Asian balance of power. Congress responded in July with the National Defense Act which gave the president the authority to place, under license, arms, munitions, critical and strategic raw materials, airplane parts, optical instruments, and metal-working machinery. To moderate the impact of such restrictions on Japan, Roosevelt omitted oil and scrap iron from his order. Later in July, however, under pressure from Stimson, Knox, Morgenthau, and Hornbeck, he added oil and scrap iron to the export license system. State Department officers, led by Hamilton, gained a compromise that limited restrictions to aviation fuel, lubricants, and heavy melting iron and steel scrap. Finally, as Japan continued its thrusts into Southeast Asia, the president, in September, terminated the sale of scrap iron and steel to Japan. Clearly such pressures only accelerated the Japanese drive into Southeast Asia, and, on September 27, 1940, Japan signed the Tripartite Pact with Germany and Italy.

Until that moment Washington had never regarded China as an ally. United States officials had scarcely treated Chinese resistance as an element in this country's security, but Japan's new identification with the Axis powers in Europe—a genuine diplomatic blunder— transformed Japan into a potential enemy and China into another ally fighting the totalitarian powers. Japanese action, at least to American interventionists, brought the Pacific war into the Atlantic. Clark M. Eichelberger, director of the Committee to Defend America by Aiding the Allies, observed in October that "Britain and China in the Pacific, with Britain in the Atlantic, now constitute our first lines of defense."[46] Grew argued against this tendency to attribute like motives and characteristics to the Japanese and German governments. For him it was essential that Washington distinguish between its immediate and

---

[46]Warren I. Cohen, "From Contempt to Containment: Cycles in American Attitudes toward China," in *Twentieth-Century American Foreign Policy*, ed. John Braeman, Robert H. Bremner, and David Brody (Columbus, OH, 1971), p. 553.

long-term goals in the Far East.[47] To avoid war in the Pacific and to counter Japan's advance into Southeast Asia, the United States, he believed, could well continue to tolerate the Japanese occupation of China.

Unconcerned with such distinctions, Roosevelt cautiously escalated the U.S. involvement in the Pacific. On November 30 he placed another $100 million at the disposal of Jiang Jieshi (Chiang Kai-shek). Aid to China now replaced the former trade with Japan. In December, Roosevelt dispatched ships and planes to the Philippines under the principle, as Hull explained it, "of letting [the Japanese] guess as to when and in what set of circumstances we would fight."[48] As late as January 1941, the president had established no goals in the Far East that reflected the nation's minimal interests, its lack of military preparations, or its determination to avoid war. Still the United States would no longer accept China's sorrows passively. China's status as an ally, moreover, would reinforce Washington's determination to encourage no Far Eastern settlement at China's expense.

V

Admiral Nomura Kichisaburo, who arrived in Washington as Japanese ambassador in February 1941, had no chance against Washington's perennial determination to place its hopes for peace in the Far East on the altar of diplomatic inflexibility. Hull reminded Nomura what the United States expected of Japan when he presented his four principles, which became the final stand of the U.S. government: "(1) respect for the territorial integrity and the sovereignty of each and all nations; (2) support of the principle of non-interference in the internal affairs of other countries; (3) support of the principle of equality, including equality of commercial opportunity; (4) non-disturbance of the *status quo* in the Pacific except as the *status quo* may be altered by peaceful means."[49] For Hull the American conditions for peace in the Pacific seemed reasonable enough; for the Japanese government, as its response of May 12 made clear, they demanded little less than a Japanese capitulation. Tokyo requested above all that the United States cooperate in establishing peace in China by requesting Jiang to negotiate under the threat of the discontinuance of all American aid should he refuse. Japan,

[47]Grew's dispatch of September 12, 1940, in Joseph C. Grew, *Turbulent Era: A Diplomatic Record of Forty Years, 1904–1945*, ed. Walter Johnson (Boston, 1952), 2:1224–29.

[48]Hull, *Memoirs*, 1:915.

[49]Memorandum of conversations between Hull and Nomura, April 16, 1941, PSF: Diplomatic Correspondence, Japan, Box 13, FDRL.

however, also asked the right to negotiate on the basis of its power and efficiency as well as the resumption of normal trade relations with the United States.[50] Hull rejected the Japanese formula because it in no measure guaranteed a peace based on his four principles. Japan would have peace on Chinese terms or not at all.

Japan responded with the determination to establish its Greater East Asian Co-Prosperity Sphere and occupy southern Indochina, whatever the obstacles involved. Roosevelt countered with a promise that, if Japan would refrain from advancing into Indochina, he would seek a multinational declaration establishing Indochina's neutralization.[51] When he received no response, on July 26 the president issued an executive order to freeze Japanese assets in the United States, thereby effectively terminating all U.S. commercial and financial relations with Japan. At last this move stopped the export of oil to Japan. Much of Washington and the press, thoroughly attuned by mid-1941 to the notion that the inflexible rejection of all Japanese gains was the surest guarantee of peace, lauded the president's decision. Assured that Japan would not fight, Roosevelt failed to attach any objectives, achievable through diplomacy, to his embargo. Thus U.S. economic sanctions, effective beyond anticipation, would force Japan, with only one year's supply of oil on hand, into a quick capitulation or an expanding war.

What troubled Tojo Hideki, the former war minister who assumed the Japanese premiership in October 1941, was the realization that Japan, now under intense economic pressure, could achieve no compromise. To avoid both costly concessions and immediate hostilities, Tojo embarked on a dual policy of continuing diplomatic efforts even while completing operational preparations for a possible war.[52] To conduct his final negotiations with Hull, Tojo dispatched Kurusu Saburo, an experienced Japanese diplomat, to Washington. The Imperial Conference of November 5 gave Kurusu until November 25 to achieve an agreement. Thereafter the question of war would go before the emperor.

In Washington, Kurusu faced the challenge of ridding Japan of its enervating war in China, at least in part on Japanese terms, as well as a renewal of U.S.-Japanese trade. For these concessions he could offer an eventual Japanese withdrawal from all Indochina. On November 20, Kurusu presented this formula to Hull in a final proposal. Hull countered momentarily with a *modus vivendi* that differed

[50]Japanese note of May 12, 1941, *FRUS: Japan*, 2:332–33.
[51]Herbert Feis, *The Road to Pearl Harbor* (New York, 1962), pp. 215–16, 238.
[52]See Chihiro Hosoya, "Japan's Decision for War in 1941," *Hitotsubashi Journal of Law and Politics* 5 (April 1967): 12–14.

only slightly from the Japanese offer, but he also had prepared a ten-point peace proposal that demanded a total Japanese withdrawal from China and Indochina in exchange for a new trade agreement. With much of the Chinese treaty structure at stake, Hull presented his modus vivendi to the British, Chinese, Australian, and Dutch ambassadors in Washington before making it a formal offer to Kurusu.[53] In this final crisis, Jiang managed to eliminate the modus vivendi. The American press, denouncing compromise as an invitation to war, joined Chinese officials in creating an intellectual and emotional barrier to negotiation that the Roosevelt administration refused to challenge. For Roosevelt, war seemed to present fewer problems than reversing a decade of U.S. intentions in the Far East. On November 26, Hull presented to Kurusu the ten-point program to bring the year's conversations to an end. For Kurusu, China's apparent control of U.S. policy was beyond comprehension.[54]

On December 1 the Imperial Conference in Tokyo made its fateful decision for war.[55] Still, even as the Japanese task force moved toward Pearl Harbor, much of the Japanese High Command scarcely antici-pated a Japanese victory. Facing the choice between total capitulation and an unending war in China, Tokyo chose the most drastic response available—a direct attack on the U.S. Pacific Fleet. Behind that deci-sion lay a desire to fight under the most favorable conditions, to gain whatever advantage might accrue from the destruction of the U.S. fleet, and to reap the special dispensation of good fortune that a display of courage might bring. It was an act of desperation.

American officials had miscalculated badly the effect of their inflexibility on Japanese decision making. Throughout the year of bur-geoning crisis in the Far East, Roosevelt's advisers had based their optimism on two factors. First, they believed Japan so vulnerable to U.S. economic power that sanctions would compel its government to stop its assault on the Far Eastern treaty structure. Indeed, Japan was vulnerable, but no Japanese government, for both psychological and political reasons, would submit to moral and economic sanctions. By narrowing Japan's alternatives and introducing the factor of time, the

[53]Memorandum of conversations among Hull, Halifax, Hu Shih, Casey, and Lou-don, November 24, 1941, between Hull and Halifax, November 25, 1941, and between Hull and Hu Shih, November 25, 1941, PSF: Diplomatic Correspondence, Japan, Box 13, FDRL.

[54]For Hull's ten-point program and the Japanese reaction see Stimson and Bundy, *Peace and War*, pp. 807–10, 811–12.

[55]See Hosoya, "Japan's Decision for War," pp. 14–19; and Hosoya, "Miscalcu-lations in Deterrent Policy," p. 112.

economic pressure merely accelerated Japan's expansion and stiffened the decision for war.[56]

Second, members of the press and the administration assured Roosevelt repeatedly that Japan would avoid war with the United States at any cost. In urging Roosevelt to avoid a top-level conference with Premier Konoe in August 1941, Hornbeck argued effectively that any settlement acceptable to Japan would infringe on American principles. Beyond that the search for an agreement was not an urgent matter. "We are not in great danger vis-à-vis Japan," he advised the president, "and Japan . . . does not possess military capacity sufficient to warrant an attack by her upon the United States."[57] Early in November a recently returned young Foreign Service officer informed Hornbeck that the embassy staff in Tokyo feared that Japan, from sheer desperation, would launch an attack on the United States. "Tell me," replied Hornbeck, "of one case in history where a nation went to war out of desperation."[58] As late as November 27, 1941, Hornbeck advised the administration that Japan, even while launching possible new offensives in the Far East, would endeavor to avoid war with the United States.[59] Armed with such assurances of American invulnerability, Roosevelt never recognized any need to pursue less than the unraveling of the whole Japanese empire. He embarked cautiously but unerringly toward a policy of escalation anchored to economic sanctions and a limited show of force. With each major increment of pressure, the country's dominant foreign policy elite anticipated a Japanese capitulation, but the capitulation never came.

[56]Stimson informed a cabinet meeting in October 1940 that "in the autumn of 1919 President Wilson got his dander up and put on an embargo on all cotton going to Japan and a boycott on her silk, with the result that she crawled down within two months and brought all of her troops out from Siberia like whipped puppies." Quoted in Hosoya, "Miscalculations in Deterrent Policy," p. 111.

[57]Hornbeck's argument of September 5, 1941, *FRUS, 1941* (Washington, 1956), 4:425–26. See also Hornbeck's memorandum of August 30, 1941, ibid., p. 412.

[58]James C. Thomson, Jr., "The Role of the Department of State," in *Pearl Harbor as History: Japanese-American Relations, 1931–1941*, ed. Dorothy Borg and Shumpei Okamoto (New York, 1973), p. 101.

[59]*FRUS, 1941*, 4:673.

The Limits of Victory*

DURING THE THREE YEARS that followed the Japanese attack on Pearl Harbor—years which for some Americans seemed an eternity—the fundamental wartime intentions of the United States emerged with remarkable clarity. With the elimination of German military power in Europe, U.S. leadership would reforge the lost world of Versailles with its established boundaries, traditional order of power, and promise of liberal democracy. For Americans in general the combined purpose of reconstructing the old balance and reviving President Wilson's precepts of peaceful change did not exceed the achievable. If the balance of power and a Wilsonian world order were not synonymous, if indeed the pursuit of one would almost of necessity eliminate the other, Washington officials managed to avoid facing the choice. For if Germany comprised the only recalcitrant European nation with the power to challenge the preferred international order, then the final barrier to its creation would be removed by that country's defeat. Pearl Harbor, bringing the accumulating power of the United States fully to bear on the Axis, presaged Germany's ultimate collapse.

Thus the times seemed unusually propitious for any program framed to establish that world of principle which had eluded the previous generation. So dominant and frightening was the Germany hegemony in Europe by 1940, yet so sure its eventual disintegration, that American aspirations transcended the mere removal of Nazi tyranny and the reestablishment of the balance of power even before the United States entered the war. American might, soon to be heavily engaged, gave an added measure of vitality to the country's crusading zeal. Alone among the world's belligerents, the United States quickly fashioned a

*Louis Martin Sears Lecture, Purdue University, January 21, 1974. Published as "The Limits of Victory," in *Studies in Modern European History and Culture* 3 (1977): 75–93. Reprinted by permission.

body of universalistic goals to give purpose and direction to its wartime exertions. Hitler's successful expansion across Europe demonstrated the limitations of policies based upon the assumption of geographic isolation. With more positive effect, it rekindled the spirit of America's sense of mission, which sought to serve the interests of all humanity by eliminating the evils of tyranny and aggression, thereby creating a free world of free men.

In 1940 a group of Western intellectuals, including such Americans as Reinhold Niebuhr, Lewis Mumford, and Van Wyck Brooks, issued a public statement entitled "The City of Man." The United States had become the repository of the civilizing virtues. "Here and here alone," declared the group, "the continuity of ancient and modern wisdom lives in a Constitution. . . . Here—more precious than all the gold in Kentucky—the treasure of English culture is guarded, as Hellenism is preserved in Rome. . . . Here, and almost nowhere else, is Europe: the Europe-America that will become 'all things to all men,' and will 'save them all.'"[1] Indeed, German tyranny had made the United States the trustee of civilization.

Building on this theme, prominent European and American liberals, shortly before Pearl Harbor, founded a new organization—the Free World Association—whose members were comprised of many Europeans who had escaped Nazi and Fascist oppression. For the first issue of the organization's publication, Archibald MacLeish wrote a poem:

> Be proud America to bear
> The endless labor of the free—
> To strike for freedom everywhere
> And everywhere bear liberty.[2]

Vice-President Henry A. Wallace in June, 1942 expanded on this need for a free world victory. "This is a fight between a slave world and a free world," he noted. "Just as the United States in 1862 could not remain half slave and half free, so in 1942 the world must make its decision for a complete victory one way or the other." During the war's early months, this universalistic design found further expression in Henry R. Luce's famed essay entitled "The American Century," as

---

[1]Paul Seabury, *The Rise and Decline of the Cold War* (New York, 1967), p. 40.
[2]Archibald MacLeish, "The Western Sky," *Free World, A Monthly Magazine* 1 (October 1941): 6.

well as in Wendell Willkie's *One World*, with sales in the United States during 1943 and 1944 rivaling those of the Bible.[3]

Months before Pearl Harbor the Atlantic Charter had grafted such goals to official American policy. This Wilsonian document unveiled a body of Anglo-American principles, but its inspiration was American. Beyond victory lay not a new balance of power but a triumph at last of liberal democracy and self-determination. In the Charter, Roosevelt and Churchill announced their decision to "make known certain common principles in the national policies of their respective nations." In the first three articles of the Atlantic Charter, the two statesmen declared that their governments sought "no aggrandizement, territorial or other," that they opposed "territorial changes that do not accord with the freely expressed wishes of the people concerned," that they respected "the right of all peoples to choose the form of government under which they will live," and that they wished to see "sovereign rights and self-government restored to those who have been forcibly deprived of them."[4] Such purposes embodied political and moral objectives of profound significance. Under the principles of the Atlantic Charter, the elimination of German and Italian power from all conquered territories would return Europe to the halcyon days of Kellogg-Briand when the major powers had supposedly accepted the decisions made at Versailles. Peace under the Charter would reestablish the European boundaries of 1919, reaffirm the faith of the West in liberal democracy, and create a peaceful moral and economic order in which aggression would have no place.

Roosevelt's specific vision embraced the triumph of his Four Freedoms, the abolition of spheres of influence, and the success of self-determination, all in cooperation with Britain and the Soviet Union.[5] What seemed to assure the fulfillment of his grand vision was the essential fact that American power was fully committed to that intent, coupled with a tremendous confidence in what American power could accomplish. This magnificent dream, shared by most Americans, proclaimed by some, and foisted by official pronouncements on all, generated the enthusiasms of the war as well as the cynicism and despair that followed. Roosevelt's dream never had the slightest relationship

---

[3]Henry A. Wallace, "The Price of Free World Victory," ibid. 3 (June 1942): 9; Henry R. Luce, "The American Century," *Life* 10 (February 17, 1941): 61–65; Wendell Willkie, *One World* (New York, 1943), pp. 202–06.

[4]Atlantic Charter, August 12, 1941, *FRUS: Diplomatic Papers, 1941* (Washington, 1958), 1:368.

[5]Roosevelt's annual message to Congress, January 6, 1941, in Samuel I. Rosenman, ed., *The Public Papers and Addresses of Franklin D. Roosevelt, 1940: War—and Aid to Democracies* (London, 1941), 9:672.

to reality, and only a leadership, compelled by overcommitment to obscuring the truth, could have misled a people even briefly into the belief that they could achieve some new international order simply by producing the elements of power sufficient to assure Germany's defeat.

II

It was clear from the beginning that the immediate objective of securing Moscow's collaboration in defeating Germany required the acceptance of Soviet policy goals which precluded the equally important but more distant objective of fashioning the kind of postwar settlement envisioned by the Western powers. Without the unlimited effort of the USSR, the defeat of Hitler's forces would have necessitated at best a long and enervating struggle, nor would a Soviet victory over Germany without Western cooperation have served the interest of the democracies. Meanwhile, Hitler's sudden invasion of the Soviet Union in June 1941 had certainly created the foundation of a promising military alliance. If, however, wartime cooperation were to be extended into the postwar era, the West would require some understanding with the Kremlin regarding the future of Eastern and Central Europe. At this intersection on the road to peace, the views of the prospective allies came into fatal collision even before the United States entered the war. Moscow did not share the Western respect for the Versailles Treaty and was neither a partner in its creation nor a beneficiary of its political and territorial provisions. The Soviets, moreover, faced specific security problems across East-Central Europe, demonstrated vividly in 1941 by the failure of the Slavic states to stall Germany's eastward advance.

Thus as early as 1941 it was obvious that American policy could not achieve both an Allied victory over Germany and a peace that would conform to the spirit of the Atlantic Charter, for Stalin never denied his intention of acquiring some tangible emoluments of victory by expanding the Soviet sphere of influence through Eastern Europe at the expense of the doctrine of self-determination. The Soviet Union's territorial aims were implicit in the entire range of its diplomacy, from the negotiation of the Nazi-Soviet Pact to Hitler's invasion in June 1941. Encouraged by his understanding with the Nazis, Stalin absorbed eastern Poland, the Baltic states of Estonia, Latvia, and Lithuania, Finland's Karelian peninsula, Bessarabia and northern Bukovina, formerly belonging to Romania. That the Kremlin attached great importance to these territorial gains became clear during the spring of 1941 when Soviet Ambassador C. A. Oumanski attempted to secure recognition of these annexations from the United States, especially those involving the Baltic states, before either country was even in the war.

This policy remained unchanged as war engulfed the USSR in the late summer and fall. Soviet diplomats continued to push the British and U.S. governments for formal recognition of their territorial gains. When the Soviet Union began to reel under the Nazi invasion, its leaders still refused to curtail their objectives or relax their diplomatic pressure.

Churchill, for the moment unmindful of Soviet ideology, responded to the Nazi assault with an immediate promise of support. "I have only one purpose, the destruction of Hitler," declared the prime minister. "If Hitler invaded Hell I would make at least a favorable reference to the Devil in the House of Commons."[6] When Stalin replied belatedly to the British overture, he reminded British leaders of the military value his country's forward positions held for those nations fighting Germany. To Harry Hopkins, visiting London late in July 1941, it seemed obvious that "Stalin had not been tremendously impressed by Britain's offer of aid, but had been concerned, from the very beginning, with the political aspects of the enforced alliance." With its very existence in peril, Hopkins recalled, "the Soviet Government appeared to be more anxious to discuss future frontiers and spheres of influence than to negotiate for military supplies."[7]

Having made clear their territorial demands to Western leaders before August 1941, the Soviets viewed the Atlantic Charter with deep distrust. They resented the fact that they had not been consulted and suspected that Roosevelt and Churchill would attempt to use the Charter and its principles to exclude them from the peace settlement. Perhaps it was this apprehension that led the Soviets to join nine other nations at London in September 1941 in signing the Charter and, similarly, on January 1, 1942 to adhere to the Declaration of the United Nations which restated the Charter's principles. In any case, the explanation of these actions as evidence of Moscow's conversion to a Western view of the postwar world was belied by events. Any expectations that the Soviet leadership would give up its territorial ambitions in conformity with the abstract principle of self-determination, which the West could not and would not enforce, simply ignored Russia's historic interests.

Shortly before Pearl Harbor, Roosevelt had occasion to frame the basic wartime approach of the United States to the question of Soviet territorial ambitions. On December 5, 1941, William C. Bullitt, former

---

[6]Churchill's conversation with John R. Colville, June 21, 1941, in Winston S. Churchill, *The Second World War: The Grand Alliance* (Boston, 1950), p. 370.

[7]For Hopkins's observations see Robert E. Sherwood, *Roosevelt and Hopkins: An Intimate History* (New York, 1948), pp. 309–11. For Churchill's concern over the Soviet delay in responding to British overtures see Churchill, *The Grand Alliance*, pp. 380–81. Churchill received no communication from Stalin until July 19, almost a month after the Nazi invasion began. In that letter Stalin asked for an immediate second front in northern France and the Arctic. Stalin to Churchill, July 18, 1941, ibid., pp. 383–84.

U.S. ambassador to Moscow, had written to the president: "Don't let Churchill get you into any more specific engagements than those of the Atlantic Charter. Try to keep him from engaging himself vis-à-vis Russia."[8] Roosevelt scarcely needed such advice. On the previous day the British Foreign Office had informed Washington that Moscow was suspicious of Western intentions, and for that reason Foreign Secretary Eden would shortly visit Moscow to reassure the Soviets that they could trust their alliance with the United States and Britain. When Washington received that communication, Secretary Hull, echoing Roosevelt's convictions, warned the British government against any secret arrangements regarding the future of Eastern Europe. American postwar policies, wrote Hull, "have been delineated in the Atlantic Charter which today represents the attitude not only of the United States but also of Great Britain and of the Soviet Union."[9] Thus Hull elevated the Atlantic Charter to the status of official U.S. policy. Under the mistaken impression that it would buttress such a policy, he had devised the formula of postponing all political and territorial decisions until the conclusion of the war and now sought to force this tactic on his allies.

London capitulated to Hull's demands. In Moscow, Eden skirted firm arrangements with Stalin by informing the Soviet leader that, because of prior obligations to the United States, "it was quite impossible for His Majesty's Government to commit themselves at this stage to any postwar frontiers in Europe." Churchill loyally, if apprehensively, agreed to this burgeoning policy of procrastination. "There can be no question whatever of our making an agreement . . . without prior agreement with the United States," he wrote on December 20. "The time has not yet come to settle frontier questions, which can only be resolved at the Peace Conference when we have won the war."[10]

Stalin did not accept Hull's formula at once. Throughout the early months of 1942 he attempted to write territorial provisions into the forthcoming Anglo-Soviet treaty of alliance. Churchill and Eden, becoming increasingly convinced that postponement was both dangerous and unrealistic, reminded Washington that necessary Soviet cooperation in the postwar world would require a body of wartime decisions that answered the needs of the USSR. Still the actual pact

[8]Bullitt to Roosevelt, December 5, 1941, President's Secretary's File: Bullitt, Franklin D. Roosevelt Library, Hyde Park, New York.

[9]Hull to John Winant, December 5, 1941, *FRUS, 1941* (Washington, 1958), 1:194–95.

[10]Eden reported Stalin's demands of December 1941 in a series of dispatches. See especially Eden to Churchill, January 5, 1942, in Churchill, *The Grand Alliance*, pp. 628–29. Churchill's reaction is in Churchill to Lord Privy Seal, December 20, 1941, ibid., p. 630; and Churchill to Eden, January 8, 1942, ibid., pp. 695–96.

signed in May between London and Moscow avoided the question of postwar frontiers. Roosevelt had made a substantial contribution to this dubious achievement. By promising Stalin a second front in Europe, and even raising hopes that it could be established before the end of the year, he had managed to divert Soviet attention from the embarrassing issue of postwar boundaries to the more immediate and essential question of maintaining an effective East-West military collaboration across Europe.

Why the USSR receded from these territorial demands and accepted from Britain a simple alliance treaty is really no mystery. Soviet leaders by no means had given up their long-range interest in an expanding sphere of influence. Instead, by an act of seeming cooperation the Kremlin acquired the needed moral and physical support of the United States, which guaranteed satisfaction of their ambitions. Without an eventual victory over Germany, an agreement on territories would matter little. With Germany's defeat, the Kremlin would be in control of those territories that it most desired. Thus Hull's "success" in postponing all territorial settlements until the conclusion of the war actually placed his country at a disadvantage. Never again throughout the war would the United States regain the diplomatic initiative from the Soviet Union, for the more complete the Allied conquest of Germany the more complete would be the Soviet control of East-Central Europe. Therefore, Hull's policy would terminate in one of two possible situations. Either the American people would accept a settlement which they had been taught to regard as unnecessary and immoral, or the Soviet people, having suffered such profound destruction at the hands of the Nazi invaders, would feel betrayed by Western leadership. From these simple alternatives, both carrying heavy political penalties, there was no escape.

III

Wartime Washington was the center not only of Allied strategic discussions but also of the national effort to frame an array of social, economic, and political institutions designed to guarantee satisfaction of the nation's ambitions in the postwar world. During the weeks after Pearl Harbor, State Department officials, supported by the distinguished Advisory Committee on Post-War Foreign Policy, which included men like Norman Davis, Sumner Welles, Leo Pasvolsky, and Dean Acheson, undertook the task of creating a four-power document on general security (to include China) designed to guarantee the peace after Germany's defeat. Conscious of the League of Nations' failure to prevent war in the late 1930s, the planners turned to the possibility of

Big Four military collaboration as a mechanism for preventing future aggression. Such a solution to the question of postwar stability was encouraged by the optimism of the times. All Western planning, beginning in 1942, simply assumed Big Four cooperation in the postwar world because any other assumption was too frightening for the architects of the future to contemplate. As Eden informed the American people by radio in March 1943, "the United Nations, and in particular the United States, the British Commonwealth, China and the Soviet Union, must act together in war and in peace." Differences were not insurmountable, he assured the Canadian parliament a few days later, because all nations desired international security so that their people could "develop their lives in freedom and in peace."[11] Thus, if they all had the same objective, why should there be any quarreling either during or after the war?

Unfortunately, postwar planning demanded more than a prescription for great-power harmony or even for a peace-keeping organization. It required also some understanding of Soviet intentions, for no international organization could function in the face of aggression on the part of one of its leading members. Therefore, it was essential for American planners to learn specifically the nature of Soviet objectives and to deal with them realistically. Why go to the trouble to frame an elaborate international organization if the likelihood existed that one of its members would not obey the rules and deliberately follow policies in conflict with the principles of that organization? In a sense, it was all too late because during the summer of 1943 the Soviet forces emerged triumphant from Stalingrad and began to prepare their counteroffensive designed to drive the Germans out of Soviet territory. Already the Kremlin had demanded land from at least six bordering neighbors and had annexed the Baltic states outright.

As Roosevelt's policy adviser, Davis believed the answer to Soviet expansionism lay in an agreement whereby the major powers, at the end of hostilities, promised to refrain from the use of military power outside their own borders except under prior international agreement. Welles disagreed and warned his colleagues that the United States could never secure a Soviet pledge to respect the territorial integrity of other nations unless the United States first agreed to revised boundaries across Eastern Europe. To him it was essential that Washington discover the precise territorial objectives of the Kremlin and to grant those boundaries in exchange for a promise from the Soviet Union to

---

[11]For a detailed discussion of Eden's conversations in Washington during March 1943 see Sherwood, *Roosevelt and Hopkins*, pp. 707–20; and Eden's speech at Annapolis, March 26, quoted in *The Memoirs of Anthony Eden: The Reckoning* (Boston, 1965), pp. 435–36.

recognize self-determination in whatever regions remained.[12] The issue sharply etched the difference in intellectual and political style between Davis and Welles. Davis, in facing the dilemmas of 1943, was not willing to concede anything to the Soviet Union. Welles, viewing the problem more realistically, insisted that under no circumstances could a permanent arrangement with the Soviet Union be effected without first recognizing the Soviet gains emanating from the diplomacy of the early months of the war. Immediate policy planning was shaped largely to conform to Davis's implacable insistence that the security of small nations in Eastern Europe would best be achieved, not by special arrangements with the USSR but by membership in an international body. Ultimately, the United States placed the principles of the Atlantic Charter on the altar of a universal collective security system.

The question has been asked whether it would not have been better if the White House had adopted the Welles rather than the Davis approach.[13] If the United States had been willing to recognize the power and natural ambitions of the Soviet Union and to come to terms with these inescapable circumstances, would it have been possible to achieve a more favorable postwar relationship between East and West? Initially, the Soviets pursued very limited objectives. What they really wanted was acceptance by the West of what they had held when the Nazis struck in 1941. This meant an approximation of their pre-World War I boundaries from the Baltic states to Romania. The legitimacy of any of these claims, or all of them, became irrelevant to the actual situation as it was shaped by American insistence on the principle that there be no wartime territorial arrangements. No deals meant not even a small one. That position was taken in an atmosphere of rekindled Wilsonianism, including the determination to recreate the shattered world of Versailles. The result was that the Soviets were never given a reasonable choice. Indeed, they were not even allowed an opportunity to negotiate on the question of what choices would be reasonable. In effect, they either could abide by the principles of the Atlantic Charter and formally renounce all their claims, as Davis would have them do, or they could defy these principles, thereby defying the United States, and involve themselves and the American people in a clash of policies that would turn out to be costly for all.

Fundamentally, however, the question does not deal with this set of choices but with a very different one: If Western leaders had been realistic and tried to deal with the Soviets, could they have limited

---

[12]Welles's argument in favor of wartime agreements with the Soviet Union, in Sumner Welles, *Seven Decisions that Shaped History* (New York, 1950), pp. 125–45.

[13]This paragraph and the two that follow are based on replies to questions from the Purdue University audience.

them to those objectives for which they were clamoring in 1941? The most measured judgment must reply that no one really knows. It may be true, but who can claim to be certain about the outcome of a negotiation that never took place? One inescapable fact is that the Soviets were never offered that choice. Another is that, when they were confronted with the alternatives actually presented, they proceeded to occupy whatever territory they had the power to penetrate. This was substantially more than they had originally demanded.

A less speculative point is that Roosevelt knew most of this by 1944, but to build a policy from that point forward on realistic assumptions would have meant turning on many people. A point has been made already concerning the great hopes, widely and fervently held as the war got under way in 1940–41, that the military effort would be a highly successful crusade for humanity and self-determination. Before the end of 1943 it was obvious, at least to the president and some of his policymakers, that this reformation of international affairs would not triumph. Still no chilling message of reassessment was feasible from the viewpoint of either American politics or previous commitments.

Eventually, Welles won many in Washington to his position, mostly those who believed there was no point in dealing with the Soviet Union unless one chose to be somewhat more realistic about Soviet ambitions. Secretary Hull, however, who was absolutely opposed to any compromise on matters of territory, demanded that any agreement signed by the Big Four include a proviso on the matter of self-determination. Accordingly, into the final draft of the Declaration of Four Nations the policy planners wrote: "[The signatory states] will not employ their military forces within the territory of other states except for purposes envisaged in this declaration and after joint consultation and agreement." The declaration, with its self-denying clause, was then approved by both Churchill and Eden at the Quebec Conference of August 14–24, 1943.

At the Tripartite Conference of Foreign Ministers, which opened in Moscow on October 19, Hull sought to place the Declaration of Four Nations on the agenda. From his point of view, this pledge of self-denial was the key to postwar agreement. He was utterly convinced that, if the Soviets would sign the declaration, they would bind themselves to abide by the principles of self-determination. The Soviets had not even bothered to put it on the agenda, but Hull persisted and managed to reinstate it. The secretary argued that such a statement was necessary to assure the lesser states of Europe that the big powers would not use military force except to win the war and to guarantee European security. In an added paragraph, Hull requested permission to invite the Chinese ambassador in Moscow to participate in the eventual signing. The skeptical Soviets agreed to that gesture also. Hull was overwhelmed by his sense of achievement at securing the Soviet signature on the declaration and confided to his *Memoirs*:

> Now there is no longer any doubt that an international organi-
> zation to keep the peace, by force if necessary, would be set up
> after the war. As I signed, I could not but recall my long personal
> battles on behalf of the old League of Nations. Now it was probable
> that the United States would be a member of the new security
> organization. It was equally probable that the Soviet Union would
> be one of the principal members.[14]

In his farewell statement at the Moscow airport, Hull pointed to an improving future: "I am convinced that the results of this Conference will become greater with the passage of time and to the degree that it is found possible to carry into effect what was decided here."[15] Even Anne O'Hare McCormick of the *New York Times* believed that Hull had found the formula that combined postwar security for all with the self-determination of peoples: "It begins to dawn on the Russians . . . and the authors of the Atlantic Charter . . . that with good will . . . ways can be found to reconcile Russia's . . . need for military security with the essential national independence of neighboring states."

On November 18 the secretary addressed a joint session of Congress. After stressing the importance of the agreement signed at Moscow and the common interests that underwrote it, he predicted the triumph of his Wilsonian convictions:

> Through this declaration the Soviet Union, Great Britain, the
> United States and China have laid the foundation for a cooperative
> effort in the post-war world toward enabling all peace-loving nations,
> large and small, to live in peace and security, to preserve the
> liberties and rights and facilities for economic, social and spiritual
> progress. No other important nations anywhere have more in com-
> mon in the present war or in peace that is to follow victory over
> the Axis powers. . . . As the provisions of the four-nation decla-
> ration are carried into effect, there will no longer be need for
> spheres of influence, for alliances, for balance of power, or any
> other of the special arrangements through which, in the unhappy
> past, the nations strove to safeguard their security or promote their
> interests.[16]

[14]Cordell Hull, *The Memoirs of Cordell Hull* (New York, 1948), 2:1307.

[15]Press statement quoted in Averell Harriman to Hull, November 5, 1943, *FRUS, 1943* (Washington, 1963), 1:699.

[16]Hull's address to Congress, November 18, 1943, Department of State *Bulletin* 9 (November 20, 1943): 343.

When the Polish ambassador in Washington complained to Hull that the Moscow Conference had not guaranteed the future of Poland, Hull responded in amazement by reciting to him the provisions of the Declaration of Four Nations, a statement, said Hull, that meant everything to Poland.[17]

On January 4, 1944, Soviet troops crossed the prewar Polish border. Several days later Moscow warned the London Polish government in exile that the status of Poland's eastern frontiers had ceased to be a subject of discussion. During March, Stalin demanded not only the Curzon line, which gave the Soviet Union large sections of eastern Poland, but also the elimination of all Polish ministers not friendly to the USSR. Churchill advised the Polish government to acknowledge its evaporating diplomatic position and to seek some compromise settlement with the Kremlin before it was too late.[18] However, on June 7, Roosevelt assured the visiting Polish premier, Stanislaw Mikolajczyk, that he could rely on the support of the United States. Poland, said Roosevelt, must be free and independent. The president informed Mikolajczyk that he had not acted openly on the Polish question because he was in an election year and dared not antagonize his Polish constituents. Eventually, Roosevelt would act as a moderator in defining and protecting Polish interests, but he advised the premier to seek an understanding with the Soviets: "On your own you'd have no chance to beat Russia, and, let me tell you now, the British and Americans have no intention of fighting Russia. But don't worry Stalin doesn't intend to take freedom from Poland. He wouldn't dare do that, because he knows that the United States Government stands solidly behind you. I will see to it that Poland does not come out of this war injured."[19]

Hull apparently remained undaunted even by Stalin's open declaration of support for Poland's pro-Soviet Lublin Committee as the core of that country's postwar government. In an address over CBS in April 1944, the secretary still promised the nation and the world that the postwar political order would conform to the principles of the Atlantic Charter. He acknowledged the fact that the road to unity was difficult but insisted that the Allies had made long strides toward agreement. They had given evidence of their unity by signing both the United Nations and the Four Nations declarations. "We look with hope and with deep faith to a period of great democratic accomplishment in Europe," concluded Hull. "Liberation from the German yoke will give

[17]Hull, *Memoirs*, 2:1315.

[18]Churchill to Eden, December 20, 1943, in Churchill, *The Second World War: Closing the Ring* (Boston, 1951), pp. 450–51; Churchill to Roosevelt, January 6, 1944, ibid., p. 452.

[19]For these exchanges see Stanislaw Mikolajczyk, *The Pattern of Soviet Domination* (London, 1948), pp. 65–66; and Hull, *Memoirs*, 2:1444–45.

the peoples of Europe a new and magnificent opportunity to fulfill their democratic aspirations, both in building democratic political institutions of their own choice and in achieving the social and economic democracy on which political democracy must rest."[20]

On May 30, 1944, British Ambassador Lord Halifax asked Hull for U.S. approval of a British plan to negotiate a wartime arrangement with the Soviet Union over the future of Romania and Greece. To London this appeared the only remaining opportunity to protect Greece from a Soviet invasion. Hull responded brusquely that Washington had little interest in departing from its established principles.

> I was, in fact, flatly opposed to any division of Europe or sections of Europe into spheres of influence. I had argued against this strongly at the Moscow Conference. It seemed to me that any creation of zones of influence would inevitably sow the seeds of future conflict. . . . I was not, and am not, a believer in the idea of balance of power or spheres of influence as a means of keeping the peace. During the First World War I had made an intensive study of the system of spheres of influence and balance of power, and I was grounded to the taproots in their iniquitous consequences. The conclusions I then formed in total opposition to this system stayed with me.[21]

Churchill repeated the British request in a special note to Roosevelt, informing him that the Soviets had already agreed in principle to some temporary arrangement for the Balkans. The president deferred to Hull who replied that any agreement, however temporary, "would inevitably conduce to the establishment of zones of influence against which we had been stoutly fighting, and against which I had spoken out at the Moscow Conference."[22] When Roosevelt rejected yet another British plea, the prime minister came back on June 11 with the proposal of a three months' trial arrangement, thereafter to be reviewed by the three big powers. This request arrived in Washington when Hull was resting at Hershey, Pennsylvania. In his absence, and without consulting him, Roosevelt agreed. During July the president confirmed his approval in a note to the Soviet government. When Hull arrived back in Washington and found out what had transpired, he recorded his apprehensions, noting that "it would be unfortunate if any temporary arrangement should be so conceived as to appear to be a departure

---

[20]Hull's speech of April 9, 1944, in Leland M. Goodrich and Marie J. Carroll, eds., *Documents on American Foreign Relations, July 1943–June 1944* (Boston, 1945), pp. 25–35.

[21]Hull, *Memoirs*, 2:1452–53.

[22]Ibid., p. 1453.

from the principle adopted by the three Governments at the Moscow Conference definitely rejecting the spheres-of-influence idea."[23]

IV

Following conversations with Vatican officials, Bullitt published his noted wartime article, in which he wrote: "Today when the moral unity of Western civilization has been shattered by the crimes of the Germans . . . Rome sees again approaching from the East a new wave of conquerors. . . . [The dominant question is] will the result of this war be the subjection of Europe by Moscow instead of by Berlin?"[24] A Soviet victory, Bullitt warned Roosevelt, must create one vast dictatorship from the Pacific to Western Europe. Again Washington scarcely required Bullitt's warning. British and American leaders knew that the Soviet Union's narrow victory at Stalingrad presaged more than an Allied conquest of Germany; it symbolized the onset of a new era in European and world history.

Stalingrad was one of the most significant battles of all time, after which Europe would never recover its historic order of power. The Soviet victory gave that nation the ultimate capacity to tear the Versailles settlement to shreds, for basic to Europe's equilibrium was the balance between Germany and the Soviet Union which could not survive the total victory of one over the other. After 1943 the Western powers could reconstruct the old order in Europe only if the USSR, for reasons of its own, chose to discard its historic ambitions in Eastern Europe. Stalin had made it clear on numerous occasions that his country had no such intention. Privately, U.S. officials recognized the post-Stalingrad realities of Western Europe's comparative weakness. When Hopkins arrived at the Quebec Conference, he carried a high-level U.S. estimate of the Soviet strategic position. The document read in part:

> Russia's post-war position in Europe will be a dominant one. With Germany crushed, there is no power in Europe to oppose her tremendous military forces. . . .
>
> The conclusions from the foregoing are obvious. Since Russia is the decisive factor in the war, she must be given every assistance and every effort must be made to obtain her friendship. Likewise, since without question she will dominate Europe on the defeat of

---

[23]Ibid., pp. 1454–55, 1458.
[24]William C. Bullitt, "The World from Rome," *Life* 17 (September 4, 1944): 95.

the Axis, it is even more essential to develop and maintain the most friendly relations with Russia.[25]

In September 1943, Roosevelt had revealed some appreciation of Soviet power, if no great sensitivity to its consequences. In conversation with Francis Cardinal Spellman of New York at the White House, the president predicted that the postwar world would be divided into spheres of influence. The Soviet Union, Roosevelt admitted, would probably dominate Europe; he hoped only that the intervention would not be too harsh and anticipated that within twenty years Europeans could learn to live with the Soviets. When Cardinal Spellman reminded the president that the United States might back the non-Communist elements in those regions threatened by Soviet control, Roosevelt responded simply that he had no intention of involving the country in any anti-Soviet maneuvers. "Be that as it may," he concluded, "the United States and Britain cannot fight the Russians. The Russian production is so big that the American help, except for trucks, is negligible."[26] Roosevelt hoped that out of a forced friendship would come a real and lasting peace. The European people had no choice but to endure Soviet domination in the expectation that in the course of time they would be able to adjust satisfactorily to these new conditions.

Thus long before 1944 Roosevelt and his advisers understood that Germany's defeat would not lay the foundations for the kind of peace originally envisioned by the Western powers and epitomized in the Atlantic Charter. Still the president refused to acknowledge fully the seriousness of the situation, and publicly he did not recognize any problems in U.S.-Soviet relations or any threat to self-determination in postwar Europe. Even privately Roosevelt apparently remained convinced that, although the grand design seemed somewhat frayed at the moment, it would come through basically intact; somehow the Kremlin's forward policies would remain subject to Western influence. Later Bullitt recalled Roosevelt's reply to his warning of Soviet expansion:

> . . . I don't dispute your facts, they are accurate. I don't dispute the logic of your reasoning. I just have a hunch that Stalin is not that kind of man. Harry [Hopkins] says he's not and that he doesn't want anything but security for his country, and I think that if I give him everything I possibly can and ask nothing from him in

---

[25]Sherwood, *Roosevelt and Hopkins*, p. 748. Churchill expressed a similar view of the USSR in a letter to Field Marshal Jan Smuts on September 5, 1943, in Churchill, *Closing the Ring*, p. 129.

[26]Robert I. Gannon, *The Cardinal Spellman Story* (Garden City, NY, 1962), pp. 223–24.

return, *noblesse oblige*, he won't try to annex anything and will work with me for a world of democracy and peace.[27]

V

Some troubled Americans, including Bullitt, remained convinced in the post-Stalingrad era that the United States and Britain still possessed the power and resources to save Europe from the Eastern peril. For these critics the answer to the Kremlin's challenge lay in continued diplomatic inflexibility, coupled with military strategies designed to establish a political and military line of demarcation separating East from West as far to the east as possible. Such political concerns were lost on U.S. military leaders, for whom strategy meant the simple quest for victory at the least possible loss of American life.

Churchill's insistence that the Western design for action in Europe encompass political as well as military objectives sustained the some-times bitter Anglo-American disagreements over the issue of the Second Front. To the end the prime minister remained skeptical of Overlord, the massive cross-Channel attack planned for June 1944. From the outset he advocated a series of peripheral landings in Norway, Den-mark, Holland, Belgium, and France but especially in Italy and the Balkans. Eventually, Churchill's tactics in the Mediterranean focused on the seizure of Rhodes and other islands in the Aegean. As a sequel to these moves, he favored operations against the Aegean mainland which, he supposed, would set off anti-Nazi revolutions in the Balkans and even bring Turkey into the war. Such strategy would not only keep the war against Germany mobile but also enable the Western powers to occupy portions of Eastern Europe in advance of the Soviet arrival. The prime minister feared that a massive accumulation of Anglo-Amer-ican power on the island of Britain, followed by a massive attack across the Channel from the west, would divide Europe between East and West at the point where their two drives met. Churchill believed that peripheral attacks coming at the Continent from several directions would avoid the necessity of splitting Europe through the middle along a single north-south line.[28]

Many military analysts and historians have agreed with Churchill that the Western allies might have enjoyed significant success had they pursued strategies specifically designed to prevent Soviet as well as German dominance of East-Central Europe. Corollary assumptions

---

[27]See Bullitt, "How We Won the War and Lost the Peace," *Life* 25 (August 30, 1948): 94.

[28]For Churchill's strategic views in late 1943 see Churchill, *Closing the Ring*, pp. 375–84, 404–05.

that Western strategy failed unnecessarily imply that the Tehran Conference of November and December 1943 marked the central disaster of the war, for it was at Tehran that the Big Three finally agreed on Operation Overlord. Isaac Deutscher, in his biography of Stalin, wrote of the Overlord decision: "This was a moment of Stalin's supreme triumph. . . . Europe had now been militarily divided in two; and behind the military division there loomed the social and political cleavage."[29] The old czarist dream of Russian hegemony over Eastern Europe was coming true. The noted student of the Second World War, John A. Lukacs, agreed, declaring that the Tehran decision of November 30, 1943 set the stage for the massive invasion of Normandy and thereby delivered Eastern and Central Europe to the Soviet Union. Similarly, General J. F. C. Fuller charged that Austria and Hungary were politically decisive areas and that the Soviet occupation of these countries ahead of the Western allies was in itself sufficient to render the whole Western war effort futile, substituting Soviet for German control of Eastern Europe.[30]

It is possible to argue that a different strategy would have prevented much of what actually happened.[31] It is equally true that much of what might have occurred, as a consequence of trying to implement Churchill's conceptions, would have been even worse, for it is by no means certain that the Western allies had the power to execute successfully such a maneuver. If there were to be a divided Europe, the West would no doubt rather have it divided the way it was than to have it fragmented in some other way. Nevertheless, it is undeniable that the Overlord strategy, following upon the failure to reach an accommodation with the Soviet Union before or early in the war, facilitated execution of the policy choice that the Kremlin had now made. One may assume that Stalin, if he had any ambitions in Eastern Europe—as by the time of the Overlord decision he evidently did—would want to keep Western troops as far from that part of the world as possible. Overlord assured him that the vast bulk of Anglo-American power would be concentrated far from Eastern Europe, and that it would approach the East from the opposite end of the Continent. Eventually, it would reach the heart of Europe, but by that time the Soviets also would be there, which explains Deutscher's reservations on the implications of this strategy. Opinions aside, the fact is that, from both the Soviet viewpoint and Stalin's ambitions to obtain a stronghold on

[29]Isaac Deutscher, *Stalin: A Political Biography* (New York, 1949), p. 508.

[30]John A. Lukacs, *The Great Powers and Eastern Europe* (New York, 1953), pp. 523–24, 556; J. F. C. Fuller, *The Second World War, 1939–45* (New York, 1949), pp. 305–13, 324–25.

[31]This paragraph is based on audience discussion.

Eastern Europe, Overlord was perfect. This is the reason why Churchill carried his regrets over strategy into his wartime memoirs.

At Tehran, Allied leaders blocked Churchill's Italian and Adriatic schemes. Even after the successful invasion of Normandy in June 1944, Churchill continued to press for a concerted Western drive through Istria and the Ljubljana Gap into the Danubian basin, thereby winning some support from Generals Mark W. Clark and Walter Bedell Smith. For Clark the U.S. decision to invade southern France, rather than push into Yugoslavia, was one of the great military mistakes of the war. In Washington, the prime minister's ideas faced obdurate opposition to the end, but he persisted nevertheless. As late as August, recalled Harry C. Butcher, Churchill expressed to Eisenhower his continuing doubts concerning American strategy: "The PM [prime minister] wants . . . to continue into the Balkans through the Ljubljana Gap, in Yugoslavia, to reach Germany through Austria."[32] Military expert Hanson W. Baldwin has acknowledged that this strategy would have presented major challenges, "yet there is no doubt in my mind that such a strategy could have succeeded had sufficient sea and air power been allocated to it and had the same number of ground troops been employed that were actually used in Italy and in the invasion of Southern France."[33]

Unfortunately, that near balance of power on the European continent, which on many former occasions had brought success to British peripheral strategy, already had been destroyed by mid-1944. When England's reliance on naval power and diversionary tactics had triumphed in the past, it was because that country had allies on the Continent capable of engaging the common enemy with armies of equal or greater effectiveness. After 1941 the only Continental power at war with Germany was the USSR, the very country whose ambitions the diversionary movements were designed to curtail. How Western occupation of portions of Eastern Europe would have affected the Soviet advance is not clear. Nor is it certain that the Soviet Union would not have exacted a heavy price for any Allied policy aimed pointedly at that country as well as Germany, for after Tehran the Kremlin did not expound its preferences from a posture of weakness. What mattered during 1944 was total power and momentum. If Austria and Hungary were indeed areas of decision, it cannot be lightly assumed that the Soviets would have permitted the Western allies to cut them out so easily. It could be assumed, however, that the Soviets, unopposed in

---

[32]Mark W. Clark, *Calculated Risk* (New York, 1950), pp. 348–49; Harry C. Butcher, *My Three Years with Eisenhower: The Personal Diary of Captain Harry C. Butcher, USNR, Naval Aide to General Eisenhower, 1942 to 1945* (New York, 1946), p. 644.

[33]Hanson W. Baldwin, "Churchill Was Right," *Atlantic Monthly* 194 (July 1954): 30.

northern Europe because of Western advances elsewhere, would have seized and held hostage regions of western Germany.

Throughout 1944 the West needed the Soviet Union to achieve its goal of defeating Germany quite as much as the USSR required Western successes to emerge victoriously from its hard-won struggle along the Eastern front.[34] Perhaps Washington pursued policies too narrowly designed to destroy Hitler's Germany. Still it is doubtful that other policies would have resurrected the Versailles world. That the Soviets reaped a greater harvest in victory than did Britain or the United States resulted far more from the accidents of geography than from the character of Western military strategy. The West, in alliance with the USSR, could destroy Germany. It could not simultaneously dispose of the German and Soviet challenges to either the European balance of power or the external dominance of Eastern Europe. To expect such a victory was utopian. The profound American dilemma of 1944 lay less in military strategy than in the limits of victory.

Admittedly, it is possible to continue the criticism of Overlord strategy by examining its execution.[35] Even if this strategy determined the division of Europe, could the points on which the bisection of the Continent depended not have been pushed farther eastward? Specifically, could the Anglo-American forces not have reached Berlin first and established forward positions beyond the Elbe River? Any analysis that attempts to deal with the entire range of wartime policy would need to include the decisions of the spring of 1945, which the critics of Roosevelt's wartime strategy have condemned. It is true that the possibilities emerging during the final drive into the heart of the Continent seemed to offer the United States access to more of Eastern Europe.

At that time, however, General Dwight D. Eisenhower, commander of Allied forces in Western Europe, was operating under military, not political, instructions. He was to move across Germany, defeat the German armies where he encountered them, and keep his own forces intact. For Berlin and Eastern Europe there was no strategy at all; the only "strategy" was to win the war. In April 1945 the concluding phase of the war was marked by almost unbelievable success of the Americans and the British as their armies, virtually unopposed, crossed Germany. Whatever power the Germans still possessed was concentrated on the Eastern Front, trying to keep the Soviets out of Berlin. American forces advanced so rapidly that they began to lose contact; those approaching the Elbe contemplated moves across it. Indeed, on

---

[34]Military analysts have concluded that four-fifths of the fighting and destruction of the European war occurred on the Eastern Front.

[35]This paragraph and the two that follow are based on responses to questions of the audience.

two fronts they did so. It was at this point that Eisenhower decided to stop the forward movement and reorganize. He therefore called his generals back and instructed them to hold the line at the Elbe. Thereafter, U.S. forces made no effort to push the Western advance beyond that point. Eisenhower was not concerned with the question of reaching Berlin before the Soviets opened their final assault against the city, but Churchill and others were. The prime minister wanted the Americans there first because he was sensitive to the political significance of the event.

To understand the U.S. response, one must return to the military situation of 1945. By April and May the basic feeling of Americans about the war was that they wanted it to end. In retrospect, it is possible to balance against this simple sentiment the weighty fact that the Soviet advance was going to mean trouble for many people, and that ultimately it would contribute to a cold war and a tremendously expensive postwar American endeavor in Europe. In those days the Soviets could not move far enough and fast enough to satisfy most soldiers in the U.S. Army. If the Soviets wanted to destroy Berlin, the disposition was to let them have the opportunity, as it was essentially a matter of ending the war. The Soviets occupied Berlin, but they lost at least 100,000 men in the assault. Later, without any casualties, the Americans marched into the shattered city. The Soviets achieved a sense of elation because they were the first to enter Berlin and subsequently maximized the propaganda advantages that flowed from their exploits. The view of Americans in the spring of 1945, however, was not shaped by such political calculations; their country had not been invaded and no bombs had been dropped on America's continental territory. The United States had losses, to be sure, but they were far fewer than Soviet casualties in the battle of Stalingrad alone. By the time the war entered its last months, the total death count in the USSR was approaching 20 million. Anyone who thought of the contrast was not inclined to quarrel with the Soviets.

The Soviet Union's burgeoning sweep toward Berlin after the Normandy invasion, Roosevelt knew, would upset Europe's historic equilibrium. It was equally clear, as George F. Kennan warned from Moscow, that the Soviets would transform much of Eastern Europe into a massive sphere of influence.[36] Nevertheless, the fundamental and irreversible decision had been made much earlier; efforts to modify its consequences after Overlord were bound to seem hazardous and inexpedient. Even as official American rhetoric assured the nation and the

---

[36]"Russia—Seven Years Later" (September 1944), in George F. Kennan, *Memoirs, 1925-1950* (Boston, 1967), pp. 519–22.

world that the principles of the Atlantic Charter would emerge triumphant, Washington stood powerless to prevent either Moscow's destruction of the European balance or Soviet repression of Eastern Europe.

In the Great War of 1914, U.S. power had succeeded, at least temporarily, in reconstituting the traditional European balance of power. By 1944 even that limited goal lay beyond the country's capabilities. With its great destructive power under full employment, the United States still was not the controlling element in European politics; the events of early 1945 would reinforce this fact. With the return of peace, that power would become even less persuasive. Long before then the possible choice between a power balance and a Wilsonian international order as the goal of victory had evaporated. To achieve the former would have required no less than a desertion of the American crusade against Germany; the latter program was always too extravagant for serious contemplation. What remained for Roosevelt was a public admission that victory over Germany would leave the nation's principles, and many of its historic interests, in tatters. That painful acknowledgment, however, exceeded his capacity for candor.

CHAPTER FIVE

A World Divided*

IN JANUARY 1945 the American people could contemplate, with deep satisfaction, the approaching end of the century's second global struggle. Tragically, German, Italian, and Japanese aggression had destroyed a previous generation's dreams of lasting peace. Throughout the war, however, the nation's leaders had seemingly addressed the mistakes of the past and framed decisions to prevent their repetition. In his Fireside Chat two days after Pearl Harbor, President Roosevelt had recounted the evidence of national failure in dealing with the aggressors, but he promised that "we are going to win the war and we are going to win the peace that follows."[1] In September 1942 he had assured an international audience of students that "we have profited by our mistakes. This time we shall know how to make full use of victory. This time the achievements of our fighting forces will not be thrown away by political cynicism and timidity and incompetence."[2] That year, recalled Hull, "virtually every American had already begun to think in terms of avoiding a recurrence of [the recent] bankruptcy in international relations." For him the promise of lasting peace lay in the creation of an effective international organization, the key to the postwar future.[3] Roosevelt's success in defending the United Nations against either American or Soviet defection seemed to guarantee the success of the new organization. The wartime goal of unconditional surrender assured

*This essay is based on a speech delivered at the annual Conference of Iowa High School and College-University Teachers of History held at the University of Iowa, Iowa City, April 1960. Reprinted by permission.
[1]Roosevelt's Fireside Chat of December 9, 1941, in Samuel I. Rosenman, ed., *The Public Papers and Addresses of Franklin D. Roosevelt, 1941: The Call to Battle Stations* (New York, 1950), 10:530.
[2]Address to the International Student Assembly, September 3, 1942, ibid., *1942: Humanity on the Defensive* (New York, 1950), 11:353.
[3]Cordell Hull, *Memoirs of Cordell Hull* (New York, 1948), 2:1634–37.

not only the necessary Allied cooperation for victory but also the elimination of unwanted aggression against the postwar peace structure.

Even before President Roosevelt departed for the Yalta Conference of February 1945, Poland was putting the wartime alliance to the
test. Early in January a Moscow broadcast announced that the Soviet
Union was recognizing its Communist-led Lublin Committee as the
provisional government of Poland. This group, by Western standards,
was not representative of the Polish people. Britain and the United
States continued to recognize the exiled Polish government in London.
The *Manchester Guardian* observed realistically that the Lublin Committee would win because the Soviets had control of Poland.[4] Some
State Department officials in Washington agreed. On January 8, John D.
Hickerson, deputy director of the Office of European Affairs, warned
the administration that much of Eastern Europe had slipped irretriev-
ably beyond Western control. To ignore this fact, wrote Hickerson,
would return Europe to the "diplomacy of the jungle." He suggested
that the government prepare the American people for a realistic settlement in Eastern Europe: "We must have the cooperation of the Soviet
Union to organize the peace. There are certain things in connection
with the foregoing proposals which are repugnant to me personally,
but I am prepared to urge their adoption to obtain the cooperation of
the Soviet Union in winning the war and organizing the peace."[5] The
West had lost all control of Eastern Europe when it failed to protect
Czechoslovakia and Poland against the Nazi-Soviet advances of 1939.
Nothing remained to counter the Soviet Union's military preponder-
ance across East-Central Europe except its signature on the Atlantic
Charter and the Declaration of Four Nations.

Soviet behavior toward Poland in January 1945 scarcely challenged the American public's utopian expectations of continued Big
Three cooperation in the postwar era. For a minority of American
officials, however, Soviet actions were both shocking and humiliating;
they threatened again to deny the American people the expected fruits
of victory. Hull recalled what the nation could expect of the Soviets:

> As Autumn, 1944, approached my associates and I began to
> wonder whether Marshal Stalin and his Government were com-
> mencing to veer away from the policy of cooperation to which they
> had agreed at the Moscow Conference, and which, with a few
> exceptions, they had followed since then. We were beginning to
> get indications that the Russians were about to drive hard bargains

[4]*Manchester Guardian*, January 12, 1945, pp. 17–18.
[5]Hickerson memorandum, January 8, 1945, *FRUS, Diplomatic Papers: The Conferences of Malta and Yalta, 1945* (Washington, 1955), pp. 94–96.

in their armistice agreements with Hungary, Bulgaria, and Rumania, which would give them something in the nature of control over those countries. . . . Accordingly I cabled Ambassador Harriman in Moscow on September 18. . . . I stated to Harriman that I should find particularly helpful his views as to the causes that had brought about this change in Soviet policy toward the United States and hardening of attitude toward Great Britain. . . . Harriman replied the following day giving a number of instances of Russia's unilateral actions or apparent unwillingness to collaborate with Britain and the United States. . . . He said it was difficult to put one's finger on the causes for the change in the Soviet attitude toward the United States and Great Britain. He thought, however, that when the Russians saw victory in sight they began to put into practice the policies they intended to follow in peace.[6]

At Yalta near the Black Sea, Roosevelt and Churchill attempted for eight days, from February 4 through February 11, 1945, to counter the burgeoning unilateralism in Soviet policy toward southeastern and Eastern Europe. Their only weapons—the abstract principles of self-determination and international cooperation—were no match for the Soviet occupying forces. Still the two Western leaders managed not only to avoid major concessions but also to obtain Stalin's signature on two documents pertaining to Eastern Europe: the Declaration on Poland and the Declaration on Liberated Europe. In these documents, Stalin agreed to permit extensive application of the principle of free elections in the creation of the postwar governments of Eastern Europe. The Declaration on Poland specified that the "Polish Provisional Government of National Unity shall be pledged to the holding of free and unfettered elections as soon as possible on the basis of universal suffrage and secret ballot."[7] When the Polish government met these requirements, it would receive the recognition of Britain and the United States. At Yalta, Roosevelt, Churchill, and Stalin agreed to the Curzon line, with minor digressions, as the eastern frontier of Poland. So great was the Western opposition to the Oder-Neisse line as Poland's western boundary that Stalin agreed to leave the western Polish frontier undefined.

Reaching agreement on Germany's future was equally troublesome. The Big Three proclaimed their agreement on principles for enforcing the unconditional surrender terms against Germany; they made no effort, in the interest of continued wartime unity, to convert those principles into concrete arrangements. They agreed to zones of

[6]Hull, *Memoirs*, 2:1459–60.
[7]*FRUS, Malta and Yalta*, pp. 973–74. For the Declaration on Liberated Europe see ibid., p. 972.

occupation for Germany, with Roosevelt proposing that France also should receive an occupation zone. Stalin denied that the French deserved a zone but eventually relented, permitting them a zone to be carved from the British and American zones. In addition, France received membership in the Allied Control Commission for postwar Germany. On the matter of German reparations, the Big Three could not agree, nor could they reach a settlement on access routes into Berlin from the Western zones. On the proposal of the United Nations, the three wartime leaders reached an accord on the veto system in the Security Council and on the admittance of two Soviet republics, the Ukraine and Byelorussia, to UN membership. The exchanges at Yalta were cordial, but unfortunately most agreements consisted of words rather than matter. The Big Three had merely transferred their disagreements to the plane of interpretation.[8]

Much of the press accepted the Yalta accords at face value. According to the *Manchester Guardian*, "the results of the Yalta meeting of the Big Three justify nearly all our hopes. . . . Certainly on the immediate political questions of the war Russia has shown herself willing to move a long way toward meeting the Western Allies' point of view." *Newsweek* asserted that Roosevelt had dominated the diplomacy that led to satisfactory compromises on all issues. *Time* viewed the meeting as a solid achievement and suggested that "all doubts about the Big Three's ability to co-operate, in peace as well as war, seemed now to have been swept away."[9] The *New York Times* declared the conference "a milestone on the road to victory and peace." For the *New York Herald-Tribune* the Big Three meeting at Yalta was simply "another great proof of allied unity, strength and power of decision." Privately and publicly U.S. officials shared the euphoria. On March 1, Roosevelt assured Congress that the Yalta Conference had found a common ground for peace. "It spells," he said, "the end of the system of unilateral action and exclusive alliance and spheres of influence and balances of power and all the other expedients which have been tried for centuries— and have failed. We propose to substitute for all these a universal organization in which all peace-loving nations will finally have a chance to join." So cordial were the outward exchanges at Yalta that Hopkins recalled: "We really believed . . . that this was the dawn of a new day. . . . We were *absolutely certain* that we had won the first great victory

---

[8]For the Declaration on Germany see ibid., pp. 970–71; evaluation of the Yalta agreements in *London Observer*, February 18, 1945.

[9]*Manchester Guardian*, February 16, 1945, p. 89; *Newsweek*, February 19, 1945, p. 37; *Time*, February 19, 1945, p. 15.

of the peace."[10] Former Senator James F. Byrnes, who attended the meeting, joined the chorus by adding that "there is no doubt that the tide of Anglo-Soviet-American friendship had reached a new high." Similarly, Secretary of State Edward R. Stettinius, Jr., believed that the meeting revealed Russia's desire "to co-operate along all lines with [the] U.S."[11]

II

Yalta raised the hope, perhaps even the possibility, that the Kremlin, as it entered a period of decision, would desert the practices and apparent intentions of previous months in its postwar design for southeastern and Eastern Europe. The declarations on Poland and Liberated Europe had promised governments based on free elections in those regions under Soviet control. When the Soviets, within days after Yalta, embarked on a methodical violation of the Yalta agreements to assure regimes in occupied areas subservient to Moscow, they imperiled not only the West's predominant role in Europe's reconstruction but also the future of U.S.-Soviet relations. On February 24, Soviet officials in Romania refused to hold a meeting of the Allied Control Commission. Three days later Andrei Vyshinsky, deputy Soviet commissar of Foreign Affairs, arrived in Bucharest and, in direct violation of the Declaration on Liberated Europe, issued King Michael an ultimatum to form a new government. On March 6, the king dismissed General Nicolae Radescu, the Romanian prime minister, and accepted a Communist-controlled regime under Petra Groza. The Soviets then signed a five-year treaty with the new government. At no time during this political revolution did Soviet officials consult the British and U.S. representatives in Romania.[12] At the same time, the Kremlin ignored the pledge of the Declaration on Poland to expand the Lublin government by including members of both the Polish underground and the London government in exile. Instead, the Soviets jailed the chief leaders of the Polish resistance and effectively eliminated them from politics. Moscow's decision to bar Allied representatives from Poland eliminated the

[10]Roosevelt's report to Congress, March 1, 1945, in Department of State *Bulletin* 12 (March 4, 1945): 361; Robert E. Sherwood, *Roosevelt and Hopkins: An Intimate History* (New York, 1948), p. 870 (emphasis added).

[11]James F. Byrnes, *Speaking Frankly* (New York, 1947), p. 45; Stettinius quoted in Walter Millis, ed., *The Forrestal Diaries* (New York, 1951), p. 35.

[12]Grew to Harriman, February 27, 1945, Berry to Vyshinsky, February 28, 1945, Berry to Stettinius, February 28, and March 2, 7, 1945, *FRUS, 1945* (Washington, 1967), 5:483, 486–88, 492–93, 502–03.

possibility that the London Poles would have some influence in determining their country's future.[13]

American reaction to Soviet policy in Romania and Poland was immediate and resentful. Ambassador W. Averell Harriman in Moscow reminded Washington that Soviet behavior in Romania was a clear violation of the Yalta agreement; to accept such conduct, he warned, "would nullify entirely the Declaration on Liberated Europe." The ambassador pressed Washington to demand a three-power meeting on Romania and to inform the Soviets that the United States would interpret any resistance to such discussions as evidence of the Soviet rejection of this declaration. On Poland, Harriman reported failure not only to negotiate changes in the Polish government but also to protect the welfare of American prisoners of war held in that country. "We must clearly recognize," he informed Stettinius on April 4, "that the Soviet program [in Eastern Europe] is the establishment of totalitarianism, ending personal liberty and democracy as we know it and respect it."[14] Harriman repeated his warning two days later: "It now seems evident that . . . they intend to go forward with unilateral action in the domination of their bordering states." Searching for the means to confront the Soviets successfully on the question of Poland, Harriman advised Washington to assert its purposes in Europe with the same determination displayed by Moscow, making the Soviets "realize that they cannot continue their present attitude except at great cost to themselves."[15] The United States could strengthen its relations with the Kremlin, he argued further, if Moscow were made "to understand specifically how lack of cooperation with our legitimate demands will adversely affect their interests." Unless the Soviets understood how their actions jeopardized satisfactory relations with the United States, the ambassador wrote, "they will become increasingly difficult to deal with."[16] Unfortunately, Soviet and U.S. interests in Eastern Europe were not sufficiently symmetrical to render American threats of retaliation effective.

During March and April, Roosevelt admitted his private misgivings about the future of U.S.-Soviet relations. He informed State Department officer Adolf Berle that he was concerned over Soviet policy toward Poland and acknowledged that the Yalta settlements did not assure the democratization of Eastern Europe. He advised Senator

---

[13]See J. M. Mackintosh, *Strategy and Tactics of Soviet Foreign Policy* (London, 1962), pp. 6–7.

[14]Harriman to Roosevelt, March 14, 1945, PSF: Russia, Box 68, FDRL; Harriman to Stettinius, April 4, 1945, ibid.

[15]Harriman to Stettinius, April 6, 1945, ibid.

[16]Ibid.

Arthur H. Vandenberg of Michigan that he was "coming to know the Russians better."[17] Finally on March 31 the president reminded Stalin that the new Polish Provisional Government of National Unity was little more than a continuation of the old Lublin regime. "I cannot," Roosevelt concluded, "reconcile this either with our agreement or our discussions. While it is true that the Lublin Government is to be reorganized and its members play a prominent role it is to be done in such a fashion as to bring into being a new Government. . . . I must make it quite plain to you that any such solution which would result in a thinly disguised continuance of the present Warsaw regime would be unacceptable and would cause the people of the United States to regard the Yalta agreement as having failed."[18]

Roosevelt's troubled reaction to Soviet policy in Romania and Poland continued to be tempered by his refusal to face the consequences of a total breakdown in U.S.-Soviet relations. His most bitter dispute with Stalin occurred in early April when Stalin learned that Nazi General Karl Wolff had met British officers near Bern, Switzerland. Immediately Stalin denounced the Western allies for engaging in secret conversations with German officers, and he accused Germany of seeking easy terms from Britain and the United States so that it could transfer additional divisions to the Soviet front. Roosevelt assured Stalin that the meeting at Bern was designed to make contact with competent German officers and not to begin negotiations of any kind.[19] Then he responded to Stalin's accusations with a sharp rebuttal: "[I]t would be one of the greatest tragedies of history if at the very moment of the victory, now within our grasp, such distrust, such lack of faith should prejudice the entire undertaking. . . . Frankly I cannot avoid a feeling of bitter resentment toward your informers, whoever they are, for such vile misrepresentations of my actions or those of my trusted subordinates."[20] Stalin reminded Roosevelt that the war was still raging on the Eastern Front. The Germans, he lamented, continued to fight savagely over every crossroad in Czechoslovakia but surrendered to Western forces without resistance. "Don't you agree," Stalin asked, "that such a behavior of the Germans is more than strange and incomprehensible?"[21] With Stalin's expression of deep concern over German conduct, the matter ended. To the end Roosevelt would not permit his

[17]A. A. Berle, Jr., "Three Roads to War," *The American Magazine* 142 (August 1946): 21, 98; Arthur H. Vandenberg, Jr., and Joe Alex Morris, eds., *The Private Papers of Senator Vandenberg* (Boston, 1952), p. 155.
[18]Roosevelt to Stalin, March 31, 1945, PSF: Russia, Box 68, FDRL.
[19]Memorandum of William Leahy to Roosevelt, March 31, 1945, Map Room, Box 23, FDRL.
[20]Roosevelt to Stalin, April 5, 1945, Map Room, Box 9, FDRL.
[21]Stalin to Roosevelt, April 3, 7, 1945, Map Room, Box 23, FDRL.

doubts concerning Soviet intentions to govern his official views. Shortly before his death on April 12 the president responded to Churchill's request for guidance on how to respond to Stalin's apology for the Bern incident. "I would minimize the general problem as much as possible," wrote Roosevelt, "because these problems, in one form or another, seem to arise every day and most of them straighten out."[22]

Despite Roosevelt's efforts to avoid it, the Soviet challenge was clear. Moscow demanded of the West nothing less than the recognition of its immediate interests in its satellite empire. If Soviet purpose appeared harsh and anachronistic, it was diplomatically feasible because it did not exceed the power that the USSR could bring to bear on international relationships. This left the Western powers with two policy choices in their defense of self-determination. They either could force the Soviet armies to withdraw to prewar Soviet frontiers or persuade them to retreat. Unfortunately, neither course was open to Washington and London. The first alternative was militarily unacceptable. It was not within the West's military capacity or interest to force a Soviet withdrawal from Eastern Europe. The second alternative was diplomatically unpromising. The West could challenge Soviet unilateralism in Eastern Europe only by establishing multiparty, democratically elected governments in regions under Soviet occupation. Moscow, however, had rejected Western interpretations of the Yalta accords; there would be no gains based simply on adherence to principle.

Unable to deflate the Soviet hegemony with either force or diplomacy, the West had two choices remaining. It could come to some agreement with the Kremlin which would recognize Soviet economic and security interests in Eastern Europe, or it could simply permit the disagreements to drift into an unknown future, unresolved. For the Truman administration the first choice was politically unacceptable. Any diplomatic recognition of the Soviet Union's new hegemony would comprise the abandonment of the principle of self-determination persistently enunciated by American officials. Truman and his advisers adopted the second course. By insisting on the fulfillment of the Yalta agreements and acting as if mere insistence were policy, the administration would avoid the necessity of bridging the gap between its utopian objectives and the realities of power politics. It could cling to the one without disregarding the other. Thus Washington defined the U.S. interest in Eastern Europe, not in terms of limited national need and the absence of means sufficiently credible to achieve its purposes without war but in terms of universal principles applicable to all mankind.

[22]Roosevelt to Churchill, April 11, 1945, Map Room, Box 9, FDRL.

Such an approach assured political success at home; it guaranteed nothing to those living under Soviet domination.

III

After mid-April 1945, President Truman faced the challenge of confronting the Soviets on the issues that troubled U.S. officials. For weeks Harriman's long reports to the State Department had outlined the shifts in Soviet policy from accommodation to unilateral impositions on the governments and peoples under Soviet control. In his report of April 6, Harriman had delineated the Soviet problem in detail:

> You will recall that at the Moscow Conference Molotov indicated that although he would inform us of Soviet action in Eastern Europe he declined to be bound by consultation with us. It may be difficult for us to believe, but it still may be true that Stalin and Molotov considered at Yalta that by our willingness to accept a general wording of the declarations on Poland and liberated Europe, by our recognition of . . . the predominant interest of Russia in Poland as a friendly neighbor and as a corridor to Germany, we understood and were ready to accept Soviet policies already known to us. . . . We have been hopeful that the Soviets would accept our concepts whereas they on their side may have expected us to accept their own concepts, particularly in areas where their interests predominate. In any event, whatever may have been in their minds at Yalta, it now seems that they feel they can force us to acquiesce in their policies.[23]

On April 13, the day after Roosevelt's death, Stettinius briefed Truman on the situation in Eastern Europe. Four days later Washington learned that Moscow planned to sign a mutual assistance agreement with the Lublin Poles. In response, the president resolved to lay it on the line when Soviet Foreign Minister V. M. Molotov visited Washington that month. Chief of Staff Admiral Leahy predicted that Molotov "would be in for some blunt talking from the American side."[24]

The Kremlin's continuing unilateralism in Eastern Europe created a policy crisis in Washington. On April 20, Truman sought the views of Harriman (recently returned from Moscow because of Roosevelt's death), Stettinius, Undersecretary Joseph Grew, and Soviet expert Charles E. Bohlen. Harriman dominated the meeting. The time

---

[23]Harriman to Stettinius, April 6, 1945, PSF: Russia, Box 68, FDRL.
[24]Stettinius's calendar notes, April 13, 1945, in Thomas M. Campbell and George C. Herring, eds., *The Diaries of Edward R. Stettinius, Jr., 1943–1946* (New York, 1975), p. 318; William D. Leahy, *I Was There* (New York, 1950), p. 349.

had come, he argued, for the United States to formulate an effective response to Kremlin policy in the border states. He urged the president to take a firm stand on the Polish question and to insist on the inclusion of London Poles in the new Polish government. Truman assured Harriman that he was not afraid to face the Soviets, declaring that "we intended to be firm with the Russians and make no concessions from American principles or traditions in order to win their favor."[25] Harriman observed that the United States could arrive at a workable arrangement with the Soviets if it abandoned "any illusion that the Soviet government was likely soon to act in accordance with the principles to which the rest of the world held in international affairs." Both sides would need to make concessions. "I agreed," Truman later recalled, "saying I understood this and that I would not expect one hundred per cent of what we proposed. But I felt we should be able to get eighty-five per cent."[26] Before his departure, Harriman spoke to the president privately: "Frankly one of the reasons that made me rush back to Washington was the fear that you did not understand . . . that Stalin is breaking his agreements. . . . But I must say that I am greatly relieved to discover that you have read [the recent cables] and that we see eye to eye on the situation."[27]

Truman's meeting with Molotov on April 22 was cordial enough. The president reminded the Soviet minister that "in its larger aspects the Polish question had become for our people the symbol of the future development of our international relations." Molotov reassured Truman that the two nations could reach the desired agreements on the Polish issue.[28] At the White House meeting on April 23, Stettinius informed the president that the subsequent conversations with Molotov had not gone well. "In fact," said the secretary, "a complete deadlock had been reached on the subject of carrying out the Yalta agreement on Poland." The Kremlin, Stettinius complained, seemed intent on imposing the Lublin Committee on the Polish people. Truman replied that "our agreements with the Soviet Union had so far been a one-way street and that this could not continue."[29] Others present urged caution.

[25]Harry S. Truman, *Memoirs*, vol. 1, *Year of Decisions* (Garden City, NY, 1955), p. 71; Millis, *Forrestal Diaries*, p. 47.

[26]Truman, *Year of Decisions*, p. 71.

[27]Ibid., p. 72.

[28]Ibid., p. 76.

[29]For the White House meeting of April 23, 1945 see Millis, *Forrestal Diaries*, pp. 50–51; and Stettinius and Truman quoted in Truman, *Year of Decisions*, p. 77. That day a State Department memorandum reminded Truman that the United States could not "agree to be a party to the formation of a Polish Government which is not representative of the democratic elements of the Polish people." See Dunn and Bohlen to Truman, April 23, 1945, Series 11, Box 721, Stettinius Papers, University of Virginia Library, Charlottesville, Virginia.

Secretary of War Stimson preferred that the United States move slowly on the Polish issue. The Soviets, he reminded the president, had carried out all their military engagements faithfully. General George C. Marshall, like Stimson, hoped that the administration would avoid an open break with the Kremlin over Poland. Truman pledged to issue no ultimatum; he would merely clarify the American position.[30]

Later that afternoon Truman informed Molotov that the American and British proposals on Poland were reasonable and embodied the maximum Western concessions. The government of the United States, the president declared flatly, would not be a party to any Polish political arrangements that did not represent all Polish elements. "The Soviet Government must realize," he said, "that the failure to go forward at this time with the implementation of the Crimean decision on Poland would seriously shake confidence in the unity of the three governments and their determination to continue the collaboration in the future as they have in the past." Molotov insisted that the USSR intended to honor the Yalta decisions, but he continued to skirt the question of Soviet compliance with the Western proposals on Poland. Truman then informed Molotov that American friendship could continue "only on a basis of mutual observation of agreements and not on the basis of a one-way street." To Molotov's complaint, "I have never been talked to like that in my life," the president retorted: "Carry out your agreements and you won't get talked to like that."[31] A week later Truman boasted to an astonished Joseph E. Davies, former American ambassador to the USSR and now his special envoy to London, that he let Molotov have it straight.

Many Washington insiders reacted favorably to Truman's toughness. Vandenberg, Republican leader in the Senate, found enough solace in Truman's words to confide to his diary that "FDR's appeasement of Russia is over." The United States and the Soviet Union could live together in the postwar world, wrote Vandenberg, "if Russia is made to understand that we can't be pushed around."[32] Admiral Leahy rejoiced at the president's new mood. "Truman's attitude in dealing with Molotov," he noted in his memoirs, "was more than pleasing to me. I believed it would have a beneficial effect on the Soviet outlook."[33] Secretary of the Navy James V. Forrestal asserted at the White House

[30]For the views of Stimson and Marshall see Millis, *Forrestal Diaries*, pp. 50–51; and Truman, *Year of Decisions*, pp. 77–79.

[31]Conversation with Molotov, April 23, 1945, in Truman, *Year of Decisions*, pp. 81–82.

[32]Vandenberg diary, April 24, 1945, in Vandenberg and Morris, *Private Papers of Vandenberg*, p. 176.

[33]Leahy, *I Was There*, p. 352.

meeting on April 23 that the Soviets had established a pattern of unilateral action throughout Eastern Europe. Therefore, he advised, "we
might as well meet the issue now as later on." In May, Forrestal
informed a member of the Senate that Soviet communism was "as
incompatible with democracy as was Nazism and Fascism."[34] In the
State Department, Undersecretary Grew had long harbored a deep
distrust of the USSR. He found nothing reassuring in its final destruction of German power. With its stranglehold on the states along its
western border, the Soviet Union, he warned, "will steadily increase
and she will in the not distant future be in a favorable position to
expand her control, step by step, through Europe. . . . A future war
with Soviet Russia is as certain as anything in the world can be certain."[35] Such top officials in the State Department as James C. Dunn,
assistant secretary for European, Asian, Near Eastern, and African
Affairs, and such regional office directors as H. Freeman Matthews
and Loy W. Henderson, shared Grew's deep animosity toward the
Soviet Union. For them any agreement with the Kremlin would merely
encourage Soviet expansionism.

Still many Americans regarded Soviet behavior in Eastern Europe,
if not desirable, at least understandable and thus not a reasonable basis
for a U.S.-Soviet conflict. Some would agree with an earlier judgment
of Arthur Bliss Lane, written when he was ambassador to Poland: "The
Eastern European area (with the possible exception of Russia) is in
itself perhaps the least important of all the areas in the world with
which the United States had to deal." Such leading analysts as Hanson
Baldwin believed that the Soviet Union faced compelling security problems which justified much of its action.[36] It was not strange that many
observers condemned the hardening attitudes in Washington. The *New
Republic* charged that too many State Department officials, including
several assistant secretaries, refused to deal with the challenges of the
postwar world except "on impossible terms of American domination
and dictation."[37] Noted news commentator Raymond Gram Swing
declared in a radio broadcast that the American diplomats who had
lost faith in U.S.-Soviet relations were all expendable. In May, Henry
Wallace, now secretary of commerce, cautioned the president not to
accept the State Department's representations on the Soviet Union
without studying them carefully. When Harriman discussed the Soviets'

[34]Millis, *Forrestal Diaries*, p. 49; Forrestal to Homer Ferguson, May 14, 1945, ibid.,
p. 57.

[35]Joseph C. Grew, *Turbulent Era: A Diplomatic Record of Forty Years, 1904–1945*, ed.
Walter Johnson (Boston, 1952), 2:1446.

[36]Hanson W. Baldwin in *New York Times*, May 28, 1945, p. 4.

[37]"A Purge Needed in State," *New Republic* 113 (July 9, 1945): 38–39.

uncompromising behavior with a number of leading journalists, Walter Lippmann walked out of the room. For Lippmann the Allied victory over Germany had divided Europe inescapably into two exclusive spheres of influence, one dominated by the United States, the other by the USSR. "No nation, however strong," wrote Lippmann, "has universal world power which reaches everywhere. The realm in which each state has the determining influence is limited by geography and circumstance. Beyond that realm it is possible to bargain and persuade but not to compel, and no foreign policy is well conducted which does not recognize these invincible realities."[38]

To restore some amity to U.S.-Soviet relations, President Truman accepted Harriman's advice to dispatch Hopkins on a special mission to confer with Stalin in Moscow on the question of Poland's future.[39] Hopkins in late May reassured Stalin that the United States did not wish to force a government on Poland that was unfriendly to the USSR, but he reminded the Soviet leader of the importance of the Polish question to the American people. He pressed Stalin to broaden the base of the Warsaw government in accordance with the Yalta agreement and to release the underground Polish leaders. Stalin recalled that Germany, in the course of one long generation, had invaded his country twice through Poland. This had been possible, he continued, "because Poland had been regarded as a part of the *cordon sanitaire* round the Soviet Union and that previous European policy had been that Polish Governments must be hostile to Russia."[40] Stalin remained adamant. Perhaps four or five London Poles, he said, could enter the Lublin cabinet. "I am afraid," Harriman reported, "that Stalin does not and never will fully understand our interest in a free Poland as a matter of principle. The Russian Premier is a realist in all of his actions, and it is hard for him to appreciate our faith in abstract principle. It is difficult for him to understand why we should want to interfere with Soviet policy in a country like Poland which he considers so important to Russia's security unless we have some ulterior motive."[41] There would be no American solution of the Polish problem. When Hopkins returned to Washington, Truman and Churchill decided to come to terms with the Warsaw government because that regime, under Soviet

---

[38]Henry A. Wallace, *The Price of Vision: The Diary of Henry A. Wallace, 1942–1946*, ed. John Morton Blum (Boston, 1973), p. 450; Charles E. Bohlen, *Witness to History, 1929–1969* (New York, 1973), p. 215; Lippmann in *New York Herald-Tribune*, May 8, 1945, p. 13.

[39]Bohlen, *Witness to History*, p. 215.

[40]Bohlen's report of the Hopkins-Stalin conversations, May 26–27, 1945, in *FRUS, Diplomatic Papers: The Conference of Berlin, 1945* (Washington, 1960), 1:26–28, 37–40. Quotation on p. 39.

[41]Harriman to Truman, June 8, 1945, ibid., p. 61.

direction, had gained complete control of Poland. On June 22, Harriman reached agreement on a provisional government for Poland. Eventually some London Poles returned to Warsaw and received minor posts; their influence proved to be temporary and inconsequential.[42]

If the differences between East and West exceeded the possibilities of total reconciliation, some American officials still hoped to moderate Soviet behavior through gentle coercion. In Washington the illusion of superiority remained strong. What gave some assurance that the administration could handle the USSR effectively was the atomic bomb. If the bomb worked, Truman remarked in July, "I'll certainly have a hammer on those boys [the Russians]." The bomb was needed, observed the new secretary of state, James F. Byrnes, not to defeat Japan but to "make Russia manageable in Europe." He added that "in his belief the bomb might well put us in a position to dictate our own terms at the end of the war."[43] Not once, however, did American officials threaten to use the atomic bomb in defense of their principles. The threatened use of force could affect Soviet behavior only if it carried credibility. The bomb had no credibility because the United States could establish no interests in Eastern Europe worth the price of war with the USSR.

For many Americans the power to control Europe's reconstruction was economic, not military. In a world of decaying economies and collapsing empires, their economy stood supreme. The United States entered the postwar era with almost half the world's total productive capacity. The Soviets, additionally, had made clear their desire for U.S. products and credits. In January 1945, Molotov handed Harriman a formal request for a $6 billion long-term loan to enable his country to purchase American industrial products such as locomotives, railroad cars, rails, oil pipes, trucks, and other heavy equipment. In forwarding the request to Washington, Harriman recommended that "the question of credit should be tied to our overall diplomatic relations with the Soviet Union and at the appropriate time the Russians should be given to understand that our willingness to cooperate wholeheartedly with them in their vast reconstruction problems will depend upon their behavior in international matters."[44] State Department officials advocated delay in granting credits until the United States could gain an adequate response from the Kremlin on matters of political adjustment. William Clayton, assistant secretary of state for Economic Affairs, feared that a large loan would result in the loss of "what appears to be the

[42]On the move toward a Polish settlement see *New York Times*, June 14, 1945, p. 1; Bohlen, *Witness to History*, p. 219; and "Solution to Poland," *New Republic* 113 (July 2, 1945): 6.
[43]Byrnes quoted in Truman, *Year of Decisions*, p. 87.
[44]*FRUS, 1945*, 5:945–46.

only concrete bargaining lever for us in connection with the many other political and economic problems which will arise between the two countries." Harriman continued to favor the Soviet loan, but he agreed that the United States should tie its economic assistance "directly into our political problems with the Soviet Union."[45] The loan issue drifted without decision in Washington until Moscow lost interest.

On May 9, 1945, Harriman advised Truman to curtail Lend-Lease shipments to the Soviet Union. During subsequent days other members of the administration agreed. Two days later, the president ordered an end to Lend-Lease shipments, explaining that Congress, with the coming of peace, had ordered the termination. Truman understood that the Soviets, although less hard hit than the British, would interpret the decision as one aimed especially at them. The Soviets indeed complained about the administration's unfriendly attitude.[46] Later Truman termed his abrupt cancellation of Lend-Lease a mistake. The termination, he explained, "should have been done on a gradual basis which would not have made it appear as if somebody had been deliberately snubbed." He complained in his *Memoirs* that Leo T. Crowley, the director of Lend-Lease, had interpreted his order too literally and had placed the embargo on shipments to the Soviet Union and other European countries without his approval.[47] The president had several days to modify his order, but did not do so. Again the Truman administration failed to bargain from its position of economic preponderence.

Churchill had reminded Washington the previous month that the advanced positions of British and American forces in Europe gave the West some advantage in challenging the Soviet political advance across Eastern Europe. He hoped, in addition, that Western forces would capture the city of Berlin. Should the Soviets take the German capital, the prime minister had warned Roosevelt on April 1, they would thereafter behave as if they had been the overwhelming contributors to the common victory: *"I therefore consider that from a political standpoint we should march as far east into Germany as possible, and that should Berlin be in our grasp we should certainly take it."*[48] Soviet pressures on Eastern Europe made it all the more essential, Churchill repeated four days later, "that we should join hands with the Russian armies as far to the east as

[45]Clayton to Stettinius, January 20, 1945, ibid., pp. 964–66; Clayton memorandum of conversation with Morgenthau, January 25, 1945, ibid., p. 966; Harriman to Stettinius, April 4, 1945, ibid., pp. 817–20.

[46]Harriman to Truman, May 9, 1945, ibid., p. 998; Truman, *Year of Decisions*, p. 228.

[47]Truman, *Year of Decisions*, pp. 228–29.

[48]Churchill to Truman, April 1, 1945, in Winston S. Churchill, *Memoirs of the Second World War* (Boston, 1959), p. 936 (emphasis in original).

possible and if circumstances allow, enter Berlin."[49] Finally, on May 12, Churchill wired Truman, urging some settlement with the Kremlin, even at the cost of principle, while Western forces still held their advanced positions:

> I have always worked for friendship with Russia [he said], but like you, I feel deep anxiety because of their misinterpretations of the Yalta decisions, their attitudes toward Poland, their over-whelming influence in the Balkans, . . . and above all their power to maintain very large armies in the field for a long time. . . . Surely it is vital now to come to an understanding with Russia, or see where we are with her, before weakening our armies mortally or retiring to the zones of occupation. . . . Of course we may take the view that Russia will behave impeccably, and no doubt that offers the most convenient solution. To sum up, this issue of a settlement with Russia before our strength has gone seems to me to dwarf all others.[50]

Truman, backed by Davies, believed Churchill too concerned with British interests on the Continent. With his advisers concurring, the president decided against the employment of advanced troop positions for the purpose of bargaining. In the summer of 1945, Truman had no desire to publicize his growing displeasure with Soviet action and thereby inform the nation that its wartime exertions had achieved a doubtful victory at best.

IV

At Potsdam in mid-July 1945, Truman, Churchill, and Stalin were no longer commanders in chief of military forces seeking victory; they were now political leaders burdened with the task of blocking out the territorial, economic, and administrative arrangements for the reconstruction of Europe. The Potsdam Conference achieved quick agreement on the establishment of the Council of Foreign Ministers; on the concrete issues posed by Soviet practices in Eastern Europe, it could agree on very little. On the question of Eastern Europe's political future, Stalin remained uncompromising. "A freely elected government in any of these East European countries," he admitted simply, "would be anti-Soviet, and that we cannot allow." The United States, Byrnes informed Molotov, "sincerely desires Russia to have friendly countries on her borders, but we believe they should seek the friendship of the people rather than

---

[49]Churchill to Roosevelt, April 5, 1945, Map Room, Box 7, FDRL.
[50]Churchill to Truman, May 12, 1945, *FRUS: The Conference of Berlin*, 1:8–9.

of any particular government."[51] The United States, Byrnes added, did not wish to become involved in the elections of other countries; it merely desired to join other nations in observing elections in Italy, Greece, Hungary, Romania, and Bulgaria. Eventually the conference implemented the Yalta declaration by agreeing that only those states of Eastern Europe with "recognized democratic governments" would be permitted to sign the peace treaties or apply for membership in the United Nations. This raised again the meaning of democracy; obviously the Soviet interpretation did not coincide with that of the West. The minor procedural agreements at Potsdam left all fundamental Eastern European issues substantially untouched. When Stalin failed to win recognition of his country's paramount position in Eastern Europe, he argued for postponement. Admiral Leahy observed later that "the only possibility of agreement would have been to accept the Russian point of view on every issue."[52]

At Potsdam the Western allies faced the task of gaining Soviet collaboration in attaining a fair and equitable settlement for Germany. During the weeks preceding the conference, the Soviets had inaugurated a program of removing from their zone what the demolition of war had missed—machines, equipment, trolleys, trains, blueprints, drawings, and all useful information from the files of ravaged companies. To resolve the pressing question of reparations, Byrnes suggested that the Soviets take industrial material and equipment from the British and American zones, provided that they pay for it with shipments of food and fuel from the Soviet zone. In addition, the Soviets could obtain 10 percent of all industrial capital equipment in the Western zones not required for the German peacetime economy. The Soviets accepted this arrangement, giving up their claim for $20 billion in reparations.[53] The Big Three established the Allied Control Commission, with headquarters in Berlin, to manage the Allied occupation of Germany by unanimous vote. From the beginning the commission failed to create a unified occupation policy for Germany. Politically, the occupation forces were to de-Nazify and democratize the country. For British and American officials democratization meant competition between free and active political parties; for the Soviets it meant political domination by Communist-controlled elements. Economically, the Allies were to disarm and demilitarize Germany but treat it as an economic unit. Instead, the Soviets continued to dismantle factories for shipment to their country

[51]Meeting of foreign ministers, July 20, 1945, ibid., 2:152–55; Byrnes, *Speaking Frankly*, p. 73.
[52]Bohlen, *Witness to History*, pp. 234–35; Leahy, *I Was There*, pp. 428–29; Department of State *Bulletin* 13 (August 5, 1945): 159.
[53]Bohlen, *Witness to History*, pp. 231–33.

and to appropriate large portions of the output of factories still in operation. Stalin gave up any effort to influence all Germany with policies aimed at German reconstruction and chose instead to turn eastern Germany into an exclusive Soviet zone, binding Poland to the USSR by assigning that country new western frontiers along the Oder-Neisse rivers at Germany's expense. Such divergent political and economic practices increased the barriers between the Soviet and the three western zones. Within months the Allied control system for Germany had all but broken down.[54]

Truman chose to cloud the failure of the Potsdam Conference. In his report to the nation, he declared that the Allies "are now more closely than ever bound together. . . . From Tehran, and the Crimea, and San Francisco, and Berlin—we shall continue to march together to our objective."[55] Actually at Potsdam world politics moved incontrovertibly toward a bipolar structure. The leading powers, already distrustful of the new United Nations Organization, established formally at San Francisco during the early summer in 1945, were beginning to seek security elsewhere. "As a result," wrote John Fischer, "most of the lesser nations are now being drawn by a sort of Law of Political Gravity into the orbit of one or the other of the two Super-Powers. So far neither Russia nor the United States has yet completed its protective belt of satellites. Some areas are being tugged both ways, like small planets caught between two great stars."[56] The regions subject to conflicting pulls, warned Fischer, were the danger spots. They would remain so until either the United States or the USSR stopped the tugging. The period of grinding adjustment without the benefit of diplomatic accommodation had arrived. To avoid war, wrote Fischer, the United States and the Soviet Union had no choice but to accept the sphere of influence of the other. Because Soviet power was dominant in Eastern Europe, he predicted that the Western nations would eventually accept the reality of a divided world with whatever grace they could muster.

At the London Conference of Foreign Ministers in September 1945, Germany again emerged as the central issue confronting the victors, yet it was already apparent that the Allies would never agree on all-German policy. For the Western powers, the rebuilding of the German economy was the necessary prelude to Germany's political

[54]Department of State *Bulletin* 13 (August 5, 1945): 153–60; *FRUS: The Conference of Berlin*, 2:210–15; "Potsdam," *London Observer*, August 5, 1945, p. 4.
[55]Truman, "The Berlin Conference," Department of State *Bulletin* 13 (August 12, 1945): 213.
[56]John Fischer, "Odds Against Another War," *Harper's Magazine* 191 (August 1945): 97–106.

independence. Lord Nathan, Britain's undersecretary of war, defined the essence of British policy before the House of Lords: "We must be careful to safeguard against a breakdown of German industry." The Soviet Union, by contrast, appeared intent on curtailing German industrial expansion for an indefinite future. Its persistent removal of German assets to the Soviet Union not only crippled the German economy in the Eastern zone but also created an enormous drain on the resources of the Western zones. If the Allies could not agree on the treatment of their common enemy, it was quite certain that they could agree on nothing fundamental.[57]

For Byrnes the problem of Eastern Europe was equally troublesome. He assured Molotov privately that the United States wanted only governments friendly to the USSR along the Soviet borders. Molotov replied that the former Radescu regime of Romania was hostile to the Soviet Union and yet received British and U.S. support, but, when the Groza government which was friendly to the USSR gained power, both the British and the Americans withdrew their support. To Byrnes's retort that the new Romanian government was the product of Soviet interventionism, Molotov responded that many of the governments of Eastern Europe had tied their destinies to Hitler. For that reason, he said, the Soviet victory "must be seen not only in the light of the defeat of German fascism but in the light of the military, political and moral defeat of fascism throughout Europe." What mattered to Molotov was the ease of the German advance across Poland, Romania, Bulgaria, and Hungary. Byrnes surmised correctly that Germany lay at the heart of Soviet insecurity. To break the deadlock over Eastern Europe, the secretary offered Molotov an agreement binding the United States to Germany's demilitarization for twenty-five years. Molotov agreed only to report to Moscow.[58]

At London the fundamental trend toward a permanently divided Europe became inescapable. In early October the *London Observer* warned that there was no "shirking from the unpleasant fact that, without agreement between Moscow and the West, a line drawn north and south across Europe, perhaps somewhere in the region of Stettin to Trieste, is likely to become more and more of a barrier separating two very different conceptions of life." For the first time administration spokesmen acknowledged publicly that U.S.-Soviet relations had become troublesome. Republican adviser John Foster Dulles reported to the nation that the Soviets, in their intransigence, were merely testing to discover how firmly the United States would support its principles. In

[57]Byrnes, *Speaking Frankly*, p. 97.
[58]Ibid., pp. 98–101.

late October, Byrnes admitted that the Soviet Union had special security interests in East-Central Europe, but, he warned, spheres of influence and special interests based on exclusion and special privilege would not bring peace.[59] President Truman in his Navy Day address again acknowledged that the United States had entered a difficult period in its external relations. The solution to world problems, he suggested, would require "a combination of forebearance and firmness."[60] The president, however, promised his listeners that America would never recognize any government established by force against the freely expressed will of the people. Clearly the conflicts of purpose dividing Europe had become matters of public concern.

During the autumn of 1945 tensions were accumulating as well outside the areas of Soviet military domination. Soviet troops in North Korea had sealed off the country north of the 38th parallel and endangered the whole American program of unifying the peninsula under free elections. Greece was torn by civil strife in which Communist-led guerrillas contested the future of the British-backed Greek government. During 1945 the Soviets repeatedly had demanded a revision of the Montreux Convention governing the Turkish Straits. Soviet troops had interfered in Iran's internal affairs. In the northern province of Azerbaijan, Soviet-backed rebels had launched a movement for autonomy. The Soviet presence in northern Iran and its growing demands for a new arrangement in the Turkish Straits suggested that the Kremlin intended to dominate the eastern Mediterranean as well as the ports, waterways, pipelines, and oil fields of the Middle East. The London Foreign Ministers' Conference had set March 2, 1946 as the date for the withdrawal of all foreign troops from Iran, but reports indicated that the Soviets had no intention of withdrawing without establishing their control at least in the north. Together with the danger of a Communist coup in Greece, Truman recalled, "this began to look like a giant pincers movement against the oil-rich areas of the Near East and the warm-water ports of the Mediterranean."[61]

Byrnes's decision to travel to Moscow in December 1945, without preparations or Republican advisers, was his own. Diplomats and columnists warned him against venturing into a conference with Stalin

[59]London Observer, October 7, 1945, p. 1; Manchester Guardian, October 5, 1945, p. 174; "Conflict in London," New Republic 113 (October 1, 1945): 423; Dulles in New York Times, October 7, 1945, in Vital Speeches of the Day 12 (November 15, 1945): 68–70.
[60]Truman's Navy Day speech, October 27, 1945, Department of State Bulletin 13 (October 28, 1945): 654–55.
[61]Truman, Year of Decisions, pp. 522–23; "What is Happening in Iran?" New Republic 113 (December 3, 1945): 731–32.

without a precise agenda agreed on in advance.[62] However, Byrnes believed, as he wrote in his defense, "that if we met in Moscow, where I could have a chance to talk to Stalin, we might remove the barriers to the peace treaties. . . . The peace of the world was too important for us to be unwilling to take a chance on securing an agreement after full discussion."[63] Byrnes's advisers at Moscow, Harriman and career officer Bohlen, agreed with him that continued nonrecognition of the Communist-led governments of Eastern Europe would achieve nothing. In October and November the United States had extended recognition to the provisional governments of Austria and Hungary. At Moscow, Byrnes made further concessions, accepting compromises on the recognition of the regimes of Romania and Bulgaria. Stalin agreed to token representation of pro-Western parties and promised early elections. If these agreements represented some retreat from previous American positions, they recognized essentially that the United States had few choices remaining. Byrnes eventually gained Stalin's support for a peace conference in 1946 but accepted the premier's demand that France and China, which always sided with the United States and Britain, be eliminated from the drafting process.[64]

V

Truman received the Moscow communiqué on December 27. "I did not like what I read," he complained. "There was not a word about Iran or any other place where the Soviets were on the march. We had gained only an empty promise of further talks."[65] Byrnes's action at Moscow, designed to arrive at some accommodation with the Soviets, signaled the end of official optimism toward the Soviet Union. When Byrnes returned to Washington, the president accused him of making concessions without any evidence that the Soviets intended to change their policies in Iran or Eastern Europe. Byrnes, he charged, had attempted "to move the foreign policy of the United States in a direction

---

[62]For George F. Kennan in the American embassy in Moscow the time had come for the United States to terminate efforts to influence the nature of the governments under Soviet control; thus, he believed that Byrnes would achieve nothing substantial in Moscow. See George F. Kennan, *Memoirs, 1925–1950* (Boston, 1967), pp. 284–86.

[63]Byrnes, *Speaking Frankly*, p. 109.

[64]Ibid., pp. 111–22. At least some members of the press regarded Byrnes's concessions at Moscow essential and believed that the Big Three could now move forward toward a general postwar settlement. See, for example, "Concessions and Confidence," *Manchester Guardian*, January 4, 1946, pp. 2–3; and "Good News from Moscow," *New Republic* 114 (January 7, 1946): 3–4.

[65]Truman, *Year of Decisions*, p. 549.

to which I could not, and would not, agree." On January 5 he presented Byrnes with his bill of particulars:

> There is no justification for [the Russian program in Iran]. It is a parallel to the program of Russia in Latvia, Estonia and Lithuania. It is also in line with the high-handed and arbitrary manner in which Russia acted in Poland. . . . There isn't a doubt in my mind that Russia intends an invasion of Turkey and the seizure of the Black Sea Straits to the Mediterranean. Unless Russia is faced with an iron fist and strong language another war is in the making. . . . I do not think we should play compromise any longer. We should refuse to recognize Rumania and Bulgaria until they comply with our requirements; we should let our position on Iran be known in no uncertain terms and we should continue to insist on the internationalization of the Kiel Canal, the Rhine-Danube waterway and the Black Sea Straits. . . . [W]e should insist on the return of our ships from Russia and force a settlement of the Lend-Lease debt of Russia.[66]

Truman later designated his memorandum to Byrnes as the point of departure in American policy. " 'I'm tired of babying the Soviets,' I had said to Byrnes, and I meant it."[67] The president complained that the Soviets had acted "without regard for their neighboring nations and in direct violation of the obligations they had assumed at Yalta." Recalling his blunt and plain language to Molotov, he continued: "I was sure that Russia would understand firm, decisive language and action much better than diplomatic pleasantries."

For some Americans the Soviets' behavior no longer had any basis in history or tradition. To Forrestal it did not serve the historic security interests of the USSR; it had become the agent of Soviet ideology, a reassertion of that country's Communist assault on free institutions everywhere. On January 2, 1946, he confided his fears to his diary: "Our task is . . . complicated by the fact that we are trying to preserve a world in which capitalistic-democratic method can continue, whereas if the Russian adherence to truly Marxian dialectics continues their interest lies in a collapse of this system." In pondering the evidence of Soviet expansionism, Forrestal wondered whether Lippmann was correct in assuming that communism and democracy could coexist satisfactorily. "[T]o me," he wrote to Lippmann, "the fundamental question in respect to our relations with Russia is whether we are dealing with a nation or a religion—a religion after all being merely

---

[66]Ibid., pp. 550–52.
[67]Ibid., p. 552.

the practical extension of philosophy."[68] The Soviet threat had become ominous indeed.

On February 9, Stalin, in a major address, raised again the old Bolshevik concept of "capitalist encirclement" and the continuing hostility between the Communist and capitalist worlds. Stalin attributed the recent war to the dialectical necessities of capitalism and suggested that those same forces would again endanger the peace. His words were not reassuring: "Our Marxists declare that the capitalist system of world economy conceals elements of crisis and war. . . . [W]orld capitalism does not follow a steady and even course forward, but proceeds through crises and catastrophes."[69] Stalin did not intimate that his country needed to establish a Communist order to prevent war, nor did he threaten an open conflict with the capitalist enemy. For many Americans, however, his references to capitalist iniquities seemed to inaugurate ideological warfare against the non-Soviet world. Several days later Justice William O. Douglas termed Stalin's speech "The Declaration of World War III."[70]

All Western efforts to reach agreement with the Soviets on the postwar reconstruction of Europe had failed. Still U.S. diplomacy with the Kremlin before 1946 had assumed generally that nothing in the Soviet outlook would prevent satisfactory relations if the administration selected the correct approach. It was left for George Kennan, in his long telegram of February 22 from the American embassy in Moscow, to explain why the West would continue to have little influence on the Kremlin. From his lengthy observations of the Soviets' behavior, Kennan argued that their policy did not reflect an objective analysis of the external world; rather, it flowed from inner necessities dictated largely by the need for domestic political repression. The Soviets, he wrote, required a hostile and menacing external world to justify the cruelties and sacrifices which they imposed on their people. Kennan advised the State Department: "[W]e are faced here with a tremendous vested interest dedicated to [the] proposition that Russia is a country walking a dangerous path among implacable enemies. [The] disappearance of Germany and Japan (which were the only real dangers) from [the] Soviet horizon left this vital interest no choice but to build up [the] United States and the United Kingdom to fill this gap."[71] With such a government there could be no successful negotiation of differences;

[68]Millis, *Forrestal Diaries*, p. 127; Forrestal to Lippmann, January 7, 1946, ibid., p. 128.

[69]Stalin, "New Five-Year Plan for Russia," *Vital Speeches of the Day* 12 (March 1, 1946): 300–01.

[70]Douglas quoted in Millis, *Forrestal Diaries*, p. 134.

[71]Kennan's long telegram of February 22, 1946, ibid., pp. 135–40.

the Soviets would yield to no form of persuasion. No longer, therefore, would Washington gain anything by hiding its disagreements with the Kremlin from general view. What remained for the Western powers was the task of drawing the line against further Soviet encroachments. In May the State Department recalled Kennan from Moscow to advise the administration on Soviet matters.

Dulles continued the analysis of the Soviet danger in a long article entitled "Thoughts on Soviet Foreign Policy and What To Do About It," which appeared in *Life* magazine in June 1946. Like Kennan, Dulles charged that Soviet foreign policy was rigid, mechanistic, uncompromising, and was pursued by men in the Kremlin who knew little about the outside world. Soviet policies, he warned, were designed essentially to undermine the strength and unity of the entire non-Communist world. Communist ideology provided the Kremlin both its objectives and assurances of ultimate success. "The foreign policy of the Soviet Union," wrote Dulles, "is world-wide in scope. Its goal is to have governments everywhere which accept the basic doctrine of the Soviet Communist Party and which suppress political and religious thinking which runs counter to these doctrines. Thereby the Soviet Union would achieve world-wide harmony—a *Pax Sovietica*."[72] William Bullitt, in *The Great Globe Itself* (1946), again described the unlimited aims of Soviet ideology: "As conquest of the earth for Communism is the objective of the Soviet Government, no nation lies outside the scope of its ambitions." The Kremlin, in working for world conquest, would turn any agreement to its advantage. To Soviet leaders peace treaties and non-aggression pacts were instruments that they might sign "merely because at some moment they consider it is their interest to sign them; and they sign with every intention of breaking such agreements when they feel strong enough to do so with impunity."[73] Bullitt concluded that the United States could stop Soviet expansionism only by threatening that country with annihilation.

This crescendo of anti-Soviet sentiment began to capture the imagination of politicians, academics, and much of the public. Congressional Republicans had supported Roosevelt's wartime policies, but they felt no hesitancy in criticizing the Democratic leadership when in the autumn of 1945 it became obvious that the Truman administration could not make the promises of the past conform to the country's postwar experience. Republicans now demanded of Truman what Roosevelt had failed to achieve: a world of justice built on the Atlantic

[72]John Foster Dulles, "Thoughts on Soviet Foreign Policy and What To Do About It," *Life* 20 (June 3, 1946): 113–26; (June 10, 1946): 119–30. Quotation in ibid., p. 119.
[73]William C. Bullitt, *The Great Globe Itself: A Preface to World Affairs* (New York, 1946), pp. 100, 102, 175.

Charter. As early as October 1945 the Senate Foreign Relations Committee pressed Byrnes to "get tough" with the Soviets. On November 1 the House of Representatives, with only two Republicans in opposition, passed an appropriations bill that barred the use of American funds in any region controlled by the USSR. The bill died in the Senate Appropriations Committee, but it revealed the decided shift in congressional opinion, especially among Republicans. Then on December 5 a committee of House and Senate Republicans issued a policy statement chiding the administration's policy toward Eastern Europe:

> We believe in fulfilling to the greatest possible degree our war pledges to small nations that they shall have the right to choose the form of government under which they will live and that sovereign rights of self-government shall be restored to those who have been forcibly deprived of them. We deplore any desertion of these principles.

Dulles, when accompanying Byrnes to Moscow, warned the secretary that any concessions to the Soviets would face the united opposition of Republican leaders. In February 1946 Representative Clare Boothe Luce criticized the Truman administration for ignoring its commitments to the Atlantic Charter, for the dismemberment of Poland, and for its failure to carry out its promise of free elections throughout Eastern Europe.[74]

Senator Vandenberg was equally troubled by Byrnes's apparent refusal to stand up to the Soviets. When it became clear early in 1946 that the new Polish government was involved in a series of political murders, Byrnes instructed the American embassy in Warsaw to "inform the Polish government that we are relying on that government to take the necessary steps to assure the freedom and security which are essential to the successful holding of free elections." Vandenberg objected immediately, declaring that it was not enough to rely on the Polish government to "vindicate the honor and the pledge of the United States of America." We must rely, he said, "on our own moral authority in a world which, in my opinion, craves our moral leadership." Such firmness, he persisted, did not mean war.

> It means, first, that we must insistently demand prompt and dependable assurances that the Yalta and Potsdam pledges in behalf of free elections be effectively fulfilled. It means, in other

---

[74]For these burgeoning partisan attacks on the Truman administration see Bradford Westerfield, *Foreign Policy and Party Politics: Pearl Harbor to Korea* (New Haven, CT, 1955), pp. 204–09; and Clare Boothe Luce in *New York Times*, February 13, 1946, p. 18.

words, that we shall lift the powerful voice of America in behalf of the inviolable sanctity of international agreements to which we are a party. If this does not suffice, it means, then, that we shall scrupulously collect our facts; draw our relentless indictment if the facts so justify; and present it in the forum of the United Nations and demand judgment from the organized conscience of the world.[75]

Vandenberg offered a direct challenge to the administration when he addressed the Senate on the growing conflict between the United States and the USSR:

If this is so . . . I assert my own belief that we can live together in reasonable harmony if the United States speaks as plainly upon all occasions as Russia does; if the United States just as vigorously sustains its own purposes and its ideals upon all occasions as Russia does; if we abandon the miserable fiction, often encouraged by our own fellow travelers, that we somehow jeopardize the peace if our candor is as firm as Russia's always is; and if we assume a moral leadership which we have too frequently allowed to lapse. The situation calls for patience and good will; it does not call for vac- illation. . . . There is a line beyond which compromise cannot go— even if we once crossed that line under the pressures of the exi- gencies of war. But how can we expect our alien friends to know where that is unless we reestablish the habit of saying only what we mean and meaning every word we say?[76]

Byrnes responded to Vandenberg's appeal for a tougher stand in his speech on February 28 before the Overseas Press Club in New York. The secretary countered the charges of weakness and quickly assumed a position as uncompromising as Vandenberg's (one wit termed the speech the second Vandenberg concerto). Unlike Vandenberg, Byrnes did not speak of U.S.-Soviet relations directly but of the obligation of the country to uphold the principles of the United Nations Charter. The United States, declared Byrnes, would use its great power "not only in order to ensure our own security but in order to preserve the peace of the world." Byrnes condemned the Soviets for keeping troops in other countries without their consent. He admitted that the status quo was not sacred or unchangeable, but the United States, he said, would not ignore "a unilateral gnawing away at the status quo . . . [or] allow aggression to be accomplished by coercion or pressure or by subterfuges such as political infiltration." Byrnes assigned the United

---

[75]Vandenberg's statement in Vandenberg and Morris, *Private Papers of Vandenberg*, pp. 244–45.
[76]Vandenberg's Senate speech, February 27, 1946, ibid., pp. 248–49.

States the role of controlling and regulating all changes in the status quo throughout the world; any change declared to be illegitimate would meet the resistance of the United States. In a warning to the Soviets the secretary added: "We must make it clear in advance that we do intend to act to prevent aggression, making it clear at the same time . . . we will not use force for any other purpose."[77] Byrnes at the end repeated his willingness to enter into give-and-take negotiations. Vandenberg and others were prepared to give the secretary the benefit of the doubt and to judge him by the success or failure of his diplomatic efforts.

Less than a week later on March 5, Churchill raised the issue of Soviet expansionism and the responsibility of the United States in meeting that danger. "With primacy in power," he declared at Fulton, Missouri, "is also joined an awe-inspiring accountability for the future." The wartime British leader alluded to an iron curtain descended across Europe from Stettin to Trieste. He did not claim to know the limits of the expansive and proselytizing tendencies of either the USSR or the Communist international. Assuring the country that he spoke for himself alone, Churchill advocated a Western defense based on a "fraternal association of English-speaking peoples, . . . the continuance of the intimate relationships between our military advisers, leading to a common study of potential dangers, similarity of weapons and manuals of instruction and inter-change of officers and cadets at colleges . . . [and] joint use of all naval and air-force bases in the possession of either country all over the world." The Soviet Union, he believed, did not desire war, but, he added, "I am convinced that there is nothing they admire so much as strength and there is nothing for which they have less respect than for military weakness."[78]

Truman, although present at Fulton, disclaimed all responsibility for Churchill's speech. White House Press Secretary Charles Ross reported that the president did not know its contents, and at the Jackson Day dinner two weeks later Truman made no reference to Churchill's address at all. Thus the president succeeded in escaping much of the bitter reaction to Churchill's plea for a new Anglo-American alliance against the Soviet Union. Members of Congress and the American people generally were still reluctant to commit their country's power to the defense of Europe or even to acknowledge that U.S.-Soviet relations had reached such a dangerous state. To the noted American

[77]Byrnes's speech of February 28, 1946, *New York Times,* March 1, 1946, p. 10. Key writers assumed that Byrnes was responding to Republican pressure. See Arthur Krock in ibid., March 1, 1946, p. 21; and James Reston in ibid., March 3, 1946, p. 3.

[78]Churchill's speech at Fulton, Missouri, March 5, 1946, *Vital Speeches of the Day* 12 (March 15, 1946): 329–32.

writer, Pearl S. Buck, speaking at Town Hall, Churchill's speech was a catastrophe because it threatened to split the world.[79] Crowds hailed and jeered the British statesman on his procession through New York City, and a liberal demonstration outside the dinner hall lasted for two hours. Senator Arthur Capper of Kansas, a leading Republican, took a parting shot at Churchill by charging him with trying to "arouse the people of the United States to commit the country to the task of pre-serving the far-flung British Empire."[80] Lippmann also attacked Churchill's speech as an appeal for support of the British Empire. Secretary of Commerce Wallace condemned it for producing distrust toward the Soviet Union and stimulating an arms race. What the prime minister's speech seemed to indicate was that most Americans, what-ever their attitudes toward the USSR, would retreat from any program that required more of the United States than an appeal to moral disapprobation.[81]

Roman Catholics had always shared some hostility toward the Soviet Union, and its absorption of the Catholic countries of Eastern Europe into the Communist world merely aggravated that hostility. American Catholics were especially troubled by the Polish question and criticized both American and British leaders for their failure to protect the interests of the Catholic government in exile. In November 1945 the *Catholic World* had declared that "the greatest menace to our hard won but still precarious peace is the Soviet ambition for a vast Communist empire," and on December 14 the *Commonweal* complained that "a spineless and policyless United States" was encouraging the Soviets to become less and less compromising and more determined to do as they pleased.[82] Thereafter, Catholic editors and writers took the lead in charging past American and British policies for the loss of Eastern Europe. James M. Gillis of the *Catholic World* observed in May 1946 that, "if the real Poland can never speak again, the shame of the democracies and the futility of the UN are both revealed. When I say the shame of the democracies, I mean the shame of our people." He chided those who led the West into war to save Poland from the Nazis and then threw the country to the Russian wolves. "That's why some of us, contemptuously branded isolationists," ran Gillis's conclusion, "are chary of assuming international obligations which we know we

[79]Buck quoted in *New York Times*, March 7, 1946, p. 5.
[80]For the demonstrations see ibid., March 16, 1946, pp. 1, 3; and Capper in ibid., March 18, 1946, p. 3.
[81]Wallace, *Prince of Vision*, p. 557; Dorothy Thompson, "U.S. Not Ready for Churchill Speech," *London Observer*, March 10, 1946, p. 5.
[82]*Catholic World* 162 (November 1945): 101; "Events Abroad," *Commonweal* 43 (December 14, 1945): 227.

cannot fulfill, and which not even the most rabid interventionists honestly intend to fulfill."[83] In June the *Commonweal* demanded a tougher line toward the Soviet Union and complained that, "while the State Department fiddles, Byrnes roams."[84] This Catholic disillusionment with U.S. policy toward Eastern Europe enabled Republican leaders to identify their own growing pressures on Washington with the demands of powerful, normally Democratic, urban groups of Eastern European and Catholic background. Herein lay the political significance of the Soviet issue in American politics.

Unfortunately, all these pressures for a tougher and more successful policy toward the USSR comprised declarations of hope, not plans for action. The new spirit of toughness, noted the *London Observer*, was in no way reflected in the determination of American leaders to check the speed of demobilization.[85] Whatever the needs of the hour, demobilization was in the air, and the majority of both parties accepted the decision to reduce the size of the U.S. military establishment. Already the dichotomy, familiar enough in the American experience, between the demands placed on policy and the almost total neglect of means had pervaded the thought of the nation's leaders. Columnist Anne O'Hare McCormick rebuked the nation for expecting achievements abroad which far outstripped its capabilities. "When Americans demand in one breath that their Government take a firm stand on principle and in the next that the bulk of our forces be withdrawn from Europe," she wrote, "they should not complain of unsatisfactory compromises. We cannot stand and move away at the same time."[86] The *New Republic* responded to Vandenberg's appeal for a tougher American policy vis-à-vis the Soviet Union: "Mr. Vandenberg's speech . . . was undoubtedly popular; the only trouble was that he did not indicate any means of carrying it out or, indeed, seem to recognize the implications involved." The writer observed that the senators who applauded Vandenberg's

[83]James M. Gillis, "First Round Goes to Russia," *Catholic World* 163 (May 1946): 102–03. For a similar charge see Alexander Janta, "A Pole Speaks His Mind," *Catholic Digest* 11 (November 1946): 18–22.

[84]Ely Culbertson, "Minutes on Our Destiny," *Commonweal* 44 (June 14, 1946): 206. In July 1946 the *Commonweal* warned that "Russian Communism cannot be appeased. Its aggression can be stopped and held in check by British and American power frankly and openly prepared and poised to strike back whenever Russia operates to take over a new area, government, or people." "Problems for Peace," *Commonweal* 44 (July 19, 1946): 324. By mid-1946 public opinion polls indicated that half the American people believed that the Soviet Union was out to dominate as much of the world as possible. See. Gabriel A. Almond, *The American People and Foreign Policy* (New York, 1950), pp. 94–95. The alleged failure of the Truman policy in Europe became an issue in the 1946 Republican congressional victories.

[85]*London Observer*, March 24, 1946, p. 4.

[86]Anne O'Hare McCormick, "Foreign Affairs," *New York Times*, July 3, 1946, p. 24.

proposed "manifestation of America's strength and 'moral leadership' have been the most vociferous in demanding that the boys come home."[87]

Perhaps this unconcern for means mattered little. Military power of any magnitude could contribute to favorable diplomatic settlements only if Washington could establish the credibility of American power in regions where the United States had no intention of fighting. At best U.S. power could stabilize the lines that separated the Soviet from the Western sphere in Europe. Any effort to deflate the Soviet hegemony with force would meet swift and determined resistance. Few Republicans who anticipated American success in freeing Eastern Europe would have demanded actions more explicit than those prescribed by Vandenberg.

VI

To reestablish a nonpartisan approach to foreign policy, Byrnes invited both Vandenberg and Tom Connally, Democratic leader in the Senate, to accompany him to the foreign ministers' meeting in Paris. The meeting opened on April 25 in the beautiful Luxembourg Palace, with little promise of success. At issue was a peace treaty for Italy as well as treaties with Hungary, Romania, Bulgaria, and Finland—the former Nazi satellites. The United States was not directly involved in the Finnish treaty because it had never been at war with the Finns. From the outset Byrnes and Molotov argued over procedure. The Soviets insisted on a rigid adherence to the stipulated agenda and opposed every effort to broaden or amend the terms of reference, always concerned with specific settlements without reference to generalizations. Byrnes, on the other hand, argued that the conference, in framing the peace treaties, seek first an agreement on general principles from which it might move on to specific settlements.[88] In their effort to frame the peace treaties, the negotiators faced the subsidiary issues of the Danube, Italian reparations, and Trieste. Molotov demanded extensive reparations from Italy; to this Byrnes objected, declaring on May 2 that, if the Soviets insisted on reparations, there would be no Italian treaty. Byrnes pressed the Soviets for the internationalization of transportation on the Danube and thus access to the trade of Eastern Europe. Soviet

[87]*New Republic* 114 (March 11, 1946): 348.
[88]"Paris," *Manchester Guardian*, April 26, 1946, p. 210; "The Atlantic Report—Europe," *Atlantic Monthly* 177 (June 1946): 13.

diplomats resisted every American effort to contest their economic hegemony in the Balkans.[89]

Trieste emerged as a special problem. This city on the Adriatic Sea had a predominantly Italian population but was surrounded by Yugoslav territory. Both the Italians and the Yugoslavs, the latter backed by the Soviet Union, claimed the city. The United States supported the Italian claim under the principle of self-determination. A special commission dispatched to Trieste reported that the inhabitants of the city preferred to belong to Italy. Molotov objected, declaring that the commission had no right to draw any conclusions from its study. He therefore sabotaged a plan to internationalize the city by insisting that the major city services, including the police, be under Yugoslav control.[90] For the Soviets, Byrnes's persistence in relying on principle, rather than bargaining, to have his way seemed quite incomprehensible. After one heated session on the question of Trieste, Bohlen, acting as adviser to the American delegation, remained behind to converse with a member of the Soviet delegation. "The Soviet representative," he reported, "said it was impossible for him to understand the Americans. They had a reputation for being good traders and yet Secretary Byrnes for two days had been making speeches about principles—talking, he said, like a professor." With all sincerity, the Soviet delegate added, "Why doesn't he stop his talking about principles, and get down to business and start trading?"[91]

At Paris almost every session ended in deadlock. Byrnes terminated one especially futile session with the observation: "Can we at least agree upon adjourning until Monday?" On another occasion Vandenberg reported that the score for the conference was "no runs, no hits, and a lot of errors (but not by us)."[92] By mid-May, Connally observed that both Byrnes and Vandenberg believed that U.S.-Soviet relations had fallen into a bottomless pit. The *Manchester Guardian* warned that "what is clear is that relations between the Big Three have now reached a perilous stage and only a great effort of statesmanship can avoid a fatal breach." On June 3 the *New Republic* complained that in "twenty-two days at Paris the Western democracies and the Soviet Union failed to find a means of living in one world with each other."

[89]Saville Davis, "Soviet Policy at Paris," *New Republic* 114 (May 20, 1946): 722; "One Year After," ibid., p. 715; Vandenberg and Morris, *Private Papers of Vandenberg*, pp. 271–72.

[90]Bohlen, *Witness to History*, pp. 253–55.

[91]Byrnes, *Speaking Frankly*, pp. 280–81.

[92]Vandenberg and Morris, *Private Papers of Vandenberg*, pp. 279, 284; Thomas T. Connally, *My Name is Tom Connally* (New York, 1954), p. 297.

Analyst Saville Davis blamed the long delay in liquidating the war on the refusal of the United States to come to terms earlier with the Soviets under the assumption "that time and smart diplomacy would alter the bargaining terms in our favor. They did not. And now the Russians in their turn have deliberately used the delays since last summer to consolidate Eastern Europe." Critics agreed that, as long as the two principal powers initiated every move and planned every maneuver from a backlog of mistrust, the negotiation would continue *ad infinitum* without result.[93] The opening session of the Paris conference recessed on May 16 without much diplomatic achievement. Byrnes hoped that the next session, to open on June 15, would make greater progress in drafting treaties and arranging a general peace conference.

Observers at the Paris meeting noted that Byrnes spent less effort in seeking accommodation with Molotov than in placing the onus for the deadlock on the Soviets. He doggedly rejected Molotov's proposals to demonstrate American toughness. Byrnes's refusal to negotiate any deals with the USSR rested on three imperatives: the need to avoid charges of weakness so easily exploitable by the administration's enemies, the genuine addiction to principle among American leaders, and the assumption that any effort to negotiate with the Soviets would fail anyway. Vandenberg lauded the toughness; the appeasement of the Roosevelt years had ended. No longer, he boasted, would the Soviets have their way at international meetings.[94] In Paris, Connally criticized Byrnes for trying too hard to please Vandenberg and for holding private conferences with him before each session. In his report to the Senate in May, Vandenberg noted that the U.S. delegation had maintained absolute unity on every issue. American policy, he said, was based on the "moralities of the Atlantic and San Francisco charters [as well as] the practical necessities for Europe's rehabilitation." That sort of foreign policy he would support under any administration. Vandenberg regretted that the negotiations in Paris had not achieved greater success, but, he concluded, "delay is preferable to error in such vital matters. We can compromise within the boundaries of principle. We can no longer compromise principles themselves."[95]

At Paris, big-power diplomacy approached a dead end, caught on issues rendered unsolvable by the Soviet occupation and political

---

[93]"A Warning," *Manchester Guardian*, May 31, 1946, p. 279; "Paris Post-Mortem," *New Republic* 114 (June 3, 1946): 788; Saville Davis, "Power Politics at Paris," ibid. 114 (May 13, 1946): 685; C. L. Sulzberger in *New York Times*, May 16, 1946, p. 1; *Newsweek*, May 20, 1946, pp. 34, 40.

[94]Vandenberg and Morris, *Private Papers of Vandenberg*, p. 285.

[95]Connally, *My Name is Tom Connally*, p. 299; Vandenberg's report to the Senate in Vandenberg and Morris, *Private Papers of Vandenberg*, p. 287.

dominance of Eastern Europe. Unable to accept the Soviet sphere in the name of principle, or to reduce it without war, the United States continued to coexist with what it could not change. What minimized the danger of this drift in policy was the actuality of a static and divided Europe. Soviet power had already resolved all specific territorial and political questions unilaterally under conditions quite tolerable to Washington. American officials never entertained any policies designed to turn the Soviets out of Eastern Europe. For that reason the American preference for self-determination was never a real threat to Soviet interests. The diplomatic exchanges of 1946 included neither proposals for compromise nor threats of reprisal.

Secretary of Commerce Wallace attempted to break this deadlock by recommending a genuine accommodation with the Soviet Union based on the reality of a divided Europe. In this quest Wallace was not alone; Clyde Eagleton also admonished the country's burgeoning anti-Soviet elements:

> One of the things for which we criticise Russia is the fact that she is trying to build up a sphere of influence. . . . At the same time, and for years back, the United States has been building up a sphere of influence reaching from the North Pole to the South Pole, and we are now talking of extending it from Dakar to Okinawa. Mr. Molotov at San Francisco, after watching how the United States worked with the other American republics to get Argentina admitted, intimated that Russia could anticipate a solid bloc of some twenty American nations, led by the United States, to vote against his country in future United Nations decisions. With half the world in our sphere of influence, the efforts of the Russians in their part of the world look positively puny![96]

Wallace, in a long memorandum dated July 23 to the president, suggested that the United States, as the world's most powerful and only undamaged country, attempt to understand "what Russia believed to be essential to her own security as a prerequisite to the writing of the peace and to cooperation in the construction of a world order." He acknowledged the administration's success in achieving bipartisan cooperation in its new tough attitudes toward the Kremlin, but he questioned whether unity built on currying conflict abroad was advisable. "I think there is some reason to fear that in our earnest efforts to achieve bipartisan unity in this country," Wallace warned, "we may

---

[96]Clyde Eagleton, "The Beam in Our Own Eye," *Harper's Magazine* 192 (June 1946): 483.

have given way too much to isolationism masquerading as tough realism in international affairs."[97]

On September 12, Wallace called for a policy of peaceful competition. What mattered, he said, were not peace treaties over Greece and the German satellites but peace between the United States and the Soviet Union.

> On our part we should recognize that we have no more business in the *political* affairs of Eastern Europe than Russia has in the *political* affairs of Latin America, Western Europe, and the United States . . . whether we like it or not, the Russians will try to socialize their sphere of influence just as we try to democratize our sphere of influence. This applies also to Germany and Japan. The Russians have no more business in stirring up native Communists to political activity in Western Europe, Latin America, and the United States than we have in interfering with the politics of Eastern Europe and Russia.[98]

Wallace's advocacy of spheres of influence offered a more realistic concept of ends than did the more ambitious purposes of his opponents; their words of boldness would never secure a Soviet retreat from Eastern Europe. Because he did not regard the USSR an immediate danger to Western Europe, Wallace denied the need for a large American military structure. Merely getting tough would not secure the fulfillment of the Yalta aspirations; toughness in the West would always be matched by that of the Kremlin. In its conflict with the United States over Eastern Europe, Wallace argued, the Soviets held the overwhelming advantage. Their defense was not based on claims and aspirations but on physical occupation and military power. His speech so antagonized Byrnes and other members of the administration that the president called for Wallace's resignation. National leaders preferred to behave as if the United States still had choices other than diplomatic compromise or perennial postponement which would free no one.

Meanwhile, Big Three disagreements over Germany had become profound. After February 1946 the Soviets ceased to cooperate with

[97]Henry A. Wallace, "The Path to Peace with Russia," *New Republic* 115 (September 30, 1946): 401–06.

[98]Wallace's Madison Square Garden speech, September 12, 1946, in *Vital Speeches of the Day* 12 (October 1, 1946): 738–41. Although members of the administration and much of the press criticized Wallace, some agreed with him that the administration was challenging the USSR to satisfy its potential Republican critics. See "After the Wallace Dismissal: Crisis in Foreign Policy," *New Republic* 115 (September 30, 1946): 395–96; Claude Pepper in *New York Times*, September 13, 1946, p. 1; and Joseph C. Harsch in *Christian Science Monitor*, October 4, 1946, p. 18.

the Allied military government of Germany as they prepared to complete the Sovietization of their zone of occupation. On April 29 in Paris, Byrnes battled the trend toward a divided Germany by repeating his proposal for a four-power treaty that would guarantee German disarmament for a period of twenty-five years. Vandenberg, who, in his noted January 10, 1945 speech to the Senate, had suggested this method of reassuring the Soviets, was delighted with Byrnes's initiative. He noted in his diary that, "if and when Molotov finally refuses this offer, he will confess that he wants *expansion* and not 'security.'. . . Then moral conscience all around the globe can face and assess the realities—and prepare for the consequences."[99] In Berlin the Allied Control Commission confronted the immediate task of determining how much industrial equipment the Soviets could remove from the Western zones without destroying the capacity of the German people to subsist without external assistance. The United States and Britain had no intention of financing heavy imports into their zones to prevent unacceptable economic hardship. The Soviets insisted that the Germans required little industry; the British, who again wanted to see Germany prosper, disagreed. Eventually the Americans sided with the British. Finally, in early May 1946, General Lucius D. Clay, the American deputy military governor of Germany, ordered a halt to all further reparations shipments from the U.S. zone. By then the ultimate solution for the German problem was clear. If a united Germany, economically powerful, would again threaten European security, the Allies had no choice but to keep Germany an economic slum or divide it, placing the Soviet zone in the economy of Eastern Europe and linking the three Western zones to Western Europe. Speaking at Stuttgart on September 6, 1946, Byrnes announced that the three Western occupying powers would proceed to merge their zones into a single economic unit. Creating a strong, united West Germany now became the essence of Western policy.[100]

VII

Byrnes and his advisers came to the second session of the Paris conference in mid-June determined to push for an early showdown with Molotov. They were convinced that the Soviets were capitalizing on Europe's prolonged political chaos. When the conference reconvened

[99]Vandenberg and Morris, *Private Papers of Vandenberg*, p. 268; "Who Failed at Paris?" *New Republic* 114 (May 27, 1946): 747–48.

[100]"East and West," *Manchester Guardian*, May 24, 1946, p. 262. Vandenberg discussed the German problem in his report to the Senate, July 16, 1946, in *Vital Speeches of the Day* 12 (August 1, 1946): 613–20. Byrnes's Stuttgart speech, September 6, 1946, in Department of State *Bulletin* 15 (September 15, 1946): 496–501.

at the Luxembourg Palace, the disagreements on Italy and Trieste were as profound as ever. *Time* had predicted in late May that, if the Soviets delayed the conference, the Western nations would proceed to organize all the areas outside the Soviet orbit on their own terms. Byrnes applied that formula when on June 22 he informed Molotov that if the Council of Foreign Ministers could not provide a peace, the Western powers would seek an arrangement through other means. No longer, at any rate, would the United States permit the Soviets to profit from the continuing delays.[101] During the first week of July, Molotov made a number of major concessions that permitted marked advances in the Balkan treaties. When he acknowledged his country's satisfaction with the progress on the treaty drafts, the foreign ministers agreed to call a general peace conference, to open in Paris in late July. Whether the twenty-one-nation conference could succeed where the Council of Foreign Ministers had not seemed doubtful. The summoning of the conference was rushed, giving the lesser nations little time to consider the partially completed treaty drafts.[102]

Byrnes had assumed that a general peace conference, through parliamentary debate and vote by opposing blocs, could bring agreement. During August the conference took up the task of completing peace treaties for Italy, Hungary, Finland, Romania, and Bulgaria. The progress on the treaties was steady and generally satisfactory. What blocked the Italian treaty was the continuing disagreement on Italian reparations and the future of Trieste. When in mid-October the conference neared its end, it had not produced a formal settlement. The *Manchester Guardian*, passing judgment on the Paris Peace Conference, wrote that its "closing stages have been more hurried than dignified. Its total achievements are unimpressive."[103] Some Americans would have preferred an American decision at Paris, taken in the name of principle, to terminate the conference and simply throw the USSR out of the community of nations.[104]

[101]"Problems at Paris," *New Republic* 114 (June 17, 1946): 853; *Newsweek*, April 29, 1946, p. 45; *Time,* May 27, 1946, p. 26; Vandenberg and Morris, *Private Papers of Vandenberg,* p. 292.

[102]For the problems and gains of the second session of the Paris Foreign Ministers' Conference see Saville Davis, "Costly Harmony at Paris," *New Republic* 115 (July 15, 1946): 38; "The Air Clears at Paris," ibid. 115 (July 22, 1946): 63; "The Atlantic Report—Europe," *Atlantic Monthly* 178 (August 1946): 3.

[103]"Paris in Review," *Manchester Guardian,* October 18, 1946, p. 202. For similar evaluations of the peace conference see "The Atlantic Report—Paris," *Atlantic Monthly* 178 (October 1946): 3–7; and "Washington," ibid., p. 15; "Byrnes, Hull and Peace," *New Republic* 115 (October 14, 1946): 467; "What Blocks World Peace?" ibid. 115 (October 21, 1946): 501.

[104]J. Alvarez del Vayo, "Will Russia Break with the West?" *Nation* 163 (August 24, 1946): 204.

With the demise of the Paris Peace Conference in October, the foreign ministers moved to New York to continue their search for agreement. There at the Waldorf-Astoria Hotel in November and December they completed the work on the treaties and resolved the troublesome Trieste issue. Even then the final settlement came hard. In a private meeting on November 25, Byrnes again warned Molotov that the United States would break off negotiations and sign its own treaties unless the Soviet government became more cooperative. During the following week, with a minimum of argument, the foreign ministers completed the draft treaties. Byrnes secured his agreement on Trieste by convincing Molotov that the Yugoslavs did not merit his long and arduous efforts in their behalf. In return for Soviet concessions on Trieste, Molotov received the promise of an early withdrawal of occupation forces. The final agreements, as compromises between rival powers, did not reflect the will of the inhabitants, nor did they follow any accepted political or economic principles. They did, however, represent the best that months of patient and enduring effort could produce.[105]

What troubled some realists was Washington's propensity throughout the Paris meetings to allow the defense of principle to carry the debate with the Soviets into issues of secondary importance, issues that the United States could never resolve to its satisfaction and which lay far outside its economic and security interests. Reinhold Niebuhr argued that the United States should

> stop the futile efforts to change what cannot be changed in Eastern Europe, regarded by Russia as its strategic security belt. It will do things there which will disturb the conscience of democrats. . . . But Western efforts to change conditions in Poland, or in Bulgaria, for instance, will prove futile in any event, partly because the Russians are there and we aren't, and partly because such slogans as 'free elections' and 'free enterprise' are irrelevant in that part of the world. . . . If we left Russia alone in the part of the world it has staked out we might actually help, rather than hinder, the indigenous forces which resist its heavy hand.[106]

Perhaps the reliance on principle in the pursuit of a Soviet retreat created the illusion of ultimate success. Nevertheless, as a substitute

---

[105]"Too Much Blue," *New Republic* 115 (November 25, 1946): 676–77; "Trieste Compromise," *Manchester Guardian*, December 6, 1946, p. 310; "Change of Mind," ibid., December 13, 1946, p. 326. For judgments on the quality of the treaty-making see *Manchester Guardian*, July 12, 1946, p. 14; Byrnes's radio address, October 18, 1946, *New York Times*, October 19, 1946, p. 15; and Vandenberg's statements at Detroit, ibid., October 20, 1946, p. 50.

[106]Reinhold Niebuhr, "Europe, Russia, and America," *Nation* 163 (September 14, 1946): 288–89.

for concrete proposals which reflected the realities of postwar Europe, it comprised largely an escape from responsibility. Lippmann analyzed succinctly why American action would continue to reap little but futility:

> Mr. Byrnes, Mr. Vandenberg, Mr. Connally, and Mr. Truman had been schooled in the Senate, and Mr. Bevin in the Trades Union Congress and in Parliament. Unable to induce or compel M. Molotov by what they regarded as diplomacy, they sought to outvote him, and to arouse public opinion against him. The theory of this procedure was that by bringing issues to a public vote an aroused public opinion would do to the Russians what it has done now and then to Tammany Hall and May Hague, to Mr. Joe Martin and Senator Taft.
>
> But to apply the methods of domestic politics to international politics is like using the rules of checkers in a game of chess. Within a democratic state, conflicts are decided by an actual or a potential count of votes—as the saying goes, by ballots rather than bullets. But in a world of sovereign states conflicts are decided by power, actual or potential, for the ultimate arbiter is not an election but war.[107]

Two disturbing trends, slowly destroying the illusion of one world, converged during the summer and autumn of 1946. The first was the unbroken increase in tension between East and West. In absence of any fundamental agreements, what had begun as a verbal dual over the future of Eastern and Central Europe had degenerated into a conflict of immense hostility. The West had refused to recognize either the Soviet Union's political gains in Eastern Europe or the legitimacy of its policies in Germany. After Byrnes's Stuttgart speech especially the Soviet attack on the West assumed a sharp and menacing tone. It seemed apparent by late 1946 that the Kremlin regarded cordial relations with the West either undesirable or simply beyond the realm of possibility. In September the *Manchester Guardian* commented on the propaganda war being waged in Paris: "Britain and the United States are no longer reproached as erring friends but are addressed as willful enemies. . . . It is this background of hostile propaganda, so ingenious, so mendacious, so unceasing, which is also most disturbing. What other conclusion is there than this: while we in the West are arguing and debating, trying to find some way of accommodation, Russia has already decided that friendship with the West is neither possible nor desirable." Byrnes himself recognized this alarming quality in the debate. "The thing which disturbs me," he observed in late October, "is not the

---

[107]Walter Lippmann, "A Year of Peacemaking," *Atlantic Monthly* 178 (December 1946): 35–40.

lettered provisions of the treaties under discussion but the continued if not increasing tension between us and the Soviet Union."[108] For Byrnes the disintegration of the Grand Alliance had come because of the constant overdemanding of the Kremlin and the refusal of the United States to yield to its demands.

Second, the deepening East-West conflict completed the structuring of a bipolar world. The United States was now in full command of the Western bloc. No longer, observed the *Manchester Guardian*, were Byrnes and Truman attempting to play the role of mediator between Britain and the Soviet Union; they had ventured fully into the arena of world politics. The president seemed to assume this new role of leadership when he had stated in April that "the United States today is a strong nation. There is none stronger. This is not a boast. It is a fact which calls for solemn thought and due humility. It means that with such strength we have to assume leadership and accept responsibility."[109] For Britain the acceptance of American leadership demanded a willing adjustment of its traditional status, for the United States and the USSR had become the world's dominant powers. British leaders agreed that a position of neutrality between the giants was untenable. As the astute *London Observer* commented on October 27, 1946, "our relations with America and Russia are not the same. Those with America, though our views and interests are far from identical, are easy and friendly, and we cannot view America as a potential menace to our existence. The same cannot, unfortunately, be said of Russia." With that admission of an unwritten Western alliance the dream of postwar big-power unity vanished. Washington, however, had not yet faced the fundamental question of whether the country's new role as leader of the Western bloc was that of repelling further Soviet expansion or pursuing the cause of the Atlantic Charter.

---

[108]"Russia's Voice," *Manchester Guardian*, September 20, 1946, p. 146; Byrnes quoted in "Stalin's Answers," ibid., November 1, 1946.

[109]Truman's Army Day speech, April 1946, quoted in ibid., April 12, 1946, p. 186.

The United States and NATO: Means Without Ends*

FOR THOSE WHO SHARED the postwar fear of Soviet expansionism, the evolution of U.S. policy toward Europe between 1949 and 1951 was nothing less than spectacular. Throughout the early postwar years, Washington had groped for a practical role that would reflect the nation's wealth as well as its interests in a militarily and politically divided Europe. The United States had emerged from the war as the richest and most powerful nation in history, yet a nation with no tradition of active participation in European affairs. By 1947 the Western world assuredly had required big-power leadership, but what could it anticipate from a country whose whole tradition had been the rejection of leadership? The initial answer came quickly in the form of the Truman Doctrine and the Marshall Plan. To some European observers even these efforts appeared piecemeal and incoherent; for the United States they comprised no less than a major revolution. With the Marshall Plan the United States turned decisively from its isolationist tradition and embarked on a costly but promising association with Western Europe. The *Economist* in January 1949 termed the offer of Marshall aid one of "the great creative acts of history."

After 1948 the European Recovery Program had created a momentum toward recovery in Western Europe. Still that program seemed incapable of surmounting the crippling effect of Europe's continuing insecurity. As Warren R. Austin explained, "today, the greatest

*Published as "The United States and the Evolution of NATO, 1949–1951," in *Teaching History* 4 (May 1970): 15–28. Reprinted by permission.

147

obstacle in the way of recovery is fear . . . that pervades the daily lives of the people of Western Europe. . . . Their plans for the future are weighed against the fear that foreign armies will again sweep across their land. . . . This sense of insecurity robs them of a vital ingredient in the recipe for recovery—confidence in the future."[1] If those fears were often exaggerated, he continued, they were not groundless, for the Soviets had used the Red Army as the instrument for creating Moscow-directed regimes across Eastern Europe. Addressing the Senate Foreign Relations Committee, the new secretary of state, Dean G. Acheson, elaborated on Europe's mood of insecurity, declaring in part:

> Western European countries have seen the basic purposes and principles of the [United Nations] Charter cynically violated by the conduct of the Soviet Union with the countries of Eastern Europe. . . . The human freedoms as the rest of the world understands them have been extinguished throughout the whole area. . . . These same methods have been attempted in other areas—penetration by propaganda and the Communist Party, attempts to block cooperative international efforts in the economic field, wars of nerves, and in some cases thinly veiled use of force itself. By the end of 1947 it had become abundantly clear that this Soviet pressure and penetration was being exerted progressively further to the West.[2]

In Britain the *Economist* took the lead in warning the West against any further trust of Stalin. "Quite apart from any question of ideological differences, or political or strategic interests," ran its conclusion, "it is well to go cautiously with a man who has shed so much blood. For better or for worse, Stalin is not a Main Street politician; he belongs among the great despots and conquerors of history, and those who have to deal with such beings should study well the nature of their power."[3] Stalin's decision to lift the Berlin blockade, many British writers agreed, was only a tactical move; the Kremlin remained as dedicated as ever to its policies of expansion in Europe.[4] Still the definition of the Soviet danger to Western Europe continued to lack precision. Soviet military control of Slavic Europe did not in itself comprise an expansionist

---

[1]Warren R. Austin's address to the Vermont Historical Society, February 24, 1949, Department of State *Bulletin* 20 (March 6, 1949): 298.

[2]Acheson's statement before the Senate Committee on Foreign Relations, April 27, 1949, ibid. 20 (May 8, 1949): 595.

[3]"Britain, France and Germany," *Economist* 156 (January 15, 1949): 91; "Mr. Truman's Stalin," ibid. (January 22, 1949): 134.

[4]"Beware the Smile," ibid. 156 (May 14, 1949): 873; see also Donald McLachlen in *Listener*, April 28, 1949, pp. 695–96.

threat. The more tangible danger lay in the USSR's huge military structure and in the commonplace assumption that the Kremlin was constantly tempted to use it.

Through the simple commitment of U.S. power to the defense of Europe, the Atlantic Alliance promised the treaty area both peace and security. As President Truman stated in his January 1949 inaugural, "if we can make it sufficiently clear, in advance, that any armed attack affecting our national security would be met with overwhelming force, the armed attack might never occur." In his letter of transmittal to the president on April 7, Acheson explained the purpose of the North Atlantic Treaty in similar terms. "It is designed," he wrote, "to contribute to the stability and well-being of the member nations by removing the haunting sense of insecurity and enabling them to plan and work with confidence in the future." Speaking over the combined Columbia and Mutual Broadcasting systems, Acheson further assured the American people that, "if peace and security can be achieved in the North Atlantic area, we shall have gone a long way to assure peace and security in other areas as well."[5]

Arguing for the North Atlantic Treaty, Acheson assured the Senate Foreign Relations Committee that the pact, supported by U.S. military assistance, would achieve the security no longer promised by the United Nations. The secretary pointed to the national affinity of purpose between the United States and Western Europe, one based on 300 years of history as well as on common institutions and moral and ethical beliefs. When committee members pressed Acheson as to the nature of the U.S. commitment, he did not evade the question. "If you ratify this pact," he told the senators, "it cannot be said that there is no obligation to help. There is an obligation to help, but the extent, the manner, and the timing is up to the honest judgment of the parties."[6] What mattered to Acheson was the success of the Western world in building a community of strength and unity against possible Soviet aggression. The alternative, he warned, was to allow the free nations to "succumb one by one to the erosive and encroaching processes of Soviet expansion." The surest hope for peace lay in the West's ability to make it absolutely plain to the USSR that aggression would not succeed.

Senators defended the treaty with an amazing display of bipartisan enthusiasm, accepting without question Acheson's assumptions

---

[5]The North Atlantic Pact, Department of State *Bulletin* 20 (March 20, 1949): 346; Acheson's address over CBS, March 18, 1949, ibid. 20 (March 27, 1949): 384; Acheson's report on the North Atlantic Treaty, ibid. 20 (April 24, 1949): 532.

[6]*Washington Post*, April 28, 1949.

of danger and assurances of success. For Republican Homer Ferguson of Michigan, American security in a highly explosive world demanded new burdens and responsibilities. "Atomic bombs, guided missiles, jet fighters, six-engined bombers," he declared, "focused attention on the need for a global policy. And our people in self-defense have come to demand it. . . . They recognize the need for our leadership, as an expression of self-interest, in a world which contains all the potentials for its own destruction unless someone will exercise the enlightened leadership necessary to head off and prevent holocaust."[7] Not all senators were convinced. What disturbed Claude Pepper of Florida and others was not the obligation to furnish arms but the obligation to fight in Europe. Republican Robert A. Taft of Ohio, NATO's leading opponent in the Senate, explained in his book *A Foreign Policy for Americans* (1951) his decision to vote against the treaty: "I opposed that feature of the Atlantic Pact which looked toward a commitment of the United States to fight a land war on the continent of Europe and therefore opposed, except to a limited degree, the commitment of land troops to Europe. . . . Nothing is so dangerous as to commit the United States to a course which is beyond its capacity to perform with success." If the U.S. obligation to Europe was unprecedented, proponents of the pact argued that the obligation was no greater than the need. Eventually the vast majority of senators agreed; they ratified the North Atlantic Treaty on July 21, 1949, by a vote of 82 to 13.

Washington's general satisfaction over the treaty scarcely exceeded that of London, for the treaty established above all the American interest in European security. President Truman's assurance of solidarity between Europe and America, no less than his open appeal for public support behind policies of cooperation, were for Europe a matter of relief and encouragement. "Whatever causes might have led to war," declared the *Economist* on March 19, "uncertainty about America's interest in western Europe can no longer be numbered among them." Similarly, Foreign Minister Ernest Bevin declared before Parliament: "This is the first time that the United States have ever felt able to contemplate entering into commitments in peace-time for joint defense with Europe, and it is a most famous historical undertaking into which they are now entering in common with the rest of us."[8] For the *Manchester Guardian* the Atlantic Pact would serve as the dike behind which the people of Europe at last could till their fields in peace.

[7]Ferguson quoted in *Congressional Record*, 81st Cong., 1st sess., July 13, 1949, pt. 7:9362–67.
   [8]*Manchester Guardian*, March 24, 1949, p. 8.

II

From the beginning of NATO, Western Europe's defense against a land invasion from the East demanded major reliance on the U.S. lead in atomic power. Western military spokesmen agreed that in any immediate war Western land and air forces would be inadequate to protect the Eastern frontiers. The creation of adequate defenses, moreover, would take time and extensive U.S. assistance. Whereas the atomic strategy offered a formidable deterrent against a conventional attack, it could not prevent the Soviet occupation of Western Europe. For that reason Western spokesmen had little choice but to assume that the Soviet danger indeed had been exaggerated or to build defenses that would guarantee the treaty area against a land invasion.

On August 8, 1949, Acheson appeared before a Joint Hearing of the Foreign Relations and Armed Services committees to argue the administration's case for military assistance to various North Atlantic Treaty countries. In October Congress authorized a military assistance program, encouraged in part by the initial explosion of an atomic device by the USSR which terminated the American monopoly. The Mutual Defense Assistance Act of 1949 first authorized the president to furnish military assistance to members of NATO, but only to countries that had requested such aid prior to the effective date of the law. Second, the president could not distribute any of the $900 million made available for Europe before the NATO allies had integrated their defenses in the North Atlantic area. Third, the law provided that any recipient nation must have entered into an agreement with the United States that embodied certain defense obligations in exchange for military assistance. The *Washington Post* lauded this effort at rearmament on October 10: "The present armament program is nothing more or less than an attempt to put more power behind peace and freedom than the Soviet Union can bring to the support of its aggressive ventures. When that has been achieved, . . . it should be possible to negotiate with the Soviet Union on a basis favorable to the free world."

North Atlantic leaders, meeting in Paris during December 1949, accepted unanimously the recommendations of NATO's Military Committee for the integrated defense of the treaty area, and in January the North Atlantic Council approved the recommendations. Shortly thereafter Truman agreed that the recommendations satisfied the need of a common defense based on the cooperative use of military resources. The recommendations, said the president, "provide further convincing evidence of the determination of these nations to resist aggression against any of them and as a definite indication of the genuine spirit of cooperation among the Treaty members."[9] Early in 1950 Washington negotiated a series of bilateral military aid agreements with NATO members whereby the latter agreed to supplement U.S. assistance with defense programs of their own.

Still the process of building unity and strength into the Atlantic world had scarcely begun. The continuing search for security soon focused on West Germany, still potentially Western Europe's most powerful nation. As early as April 1949, Acheson had made the integration of West Germany into Europe's burgeoning security system the ultimate objective of United States defense policy. Henry A. Byroade, director of German and Austrian Affairs, informed the Southern Newspaper Publishers' Association late in October that "we are determined to do all within our capacity to bring about the assimilation of Germany into a free Europe and the assumption of cooperative responsibilities by the Germans in the European community."[10] With the establishment of the German Federal Republic in 1948, the occupation governments had continued to control Germany's military and foreign affairs as well as all of its foreign trade policies. What mattered thereafter was the extent to which Britain, France, and the United States chose to exercise their powers.

Still many Western writers and officials alike had argued against German membership in NATO. To commit West Germany to the North Atlantic Alliance, warned American critic James P. Warburg in May 1949, would not only involve the United States in the rearming of Germany but also would solidify the Eastern bloc. To arm West Germany, declared George Kennan, would create an unacceptable threat to the USSR and divide Germany permanently into a Western and Soviet sphere. Never would the Kremlin tolerate a united Germany armed and free to pursue its own destiny. British writer Kingsley Martin argued that the desire to be on good terms with Germany reflected essentially a fear of the Soviet Union. An armed Germany would contribute nothing to European security, for the only effective deterrent against Soviet expansion was the U.S. commitment to Europe's defense.[11] French leaders especially opposed German rearmament. Their demand for adequate guarantees against the rebirth of German military power had already produced a deadlock in constitution making in Bonn, the

[9]Mutual Defense Assistance Agreements, Department of State *Bulletin* 22 (February 6, 1950): 198.

[10]Acheson's address to the American Society of Newspaper Publishers, New York, April 28, 1949, ibid. 20 (May 8, 1949): 585; Byroade's address to the Southern Newspaper Publishers' Association, Mineral Wells, Texas, October 31, 1949, ibid. 21 (November 7, 1949): 702.

[11]*New Statesman and Nation*, July 30, 1949, p. 115.

West German capital. Still the arguments for German membership in NATO continued to accumulate, for West Germany lay geographically within the Western defense area. Eventually the French would accept them.

What established the necessary level of Western concern to resolve the German question was the outbreak of the Korean War. The North Korean attack on June 25, 1950 seemed to prove two basic assumptions on which NATO rested: that the USSR would probe every weak spot in the long line that separated the Communist from the non-Communist worlds and that the United States would come to the assistance of any victim of Communist-led aggression. Korea also turned containment from a matter of diplomacy into one of military reality, for its demonstrated that Western intent had fallen increasingly out of step with military strategy. No longer could the NATO countries limit their defense expenditures to what they believed they could afford; the emergency seemed clear. Still it was essential that the military requirements not be exaggerated. As the *Economist* warned, "over and over again it must be repeated that the job is not to fight and win a war—when the sky is the limit—but to prevent one—in which time is of the essence."[12] Therefore, what mattered was speed, not a complete defense system in 1953 or 1954 but an adequate defense available in six months. This timetable of military planning required a sense of urgency; in Europe that sense of urgency did not exist.

In Washington, however, the reaction to Korea was overwhelming. During July Congress, with little debate, accepted the second installment of $1 billion for North Atlantic military aid. The vote in the House was 361 to 1; in the Senate, 66 to 0. In addition, Truman requested $10 billion for an expanded American arms program. The new mobilization measure called for an increase in the U.S. Army from ten understrength divisions to eighteen full-strength divisions, with air and seapower increased in proportion. Washington planners based their new requests on the need of larger and more effective mobile striking forces, enough to demonstrate the American resolve to counter military adventuring anywhere on the globe. These preparations nevertheless did not approach the point of no return where the country accepted the inevitability of a general war.

Following their September 1950 meeting in New York, the foreign ministers of Britain, France, and the United States announced their decision to rearm Germany. The standard that they followed Byroade had marked clearly in August over CBS: "Everything we do in Germany

---

[12]"Strength with Speed," *Economist* 159 (July 8, 1950): 58; "Priorities for Containment," ibid. 159 (July 22, 1950): 154.

must be measured in terms of its effect on . . . the great and rising menace from the East." In their communiqué the ministers spelled out their intention to strengthen Western Europe through the further integration of the Federal Republic into the Atlantic community. The USSR had established large military units in its zone of occupation. Now the three allies would not only strengthen their forces in Germany but also invite German participation in an integrated Western European force. How Germany would participate in this common defense was too divisive an issue to permit an immediate decision. France completely refused to accept the creation of an independent German army, insisting instead that German contingents, limited to battalion size, be incorporated into a European army. Meanwhile, the Federal Republic regained control of its foreign affairs, with the right to establish diplomatic relations with other countries as well as increased freedom over all internal and external economic matters.[13]

III

The American response to the challenge of Soviet power after 1949 had seemed impressive indeed. Still the general trend of U.S. policy, and especially the rhetoric employed to explain and defend it, disturbed many British and American observers. Some who accepted the need of Western rearmament rejected the customary definition of the Soviet danger employed to justify it. By mid-century American officials habitually depicted the Soviet problem in ideological rather than imperialist terms. Former Ambassador to the Soviet Union Walter Bedell Smith, for example, had warned the nation in June 1949: "It is extremely important for the democracies, and especially the United States, never to lose sight of the fundamental fact that we are engaged in a constant, continuing, gruelling struggle for freedom and the American way of life that may extend over a period of many years." In time Acheson shared this view that the Soviet Union endangered American civilization itself. What made the Soviet threat so serious was less the traditional struggle for power than the Communist ideology that determined Kremlin policy. "This fanatical doctrine," he had declared in April 1950, "dominates one of the greatest states in this world, a state which, with its satellites, controls the lives of hundreds of millions of people and which today possesses the largest military establishment in existence." The

[13]Byroade's television broadcast over CBS, August 20, 1950, Department of State *Bulletin* 23 (September 11, 1950): 427; report on the foreign ministers' meeting, September 19, 1950, ibid. 23 (October 2, 1950): 530–31.

threat was especially dangerous because the Kremlin had singled out the United States as the principle target of attack, convinced that it was the productive power and vitality of this country that stood between the Soviet Union and dominion over the entire world. "We are faced with a threat," Acheson continued, "in all sober truth I say this—we are faced with a threat not only to our country but to the civilization in which we live and to the whole physical environment in which that civilization can exist."[14]

That the Soviet threat to Western security was genuine and of unprecedented magnitude few critics at mid-century would deny, but they wondered how policies of military containment, whatever their cost, could resolve a danger described largely as ideological. Even if preponderantly military, the Soviet problem appeared serious enough. To commit policies of containment to the destruction of an opposing ideology encumbered them with added burdens of fear and recalcitrance under conditions that were already both financially and intellectually demanding. The British *New Statesman and Nation* had attributed American fears of communism to the requirements of Washington politics. "One of the difficulties, indeed," ran its editorial of March 19, 1949, "is that anti-Communist propaganda has constantly to be stimulated by the American press and radio in order to overcome the traditional anti-imperialism of Americans and the American businessman's detestation of high taxation."

For some frightened Americans the struggle with the Soviet Union had become so limitless and so intense that successful coexistence no longer seemed possible. To many students of world affairs, however, such fears even in 1950 simply confused possible aggression by the Soviet Union, which few Americans or Europeans regarded a likely occurrence, with the spread of communism which advanced through social revolution and against which a military alliance was no defense. The Yugoslav defection from the Soviet bloc in 1948 had made clear that Soviet control of Communist parties did not extend beyond the reach of the Red Army. Moreover, the Communist regimes in Eastern Europe—those actually held in power by the Soviet military presence—would soon demonstrate their preferences for national, not international, concerns. If Western preparedness promised to contain the armed might of the USSR, defense against Soviet ideology lay in the overall performance of non-Communist societies. Even in the critical area of national performance, Western Europe's future seemed assured, for by mid-century that region, under impressive leadership, had entered a

---

[14]Department of State, *Strengthening the Forces of Freedom* (Washington, 1950), p. 1.

period of unprecedented internal economic expansion, stimulated and sustained in large measure by the burgeoning U.S. expenditures. Confident of American power to discourage aggression and of the capacity of their own societies to curtail the encroachments of communism, Europeans generally rejected the assumptions of danger which underlay much of the American Cold War rhetoric.

IV

Beyond creating a system of military deterrence, what was the Western buildup of power to achieve? Power is a means, not an end. If the immediate goal was security, the ultimate end could only be a negotiated settlement or war. Still official Washington was determined to avoid both latter alternatives. It was compelled, therefore, to rationalize its preoccupation with power as a temporary condition preparatory to an eventual resolution of the Cold War largely on Western terms. Early in 1950, Acheson, at the president's request, had reviewed the commitments and intentions of the United States in a series of public statements. To give the nation's defense policies the needed sense of direction, he developed the promising concept of negotiation from strength. Acheson first advanced this theme in a press conference:

> What we have . . . observed over the last few years is that the Soviet Government is highly realistic, and we have seen time after time that it can adjust itself to facts when facts exist. We have seen also that agreements reached with the Soviet Government are useful when those agreements register facts. . . . So it has been our basic policy to build situations which will extend the area of possible agreement; that is, to create strength instead of weakness which exists in many quarters. . . . Those are illustrations of the ways in which, in various parts of the world, we are trying to extend the area of possible agreement with the Soviet Union by creating situations so strong they can be recognized and out of them can grow agreement.[15]

Acheson again gave the formula precise definition in a speech at the White House on February 16. "We must realize," he said, "that the world situation is not one to which there is an easy answer. The only way to deal with the Soviet Union, we have found from hard experience, is to create situations of strength. Wherever the Soviet detects weakness or disunity—and it is quick to detect them—it exploits

---

[15]Acheson's press conference, February 8, 1950, Department of State *Bulletin* 22 (February 20, 1950): 273.

them to the full. . . . When we have reached unity and determination on the part of the free nations . . . we will be able to evolve working agreements with the Russians." The time for negotiation had not arrived. To attempt it would raise false hopes in some and fears in others. "The Russians," continued Acheson, "know that we are ready . . . to discuss with them any outstanding issue. . . . It is clear that the Russians do not want to settle those issues as long as they feel there is any possibility they can exploit them for their own objectives of world domination. It is only when they come to the conclusion that they cannot so exploit them that they will make agreements, and they will let it be known when they have reached that decision."[16] In what quickly evolved as accepted phraseology, Ambassador at Large Philip C. Jessup repeated the promise of an eventual Cold War settlement. "In the face of such an aggressive imperialist system as that of the Soviet Union," he had reminded the nation in June 1950, "there is a prerequisite to negotiation. The prerequisite is strength." When the West had created the necessary strength, negotiations would succeed.[17]

Acheson's promise of negotiation from strength followed hard on the heels of President Truman's announcement of January 31, 1950 that the administration would push the development of the hydrogen bomb. This decision, for whatever reason, exposed much of the private concern, especially among leading scientists, over the direction of American policy. Since September a group of distinguished nuclear physicists, led by J. Robert Oppenheimer, had argued in private against the hydrogen project. Professor Albert Einstein added his disapproval, warning that the effort to achieve security through the pursuit of military predominance was a "disastrous illusion." For him the arms race, based on hysteria and conducted in secrecy, had already led to the "concentration of tremendous financial power in the hands of the military, militarization of the youth, close supervision of the loyalty of the citizens, . . . intimidation of the people of independent political thinking, indoctrination of the public, . . . [and] growing restriction of the range of public information under the pressure of military secrecy." The H-bomb, if successful, would poison the atmosphere with radioactive fallout, making the annihilation of life on earth a technical possibility. Einstein saw hope only in a renunciation of violence and the creation of embryo world government.[18]

Such pressures on the administration continued through February

[16]*Strengthening the Forces of Freedom*, pp. 16, 18–19.
[17]Jessup's speech at Hamilton College, Clinton, New York, June 11, 1950, Department of State *Bulletin* 23 (July 3, 1950): 29.
[18]Quoted in "Agreement Through Strength," *Economist* 158 (February 18, 1950): 353–54.

1950. That month twelve renowned scientists requested a public assurance that the United States would never initiate a nuclear exchange. Senator Brien McMahon, chairman of the Joint Congressional Atomic Energy Committee, suggested that the Senate offer a five-year worldwide Marshall Plan, with a U.S. commitment of $50 billion, in exchange for a firm agreement on the control of atomic energy. Millard E. Tydings, chairman of the Senate Armed Services Committee, recommended on February 6 that the United States call a world disarmament conference before it embarked on an expensive, long-term dangerous arms race.[19]

This outburst of concern did not alter the established course of policy. Convinced that the balance of power had swung against the West, Truman and Acheson continued to place their emphasis on strength, not on diplomacy. Acheson's public statements after February 1950 did not rule out negotiation, but whether there would ever be an agreement depended on the behavior and intentions of the Soviet Union. What mattered, he made clear in March, was not the specific issues in conflict but the evidence that the Soviets had given up all forms of aggression—military attacks, propaganda warfare, and subversion. "If, as, and when the idea of aggression, by one means or another, can be ruled out of our relations with the Soviet Union," he said, "then the greatest single obstacle to agreement will be out of the way."[20] Serious negotiation required at the outset some assurance that all participants would honor their agreements; that assurance could not exist, argued Acheson, until the Soviets adopted a "live and let live" philosophy. Only thereafter would any free world approach, however imaginative, resolve the European conflict.

Unfortunately, international settlements hinge less on attitudes than on precise national objectives. Was the Western military establishment being expanded to negotiate a suitable division of interests in Europe or to secure the capitulation of the Soviet Union? For the Truman leadership the existing facts which divided the Continent lay totally outside the area of legitimate discussion. The president had made that clear when he declared in January 1949 that "the American people desire, and are determined to work for, a world in which all nations and all peoples are free to govern themselves as they see fit and to achieve a decent and satisfying life." That month Charles Bohlen

---

[19]For an excellent discussion of these pressures see Coral Bell, *Negotiation from Strength: A Study in the Politics of Power* (London, 1962), pp. 15–16.

[20]Acheson's address to the Harvard Alumni Association, Cambridge, June 20, 1950, Department of State *Bulletin* 23 (July 3, 1950): 16.

reminded the country that the USSR had not lived up to its international agreements in imposing its will on Eastern Europe. What separated the world, therefore, was less a conflict of interests than a conflict of principles which no agreement could bridge. Perhaps there could be settlements on practical issues but, until the Kremlin accepted Western notions regarding human rights, agreements would be no more than compromises of doubtful validity.[21]

No more than most Washington officials was Acheson prepared to use negotiations as a means of altering the facts. When the secretary, in his noted speech at Berkeley on March 16, 1950, dwelt at length on the necessary conditions for negotiation, he pointed less to Soviet designs on Western Europe and Asia than to the Soviet hegemony in Eastern Europe and the policies of obstructionism which the Kremlin pursued in the United Nations to protect that hegemony against overwhelming majority opposition. American purpose, Acheson reminded a Cambridge, Massachusetts, audience in June 1950, had been consistent; "we continue to strive," he said, "for the fulfillment of the aspirations to which we dedicated ourselves in the war. We seek . . . the advancement of the well-being of mankind." Settlements required concessions but, as Ambassador Jessup explained that month, "not concessions at the expense of principles or of the rights of others."[22] Washington had demonstrated its primary concern for religious and political change in Eastern Europe when early in 1950 it rebuked and finally broke diplomatic relations with several Iron Curtain countries.[23]

V

For many this revisionism in the American intent toward Europe reduced the area of profitable negotiation to the vanishing point. If Kennan in his July 1947 article in *Foreign Affairs* had attached the principle of containment to revisionist expectations, by 1950 he had discarded his earlier optimism regarding change in the USSR and had accepted the need of seeking some modification of the political and military structure of Europe through diplomacy. There existed the possibility, even in the Truman years, that the Cold War would gradually disappear through

[21]Bohlen's address before the New York State Bar Association, January 28, 1949, ibid. 20 (February 6, 1949): 158; The North Atlantic Pact, ibid. 20 (March 20, 1949): 346.

[22]Jessup's Hamilton College address, June 11, 1950, ibid. 23 (July 3, 1950): 26.

[23]The peace treaties with Bulgaria, Hungary, and Romania had provided that these countries take measures to guarantee human rights to their peoples. The failure of these governments to adopt democratic procedures gave Washington the needed rationale to sever relations.

the mutual acceptance of the unchanging realities of Europe without any formal settlement at all. The alternative to some agreement, whether formal or not, remained that of military competition conducted at an ever rising level of expenditure. Still the potential costs inherent in drift were scarcely a subject of public debate, for the national consensus on foreign policy had welded the emotions of fear and expectation into a single intellectual pattern. Indeed, the greater the dread of Soviet expansion among some Americans, the greater their determination to settle for nothing less than a victory for self-determination in Europe.

So reliant was Europe on American power that its official spokesmen generally refused to challenge Washington's revisionist goals. Most were content to laud the administration for its leadership in building the Western defense structure, but to Churchill, no less than to Kennan, diplomacy was as an agency for effecting change as well as for recording facts that already existed. If negotiation was the only acceptable end of power in a nuclear age, delay would serve no purpose. Churchill was convinced that the West was as strong vis-à-vis the Soviet Union in 1950 as it was likely to become. Reacting to Acheson's press conference of February 8, the prime minister, in a speech at Edinburgh a week later, raised the question of negotiation:

> It is my earnest hope that we may find our way to see more exalted and august foundation for our safety than this grim and sombre balancing power of the bomb. . . . I cannot help coming back to this idea of another talk with Soviet Russia upon the highest level. The idea appeals to me of a supreme effort to bridge the gulf between the two worlds, so that each can live their life if not in friendship, at least without the hatreds and maneuvres of the cold war. . . . It is not easy to see how things could be worsened by a parley at the summit if such a thing were possible.[24]

Shortly thereafter Churchill, with even greater urgency, put his case before the House of Commons. "Time and patience, those powerful though not infallible solvents of human difficulties," he declared, "are not necessarily on our side. . . . Therefore, while I believe there is time for a further effort for a lasting and peaceful settlement, I cannot feel that it is necessarily a long time, or that its passage will progressively improve our own security. Above all things, we must not fritter it away." Bevin defended the government by repeating Acheson's formula of negotiation from strength. The evolution of NATO, he assured the House, "will create a situation that will leave no alternative but to

---

[24]Quoted in Bell, *Negotiation from Strength*, p. 17.

negotiate and to settle once and for all this problem that has cursed the world for so long."[25]

Acheson, unlike Churchill, had assumed that in time the Western powers would outstrip the Soviet bloc in military strength. Herein lay the essential hope for the policy of negotiation from strength. It was immediately clear, however, that the Truman administration would never modify the nation's priorities to the extent that Acheson's concept of "total diplomacy" required. In Europe the Allies were even more reluctant to spend for defense. Throughout the spring of 1950, NATO's proponents in government and the press noted the slow pace of Western military preparedness. With the outbreak of the Korean War, Acheson reemphasized the need for power as the foundation of a desired settlement. On September 10 he declared over national television: "The goal for which we are struggling is to settle, so far as we can, the great issues between East and West. To settle these differences we have got to talk on equal terms. We cannot have one party very strong in terms of armament, and the other party very weak."[26] That month the secretary warned Atlantic Pact members that their military plans were far too modest to convince Congress of their good faith. Unless Europe gave convincing evidence of its intention to rearm, Congress would refuse to reinforce American troops in Europe or send additional supplies and equipment.[27]

Still the power for negotiation remained elusive. To overcome Europe's reluctance to create the fifty-division integrated defense force recommended by the NATO chiefs of staff, European leaders invited General Eisenhower to return to Europe as supreme commander of all NATO forces. It was hoped that his presence would serve as a pledge of the American commitment to Europe and give NATO the prestige and leadership required to overcome those vested interests which undermined its unity and purpose. When the Brussels meeting in December affirmed both Eisenhower's appointment and West German membership in NATO, everything practical in building Europe's defense remained to be done. At that moment Europe had ten active divisions, scarcely enough to slow a Soviet invasion, nor would that situation change markedly.

Obviously any Western negotiation with the Kremlin held greater promise of success if conducted from a position of strength. Still the *New Statesman and Nation* detected early the central fallacy in the concept: "The difficulty is that while countries dare not negotiate when they

---

[25]*H. C. Debates*, 5th series, vol. 473, col. 33, 199 seq., quoted in ibid., pp. 20–21.
[26]Quoted in *New York Times*, September 10, 1950.
[27]"Germans and Russians," *Economist* 159 (December 23, 1950): 1125–26.

are weak, they are apt not to think it worth while when they feel strong."[28] That the West lacked the will to build a predominant military structure mattered little. There would be no negotiation from strength, not because power was elusive but because the aims of Western diplomacy were unattainable. No level of preparedness would dismantle the Iron Curtain without war for the reason that the West could never establish an interest in Eastern Europe substantial enough to lend credibility to any threat of force. Washington had managed to place the nation's goals beyond Western military capabilities. Consequently, the West faced the simple choice of indefinite coexistence with the Soviet world or resort to war. Those who, in the interest of security or principle, condemned coexistence as a measure of national failure advocated either nothing or war.[29]

With no prospect of diplomatic settlement in sight, critics by 1951 feared that the American pursuit of power would become an end in itself. "Foreign policy in [Acheson's] regime," complained the *Washington Post* in April 1951, "has become merely a carbon copy of Pentagon strategy without regard to policy or principle. A military man has to think of war tomorrow, but not a diplomat." Similarly, the *New Statesman and Nation* predicted that Washington, in its search for security, would never reach the time for negotiation:

> The Americans are now arming on a scale which may make them forget that peace is the only object of arming; they have acquired, and are extending, military bases all round the world, and in their dealings with Spain, Germany and Japan are throwing to the four winds all considerations save those of strategic advantage. Any one who suggests that strength without purpose leads to war . . . are dismissed as pro-Soviet or faint-hearted or mere passengers on the gravy train of the American alliance.[30]

For most Americans in 1951, however, the pursuit of power in a divided and seemingly dangerous world still outweighed in importance the character or timing of some ultimate Cold War settlement. Negotiation from strength established the hope that the buildup of Western power would terminate at some appropriate time in a satisfactory agreement. Meanwhile, in the absence of a direct clash of interests across the Iron Curtain, neither the peace nor the stability of Europe demanded an immediate diplomatic settlement. Power in itself would not produce

---

[28] *New Statesman and Nation*, August 18, 1951, p. 170.
[29] Kennan developed this theme in a perceptive article that appeared in *New York Times*, February 25, 1951.
[30] *New Statesman and Nation*, August 18, 1951, p. 170.

change or assure the triumph of self-determination, but it could add an essential element of stability to a situation already established. Thus NATO would sustain the military division of Europe with a vengeance; it would not do more.

CHAPTER
SEVEN

Global Containment: The Truman Years*

AT MID-CENTURY that pattern of challenge and response in international affairs known as the Cold War was three years old. The fear of Soviet expansionism, incited in large measure by a powerful, if ill-defined, combination of Communist ideology and Soviet totalitarianism and power had produced a full-scale American response aimed at restricting Soviet political dominance to the regions of East-Central Europe where it then existed. American involvements in East Asia during the immediate postwar years, extensive as they were, had brought the United States into no direct conflict with Soviet purpose. The Truman Doctrine of March 1947 had announced a sweeping U.S. commitment to intervene everywhere in the world where governments might be threatened by communism regardless of the security interests involved or the prospects of success for any American effort. In practice, however, the Truman Doctrine had been limited to Greece and Turkey, and Secretary of State George C. Marshall had pointedly refused in 1948 to extend it to China. The emerging Cold War, whatever its demands on American emotions and resources, remained largely a European phenomenon.

Perhaps the comparative complacency with which Americans viewed the Far East was natural enough. For two long generations Japan had been the major, if not the exclusive, threat to a balanced and stable Orient, but the Japan of the late 1940s was an occupied nation, its military power broken. The continuing collapse of European colonialism in South and Southeast Asia threatened that region's historic stability. Power might abhor a vacuum, but to American analysts

---

*Published as "Global Containment: The Truman Years," in *Current History* 57 (August 1969): 77–83. Reprinted by permission.

165

in general even the Communist-led revolution in Indochina represented the ideal of self-determination far better than did French colonial policy. No aggressor had appeared anywhere on the scene to challenge the independence of the new Asian states, whatever their internal weakness.

China was the critical problem of the Far East. Almost from its inception the rise of Mao Zedong (Mao Tse-tung) to power in China separated Americans on matters of causation and meaning as had no previous external episode in the nation's history. Initially, even as Jiang Jieshi went down before Mao and his Chinese Communists in 1948 and 1949, the U.S. government did not recognize in this grinding transferal of power in China any threat of aggression or danger to the United States. Indeed, until 1949 Washington did not reject the possibility of establishing normal and satisfactory relations with the new regime. As Mao took control of the China mainland, the United States did not withdraw its officials from their posts. What determined all official attitudes toward the Chinese civil war was the conviction that the Chinese Communist success manifested a clear expression of self-determination, not evidence of Soviet subversion or any unusual Soviet influence. Nothing illustrated better the official American tendency to view the Communist victory as the legitimate expression of popular approval, and thus no real challenge to Asian stability or American interests, than the famous White Paper, published in August 1949. In his letter of transmittal, which prefaced the White Paper, Secretary of State Acheson explained that a policy of military intervention would have antagonized the Chinese people; he assigned the responsibility for China's problems to the Chinese themselves.[1] His denial that the United States could or should attempt to control the internal affairs of China denied also that the United States had any special security interest in the continuation of Nationalist control in China. Thus at no time did the Truman administration make any effort to apply its burgeoning containment policy to China. The country was too large, the potential financial and military burden too great. There was no possibility, moreover, of building a stable Orient through cooperation with a disunited and warring China. What mattered after 1948 was the rebuilding of a strong and friendly Japan.[2]

---

[1] U.S., Department of State, *United States Relations with China* (Washington, 1949), pp. xiv, xv. Viewing the Chinese upheaval as an indigenous conflict, many officials were prepared to accept the extension of Communist authority to Taiwan where the Nationalists were then establishing themselves as a government in exile.

[2] By 1947 the United States, through General Douglas MacArthur's leadership, had completed its basic program for redirecting Japanese society. During 1948 the program for Japan shifted to one of restoring that country so that it could contribute to

To the extent that numerous Americans and potential critics anticipated the Communist victory in China with deep regret, they regarded the new Chinese leaders as dangerous to Chinese traditions and to China's historic relations with the United States. They feared above all that Mao might slam shut the Open Door and thus deprive American scholars, missionaries, travelers, officials, and merchants of their former access to a country which for them was a region of immense charm. Even for the friends of China and of Nationalist leader Jiang, the closing of the Open Door and the subsequent mistreatment of American officials in China was not necessarily evidence of Mao's aggressive intent toward China's neighbors. Communist influence and behavior in China might be tragic, but it still comprised no threat to American security interests. Therefore, the final collapse of the Guomindang (Kuomintang), the Nationalist Chinese government, in late 1949 did not automatically bring the fear of aggression and with it the introduction of a body of Cold War attitudes, assumptions, and policies into U.S.-Far Eastern relations.

Still there existed in 1949 a marked ambivalence in American attitudes toward the impending retreat of Jiang to the island of Formosa. Some Americans recalled V. I. Lenin's alleged blueprint for expansion: "First we will take Eastern Europe, then the masses of Asia. Then we will surround America, the last citadel of capitalism." The Western world could not ignore the fact that soon 900 million people would be living under Communist-led governments. Indeed, with the collapse of Nationalist China the United States entered a period of deep intellectual crisis. What mattered during these critical months of decision was the role that American officials, editors, and political leaders—the creators of public opinion—chose to assign to the USSR in the triumph of Communist power in China. What had once appeared indigenous suddenly appeared to many in Washington as possibly the initial triumph of Soviet aggression as it moved into the Asian sphere.

Late in January 1949, John M. Cabot, U.S. consul general in

---

the stability and prosperity of the Far East. George F. Kennan, as head of the State Department's Policy Planning Staff, discussed the need for a new Japanese policy with MacArthur in Tokyo. In his *Memoirs*, Kennan concluded that his visit with the general in 1948 and the directives that finally emanated from Washington "represented in their entirety a major contribution to the change in occupation policy that was carried out in late 1948 and 1949; and I consider my part in bringing about this change to have been, after the Marshall Plan, the most significant constructive contribution I was ever able to make in government." See Kennan, *Memoirs, 1925–1950* (Boston, 1967), p. 393. For additional information on the new policy toward Japan see Shigeru Yoshida, *The Yoshida Memoirs*, trans. Kenichi Yoshida (Boston, 1962), p. 161; and Owen Lattimore, "Japan is Nobody's Ally," *Atlantic Monthly* 183 (April 1949): 54–58.

Shanghai, noted that the Chinese Communists had endorsed a Cominform communiqué which denounced Yugoslavia for its refusal to follow orders from Moscow. This suggested strongly to Cabot that Mao indeed followed the Kremlin's orders. It was to protect the Chinese people from such foreign domination, said Cabot, that the United States had furnished aid to the Nationalist government.[3] Moreover, Kennan later declared over CBS that the new Chinese leadership, whether sincere or not, was committed to unrealistic doctrines which had induced the Chinese people "to accept a disguised form of foreign rule."[4] Even Acheson's letter of transmittal in the White Paper called attention to the danger of Soviet imperialism in the Far East and reaffirmed U.S. opposition "to the subjugation of China by any foreign power, and to any regime acting in the interest of a foreign power, and to the dismemberment of China by any foreign power, whether by open or clandestine means."[5] For him to speak in his preface of Chinese subservience to a foreign power appeared totally inconsistent, for the overriding purpose of the White Paper was to reassure the American people that the collapse of the Guomindang posed no threat to this nation's security.

During July 1949, Acheson designated Ambassador Jessup to conduct an objective appraisal of Far Eastern problems and make recommendations for the formulation of an American strategy for Asia. Whereas it was quite clear that the administration would do nothing to save Jiang, Acheson, in a top-secret memorandum, instructed Jessup:

> You will please take as your assumption that it is a fundamental decision of American policy that the United States does not intend to permit further extension of communist domination on the continent of Asia or in the southeast Asia area. . . . I fully realize that when these proposals are received it may be obvious that certain parts thereof would not be within our capabilities to put into effect, but what I desire is the examination of the problem on the general assumptions indicated above in order to make absolutely certain that we are neglecting no opportunity that would be within our capabilities to achieve the purpose of halting the spread of totalitarian communism in Asia.[6]

This statement, dated two weeks prior to the release of the White Paper,

[3]Cabot's address to the American University Club, Shanghai, January 26, 1949, Department of State *Bulletin* 20 (February 13, 1949): 183.

[4]For Kennan's CBS address of August 22, 1949 see ibid. 21 (September 5, 1949): 324.

[5]See Acheson's comments on the White Paper in ibid. 21 (August 15, 1949): 236.

[6]Acheson to Jessup, July 18, 1949, Committee on Foreign Relations, *Hearings on the Nomination of Philip Jessup to be U.S. Representative to the Sixth General Assembly of the United Nations*, 82d Cong., 1st sess., 1951, p. 603.

revealed again the extent to which the U.S. government was prepared to accept the notion that Communist power in China represented Soviet expansion more than an indigenous revolution.

This was only the beginning, however. Republican congressmen, who now opened their assault on the Truman administration for its alleged loss of China, accused the chief executive of undermining U.S. security by rendering all Asia vulnerable to Soviet conquest. In their attack of August 1949, Senator Kenneth Wherry of Nebraska, joined by other Republicans, charged that the State Department's White Paper was "to a large extent a 1,054 page whitewash of a wishful, do-nothing policy which has succeeded only in placing Asia in danger of Soviet conquest with its ultimate threat to the peace of the world and our own national security."[7] If the objective of American policy was the containment of communism the world over, they said, then that policy should be applied to Asia as well as Europe by giving adequate military aid to Jiang. Similarly, Senator William F. Knowland of California declared in September 1949 that, since communism was global in character, "it did not make sense to try to keep 240,000,000 Europeans from being taken behind the Iron Curtain while we are complacent and unconcerned about 450,000,000 Chinese going the same way, when, if they should go that way, it would probably start an avalanche which would mean that a billion Asiatics would be lined up on the side of Soviet Russia and in the orbit of international communism."[8]

Stung by such charges that it was weakening the nation's security, the administration continued to search for a definition of the Asian problem. To that end, early in October it called the special Washington Roundtable Conference, attended by leading businessmen, political leaders, and scholars with a known interest in Chinese affairs, to examine the question of U.S. policy toward Communist China. In part, the discussion revolved around the question of Soviet ambitions in Asia. In November, George C. McGhee, assistant secretary for Middle Eastern, South Asian, and African Affairs, acknowledged again the official fear of Communist aggression in Asia when he declared at Chattanooga, Tennessee, that the rapidity of the Communist advance in China compelled the Soviet Union "to define the nature and extent of its influence over the Chinese Communists, and then to consolidate this vast area within the Soviet orbit."[9] That same month Foreign Service officer Karl Lott Rankin warned from Hong Kong that Communist China, through

---

[7]*Congressional Record*, 81st Cong., 1st sess., August 22, 1949, pt. 15: A5451-53.

[8]Knowland's statement in *Congressional Record*, 81st Cong., 1st sess., September 9, 1949, pt. 10:12,755, 12,758.

[9]McGhee's Chattanooga speech, November 19, 1949, Department of State *Bulletin* 21 (November 28, 1949): 826.

subversion, would attempt to extend its influence through South and Southeast Asia. "Now that communist control of China proper is all but assured," wrote Rankin, "it may be taken for granted that efforts will be redoubled to place communist regimes in power elsewhere in Asia. . . . China may be considered weak and backward by Western standards, but . . . in Eastern terms, communist China is a great power, economically, militarily, and politically. Supported by communist dynamism, China might well be able to dominate not only Indochina, Siam, and Burma, but eventually the Philippines, Indonesia, Pakistan, and India itself."[10]

These conflicting trends in official American thought—one accepting the indigenous, non-Soviet nature of the Chinese revolution, the other detecting Moscow's burgeoning influence in Chinese and Asian affairs—collided in Acheson's noted speech before the National Press Club on January 12, 1950. The secretary explained the fall of Jiang Jieshi in terms of an indigenous revolution: "What has happened . . . is that the almost inexhaustible patience of the Chinese people in their misery ended. They did not bother to overthrow this government. There was really nothing to overthrow. They simply ignored it. . . . They completely withdrew their support from this government, and when that support was withdrawn, the whole military establishment disintegrated."[11] Again Acheson assured the nation that the Communist victory in China did not constitute a threat to the rest of Asia. He pointedly eliminated South Korea, Formosa (now Taiwan), and Southeast Asia from the U.S. defense perimeter.

At the same time Acheson recognized a powerful Soviet encroachment on China: "The attitude and interest of the Russians in north China, and in these other areas as well, long antedates communism. . . . But the Communist regime has added new methods, new skills, and new concepts to the thrust of Russian imperialism. These Communistic concepts and techniques have armed Russian imperialism with a new and most insidious weapon of penetration." Acheson pointed out that through such techniques the Soviets possibly had detached several northern provinces of China—Manchuria, Inner Mongolia, Outer Mongolia, and Xinjiang (Sinkiang)—and had added them to the USSR. "The consequences of this Russian . . . action in China," warned Acheson, "are perfectly enormous. They are saddling all those in China who are proclaiming their loyalty to Moscow, with the most awful responsibility which they must pay for. Furthermore, these actions of the

---

[10]Karl Lott Rankin, *China Assignment* (Seattle, 1964), pp. 35–36.
[11]Acheson's National Press Club speech, Department of State *Bulletin* 22 (January 23, 1950): 113–14.

Russians are making plainer than any speech, or any utterance, or any legislation can make throughout all of Asia, what the true purposes of the Soviet Union are and what the true function of communism as an agent of Russian imperialism is."[12]

That the Chinese had indeed become puppets of the Moscow Politburo appeared to pass beyond any shadow of doubt when in February 1950 the world read the terms of the new Sino-Soviet Treaty of Friendship, Alliance and Mutual Assistance. By its terms the Soviets promised China considerable financial and technical aid. Acheson admitted that the Chinese people might welcome such promises, but, he added, "they will not fail, in time, to see where they fall short of China's real needs and desires. And they will wonder about the points upon which the agreements remain silent." He warned the Chinese that whatever China's internal development, they would bring grave trouble on themselves and the rest of Asia "if they are led by their new rulers into aggressive or subversive adventures beyond their borders."[13]

II

This concept of a single conspiracy, global in its pretensions and centering in Moscow, had not won universal acceptance. Indeed, many American scholars at mid-century rejected the notion completely. Walter Lippmann, speaking before the Chicago Council on Foreign Relations on February 22, 1950, reminded his audience that "while it is true that we have lost our power and for the time being most of our influence in China, it by no means follows that Russia has won control of China or has achieved an enduring alliance with China." Most American writers on Far Eastern subjects agreed with Acheson's warning of January that the United States should not introduce the use of military force into Asia. The final Communist victory in China, however, added to the interpretation of the Sino-Soviet Pact which official Washington ascribed to that document, propelled the administration logically toward the extension of the containment principle to the Far East. By March the Chinese revolution alone seemed sufficient to demonstrate Soviet expansionist tendencies toward Asia.

Acheson took the lead in defining the new challenge to Asia and in formulating the requirements of American policy in the Far East. When China appeared to be achieving true national independence, he told the Commonwealth Club of California, its leaders were forcing it

[12]Ibid., p. 115.
[13]Acheson's address before the Commonwealth Club of California, San Francisco, March 15, 1950, ibid. 22 (March 27, 1950): 468.

into the Soviet orbit. "We now face the prospect," he admitted, "that the Communists may attempt to apply another familiar tactic and use China as a base for probing for other weak spots which they can move into and exploit." He warned the people of Asia that they "must face the fact that today the major threat to their freedom and to their social and economic progress is the attempted penetration of Asia by Soviet-Communist imperialism and by the colonialism which it contains."[14] To meet this challenge of Communist aggression in Asia, Acheson stressed the importance of President Truman's new program of military and economic aid to the free nations—Japan, Korea, the Philippines, Indonesia, and Thailand—along the Chinese periphery. Whatever the limits of prudent action, Acheson assured his listeners that the nation would extend the kind of aid that appeared most appropriate to protect the independence of the weak Asian states. The secretary announced the special assignment of R. Allen Griffin, formerly deputy head of the China Economic Cooperation Administration mission, to Southeast Asia to discover, through special surveys, the nature of those projects which might meet the immediate needs of containment. Nevertheless, the purpose of U.S. policy in Asia, Acheson insisted, was not merely to halt the spread of communism but rather "to make possible a world in which all peoples, including the people of Asia, can work in their own way toward a better life."

American officials in Asia joined the secretary in giving form and unity to this burgeoning concept of containment. Ambassador Loy Henderson admitted before the Indian Council of World Affairs that the United States, with its long tradition of involvement in the Atlantic world, understood better the culture of Europe than that of Asia. Recent events in Asia, however, had given the American people a new and enlarging interest in the region. "It should be borne in mind, in considering various policies of the United States in respect to Asia," he said, "that the United States does not pursue one set of policies with regard to the Americas or Europe and another with regard to Asia. The foreign policies of the United States by force of circumstances have become global in character."[15] Henceforth, the United States would approach the problems of Asia on the basis of the established policies of containment.

Upon his return to the United States, Ambassador Jessup addressed the nation in April 1950. Again he cited the requirements for a larger and more pervading policy to stem the tide of aggression

[14]Ibid., pp. 469–72; see also Dean Acheson, "New Era in Asia," *Vital Speeches of the Day* 16 (April 10, 1950): 356–57.
[15]Henderson's speech at New Delhi, March 27, 1950, Department of State *Bulletin* 22 (April 10, 1950): 562.

in Asia: "There is no need for me to tell you that what is going on in Asia is of tremendous importance to the United States. I think most Americans realize that Asia is important not only because Soviet communism is clearly out to capture and colonize the continent. . . . Asia is important . . . because a great continent and great peoples are anxious to build not only a free but also an abundant society." Jessup reported an Asian continent in turmoil, with tension, fear, disorder, and poverty. These were weaknesses, he warned, on which communism thrived, and Communist pressure was especially strong in those Asian nations bordering China as well as among the Chinese minorities scattered throughout Southeast Asia, the latter of which were subject to Chinese propaganda and blackmail. Everywhere, Jessup informed the nation, Asians relied on the United States to defend their independence.[16] To help these nations achieve stability in the face of subversive and guerrilla activity, the United States should supply them with both small quantities of highly selected military equipment and a program of technical cooperation.

During the spring of 1950 the Truman-Acheson leadership pushed the concept of containment, still anchored to programs of economic and military aid, beyond the realm of mere conceptualization. The administration adopted limited programs of technical assistance for such Asian nations as Indonesia, the Republic of China on Taiwan, and Korea. It shipped military aid to Korea and the Philippines to help them dispose of pressures against their political integrity, while insisting that Japan had progressed to the point where that nation should regain responsibility for managing its own affairs. Addressing Congress in June on the subject of military assistance, President Truman made it clear that American security hinged on the containment of Communist expansion in Asia. Military aid, he admitted, would not permit the same precise results in Asia that it had achieved in Europe. Still such aid, where it could be used effectively, was now essential to protect Asian and American security. "The interests of the United States are global in character," Acheson repeated. "A threat to the peace of the world anywhere is a threat to our security."[17]

III

Much of the fear of further Soviet aggression centered on Indochina where the French continued to fight for their Asian Empire against the determined opposition of Ho Chi Minh. The United States had once

---

[16]Jessup's ABC address, April 13, 1950, ibid. 22 (April 24, 1950): 627.
[17]Truman's message to Congress, June 1, 1950, ibid. 22 (June 12, 1950): 938–40. Quotation is from Acheson's statement of June 2, ibid., p. 944.

supported Ho outright and as late as 1946 had revealed no official interest in his defeat. Within the context of the expanding concept of containment, however, the fact that Ho was a Marxist and Moscow-trained made him sufficiently suspect as an agent of Soviet imperialism to bring the full weight of U.S. policy against him. What embarrassed American leadership, however, was the French reluctance to grant the region its independence. In December 1947, Bullitt had argued con-vincingly that the French had permitted Communists to capture the Indochinese struggle for independence. Not one Annamite in one hundred was a Communist, he insisted, but all wanted their indepen-dence. To achieve independence they had no choice, under French policy, but to fight under Ho. If this continued, predicted Bullitt, the result would be disastrous. "Since Viet Nam is the extension of South China," he wrote, "Communist control of Viet Nam would add another finger to the hand that Stalin is closing around China." What French policy required was the cooperation of Indochinese nationalism. The two forces, fighting together for the genuine independence of the region, would soon eliminate the Communists. By promising the Indochinese people their ultimate independence and making clear their determi-nation to keep the country out of the hands of Soviet agents, Bullitt predicted, the French would turn Indochinese nationalism loose on the Communists and secure an easy victory for self-determination.[18]

By the Élysée Agreements of March 1949, the French government had promised independence to Indochina. As spokesman for the new state of Vietnam, it selected Bao Dai, whom Bullitt had recommended to French officials in Paris. The United States accepted Bao Dai with enthusiasm, for here was the Nationalist answer to Ho Chi Minh. In June the State Department welcomed the creation of the new state and expressed the hope that the March agreements would "serve to hasten the reestablishment of peace in that country and the attainment of Viet Nam's rightful place in the family of nations."[19] Meanwhile, the French,

[18]William C. Bullitt, "The Saddest War," *Life* 23 (December 29, 1947): 64–69.

[19]For the Élysée Agreements of March 8,1949 see Gareth Porter, ed., *Vietnam: The Definitive Documentation of Human Decisions* (Stanfordville, NY, 1979), 1:184–85. For the statement on the formation of the new state of Vietnam see Acting Secretary of State to Certain Diplomatic and Consular Officers Abroad, June 14, 1949, *FRUS, 1949* (Wash-ington, 1975), 7:54. Actually American doubts regarding French policy were profound. See Theodore C. Achilles to John D. Hickerson, March 25, 1949, in Porter, *Vietnam*, pp. 194–95; and memorandum by the Department of State to the French Foreign Office, June 6, 1949, *FRUS, 1949*, 7:39–45. This memorandum was so critical of French policy that the American ambassador in Paris, David Bruce, advised that it not be delivered to the French government. See Bruce to Acheson, June 13, 1949, ibid., pp. 45–46; and Bruce to Acheson, June 29, 1949, ibid., pp. 65–66. Despite official doubts in Washington, the U.S. government could find no alternative to continued support for Bao Dai and French policy in Indochina.

conscious of the growing American fear of Communist power in Asia, now insisted that they were fighting for Western security in the Far East and therefore deserved U.S. military aid. Only the refusal of the French National Assembly to ratify the Élysée Agreements stalled the final French request for U.S. military support in Asia.

The events of January and February 1950 finally rendered Ho Chi Minh a mortal enemy of the United States. On January 14, to meet the challenge of Bao Dai and French policy, Ho declared the establishment of the Democratic Republic of Vietnam, under his control, as the only lawful government representative of the Vietnamese people. At the same time, he announced that his nation would "consolidate her friendly relations with the Soviet Union, China and other People's Democracies, actively to support the national liberation movements of colonial and semi-colonial countries." Before the end of the month both China and the USSR had recognized the Democratic Republic. In Moscow, *Pravda* followed the Soviet decision with an editorial that not only accused the French of supporting a puppet regime in Vietnam but also the United States for attempting to make Indochina "a base for aggression directed against people's democratic China, against the national liberation movement of the Asiatic peoples." In a press release Acheson declared that the Soviet recognition of Ho's Democratic Republic revealed Ho "in his true color as the mortal enemy of national independence in Indochina."[20]

Meanwhile, the French Assembly ratified the agreements which established the new State of Vietnam, the Kingdom of Laos, and the Kingdom of Cambodia as independent states within the French Union. On February 6, Ambassador Jessup declared in Singapore that the United States would view any armed Communist aggression against the new states of Indochina as a matter of grave concern. On the following day the United States and Britain extended de jure recognition to the Associated States of Laos, Vietnam, and Cambodia and sent a note of congratulations to Bao Dai, chief of the new Vietnam state. The notion that Bao Dai had better claims to Vietnamese leadership than Ho and that he would ultimately triumph became official doctrine in Washington. Ambassador Henderson expressed the new American faith when he said:

> The United States is convinced that the Bao Dai Government of
> Viet Nam reflects more accurately than any rival claimants to
> power in Viet Nam the nationalist aspirations of the people of that

[20]Acheson's statement on the Soviet recognition of the Democratic Republic of Vietnam, February 1, 1950, Department of State *Bulletin* 22 (February 13, 1950): 244.

country. It hopes by its policies with regard to Viet Nam, to
contribute to the peaceful progress of Vietnamese people toward
the realization of the fruits of self-government. . . . My government
is convinced that any movement headed by a Moscow-recognized
Communist such as Ho Chi Minh must be in the direction of
subservience to a foreign state, not in that of independence and
self-government.[21]

Nevertheless, it was apparent that Bao Dai's efforts had produced no
defectors among the Vietminh. Jessup admitted in April that Ho, still
capitalizing on the Nationalist, anti-French sentiment of the people,
controlled most of the North although he had no capitol or regular
government.[22]

In Indochina the United States faced a dilemma which belied its
stated faith in either Bao Dai or the French. To give military aid to
the French would lend additional credence to the charge that this
nation's policy in Asia was primarily military and strategic, with little
or no genuine concern for the political advancement of the Vietnamese
people. To channel aid to the government in Saigon, with Bao Dai
spending his time at Dalat far removed from the activities of his government, gave no promise at all of effective utilization. Asia generally
refused to recognize him. Finally, on May 8, 1950, Acheson, with French
Foreign Minister Robert Schuman, negotiated an arrangement whereby
France and the governments of Indochina together would carry the
responsibility for Indochinese security and development; American aid
would simply contribute to that objective. Again the motives of containment were clear. "The United States Government," wrote Acheson,
"convinced that neither national independence nor democratic evolution exist in any area dominated by Soviet imperialism, considers the
situation to be such as to warrant its according economic aid and
military equipment to the Associated States of Indochina and to France
in order to assist them in restoring stability and permitting these states
to pursue their peaceful and democratic development."[23] In defending
the president's request to Congress for military assistance funds in June,
Acheson acknowledged the nation's determination "to preserve the
freedom and integrity of Indochina from the Communist forces of Ho
Chi Minh."[24] In December 1950 the United States would sign a Mutual

[21]Henderson in ibid. 22 (April 10, 1950): 565.
[22]Jessup in ibid. 22 (April 24, 1950): 627.
[23]Acheson's statement on Indochina, issued in Paris, May 8, 1950, ibid. 22 (May 22, 1950): 821.
[24]Acheson's statement before the Senate Foreign Relations and Armed Services committees, June 2, 1950, ibid. 22 (June 12, 1950): 944.

Defense Assistance Agreement with France, Vietnam, Cambodia, and Laos for indirect military aid to the three states of Indochina.

Unfortunately, the U.S. policy of opposition to Ho Chi Minh demanded the full cooperation of France in Southeast Asia, yet the French involvement in Vietnamese affairs would always undermine the Nationalist appeal of any regime that France supported in direct proportion to its military successes. Whatever this nation's purpose, its identification with French policy placed it, in Asian eyes, on the side of colonialism. John Cady, formerly head of the State Department's research branch for South Asia, saw the dilemma clearly. "While admitting the risks involved in offering major political concessions to Ho Chi Minh," he wrote, "one must recognize also the greater perils involved in supporting the French-sponsored regime, for such policy would . . . stimulate distrust of the United States on the part of the very peoples of Southern Asia whom the policy of containment of Chinese Communism is supposed to benefit." Similarly, Raymond Fosdick challenged the trend of U.S. policy toward military and economic containment in Asia: "[I]t is our revolution with which American sympathies and creative capacity ought now to be actively identified. Instead of that, communism has moved in to take the initiative away from us. . . . [W]e find ourselves in the unhappy position of seeming to oppose some of the objectives of the revolution which . . . should have our complete understanding and support."[25]

IV

Late in June 1950 the Asian containment policies of the United States required a commitment of ground forces to prevent a Communist-led country from erasing its boundary with a non-Communist neighbor. Within the context of the recent conceptualization of Communist aggression in Asia, the rationale for American involvement in Korea was clear enough. The immediate concern of the Truman administration was the defense of a small Asian nation against external aggression. The people of South Korea, the administration insisted, had the right to choose their own form of government. For months U.S. officials had praised the achievements of South Korean President Syngman Rhee. For the Communist North Koreans this experiment in human freedom had to be terminated, but more than the independence of South Korea was at stake. To the Truman administration the North Korean invasion

[25]John Cady, "Challenge in Southeast Asia," *Far Eastern Survey* 19 (February 8, 1950): 27; Raymond B. Fosdick, "Asia's Challenge to Us—Ideas, not Guns," *New York Times Magazine*, February 12, 1950, p. 41.

of South Korea was proof of Soviet imperialistic designs on Asia. "The attack upon the Republic of Korea," said the president on July 19, "makes it plain beyond all doubt that the international Communist movement is prepared to use armed invasion to conquer independent nations. We must, therefore, recognize the possibility that armed aggression may take place in other areas."[26] Similarly, State Department adviser John Foster Dulles assured the nation that the North Koreans did not attack "purely on their own but as part of the world strategy of international communism."[27]

For Washington the challenge was obvious: if the United States failed to repel this invasion, Communist aggression would conquer one nation after another until it would render a third world war inevitable. The United States was fighting not only the age-old struggle for freedom but also those tendencies that endangered the peace of the world. "If the history of the 1930's teaches us anything," the president warned, "it is that appeasement of dictators is the sure road to world war. If aggression were allowed to succeed in Korea, it would be an open invitation to new acts of aggression elsewhere."[28] Thus official U.S. rhetoric quickly elevated the contest for Korea to the level of a preventive war. On the success of American policy hinged the territorial status quo throughout Asia. To meet this challenge of Soviet aggression, Truman ordered the U.S. Seventh Fleet to defend the island of Taiwan and accelerated military assistance to Indochina and the Philippines. The attack on the Republic of Korea, the president warned Europeans as well as Asians, made it essential that all the free nations increase and unify their common strength to deter potential aggression. In Korea itself, however, the actual U.S. response had little relationship to the notion that the Communist threat was overwhelming and global, for the Truman administration assumed that, with a limited military commitment, it could localize the war in Korea and resolve the contest of power there. Indeed, at the level of strategy it regarded the danger so minimal that it adopted and pursued President Rhee's goal of the reunification of Korea under a non-Communist government. From the beginning of the Korean War, there was little relationship between the declared ends of policy—to keep all of Asia out of Soviet hands—and the means which the nation intended to employ.

American officials, in attributing the Korean War to Soviet imperialism, placed enormous faith in the Chinese refusal to become involved, with the hope that this would demonstrate China's ability to withstand

[26]Truman's statement of July 19, 1950, Department of State *Bulletin* 23 (July 31, 1950): 165.

[27]Dulles's CBS interview of July 1, 1950, ibid. 23 (July 10, 1950): 49.

[28]Truman's radio address, September 1, 1950, ibid. 23 (September 11, 1950): 407.

the demands of the Kremlin. Acheson revealed his confidence in the good judgment and resistance of the Chinese nation. For the Chinese to enter the war, he said, would be sheer madness. "And since there is nothing in it for them," he added, "I don't see why they should yield to what is undoubtedly pressures from the Communist movement to get into the Korean row."[29] Similarly, Senator Tom Connally, chairman of the Foreign Relations Committee, pointed to the logic of Chinese abstinence from involvement in the Korean War: Mao Zedong "must know all about Russian ambitions in the Far East. He must know the master planners in the Kremlin would like to dismember his country. He must know it would be folly for China to yield to Communist pressures and go to war against the free countries which have always been friends of the Chinese people."[30]

At Wake Island in October 1950, General Douglas MacArthur assured Truman that China would not enter the Korean War. Such expressions of hope proved to be a poor prediction of the future, but they explain why the Chinese advance across the Yalu in November produced a traumatic reaction among Washington officials. The Chinese action seemed to demonstrate at last not only Chinese irrationality but also the absolute control that Moscow had gained over China and its external policies. This new situation, noted Acheson in a Washington broadcast, created a situation of unprecedented danger. The international Communist movement, it was now clear, gave the USSR both its fundamental design and its fantastic power. "All governments which are now free and all responsible citizens of free societies," Acheson warned, "must face, with a sense of urgency, the capabilities for conquest and destruction in the hands of the rulers of the Soviet Union."[31] If the new attack in Korea were successful, ran a White House press release in December, "we can expect it to spread through Asia and Europe to this hemisphere. We are fighting in Korea for our own national security and survival." With the Soviets in control of China, where would aggression end?

It was left for Dean Rusk, assistant secretary of state for Far Eastern Affairs, and Dulles, consultant to the secretary of state, to carry the fears of Soviet aggression in the Far East to their ultimate conceptualization. As top spokesmen for the State Department, they both accepted without question the existence of a monolithic Communist

[29]Acheson, CBS television interview, September 10, 1950, ibid. 23 (September 18, 1950): 463.

[30]Connally's address to the Senate, September 22, 1950, ibid. 23 (October 9, 1950): 565.

[31]Acheson's broadcast from Washington, November 29, 1950, ibid. 23 (December 11, 1950): 964.

enemy, with its center in Moscow, promoting what Stalin had once called the amalgamation of all Asia under Soviet power. Stalin, from his studies of Leninism, observed Dulles, had seen the possibility of weakening the West mortally through "the revolutionary alliance with the liberation movement of the colonies and dependent countries against imperialism." To achieve the transformation of the revolutionary liberation movement of Asia into a reserve of the revolutionary proletariat of the Soviet Union required a two-phased program. In the initial phase, Dulles contended, the USSR would "whip up and support the nationalist aspirations of the people so that they will rebel against their colonial rulers." Before that aroused nationalism might become a barrier to amalgamation, the Soviets would embark on the second phase of their program in which they would war successfully against those revolutionaries who preferred to maintain their national insularity and thus assure "the subsequent amalgamation of all nations." Actually the liquidation of colonialism had proceeded so rapidly that Soviet communism, Dulles warned, was already rushing into its second phase to break down the drive for national independence in Asia before it became an obstruction to the planned transfer of this region into the Soviet orbit.[32] Rusk, speaking in February 1951, acknowledged this Soviet assault on Asian nationalism when he said that "communism has appeared in Asia not as a Russian preaching the tyranny of the Kremlin but as an Asian preaching nationalism and promising Utopia."[33] Such analyses transformed nationalism as a legitimate quest for self-determination into a fraudulent device for Soviet expansion.

To achieve its ultimate success in Asia, Dulles and Rusk agreed, the Soviet Communist program first required the amalgamation of China's millions. "To this end," Dulles informed a New York audience in May 1951, "a Chinese Communist Party was formed under the guiding direction of the Russian, Borodin. That Party, Soviet Russia has nurtured until it has matured into today's regime of Mao Tse-tung which serves as the instrument of Soviet communism." Certainly, he concluded, the Soviet government would not have paid so great a price to bring the Chinese Communists to power unless thereby it intended to serve the Soviet interest. "By the test of conception, birth, nurture, and obedience the Mao Tse-tung regime is a creature of the Moscow Politburo, and it is in behalf of Moscow, not of China, that it is destroying the friendship of the Chinese people toward the United States." Ostensibly, the Chinese Communists had whipped up anti-American

[32]Dulles's statement at the United Nations, November 21, 1950, ibid. 23 (December 4, 1950): 908–09.
[33]Rusk's Philadelphia address, February 9, 1951, ibid. 24 (February 19, 1951): 297.

sentiment in the interest of national independence, but actually, Dulles informed his listeners, the hysteria was merely the front behind which the Chinese people were "being betrayed into amalgamation with the mass which serves Moscow."[34]

This pattern of Soviet conquest now appeared equally clear else-where in Asia. Disturbances throughout the Pacific and Asian area, from the war in Korea to the activities of the Communist-controlled U.S. maritime unions, said Dulles, were "part of a single pattern . . . of violence planned and plotted for 25 years and finally brought to a consummation of fighting and disorder in the whole vast area extending from Korea down through China into Indochina, Malaya, the Phil-ippines, and west into Tibet and the borders of Burma, India, and Pakistan."[35] Moreover, Rusk noted that the year 1950 had marked a new phase in the Soviet Union's aggressive policy: "First it has clearly shown that it is prepared to wage war by satellites so far as that becomes desirable to further its objective—not only wars by small satellites such as the North Koreans, but full-fledged war by Communist China, a major satellite. Second, the Soviet Union has shown that it is itself prepared to risk a general war and that it is pushing its program to the brink of a general war."[36]

During 1951 much of the official American concern focused on Southeast Asia where, according to Rusk in November, the real issue was whether the people of Indochina would be permitted to work out their own future or "whether they will be subjected to a Communist reign of terror and be absorbed by force into the new colonialism of a Soviet Communist empire."[37] Meanwhile, the French, increasingly hard pressed in Indochina, supported their claims to additional U.S. aid by insisting that they were as much involved in fighting international communism there as was the United States in Korea.[38] The Truman administration therefore strengthened its Asian containment policy with a new Japanese treaty designed to rebuild Japan into a strong nation; new alliances with the Philippines, Australia, and New Zealand; and larger commitments of military aid for the French and the Associated States of Indochina as they carried the chief burden of containment in Southeast Asia.

With the outbreak of the Korean War, Washington officials pushed

[34]Dulles's address in New York, May 18, 1951, ibid. 24 (May 28, 1951): 844.

[35]Dulles's speech before the Philadelphia *Evening Bulletin* forum, March 14, 1951, ibid. 24 (March 26, 1951): 484.

[36]Rusk, "The Strategy of Freedom in Asia," Philadelphia, February 9, 1951, ibid. 24 (February 19, 1951): 295.

[37]Rusk's speech at Seattle, November 6, 1951, ibid. 25 (November 19, 1951): 823.

[38]Jacques Soustelle argued the French case effectively in "Korea and Indochina: One Front," *Foreign Affairs* 29 (October 1950): 56–66.

U.S. rearmament in Europe and Asia toward a new state of urgency under the assumption that the non-Soviet world had entered a period of great peril and had but a short time to prepare before the enemy reached the peak of its power. In the president's budget message of 1951, military aid became an established policy of the United States. The Mutual Security Act, adopted that year, implied that thereafter economic aid would be used primarily to expand the military base of the recipient countries. During 1952 military assistance to Asia grew in importance relative to Europe. The bulk of the military aid channeled into Asia went to four countries regarded especially vulnerable to Soviet-Chinese aggression: the Republic of China on Taiwan, the Republic of Korea, the Republic of Vietnam, and Japan. In Korea, the United States supported one of the largest non-Communist armies in the world at a cost of almost $1 billion per year. In Indochina, the United States eventually underwrote 80 percent of the financial cost of the French effort.

That the globalization of containment would produce diminishing returns was evident even as the policy unfolded. Containment in Europe had promised success because the threat was purely military: the danger of a Red Army marching westward. The region guaranteed by NATO, moreover, comprised the seat of an ancient civilization with a tradition of political, economic, and military efficiency. In Asia and the Middle East, the danger was less that of marching armies than of guerrilla warfare and subversion. This reduced containment to a matter of political, not military, effectiveness, for no government that failed to establish a broad governing base would long remain in power whatever moral and physical support it received from the United States. Even as a venture in power, containment in Asia was prejudiced from the start. Unlike the nations of Europe, the Asian nations lacked the skilled manpower and industrial bases to develop self-sustaining military strength. Whereas the military structures of such countries would never be strong enough to resist aggression, they would always exceed in cost what the Asian economies could support. Thus they threatened the United States with an endless financial drain without contributing much useful defense.

It was essentially the absence of political stability that rendered the borderlands along the Asian periphery of the Soviet Union and China an unfortunate area in which to establish the barriers against Communist expansion. Such an effort at containment, warned Lippmann, would compel the United States to stake its policies

> upon satellites, puppets, clients, agents about whom we know very little. Frequently they will act . . . on their own judgments, presenting us with accomplished facts that we did not intend, and

with crises for which we are unready. The 'unassailable barriers' will present us with an unending series of insoluble dilemmas. We shall have either to disown our puppets, which would be tantamount to appeasement and defeat and the loss of face, or must support them at an incalculable cost on an unintended, unforeseen and perhaps undesirable issue.[39]

From such dilemmas there would be no escape, for through the critical years from 1949 to 1951 U.S. officials had created an image of Asia which would not die, an image calculated to introduce the element of fear on a massive scale into the American conceptualization of the challenges that the United States faced. Global containment, responding to the challenge of an insatiable Soviet-based Communist monolith, elevated every Communist-led maneuver to first-level importance even where U.S. security interests were unclear and strategic conditions unfavorable. The policy would ultimately exact its toll in costly military involvements and a deeply divided nation.

[39]Walter Lippmann, *The Cold War* (New York, 1947), p. 16.

CHAPTER EIGHT

Eisenhower and the New Isolationism*

THE TERM "new isolationism" refers to that powerful body of American opinion, lodged predominantly in the Republican party, which proclaimed that the Truman foreign policies, as they evolved between 1947 and 1952, were at once overdemanding of the country's resources and less than effective abroad. Even as those policies drained the federal treasury and imposed unprecedented obligations on the United States in Europe, they did not, declared Republican critics, assure the deflation of the Soviet hegemony in Eastern Europe or a certain defense against possible Soviet expansion. Nor had the Truman policies prevented the alleged American failure in China or the Korean War, rendered dangerous by China's entry in late 1950. It was left for Wisconsin Senator Joseph R. McCarthy to attribute the "loss" of China to Mao Zedong and the frustrations of the Korean War, not to Democratic incompetence but to Democratic disloyalty, suggesting that new patriotic leadership could easily set things right in the Far East. Most of the Republican Old Guard fell into line behind McCarthy because he filled the party's needs of the moment. The burgeoning new isolationism swept Republican nominee Dwight D. Eisenhower toward the adoption of its assumptions and expectations for a more successful, and less costly, national performance abroad. As president, he faced the task of creating a body of foreign policy that would achieve his campaign promises of liberating both Eastern Europe and China, terminating the Korean War successfully, and achieving the essential budgetary restraints.

*Published in *The New Isolationism: A Study in Politics and Foreign Policy Since 1950* (New York, 1956). Reprinted by permission.

Eisenhower learned at least one notable lesson from the rough-and-tumble politics of the previous administration: partisanship can have a destructive effect on the nation's foreign relations. He appeared determined to avoid the political attacks on his administration which had helped to weaken the leadership of Truman and which subsided only with the 1952 election. In keeping with this purpose, Eisenhower, in his first State of the Union message, called for a policy developed between the executive and Congress "in the spirit of true bipartisanship."[1] Perhaps he had no alternative. Despite his enormous personal triumph that year, Eisenhower was not assured enough Republican support for any sustained foreign policy; the Republican majority was very narrow. Even more significant were the apparent differences of opinion toward Europe and Asia between the new president and the powerful neoisolationist wing of the Republican party. The Old Guard element comprised about two-thirds of the party membership in both houses of Congress. Without Democratic votes it seemed doubtful if the new administration could carry out any realistic foreign policy program at all. Republican Congressman John M. Vorys of Ohio observed that the Republicans were not like-minded or disciplined enough to "jam through foreign policy measures on a party responsibility basis, even under the lead of President Eisenhower."[2]

During his campaign Eisenhower had endorsed all the extreme demands of the Republican Old Guard toward Eastern Europe, China, and Korea. Still his overwhelming victory indicated that millions of Americans who voted for him never questioned his devotion to the basic Truman policies. The congressional elections brought the most significant victories to those who favored the established Cold War policies of the Truman years. Only two Republican senators, Irving Ives of New York and John Sherman Cooper of Kentucky, ran conspicuously ahead of Eisenhower, and both were well-known moderates. Such neoisolationists as McCarthy and William Jenner of Indiana ran far behind him, while others like James P. Kem of Missouri, Harry P. Cain of Washington, and Zales N. Ecton of Montana were defeated. Eisenhower's initial foreign policy appointments gave evidence of his personal adherence to past policy. They included Henry Cabot Lodge to the United Nations; James B. Conant, former president of Harvard University, to Germany; and Charles Bohlen to the USSR. Furthermore, Eisenhower and Secretary of State John Foster Dulles included key Democrats in their early foreign policy conferences.

[1]Eisenhower's State of the Union message, February 2, 1953, *Newsweek*, February 9, 1953, p. 17.
[2]John M. Vorys, "Party Responsibility for Foreign Policy," *The Annals of the American Academy of Political and Social Science* 289 (September 1953): 171.

Democratic leaders pledged their support of the new administration, as did both Truman and defeated Democratic candidate Adlai E. Stevenson. Richard B. Russell of Georgia, key Democratic spokesman in the Senate, declared: "My disposition is to try to help General Eisenhower in every possible way. Our big objective now is world peace and times are too perilous to indulge in partisanship for the sake of partisanship." Such Democratic declarations of purpose gave evidence of innumerable opportunities for cementing strong bipartisan relationships under the Eisenhower administration that would be reminiscent of the Truman-Vandenberg alliance. Only a policy that directly or indirectly flogged previous Democratic administrations or shifted the emphasis of U.S. action from Europe to Asia through a blockade of the China coast or the bombing of Manchurian bases would meet the determined opposition of congressional Democrats. Eisenhower's personal spirit of goodwill convinced many observers that he would destroy completely all previous American animosity over foreign policy and reunite the nation again behind one realistic program that would ease world tensions.

For Republican leaders, however, the dichotomy within their party on foreign policy matters made the genuine promise of bipartisanship disquieting. Real interparty cooperation could exist only through a strong coalition of moderate Republicans and the great bulk of congressional Democrats. Any attempt by Eisenhower to employ this combination in the creation of what might be sound and workable policy would alienate completely the Republican Old Guard and widen the internal cleavage within the party. For those who believed the president above party, such action did not exceed their expectations, but they failed to perceive that Eisenhower would soon prove himself a far better Republican on domestic policies than they had anticipated. From the beginning of his administration, the president gave evidence of a deep concern for the strength and welfare of his party. Whatever problems it might create in the formulation of foreign policies, the Republican high command could not ignore the continuing task of building political fences.

Presidential politics in 1952 had revealed a significant discrepancy between Eisenhower's popularity and that of his party. Few presidents had been elected so easily. His widely publicized and genuine personal charm, added to an illustrious military reputation at a time when such a reputation had some relevance to successful leadership, made his nomination at Chicago almost synonymous with election to the White House. The November returns, however, also demonstrated a general reluctance among the American people to accept his party with comparable enthusiasm. In essence, the victorious Republican party, with its heavy obligation to American business, had to prove to millions of Eisenhower voters that its economic policies, whatever their nature, were operating in the broad interest of the people. It appeared doubtful in 1953 that the Republican party could devise any program of social or economic betterment that could be carried through Congress except with a generous portion of Democratic votes, nor did the times call for action on the domestic front vigorous enough to solidify Republican gains. Additional victories required the maintenance or creation of political appeals that would help to tie a liberal vote to a traditionally conservative party. Unless Republican leaders could exploit further those foreign policy issues of 1952 which had proved politically successful, it seemed doubtful that the Republican party could expand, or even maintain, its narrow congressional majority.

Thus there could be no abatement in the intense partisanship over the foreign policy that had characterized the late Truman years. The very success of the China, Korea, and loyalty issues in aggravating and exploiting the American inclination toward isolationism and nationalism, particularly in the Midwest, meant that the attack on the past would continue. The Republican victory did not bring the Old Guard into power either within the party or in the nation. During the campaign, foreign policy comprised the one genuinely partisan contribution to the Republican position. It was the one party issue that transcended the appeal of the man whose nomination the Old Guard had fought at Chicago. The foreign policy question alone gave promise of future Republican victories when the party could no longer rely on Eisenhower's popularity. Senator Taft engineered the renewed attack on the Truman policies when he admitted that additional GOP victories would not be won solely by efficiency, honesty, and frugality in government. In April 1953, Taft recommended a political course that would ensure additional Republican victories:

> The particular job to be done is to publicize constantly the contrasts between the present administration and the Truman administration. This is the picture which must be kept before the voters. That means that the mistakes at Yalta and other policies that bequeathed us the Korean War must be constantly developed and brought out. . . . In one way or another, there must be presented to the people the failures in the conduct of the Korean War itself— the lack of ammunition, the mishandling of prisoners, armistice negotiations which enabled the Chinese Communists to build up a tremendously strong force and remedy all their deficiencies, and the outrageous dismissal of MacArthur because he thought that the only purpose of war was victory.[3]

[3]Robert A. Taft, "What the G.O.P. Must Do To Win in 1954," *Look* 17 (April 21, 1953): 44.

For the Taft Republicans foreign policy had become the pawn in a conservative revolution, with the failures of American policy in the Orient and Europe attributable not only to past subversion but also to the very philosophy of New Dealism and Fair Dealism. Through congressional investigations the Old Guard hoped to delve into everything from past treason and corruption to the alleged futility of the Korean War. Fundamentally, however, the Republican strategy was still moored to the concept that President Eisenhower held the affection and trust of the American people and that, whatever was done to perpetuate past national antagonisms, nothing dared deflate the president's stature. Eisenhower's philosophy toward his office made this dual objective totally feasible. His broad tolerance toward congressional action permitted Republican leaders a wide range in which to establish the assumptions on which U.S. foreign policy would be founded without destroying the illusion that the president, in fact, was charting the nation's course.

II

Eisenhower's promise of a new and dynamic foreign policy that would deflate the Soviet and Red Chinese empires at reduced cost placed an enormous burden on American diplomacy. Enough crusading zeal had accompanied the creation of the Truman Cold War policies to rule out all hope of immediate accommodation with the Soviet bloc. The Republican platform of 1952, having attributed the enslavement of hundreds of millions of Europeans and Chinese to the handiwork of Democratic officials, however, had made the destruction of the Communist hegemony in Asia and Eastern Europe the moral commitment of the Republican party. The continued insistence that such illusive goals were actually attainable effectively eliminated all diplomacy. The promised success in foreign affairs required nothing less than unconditional surrender from the enemy, yet neither Eisenhower nor Dulles would defy the promises of 1952 by compromising their high expectations of rolling back the Iron Curtain. Dulles himself affirmed the administration's goal of liberation when he said that "it is of utmost importance that we should make clear to the captive peoples that we do not accept their captivity as a permanent fact of history. If they thought otherwise and became hopeless, we would unwittingly have become partners to the forging of a hostile power so vast that it could encompass our destruction."[4] The secretary promised the American people at the outset that there would be no diplomacy on the basis of the status quo in Europe.

---

[4]Dulles's speech before the American Society of Newspaper Editors, April 18, 1953, Department of State *Bulletin* 28 (April 27, 1953): 606.

President Eisenhower, in his State of the Union message of February 2, 1953, criticized the American agreements which allegedly had brought Soviet dominance to millions of Europeans. He would ask Congress, he said, to pass a resolution making it clear that the government of the United States recognized no past accords which condoned such enslavement. This proposed resolution, by previous agreement with influential Democrats, did not approach repudiation of Yalta. When it condemned the USSR rather than the Roosevelt leadership, the Senate Republicans rejected it. Taft demanded no less than the specific repudiation of the Yalta agreement; Senator Arthur Watkins of Utah reminded his Republican colleagues of the campaign pledges. Dulles refused to defend the resolution in its original form and the entire project collapsed. Dulles's Democratic supporters discovered early that the secretary was unprepared to defend them in their quarrels with Republican neoisolationists in Congress.[5]

Congressional Republicans never relented in their exertions to limit all diplomacy with the Soviet Union until that nation agreed to release its control over the peoples of Eastern Europe. Tehran, Yalta, and Potsdam—all symbols of failure—should militate, they agreed, against any further conferences unless the Kremlin made all possible guarantees for successful negotiations in advance. Senator Bourke Hickenlooper of Iowa warned against "round robin" discussions with the Soviets. Former President Herbert Hoover charged that American "acquiescence" to Soviet annexationist policy had "extinguished the liberties of tens of millions of people" in Eastern Europe and should not be recognized by the Republican administration. In May, Taft rebuked the British and French for their willingness to abandon the Poles, Czechs, Hungarians, and Romanians to the mercies of the Soviets, and Senator McCarthy advised the administration late that year against adopting the Truman-Acheson policy of "perfumed notes" and "whining, whimpering appeasement."[6]

President Eisenhower resisted the Bermuda Conference of December 1953 but attended it finally as a tough bargainer. Shortly before the meeting Dulles assured a House committee that the United States would welcome the opportunity to settle specific disputes with the Soviet Union, but, he added, "we do not look on the conference table

---

[5]For a brief history of the anti-Yalta resolution see *Time*, February 9, 1953, p. 15; *Newsweek*, March 9, 1953, pp. 21–22, and March 16, 1953, pp. 36–37; *San Francisco Chronicle*, February 22, 1953, p. 8; and William S. White in *New York Times*, May 9, 1954.

[6]Republicans continued to exert pressure on the Eisenhower administration to create a tougher, more effective stance toward the Soviet Union. For example, California Senator William F. Knowland warned the administration in December 1954 to avoid any conference in which the Western allies might recognize the Iron Curtain: "I think that is a direct contradiction of the party platform of 1952 under which the Republicans came to power." *New York Times Magazine*, December 5, 1954, p. 13.

as a place where we surrender our principles, but rather as a place for making principles prevail."[7] If Churchill and Premier Joseph Laniel of France hoped to extract an accommodating policy from the United States toward the Kremlin, they were disappointed. The Bermuda declaration repeated the American rollback policy toward the USSR. In its reassurance to the enslaved peoples behind the Iron Curtain it declared: "We cannot accept as justified or permanent the present division of Europe. Our hope is that in due course peaceful means will be found to enable the countries of Eastern Europe again to play their part as free nations in a free Europe."[8] Unfortunately, liberation required the withdrawal of Soviet forces and political influence from Eastern Europe. What peaceful means could achieve such purpose was not clear. Liberation meant the risk of war or it meant nothing.

Eventually the Eisenhower-Dulles revisionism focused on the issue of German reunification; anything less would upset West Germany's internal stability. For political reasons the West German government would not accept as permanent the Soviet subjugation of 17 million East Germans. Few American leaders entertained much hope of immediate reunification, but they were determined to prevent the Western alliance from using the East Germans as pawns in East-West diplomacy. As early as July 1953, Eisenhower had declared that an honorable European peace would require the reemergence of a united German republic, dedicated to the welfare of its own people and to the peace of Europe. "The continued partition of Germany," Dulles declared more forcefully in September, "is a scandal. It is more than that. It is a crime. . . . [I]t is not only wrong to the Germans; it is a menace to the peace."[9] In February 1954, Dulles, with Allied approval, made German reunification the central issue at the Berlin Conference. "I am firmly convinced," he said, "that a free and united Germany is essential to stable peace in Europe. . . . It is the disagreement of our four nations which perpetuated the present division of Germany, and it is only we who can end this division of Germany." He condemned the Soviet effort to defend its interests in a regime placed in power and held in power by the presence of Soviet divisions and, in his central argument, denied that such a regime had the right to negotiate with the West German government on equal terms.[10] Dulles's goal of free German elections far exceeded the limits of diplomatic possibility.

Ultimately, American diplomacy, characterized by Dulles's

[7]Quoted by Richard Wilson in *Des Moines Register*, December 1, 1953.

[8]The Bermuda Declaration of December 7, 1953, Department of State *Bulletin* 29 (December 21, 1953): 852.

[9]Department of State, *American Foreign Policy, 1950–1955: Basic Documents* (Washington, 1957), 2:1747–48, 1843–44.

[10]Ibid., pp. 1850–52, 1854–55.

inflexibility, could not even save the European Defense Community (EDC). In February 1953 the secretary had visited six EDC countries and Great Britain to warn them that a policy of drift and disunity would dry up the sources of U.S. military and economic aid; he urged the countries of Europe to perfect the EDC. The EDC proposal, as finally adopted by the NATO governments in May 1952, had provided for a German contribution of twelve divisions to Europe's defense, with all military units above division level under multinational control. In addition, EDC would deny Germany the right to manufacture aircraft, heavy ships, or atomic, chemical, and biological weapons unless the NATO Council approved such production unanimously. France had demanded these restrictions on Germany's military power, yet in Paris the French Assembly balked at its own government's proposal. Having revived the project, Dulles predicted that its completion would soon be realized. It had become, he informed the American nation, "the livest single topic before the six parliaments of continental Europe." Unless the French approved EDC quickly, he warned, the United States would undertake an "agonizing reappraisal" of its commitment to Europe's defense.[11] Europe recognized in these demands a veiled threat that the United States either would return to this hemisphere and rely on airborne striking power or it would proceed to rearm West Germany without French approval. To European observers such strong alternatives appeared unreasonably severe.

In August 1954 the French Assembly finally delivered its coup de grâce to EDC, a resounding defeat for Dulles's policy of acting tough. It left the West scrambling for the means to tie Germany to an integrated Western Europe and to utilize German power in Western defense. Into this vacuum moved the British, deserting their traditional isolation from the Continent. Britain feared that any U.S. move to rearm Germany by by-passing France would expose that country even more to bitterness and internal dissension. Britain, moreover, shared France's dread of German power and viewed with disapproval a combination of uncontrolled German and American forces in Western Europe. British leaders wanted no further pressure on the Soviet Union. They never accepted Dulles's purpose of rolling back the Iron Curtain, nor did they share the moral scruples of the United States regarding the Soviet position because they never believed it to be the creation of Yalta.

In the crisis Sir Anthony Eden committed four British divisions to the Continent "as long as a majority of the Brussels partners want

---

[11]See Dulles's speech of April 18, 1953, Department of State *Bulletin* 28 (April 27, 1953): 604.

them there." He saved NATO by placing curbs on Germany satisfactory to the French. Suddenly Western Europe enjoyed more unity than had existed earlier. Eisenhower lauded the new accord as perhaps "one of the greatest diplomatic achievements of our time." At the nine-power conference in London in September 1954, American policy revealed a more compromising tone. Dulles remained calm at French demands for arms control and did not threaten to pull the United States out of the meeting. During the following month the foreign ministers met in Paris to approve the new agreements with Germany. The West German state received independence and membership in the Atlantic community as an equal partner, and the United States received what it had long desired: the full integration of German power into the Western alliance. In May 1955, West Germany became the fifteenth member of NATO and, supported by U.S. military assistance, that country soon embarked on an ambitious program of rearmament.[12] The Soviet Union responded to the challenge by organizing its Warsaw Pact across Eastern Europe.

NATO might stabilize the lines of demarcation between Western Europe and the Soviet sphere, but British and American observers questioned the revisionist goal of liberation that determined U.S. objectives in Europe and eliminated any search for accommodation with the Kremlin. Sharing a more modest evaluation of Western interests and power in East-Central Europe, they rejected the Eisenhower-Dulles preference for sweeping settlements or no settlements at all. Churchill objected to the goal of liberation before the House of Commons on May 11, 1953: "It would, I think, be a mistake to assume that nothing can be settled with Soviet Russia unless everything is settled. Piecemeal solutions of individual problems should not be disdained or improvidently put aside." The *London Observer,* in its editorial of May 17, also decried American purposes in Europe. Perhaps the West might secure some liberalizing of the satellite regimes, but no more. The writer declared that "the best we can hope for—and this is not a wholly unreasonable or unrealistic hope—is that a period of peace may reduce Russia's iron grip on her neighbors which six years of cold war have merely tightened." Sebastian Haffner, the British writer on international affairs, further believed that any policy that appeared to encourage revolution was grossly dishonest and "criminally irresponsible."

[12]Drew Middleton noted Dulles's efforts to find the necessary compromises in *New York Times,* October 3, 1954. For the U.S.-West German mutual defense agreement of June 30, 1955 see Department of State *Bulletin* 33 (July 25, 1955): 142–44; James B. Conant, ambassador to the Federal Republic, discusses U.S.-West German relations, March 23, 1956, ibid. 34 (April 9, 1956): 585–87.

The president, he charged, knew that the United States would do nothing to liberate Eastern Europe, even if the satellites themselves revolted. If diplomatic intransigence would merely perpetuate the subjugation of the region, then any liberation would require concessions from the West. "The present American government," he concluded, "seemed to be in the curious position of having to confess that it can do nothing for Eastern Europe by force, and yet at the same time being too proud to do something for Eastern Europe by diplomacy."

Meanwhile, Eisenhower, to fulfill his campaign promise of tax reduction, searched for a defense structure that would maximize the nation's strength at a minimum of expenditure. As early as February 1953, the president had stated clearly his purpose of tailoring military power to budgetary requirements: "Our problem is to achieve military strength within the limits of endurable strain upon our economy." By May he was speaking of a budget cut of $8 billion to achieve the objective of creating a situation of "maximum military strength within economic capacities." He recognized the necessity of maintaining the true military power of the country, but, he added, "the overwhelming majority of the people of the free world appreciate the fact that a healthy economy and a functioning economy . . . are inseparable from true defense."[13] Republican leaders, with their traditional concern for balanced budgets, found Eisenhower's emphasis on budgetary restraint highly attractive. Senator Knowland warned that prolonged defense spending would permit the Kremlin to achieve its objectives without moving a division across one international frontier.[14]

The "New Look" in military policy spelled out the administration's effort to find a working arrangement whereby it could reduce taxes and at the same time answer the charge that the national leadership was neglecting the country's defense. The new accent on air-atomic-sea power assured not only greater mobility in the employment of force but also augmented destructive power at reduced cost. The trend toward air-atomic defense fitted precisely the predilections of Secretary of the Treasury George M. Humphrey, for he represented the powerful business pressure being exerted on the Eisenhower administration to reduce taxes. Humphrey insisted that the United States had "no business getting into little wars. If a situation comes up where our interests justify intervention," he said, "let's intervene decisively with all we have got or stay out." New isolationists such as Hoover and Taft lauded the New Look because they had always favored a

---

[13]*Newsweek*, May 11, 1953, p. 28.
[14]William F. Knowland, "The 'Instant Retaliation' Policy Defended," *New York Times Magazine*, March 21, 1954, p. 74.

major national reliance on sea and air power. Under the direction of such noted industrialists as Charles E. Wilson and Roger Kyes of General Motors, who became secretary and deputy secretary of defense, the administration reduced military expenditures while it claimed that greater efficiency brought the nation additional defense. Perhaps the United States received more for its defense dollar, but the level of preparation for conventional warfare was lower than it had been under the previous administration. Because the Eisenhower administration did not argue that Truman and his advisers had overrated the Soviet threat, military expert Donald W. Mitchell concluded that "the New Look accepts voluntarily, for the sake of cutting government costs, greater risks than were formerly regarded as acceptable."[15]

Military writers doubted the wisdom of a military program dictated by economy rather than combat effectiveness. To such analysts as Hanson Baldwin, it appeared that Humphrey, rather than the Joint Chiefs of Staff, was dictating policy. He charged the administration with "putting a price tag on national security."[16] He wondered whether manpower reductions were essential to a sound American economy, or whether the United States was really getting more combat power at less expenditure. To military critics everywhere the concentration on air-atomic-sea power seemed to leave little preparation for any eventuality other than a policy of nonresistance or a program of annihilation.[17] Politically, the New Look, with its assurance that fighting in mud and foxholes had been outmoded, had unquestioned appeal (Elmer Davis remarked that in Washington it was generally understood that only ground troops have mothers).[18] Still it was doubtful whether any level of defense could really settle the outstanding issues of the Cold War unless American expectations abroad were significantly downgraded.

III

In the evolving new isolationist pattern under Eisenhower's leadership, Asia continued to receive top billing. This emphasis on the Far East stemmed logically from the fixed orthodox belief that the Truman administration had planned the collapse of Jiang Jieshi and had refused to win the Korean War against the advice of General MacArthur. "So

[15]Donald W. Mitchell, "The 'New Look,' " *Current History* 27 (October 1954): 219.
[16]Hanson W. Baldwin in *New York Times*, November 1, 1953.
[17]Baldwin in ibid., January 24, 1954; Dean Acheson, " 'Instant Retaliation': The Debate Continued," *New York Times Magazine*, March 28, 1954, p. 78; Thomas R. Phillips, "Our Point of No Return," *Reporter* 12 (February 24, 1955): 14–18.
[18]Elmer Davis, *Two Minutes Till Midnight* (Indianapolis, 1955), pp. 36–37.

we now reap the harvest," ran the judgment of Frazier Hunt, the noted journalist, "of our stupidity and our moral cowardice, from the northern reaches of the Western Pacific to the warmer waters of the Indian Ocean." This conviction that the United States could have had its way in the Pacific reached the extreme in vituperation when Senator Jenner asserted that President Truman had sent U.S. troops into Korea for the specific purpose of having them defeated. The Democratic administration, he charged, "had ordered American youth to engage in a war halfway 'round the earth, in territory the Fair Dealers had carefully stripped beforehand of every American soldier and virtually every American gun," leaving the South Koreans to stand at the Soviet frontier "armed only with policemen's pistols." The administration then deprived American troops of air support and naval blockade and finally removed their general in the midst of the campaign. When the American forces, not knowing that they were supposed to lose, proceeded to win the war, the Truman administration "gave away the victory our men had won with their blood."

Such neoisolationists refused to believe that victory need be denied American forces, even in the spring of 1953. General James A. Van Fleet informed the nation that it could still gain an easy victory in Korea. "[W]e are . . . thoroughly and completely superior to the Chinese Reds in North Korea," he observed upon his return from the Far East; "all we have to do is to start an all-out effort in Korea, and the Reds will come begging to us. . . . Any time we want to beat the Reds in Korea . . . I guarantee you it can be done."[19] American and South Korean forces, he argued, had almost destroyed the enemy in the late spring of 1951. Another assault at that critical moment would have brought the needed victory in Korea. "Then our government's high policy intervened," the general recalled, "and we were ordered not to advance any further. The stalemate began, and then the long and futile armistice talks."[20] Eventually most of the high-ranking American officers in Korea accepted General Van Fleet's contention that the Truman administration had needlessly denied success to the U.S. forces in Korea. General Courtney Whitney charged the Truman leadership with "timidity and abject wheedling," after the Chinese Communists entered the war. General Edward M. Almond declared that the Chinese would never have entered the war had they not received some assurance that

[19]General James A. Van Fleet, "The Truth About Korea, Part I: From a Man Now Free to Speak," *Life* 34 (May 11, 1953): 127–28; Van Fleet, "The Truth About Korea, Part II: How We Can Win with What We Have," ibid. 34 (May 18, 1953): 169. Van Fleet declared that Jiang Jieshi, with some American help, could liberate the mainland. Ibid., p. 172.

[20]Ibid. 34 (May 11, 1953): 127.

their bases across the Yalu would not be destroyed.[21] Both officers agreed that the United States was deprived of victory by the dual opposition of the enemy in Korea and the administration in Washington.

Not all American officers accepted such notions of American superiority in the Far East. General Matthew B. Ridgway replied "casualties unacceptable" when in June 1952 the Pentagon had sought his views on a general Korean offensive. Ridgway was convinced that the United States would suffer 350,000 to 400,000 dead and wounded if it attempted to reach the Manchurian border and that, if American forces pursued the war into China, the figures would become astronomical. "If we had been successful in a drive to the Yalu," added General Robert Eichelberger, "we would have faced millions of Chinese and Russia's best—its Siberian Army. Napoleon and Hitler fell into a similar trap in Europe and we [were] lucky to have avoided one in Asia."[22]

Those who accepted the doctrine of American invincibility in the Far East believed that the time had arrived in the spring of 1953 for the United States to firm up its Korean policy and break away from the limitations imposed by the European allies. The popular denial of opposing power in the Orient made logical two normally incompatible hopes: that the United States could secure what it wanted of China merely by demanding it and that it could actually achieve such an illusive objective by "going it alone." At Cincinnati, Taft declared that this nation "might as well forget the United Nations so far as the Korean War is concerned." Others agreed that the time for unilateral action had come. Congressman Lawrence H. Smith of Wisconsin declared that Taft's was "the lone voice that dares to challenge a policy of drift and equivocation in the state department." David Lawrence assured his readers that Taft's position was not isolationism but that the senator "just doesn't believe in sitting by and letting America get buffeted about by allies."[23] War in Korea had convinced few new isolationists that the West, even at small cost and effort, need require less than absolute surrender of its adversaries in the Far East.

Official U.S. purpose in Asia, as defined by Secretary Dulles in March 1953, was that of "disengagement." The administration believed that another ground war in Asia would again pin the United States down and give the Soviets a free hand elsewhere. In the Korean truce of July 1953, the administration achieved its first step in its policy of

[21]Almond in *U.S. News & World Report*, December 10, 1954, p. 94; General Courtney Whitney, "The War MacArthur Was Not Allowed to Win," *Life* 39 (September 5, 1955): 63. For a similar view from another high-ranking officer see General Mark W. Clark, "The Truth About Korea," *Collier's* 133 (February 5, 1954): 34–35.

[22]Eichelberger in *Newsweek*, August 3, 1953, p. 20.

[23]Lawrence in *U.S. News & World Report*, June 3, 1953, p. 84.

disengagement. Both Eisenhower and Dulles created the illusion that they were willing to use stronger methods to bring an end to the war. When Eisenhower returned from Korea in January, he had admitted publicly in New York that "we face an enemy whom we cannot hope to impress by words, however eloquent. But only by deeds—executed under circumstances of our own choosing." As the negotiations continued through the early months of 1953, Dulles informed the Chinese that, unless they agreed to some truce, the United States would strike at their Manchurian bases. Nor would the administration accede to the Chinese insistence on "compulsory repatriation" for all prisoners of war. The eventual compromise granted each prisoner his own choice.[24] Agreement in Korea came hard and promised only temporary relief. What complicated the negotiations for the administration was its commitment to a reunited peninsula under President Rhee. That objective both the Chinese and North Koreans rejected totally. The Korean negotiations also placed the Eisenhower administration in the embarrassing position of dealing with a Chinese regime whose existence it could not recognize and to whose downfall it was politically and morally committed.

Eisenhower and Dulles rightly hailed the Korean truce as a triumph for both the United States and the United Nations. Amid the universal relief, the administration appeared to overlook certain aspects of the new status of Asia as it contemplated future policy: the United States had not defeated the Chinese army, it had not reunited Korea, it had not created policy acceptable to the spokesmen of free Asia, it had not settled the Chinese civil war, and it had agreed to truce terms so loosely drawn that they could be intentionally misinterpreted. Hans J. Briner, the Swiss member of the Neutral Nations Supervisory Commission selected to carry out the armistice terms, concluded, after his frustrating experiences in Korea, that the implied promise of a quick settlement in 1952 had so weakened the bargaining position of the United Nations that the formula it had secured was actually unworkable.[25] Whether the United States could extract itself completely from the remaining problems of the Orient without recognizing certain claims of mainland China was not clear. Washington correspondent Joseph C. Harsch posed this question in September 1953: "If Secretary Dulles is firmly set on a policy of 'disengagement' from the Far East and if Ambassador Lodge really expects to get American troops out of Korea, then both of them must contemplate the possibility of some sort of progression from the

---

[24]See James Reston's analysis of Eisenhower's tough approach to Korea in *New York Times*, February 1, 1953.

[25]Hans J. Briner, "The Strange Neutrals of Panmunjom," *Korean Survey* 4 (November 1955): 3.

Korean peace conference which would lead to a seat for Communist China in the UN."[26]

Jiang Jieshi's supporters in the United States declared openly that Eisenhower's election was a mandate that the new administration abrogate the Truman policy toward China and give all possible assistance to the Nationalists. A *Life* magazine editorial asserted that the first requirement of a sound China policy was the need of binding "free China's fate and policy to ours with hoops of steel. Only on that basis will there be anything to defend." *Life*'s editor Henry Luce, after a visit to Taiwan, declared that the Nationalists were living completely for the purpose of liberating China from the Communist regime. The time had come, he believed, to join hands with the Guomindang in its struggle to free the mainland. Similarly, Geraldine Fitch added real expectations of success to the proposed venture by asserting that the overwhelming majority of the mainland Chinese were "working, watching and praying" for Jiang's return.[27] Any integrated invasion by 600,000 to 800,000 Nationalist troops, she wrote, would make "the liberation crusade snowball from South China to Manchuria."

Throughout 1953 members of the Nationalist China bloc in Congress attempted to force the China issue to its ultimate conclusion. These Republicans repeated their charges that coexistence with the Beijing (Peking) regime was tantamount to total surrender, that war with Red China was inevitable, and that the Guomindang was the last hope for American security in the Far East. "Let us face one simple fact," Jenner warned in the Senate. "There can be no American policy for the Pacific if the Communists are allowed to retain the heartland of Asia. . . . All American policy must start from a firm decision to reestablish the legitimate anti-Communist government on the China mainland."[28] Knowland could no longer visualize any long-run alternative to military action against Red China and, in his *Collier's* article of January 1954, was to note that any American failure to take a strong stand behind the Nationalists on Taiwan, in effect, would hand all Asia to the Communists.[29]

Jiang's Republican supporters denied that a successful war against Red China would require more than American air-atomic-sea power. Bullitt predicted that the United States could turn the balance of power

[26]Joseph C. Harsch in *Christian Science Monitor*, September 3, 1953. For a superb analysis of U.S. Far Eastern policy in 1953 see Vincent S. Kearney, "Whither U.S. Policy in the Far East?" *America* 90 (November 7, 1953): 147–49.

[27]Geraldine Fitch, *Formosa Beachhead* (Chicago, 1953), pp. 258–59, 262.

[28]William Jenner in *Congressional Record*, 83d Cong., 1st sess., August 3, 1953, pt. 8:11,001.

[29]For a similar view see Delia and Ferdinand Kuhn, "Who Can Save Asia?" *Collier's* 135 (April 1, 1955): 46–47.

against the Communist world "by a concerted attack on the Chinese
Communists, employing no American soldiers except those in Korea,
but using the American Navy to blockade the China coast and the
American air force to bomb appropriate targets, while assigning the
great burden of the ground fighting to the Koreans and the Free
Chinese."[30] President Rhee agreed and informed a joint session of the
U.S. Congress that the Red Chinese could be overwhelmed with American sea and air power supported by South Korea and the Republic
of China on the ground. The conquest of Red China, he emphasized,
would terminate the tensions of Asia by swinging "the balance of power
so strongly against the Soviet Union that it would not dare seek war
with the United States."[31] McCarthy believed that a sturdy administration could upset the Red regime with no application of power at all.
"We can bring the enemy to their knees," he said in late 1953, "without
firing a single shot."

Republican stalwarts quickly committed the administration to
the indefinite nonrecognition of the Beijing regime. During June 1953
they closed in on Eisenhower and Dulles by attaching a rider to an
appropriation bill which declared that the United States would cut off
all financial support to the United Nations if it should seat a Red
Chinese delegation. Senator Knowland soon monopolized the headlines
when he announced that he would resign his position as majority leader
in the Senate and devote his full efforts to seek the withdrawal of U.S.
membership if the United Nations admitted the Beijing regime. Eventually the new isolationists relaxed their pressure on the president but
only after he had assured them personally that he would oppose vigorously any effort to bring the Beijing government into the world organization. The irreconcilables in Congress remained committed to the
restoration of Jiang Jieshi, although they never made clear how they
intended to accomplish that purpose. Still no one in high places challenged them or their approach to the China question.

President Eisenhower improved his liaison with the China bloc
by appointing Walter S. Robertson to the position of assistant secretary
of state for Far Eastern Affairs. In China after the war, Robertson had
opposed a coalition government for that country. Upon his return to
the United States, he allied himself with such friends of Jiang as Senator
Knowland, Congressman Walter Judd of Minnesota, and General
Albert C. Wedemeyer who by 1953 had moved far from the views of
an exhaustive 1947 report on the deficiencies of Nationalist China. In

    [30]William C. Bullitt, "Should We Support an Attack on Red China?" *Look* 18
(August 24, 1954): 33.
    [31]Rhee quoted in Davis, *Two Minutes Till Midnight*, pp. 136–38.

his appointment of Admiral Arthur W. Radford as chairman of the Joint Chiefs of Staff, the president placed in a high advisory position another powerful member of the Nationalist China bloc. Radford had made no secret of his belief that the Red China regime must be destroyed even if it required a fifty-year war to accomplish it. Demanding relentless opposition to Red China, these men, along with Secretary Dulles, comprised a strong voice in the top echelons of the Eisenhower administration. Thus nowhere was it evident that the new administration was ready to come to grips with the most significant alternation of power at mid-century—the consolidation of Communist authority over the mainland of China. The president readily admitted to newsmen and even to his cabinet that the United States could not eliminate the Red regime and therefore needed to seek the means to coexist with it peacefully. In his diplomacy, however, he preferred to keep the question in limbo through continued indecision and temporizing. Officially, he remained committed to Jiang Jieshi.[32]

Eisenhower had assured the country, in his special foreign policy message of February 2, 1953, that the free world would not remain indefinitely "in a posture of paralyzed tension," for it left the initiative of time and place for future conflict to the aggressor. The administration had "begun the definition of a new, positive foreign policy. . . . Our foreign policy," he added, "must be clear, consistent and confident."[33] For Asia this new policy of recapturing the initiative became real with the "unleashing" of Jiang. Dulles announced in April that the United States was accelerating its military assistance to Nationalist China, had already stationed an ambassador at Taipei, Taiwan, and had instructed the Seventh Fleet to terminate its protection of the Chinese Communists on the mainland. Truman had placed the fleet in the Formosa Strait early in the Korean War to protect Formosa from the mainland Chinese, but now Eisenhower noted emphatically that the United States had "no obligation to protect a nation fighting us in Korea." To add reality to the concept that the Nationalists, now supposedly unleashed, would shortly seize the offensive against the mainland, the administration pressed Jiang hard to put regular troops on the Tachens. At first he resisted, believing these islands too distant from Taiwan. Eventually Jiang conceded and placed his Forty-sixth Division under one of his ablest generals on these distant outposts.

[32]See Robert J. Donovan, *Eisenhower: The Inside Story* (New York, 1956), p. 132. For the standard view of the China question see that of Radford in *Atlantic Monthly* 195 (April 1955): 6.

[33]Eisenhower's State of the Union message, February 2, 1953, *Newsweek*, February 9, 1953, p. 17; *Time*, February 9, 1953, p. 15. For Eisenhower's instructions to the Seventh Fleet see ibid., pp. 15–16.

Eisenhower's promise of a new and more positive policy toward China met with broad acclaim. Congressional affirmation was most acute among those who had opposed Truman's neutralization of the Formosa Strait in 1950. Senator Taft thought the policy "a step in the right direction," and Admiral Leahy termed it a "bright idea" to let the Chinese Nationalists help in settling "problems along the China coast." General MacArthur said it would "correct one of the strangest anomalies known to military history"; it would strengthen the American position in the Far East by releasing the Nationalists for raids on the Chinese coast and would give notice to the Reds that their unprecedented sanctuary would now come to an end. "The modification of the Seventh Fleet's orders," he concluded, "should be supported by all loyal Americans irrespective of party."[34]

IV

Having cast its lot with Jiang, the United States was assured from 1950 onward that eventually it would be trapped in a renewal of the Chinese civil war. It required no more than the heavy fire by Chinese Red artillery and air bombardment on the Nationalist-held offshore islands in September 1954, especially in the vicinity of Quemoy and the Tachens, to involve the United States in another Far Eastern crisis. What made the attacks particularly disconcerting was the assertion by Chinese leaders that these were a prelude to the conquest of Taiwan.[35] After a lull, mainland leader Zhou Enlai (Chou En-lai) announced on January 24, 1955 that "the government of the People's Republic of China has repeatedly and in solemn terms declared to the world that the Chinese people are determined to liberate their own territory of Taiwan [Formosa]. . . . Taiwan is an inalienable part of China's territory."

The threatened assault on the Nationalist stronghold created a situation of immense tenseness in Washington. First, the island of Taiwan was symbolically the key to America's Pacific defenses from the Japanese islands to the Philippines. Second, the United States had direct commitments to the defense of Taiwan as the seat of the Republic of China. On December 1, 1954, Dulles had announced a new security pact with China which made it clear that the United States would defend Taiwan and the Pescadores as well as other Nationalist-held islands. In exchange, Jiang agreed not to attack the mainland without

[34]William Henry Chamberlin, *Beyond Containment* (Chicago, 1953), p. 372; MacArthur quoted in *San Francisco Chronicle*, February 1, 1953. *Time* lauded the decision to "unleash" Jiang Jieshi, February 9, 1953, p. 16.
[35]"The Week in Review," *New York Times*, November 28, 1954.

previous consultation with Washington. With the renewal of the Communist threat on Taiwan in January 1955, Dulles again assured Jiang and the world that the Nationalists on Taiwan would not "stand alone" against any invasion from the Asian continent. This purpose was totally acceptable to the non-Communist world, except among Asiatic leaders who had no interest in Jiang or in American defense commitments. Strategically, the Dulles declaration seemed feasible because it was based on this country's power to control the sea and the air in the Formosa Strait. Legally the United States had a defensible claim based on the fact that Taiwan had been returned to the victors in the Pacific war and not necessarily to China. At worst, Taiwan's legal status was uncertain. With that country protected from the mainland by one hundred miles of water, the U.S. commitment did not appear to Europeans as particularly dangerous.

What quickly subjected the Eisenhower administration to open criticism all over the free world was the doubtful posture that it assumed on the question of the offshore islands.[36] With the president's decision to order a retreat from the exposed Tachens went the tacit promise to Nationalist Foreign Minister George Yeh that the United States would defend Quemoy and Matsu, the offshore islands along the China coast facing Taiwan. Even then American policy remained vague. Dulles announced that the United States would fight for these islands if their seizure appeared a step toward an attack on Taiwan itself. Unfortunately, the future course of Chinese policy could hardly be determined with any certainty by an attack on Quemoy and Matsu. Perhaps Dulles had two purposes in mind, both designed to prevent trouble. By avoiding a firm stand he seemed to be telling the world that the offshore islands were really negotiable and that they would be released in exchange for a cease-fire. On the other hand, the American posture of doubt might deter the Reds from attacking and thus prevent war, saving the islands for Jiang. Dulles even intimated that the United States might use some form of "massive retaliation," including the tactical use of atomic bombs, to defend the offshore islands.[37]

Furthermore, the administration's request to Congress in January 1955 for a resolution to grant the president permission to employ U.S. armed forces in the defense of Taiwan and the Pescadores did not clarify the official American position. Eisenhower agreed to use forces

---

[36]For the beginning of the ambivalence in administration policy toward the offshore islands see Reston in ibid., September 12, 1954.

[37]Republican pressures on Eisenhower and Dulles to remain firm on the offshore island issue was intense. See Harlan Cleveland, "Troubled Waters: The Formosa Strait," *Reporter* 12 (January 13, 1955): 9–10; Max Ascoli, "What Price Peace?" ibid. 12 (March 10, 1955): 12–13; Baldwin in *New York Times*, January 30, 1955.

only in situations which were recognizable as part of a general assault on the main Nationalist position. His purpose was to demonstrate the unity and determination of the American people to maintain the country's commitment to the defense of Taiwan.[38] Congress neglected to demand a precise definition of what that commitment might be in a crisis. Such indecision assumed a calculated risk, and Dulles himself admitted to newsmen that the Reds were amassing enormous forces of air and man power along the coast opposite the offshore islands. He predicted that an assault could come at any moment, yet any Chinese attack would have left the United States two alternatives, neither of which would have been wholly in the nation's interest. If American forces rushed to the aid of Jiang's exposed position on the offshore islands, the United States would have entered another open conflict with China; if it, as Dulles had warned, used atomic weapons, the world might shortly be involved in a general war. If, on the other hand, the United States backed down and deserted Jiang, as it did in the Tachens, it would suffer another tremendous, if unnecessary, loss of prestige. The secret of successful diplomacy has always entailed the avoidance of the hard decision between war and diplomatic defeat, yet any all-out Chinese attack on Quemoy or Matsu would have placed the United States in exactly that dilemma.[39]

This crisis in the Formosa Strait demonstrated again the irony of the new isolationist posture toward China. It was not the strength but the weakness of the Nationalist regime that forced the administration to risk war over the defense of two tiny islands hugging the China coast, islands not even remotely required for the defense of Taiwan. After a visit to that country, Cyrus L. Sulzberger of the *New York Times* reported from Tokyo: "Chiang Kai-shek would like to see a battle for the strategically unimportant offshore islands developed into a world war so he could gamble on returning to the mainland. But as far as we are concerned they have no military value."[40] It was not strange that Eisenhower's decision to remain in the thick of the Chinese civil war soon isolated American policy from the bulk of non-Communist

[38]Eisenhower's message to Congress, January 24, 1955, Department of State *Bulletin* 32 (February 7, 1955): 212.

[39]See Adlai Stevenson in *Des Moines Register*, April 12, 1955.

[40]Thomas R. Phillips, "Quemoy and Formosa as I Saw Them," *Reporter* 12 (April 21, 1955): 34; Cyrus L. Sulzberger quoted in ibid. 12 (April 7, 1955): 2; Phillips, "An Important Link in the Chain," ibid. 12 (March 10, 1955): 19–20. For a similar view see Reston in *New York Times*, April 3, 1955: "To argue that the defense of the offshore islands is necessary to the defense of Formosa . . . is almost like arguing that the loss of Staten Island, a ferry-boat ride from Manhattan, would jeopardize the defense of Bermuda. Yet this argument is made in the face of testimony by the Joint Chiefs of Staff that they can defend Formosa even if Quemoy and Matsu are taken."

opinion. In the House of Commons, Eden was bitterly critical, as was both the *Times* and the *Manchester Guardian* which openly lectured the United States and Jiang on the folly of trying to hold the offshore islands.[41]

To Jiang the offshore islands, as stepping stones to the Continent, were symbols that the Nationalists would again one day return to power over all China. With a fourth of his best troops on Quemoy and Matsu, placed there largely at the request of American officials, he continued to assert his right to hold the islands as essential for his ultimate victory in the Chinese civil war. Without such anticipation of success, his regime was in danger of disintegration. Tingfu F. Tsiang, Chinese representative to the United Nations, defended the Guomindang position in June 1955: "We cannot do that [give up the offshore islands] because withdrawal from Matsu and Quemoy weakens our material strength and undermines our moral position." Any effort to force compromise on the Nationalists would "liquidate the Republic of China."[42] The administration had admitted in its arrangements with Jiang in December 1954 that he would not return to the mainland, yet it agreed that any U.S. policy that reflected this conclusion would inflict such damage on Nationalist morale that it would produce wholesale desertions of Guomindang forces and their return to the mainland. Said Lippmann of American policy: "If, as a matter of fact, the internal strength of Nationalist China rests on the fantasy that Chiang Kai-shek will some day return to China, we are headed for trouble."

For its critics—and they were legion—the Eisenhower-Dulles posture toward China appeared as unpromising as it was dangerous. The hard stand on nonrecognition and the offshore islands sustained the promise of liberating the mainland and thereby pacified the China bloc. Many wondered, however, what the perennial nonrecognition of China would achieve except to aggravate the Cold War in the Far East. British philosopher Bertrand Russell declared that the "recognition of the existing Government of China is an essential step in diminishing tension of the Cold War, and no legitimate purpose of statesmanship is served by postponing it."[43] Harold Macmillan, former British foreign secretary, was equally critical. "Recognition of a government," he observed, "never used to be a sort of diploma or certificate of approval. I think

[41]For European views of Eisenhower's Taiwanese policy see Drew Middleton in *New York Times*, January 30, 1955. A. M. Rosenthal discusses Indian views in ibid., February 13, 1955.

[42]See C. H. Lowe in *Commonwealth* (Commonwealth Club of California), October 4, 1954, p. 213; Tingfu F. Tsiang in ibid., June 27, 1955, p. 156.

[43]Bertrand Russell, "A Prescription for the World," *Saturday Review*, August 28, 1954, p. 39.

rather a false diplomatic doctrine has grown up about all this in recent years. We do it, to be frank, to benefit ourselves—not to please them. This was the older doctrine and I think the right one." Clement Attlee, recently British prime minister, termed it ironic that the United States insisted on viewing Jiang Jieshi's China as a great power and placing it on the Security Council but denying mainland China a seat when it evolved into a nation of considerable importance.[44] Indian leader Jawaharlal Nehru, regarded generally as free Asia's leading spokesman, asked: "Why should the United States *not* recognize China?" Apart from liking or disliking the Chinese regime, he declared, one could scarcely ignore its existence or its place in Asian affairs. If diplomatic courtesies implied approval, observed C. Northcote Parkinson of the University of Malaya, Britain would not have recognized the independence of the United States.[45] Asia, like Europe, had deserted Jiang.

Critics argued that nonrecognition contributed to the diplomatic advantages of both Moscow and Beijing and sustained a highly artificial friendship between them. Spokesmen of the administration met such arguments head-on despite the president's private convictions that they might be correct.[46] Robertson denied that any break between China and the Soviet Union was possible. He reportedly declared in a long conversation with Dulles: "There is as much chance of winning them [the Chinese] away in 10 years—or a 100 years—as there is, Foster, that you will become a Communist!" If Robertson's suppositions were highly questionable, they expressed the administration's official outlook. So completely did nonrecognition tie China's voice to that of the Soviet Union that observers wondered why the Soviets brought the issue of recognition before the United Nations each year. One Yugoslav diplomat supplied an answer: "Obviously because she thinks the effect in China will be to increase anti-Western sentiment. And why does she always seem to bring it up at a time when it is most likely to call for a particularly sharp turndown from the United States? Obviously to create trouble between the Western allies and to convince the world that America is anti-Asian."[47] Thus for Beijing there were advantages

---

[44]Macmillan quoted in *Commonwealth*, July 4, 1955, p. 163; Attlee quoted in *New Republic* 128 (June 8, 1953): 17.

[45]For Nehru's neutralism and strong ties to China see "Diffidence in the East," *Commonweal* 60 (May 15, 1954): 131; and *Time*, October 25, 1954, pp. 22–23. Nehru was Asia's leading critic of U.S. attitudes toward China.

[46]For a good example of the administration's arguments for nonrecognition see Walter P. McConaughy, "China in the Shadow of Communism," Department of State *Bulletin* 30 (January 11, 1954): 39–41; and Alfred le Sesne Jenkins's address before the American Academy of Political and Social Science, April 2, 1954, ibid. 30 (April 26, 1954): 624–27.

[47]See Chester Bowles, "A Bipartisan Policy for Asia," *Harper's Magazine* 208 (May 1954): 25.

too; its Communist leaders understood well that U.S. policy was a constant affront to Asian sentiment.

British experts on the Soviet Union and China agreed with some in the United States that the Moscow-Beijing axis was tenuous at best. The fact that Mao Zedong owed little or nothing to the Soviets for his success; that China was large and fiercely independent in tradition, with a strong sense of nationalism; that its long common boundary with the Soviet Union was a constant source of irritation; that China was overpopulated and Siberia was not; and that in the long run China would require more technology than the USSR could supply, indicated that the alliance between Moscow and Beijing was neither stable nor permanent. The words of Soviet Foreign Minister Sergei Sazonov, uttered in 1912, still had meaning: "Germany is interested in China as a market and she fears China's disintegration. . . . Russia, on the contrary, as a nation bordering China, and with a long, unfortified frontier, cannot wish for the strengthening of her neighbor: she could therefore view with equanimity the collapse of modern China."[48] The China bloc, both inside and outside the Eisenhower administration, had far less trouble in monopolizing the official posture of the United States toward China than in framing policies that would accomplish its purposes.

V

Indochina loomed as the third important crisis area to challenge the Asian policies of the Eisenhower administration. There was nothing strange or unique in the Indochinese situation of 1953. For seven years Saigon, Indochina's beautiful, French-architectured capital, had been the nerve center of a ruthless civil war. The region's Nationalist movement, vastly strengthened by the Japanese successes in Southeast Asia during World War II, had been captured by the Marxist Ho Chi Minh. With the collapse of the Japanese Empire in 1945, Ho expected to fill the political vacuum with the creation of an independent republic, but the French had other plans. By 1946 French forces, with British help, had recaptured control of Saigon and soon came face to face with Ho and his Vietminh forces to the north.

France was in no mood to see its declining prestige in the Orient vanish with the loss of Indochina, and the French constitution of 1946 had anticipated neither independence nor dominion status for the noted colony. As French relations with Ho gradually disintegrated into civil

---

[48]Quoted in Edward Crankshaw, "China and Russia," *Atlantic Monthly* 197 (June 1956): 27.

war, the United States sided with the French and by 1950 had recognized the French puppet regime of Bao Dai. From the beginning
American observers predicted eventual French defeat because it was
clear that Indochina's powerful nationalistic upheaval was working for
Ho. For Washington officials, however, the struggle for Indochina
remained a matter of international Communist aggression emanating
from Moscow and Beijing which only military power would resolve.

Unfortunately, the employment of military force in Indochina
was not promising. Beyond Korea the problems of defense would become
difficult indeed. In Indochina, for example, a war similar to that of
Korea would confront the United States with problems of transporting
men and materiel two thousand miles, fighting in a more rugged terrain
and climate, and maintaining military lines that would always melt
into the jungle. In the interior of Southeast Asia, the burdens involved
in bringing U.S. military power to bear would become even heavier.
Since the threat to the status quo in regions such as Indochina would
stem from internal revolt rather than external aggression, the United
States, unlike in Korea, would find itself in a welter of public apathy
or outright resistance. Even the Indochinese Communists, sometimes
amazed at their own success, admitted that an army fighting without
the support of the indigenous population was like a fish fighting on dry
land. Whether the employment or threatened employment of American
military power in 1953 had presented a realistic answer to the challenge
of Asia was subject to doubt.

Repeatedly after the Korean armistice Dulles warned the Chinese
of "grave consequences" if they transferred their forces from Korea to
Indochina where, despite extensive and continued American military
aid, the French forces were still in retreat.[49] Nowhere on the horizon
was there any coalition of power sufficiently in sympathy with the
French purpose to resist the thrusts of Ho Chi Minh and his allies.
The free nations of Asia had no interest in the war, except to see the
French driven out. Even the French, after seven costly years of futility,
were ready to compromise with the Vietminh forces and retire from
Indochina. Nor could the United Nations step into the breach, for the
American maneuvers toward involvement had been unilateral and no
other power had enough concern to invoke the good services of the
world organization. Still the growing threat of a Communist victory in
Indochina found the administration in an uncompromising mood. During his tour of Indochina in late 1953, Vice-President Richard M. Nixon
had warned the French: "It is impossible to lay down arms until victory

[49]Dulles's speech before the American Legion, September 2, 1953, Department
of State *Bulletin* 29 (September 14, 1953): 342.

is completely won. . . . If your country [Indochina] is to be independent and free, it is first necessary to defeat the representatives of Communist imperialism on your soil. . . . Those who advocate [removal of the French troops from Indochina] must know that if such a course is adopted it will mean not independence but complete domination by a foreign power."[50] So patent was the American drive to stop at nothing in blocking Communist success in Indochina that Eden at Bermuda felt compelled to caution the American leaders not to "go it alone" and thus destroy the entire working alliance of the West.

Indochina confronted the Eisenhower administration with its gravest foreign policy dilemma. Dulles had to reassure those who feared the Communist domination of all Southeast Asia that the United States would remain firm. At the same time, he had to reassure moderate Republicans, Democrats, the British, and free Asians everywhere that American policies would not involve the world in another war. Daily the French promises of victory proved to be false. In the crisis Dulles required a coalition of powers if he would hold the line, but the nations of Europe and Asia had no sympathy for official American objectives in Indochina. Having repeatedly agreed with the new isolationists that the French province was the key to all Southeast Asia and more, the secretary had no choice but to revise downward the American estimation of its strategic importance or to commit the United States to a policy of defending the region alone. His response to the challenge was clear: if the Red pressure continued, the United States would draw deeply enough on its air-atomic resources to counterbalance its shortage of allies.[51]

Dulles, amid the burgeoning crisis in Southeast Asia, announced that the United States would fill the vacuum in Western policy by placing new emphasis on the "deterrent of massive retaliatory power" to supplement the reliance "on local defensive power." The free community now would depend on its willingness and ability "to respond vigorously at places and with means of its own choosing."[52] This implied the bombing of areas beyond the range of immediate aggression; the places of American choosing were assumed to be the cities of China and the Soviet Union. Critics in the United States, Europe, and Asia predicted that such a strategy would narrow the freedom of choice to either complete inaction or the mushroom cloud. In April 1954, Dulles explained his original statement more fully:

[50]Upon his return from the Far East, Nixon repeated that warning over radio and television, December 23, 1953, ibid. 30 (January 4, 1954): 12.
[51]Dulles's address to the New York Council on Foreign Relations, January 12, 1954, ibid. 30 (January 25, 1954): 108–09.
[52]Ibid., p. 108.

The essential thing is that a potential aggressor should know in advance that he can and will be made to suffer for his aggression more than he can possibly gain by it. This calls for a system in which local defensive strength is reinforced by more mobile deterrent power. The method of doing so will vary according to the character of the various areas. . . . [L]ocal defense is important. But in such areas the main reliance must be on the power of the free community to retaliate with great force by mobile means at places of its own choice.[53]

He assured Congress that the capacity to retaliate instantly did not impose the necessity of unleashing atomic power in every instance of attack; he concluded that "it is not our intention to turn every local war into a general war."

Massive retaliation conformed perfectly to the official American dogma, vigorously supported by the new isolationism, that all Communist gains in Asia had resulted from pure military aggression emanating from the Soviet Union and China. Such aggression had allegedly driven Jiang onto Taiwan; now it threatened to overrun Indochina as well. Nixon had described the struggle within Indochina as a simple matter of Communist imperialism on French soil. Dulles himself limited the threat to "the mighty land power of the Communist world." It was this great landed force that demanded "the further deterrent of massive retaliatory power," for otherwise a potential aggressor, glutted with manpower, "might be tempted to attack in confidence that resistance would be confined to manpower." Knowland voiced the theme more succinctly when he said that "Communism is a global and not a mere area menace"; it advanced on the conspiracy to destroy freedom everywhere.[54] Massive retaliation satisfied those Americans who were determined to hold the line in the Far East while they avoided jungle wars and reduced military expenditures in the United States. Essentially it offered an inexpensive and generally risk-free method whereby the nation could have its way all over the world. As many predicted at the outset, the new strategy disturbed the European allies and the free nations of Asia more than it did Ho Chi Minh and the Red Chinese who called the bluff and proceeded unhindered in their assault on the French position in Southeast Asia.

Somehow the very simplicity of massive retaliation raised serious doubts because it guaranteed too much. It promised to hold the line against the Russo-Chinese alliance on the vast continent of Asia with

[53]John Foster Dulles, "Policy for Security and Peace," *Foreign Affairs* 32 (April 1954): 358–59.

[54]Knowland, "The 'Instant Retaliation' Policy Defended," p. 69.

primarily air-atomic power, without effective allies, even while it permitted reductions in both available manpower and the military budget. Many challenged Dulles's statement that the United States could afford no more conflicts like the Korean War. For them there was no other type of war that the nation could afford. Hans J. Morgenthau, the noted political scientist at the University of Chicago, averred that "a Korean war, even one fought in perpetuity, is cheaper in every respect than an atomic war."[55] Lester B. Pearson, Canada's secretary of state for External Affairs, accepted massive retaliation as one component in democratic strategy but opposed the use of more force than necessary to stop an aggressor. He argued instead for limited wars ending in negotiated settlement. "If hostilities ever again break out," he warned, "surely every effort must be made, not only to prove that aggression does not pay by repelling and defeating the aggression, but also to localize the hostilities, to bring them to an end as soon as the limited objective is accomplished; and then to work at once for a peace which will be just but not savage, the kind of peace that will not have planted in it the seeds of future war."[56]

Critics predicted that Dulles's policy of massive retaliation would prove a failure in action as well as in concept. They saw that under conditions of revolutionary change sweeping the Orient, whether successfully exploited by Communist spokesmen or not, the real challenge to the status quo would always be the quest for independence and a better existence, one that arose wholly out of indigenous conditions. It was such issues in Indochina that gave power to the straggling forces of Ho Chi Minh, and it was not clear how the dropping of bombs on such Asiatic targets could ease the demand for change that was exerting itself not through overt military aggression but through an internal upheaval anchored to emotion and spirit. Since purely military and industrial installations would be hard to find, the bombing of human targets in Asia appeared certain to alienate millions of Asians. It was doubtful if the coolies of Shanghai would understand that they were being vaporized for the brutal and sadistic treatment meted out to U.S. prisoners in some distant Chinese camp. Chester Bowles, recently ambassador to India, queried: "Would not the atomic destruction of defenseless Chinese cities—while Russian cities remained untouched—turn all Asia into our bitter and unrelenting enemies?"[57] Nor was it

---

[55]Hans J. Morgenthau, "Will It Deter Aggression?" *New Republic* 130 (March 29, 1954): 11–14.

[56]Lester B. Pearson, *Democracy in World Politics* (Princeton, NJ, 1955), p. 30. This quotation appears in an essay entitled "Proportions of Force."

[57]Chester Bowles, "A Plea for Another Great Debate," *New York Times Magazine*, February 28, 1954, p. 64.

certain that massive retaliation could guarantee a cheap and easy victory. It assumed zero enemy capability from an enemy with access to atomic bombs, and it ignored the oft-stated fact that "preventive war is war." Dulles's policy of instant retaliation, finally, defied the primary rules of coalition diplomacy. In his speech announcing his new policy, the secretary stressed the need for joint action: "We need allies and collective security. Our purpose is to make these relations more effective, less costly."[58] If indeed he believed that the free nations would respond favorably to his use of power as a substitute for diplomacy, he overlooked their fear of atomic warfare and their lack of sympathy for the goals and the inflexibility of American purpose.

From the besieged Indochinese fortress of Dienbienphu in March and April 1954, the crucial test came for Dulles's new Asiatic policies. General Paul Ely, French chief of staff in Indochina, informed American leaders that the time for Allied intervention had arrived. In response, Dulles called for the internationalization of the Indochinese war, warning that the "imposition of Southeast Asia of the political system of Communist Russia and its Chinese Communist ally, by whatever means, would be a grave threat to the whole free community. The United States feels that the possibility should not be passively accepted, but should be met by united action. This might involve serious risks. But these risks are far less than those that will face us a few years from now, if we dare not be resolute today."[59] Numerous Americans, especially political and military leaders who recognized in this new crisis the opportunity (denied them in Korea) to destroy the Beijing regime, demanded that the United States save the French province. Nixon informed newsmen in Washington that the fall of Dienbienphu would be catastrophic. To Knowland the free world had reached the "jumping off place," and, if it did not react properly, it would witness the loss of all Southeast Asia. Dulles even warned that a situation might arise in which the United States might be forced to act alone. President Eisenhower affirmed Dulles's stand that this nation must block Communist expansion by whatever means were available; if one more nation went down, the others, like a row of dominoes, would follow.[60]

During the crisis month of April the public statements of national leaders became more strident, if less consistent. On April 7 the president was quoted at a press conference as saying that "we simply cannot afford to lose Indochina." Nixon, on April 16, told the American Society

[58]Dulles's address of January 12, 1954, Department of State *Bulletin* 30 (January 25, 1954): 108–09.

[59]Dulles's speech before the Overseas Press Club, New York, March 29, 1954, ibid. 30 (April 12, 1954): 539–40.

[60]Eisenhower's press statement of April 7, 1954, *Time*, April 19, 1954, p. 19.

of Newspaper Editors: "If, to avoid further Communist expansion in Asia and Indochina we must take the risk now by putting our boys in, I think the Executive has to take the politically unpopular decision and do it." So violent was the reaction to his speech among Republican editors that the administration demurred. Four days after Nixon's statement, Dulles admitted that the administration believed it unlikely that American troops would be employed in Indochina.[61] Meanwhile, Dulles and Radford, who admitted that he was not speaking for the Joint Chiefs, had moved to obtain congressional support for an air strike to relieve the embattled French at Dienbienphu.[62] Then to secure British approval for his policy of "united action," Dulles conferred with Churchill and Eden in London. The eve of the Geneva Conference in late April still found the French seeking military aid from Radford and Dulles in Paris. At the eleventh hour, however, the British cabinet rejected the plan for united action, while the British chiefs of staff predicted that within forty-eight hours after the initial air attack the demand for ground forces would become irresistible. The British feared that Allied intervention would provoke a direct countermove by the Chinese Reds and greatly enlarge the Asian war. Facing consistent opposition in both Britain and the United States, Dulles's plan for military involvement ground to an abrupt halt. With the fall of Dienbienphu in May 1954, the struggle for Indochina was transferred to the conference table at Geneva.[63]

Throughout the siege of the fortress, the reality that Indochina lay at the extremity, not the center, of America's vital interests became increasingly the basic determinant in U.S. action. Many congressmen and members of the press argued that the United States dared not become bogged down alone in another war on the Asian continent. To the end some of the congressional extremists were willing to "go it alone," but not the administration. As April wore on the president became more responsive to the views of Generals Ridgway and Nathan F. Twining of the Joint Chiefs, key members of Congress, and leading editors, all of whom were opposed to American intervention. Radford and Dulles did not have their way.

Dulles attended the Geneva Conference, limited by his own attitudes and those of Republican leaders at home. Without either allies or complete congressional backing, he had the choice of bluffing or compromising. Unable to exert pressure on the Chinese, he had recourse only to negotiation. American leadership at that moment required a

[61]*New York Times*, April 21, 1954, p. 4.
[62]Chalmers, M. Roberts, "The Day We Didn't Go to War," *Reporter* 11 (September 14, 1954): 31–35.
[63]Survey of the Indochinese crisis in *Des Moines Register*, June 13, 1954.

secretary of state with the freedom to discuss, negotiate, and bargain. Instead, Dulles's diplomatic powers were completely circumscribed; he had been warned by powerful congressional new isolationists, whom the administration would not defy, against an Asian "Munich" or a "sell-out." These political restraints ruled out even a glance at the Chinese delegation, and Dulles could assure Republican leaders upon his return that he had acceded to their demands. At Geneva he could do nothing but call for free elections and a reunified Korea and then disengage himself from the conference as quickly as possible.[64] With this nation on the sidelines, the French were forced to negotiate alone. The American failure of leadership seemed to prove the Soviet and Chinese contentions that, if the free nations would ignore the United States, the great tensions of the world could be resolved. Many writers were critical of this undermining of U.S. diplomacy by the irreconcilables in Washington. "They have raised the false hopes which have then to be denied," Lippmann charged. "They have made a united front impossible by their extremism, their contempt for negotiation, their advocacy of a big war. They have frightened off, indeed they have lined up against us, all the important nations that were needed if there was to be a united front." Such diplomatic setbacks would be repeated, he believed, as long as the State Department remained a "paralyzed instrument of policy" and a "bureaucracy intimidated by demagogues."

After May 1954, Eisenhower and Dulles modified their domino theory by declaring their intention to strengthen the other nations of Southeast Asia so that if Indochina should fall the others would stand. From his failure to uphold American purpose and prestige at Geneva, Dulles struck back with the Manila Pact of September 1954 which established the Southeast Asia Treaty Organization (SEATO). The new alliance, which included the United States, Britain, France, Australia, New Zealand, Pakistan, Thailand, and the Philippines, was designed to ensure Southeast Asia against further encroachment of Communist power. The eight signatories promised only to confer in the event of "any fact or situation which might endanger the peace of the area" south of Taiwan. As a military arrangement it demonstrated the weakness, rather than the strength, of American policy, for the only countries that could have made it a success in building the needed balance of power in the Orient refused to join. Collective defense in Southeast Asia without the allegiance of India, Burma, Ceylon, and Indonesia, observed Drew Middleton of the *New York Times*, was as absurd as NATO without France and Italy. The Asian bloc, represented

[64]Dulles's address on Korea at the Geneva Conference, April 28, 1954, Department of State *Bulletin* 30 (May 10, 1954): 704–07.

by the Nehru school, charged SEATO with violating the neutralist third force tactics of free Asia. This middle way, Asian spokesmen believed, would serve as a brake on the two power groups and would best protect Asia against involvement in another general war. To them communism was not an external military threat but rather the product of economic misery and political misrule that could be dealt with only by eliminating the conditions.

VI

Both in Europe and in Asia the Eisenhower-Dulles policies embodied objectives that lay outside the interests and the genuine intent of national action. This proclivity to pursue the unachievable reflected, at least in part, the president's determination to coexist with the demands imposed on him by congressional Republicans. Eisenhower refused to attack forthrightly the fundamental new isolationist assumption of American invincibility. Thus the attacks on the State Department had to continue, for here allegedly was the real danger to American security. Critics of past policy grew restive at the retention of Truman-Acheson holdovers. That regime was thoroughly discredited, so the argument ran, and all connected with it should be removed from office. "Most Americans," wrote columnist George Sokolsky, "desire a pro-American State Department and hope that they will get it in due course." Republican irreconcilables in the Senate vigorously opposed the appointments of Bohlen to the USSR and Conant to Germany because both had served under the Truman administration. When a Senate fight loomed, the administration ran out on the appointment of Mildred McAfee Horton. Nor did it oppose the relentless pursuit of Foreign Service officers who were associated with U.S. policy on China before 1949.[65]

It required only a few weeks for the Eisenhower administration to arrive at a modus operandi with Republican leaders in Congress. After Senator McCarthy in the spring of 1953 had launched his crusade against the Voice of America and the Overseas Books Program and negotiated his agreement with Greek shipowners, he acknowledged publicly, after a luncheon with Dulles, that foreign policy was an executive function. While the administration thereafter defended nothing that occurred prior to January 20, 1953, the date that it assumed office, the senator and other congressional investigators had begun to limit their attacks to events and personalities of the Truman and Roosevelt

---

[65]On McCarthy and the Senate see William S. White, "Joe McCarthy, the Man with the Power," *Look* 17 (June 16, 1953): 30–31; and John B. Oakes, "Inquiry into McCarthy's Status," *New York Times Magazine*, April 12, 1953, p. 9. On the Bohlen nomination see *Time*, March 23, 1953, p. 24, and March 30, 1953, p. 14.

administrations. When McCarthy, for example, was frustrated during an investigation of the armed forces during the late summer of 1953, he was specific in naming the culprits. The army, he had charged, was doing "what they did under the Truman administration." While there was a better attitude after Eisenhower assumed office, "the political carry-overs are still functioning to cover up, protect, and white-wash."

It was strange, in a sense, that the administration refused to defend the Voice of America, for it had special significance as an agency in the new Dulles policy of liberation. Dulles himself had written: "[W]e have spent little on the war of ideas in which we are deeply engaged and are suffering reverses that cannot be canceled out by any amount of military power."[66] He informed Congress shortly before he took office that on the effectiveness of an American program to convey truth to the world "may hang the question of war or peace." What the attack on the Voice accomplished was not clear. Raymond Aron, the distinguished Parisian journalist, wrote in the *New Yorker* that the attack had a purely political objective and that, since there had been no charges of Communist activity in the Voice of America staff, the search was not for subversives but for "a cheap political victory against a group of dedicated anti-Communists." So prompt were the State Department's reversals of policy on the Overseas Books Program, resulting from pressure exerted by McCarthy, that William S. White observed: "No greater series of victories by a Congressional body over a senior Executive Department in so short a time is recalled here."[67]

Perhaps the most disquieting account of those early topsy-turvy days of the Eisenhower administration can be found in Martin Merson's *The Private Diary of a Public Servant* (1955). In this brief volume Merson, consultant to Robert L. Johnson, President Eisenhower's appointee to head the International Information Administration (which included the Voice of America), described the dismal record of false accusations,

[66] John Foster Dulles, *War or Peace* (New York, 1950), p. 249.
[67] White in *New York Times*, February 22, 1953. Leading Democrats felt powerless to defend those accused by McCarthy. Because Eisenhower had been elected overwhelmingly by the American people, they believed that it was the responsibility of the administration to defend those unjustly accused; any Democratic efforts would be attributed to partisanship unless they had the support of the president. Such views appear in Franklin D. Roosevelt, Jr., to Mrs. Sherrett S. Chase, March 5, 1953; and J. William Fulbright to Chase, February 27, 1953, letters in possession of the author. Reston noted as late as October 1953 that McCarthy, because Republican leaders continued to defer to him, still controlled the foreign policy debate in Washington. See Reston in *New York Times*, October 7, 1953. Not until McCarthy in late 1953 accused the administration of sending "perfumed notes" did Dulles receive Eisenhower's permission to acknowledge the administration's displeasure with the senator. See *Des Moines Register*, December 2, 1953; and Department of State *Bulletin* 29 (December 14, 1953): 811–12.

ubiquitous resignations under fire, the disintegration of the Voice of America, and the refusal of the White House to oppose McCarthy or defend anyone who challenged him. By July, Merson, along with Johnson, had resigned, puzzled by the refusal of Eisenhower to seek out the American people rather than to accommodate himself to congressional pressure, compromise, and expediency.

With Executive Order 10450 the Eisenhower administration sought to fulfill the campaign pledge to rid the government of "security risks." It appointed Scott McLeod, a close friend of McCarthy and former assistant to Senator Styles Bridges, to administer the order. McLeod soon discovered that he could remove, without difficulty, old Acheson associates under the new order because it enumerated about seventy characteristics for which a government employee could be termed a security risk. These demanded such rigid standards of political conservatism, previous associations, attitudes, and sexual behavior that few statesmen since George Washington could have met all the requirements.[68] Under the new security system the administration became involved in the "numbers game." As hundreds were released from federal service, the national leadership was never clear on the number of actual subversives found in the State Department. McLeod demurred when questioned: "I don't think that people are concerned with any breakdown. They don't care if they are drunks, perverts, or Communists—they just want us to get rid of them." In February 1954 he told a Lincoln Day rally in Worland, Wyoming: "In the twenty years from 1933–1953, traitors had free run in high places and low. It is not for me to tell you why—it is up to those who permitted it to tell you why. . . . I wish they would stop squalling 'smear' and stand up like men and offer an explanation if they can."[69]

Actually in the first seven months under Executive Order 10450 somewhat less than two hundred security risks were removed from the State Department, one of whom was a suspected but unproved subversive. In June 1954, Undersecretary Walter Bedell Smith testified that not one Communist had been found in the State Department under the Eisenhower order. The administration did nothing to correct this discrepancy; if it had uncovered any subversives it did not reveal them. The new security system, although thousands lost their posts under it, did not turn up a single traitor, spy, or subversive whom the government was willing to indict. This lack of evidence gradually led many to

[68]Henry Steele Commager, "The Perilous Delusion of Security," *Reporter* 13 (November 3, 1955): 34.

[69]Quoted in Charlotte Knight, "What Price Security?" *Collier's* 134 (July 9, 1954): 67.

wonder whether there ever was any betrayal in the State Department.[70] Whatever the responsibility of the State Department in the creation of the country's external problems, it was still in January 1953 a useful policy instrument. Many of its top- and middle-level officers were men of such experience, ability, and competence that it was doubtful if they could be replaced by a team of equal quality, yet during the next two years many of these officers either had been dismissed or had resigned voluntarily. The disintegration of the China Service began under President Truman; by 1954 congressional attacks had almost denuded the government of experts on China and the Soviet Union. These years of political assault, plus the refusal of the administration to protect the State Department and Foreign Service from congressional cannonading, had reduced morale so drastically that it was doubtful if these agencies still had the capacity to serve as the eyes, ears, and brains of the United States in the area of foreign affairs. Foreign Service officers abroad felt deserted in high places, and many became bitter toward Dulles for not defending them. As one officer declared, "if you can't count on your own Secretary of State to stand up for you, what can you count on?"[71]

As a final gesture to those in pursuit of Foreign Service officers connected with China policy, Dulles dropped the distinguished and popular John Paton Davies from the service. The secretary made it clear that Davies's loyalty was not in question, but under 10450 it was "not enough that an employee be of complete and unswerving loyalty. He must be reliable, trustworthy, of good conduct and character." What made Davies vulnerable was the accuracy of his reporting preceding the collapse of Jiang Jieshi and his refusal to agree that the Nationalists could recapture the mainland. Having accepted the rationale of the Nationalist China bloc on matters of China policy, the secretary had no choice but to accede to its pressure. Critics believed that the Davies case would "complete the wreckage of the Service morale." Former official George Kennan predicted that it would produce "great sadness and discouragement." Even the administration's staunch supporter, Arthur Krock of the *New York Times,* described the case as "deplorable," and Roscoe Drummond of the *New York Herald-Tribune* predicted that "if the government keeps this up . . . it won't have a Foreign Service

---

[70]Ibid., pp. 58–67; Commager, "The Perilous Delusion of Security," pp. 34–35; Allen Drury in *New York Times,* October 2, 1955.

[71]Dorothy Fosdick, "For the Foreign Service—Help Wanted," *New York Times Magazine,* November 20, 1955, p. 65. On the decline of the Foreign Service see Eric Severeid, "Shooting Our Own Sentries," *Reporter* 13 (November 17, 1955): 31; Hans J. Morgenthau in *Des Moines Register,* May 1, 1955; and Perry Laukhuff, "How to Bargain with Russia," *Harper's Magazine* 210 (June 1955): 30.

worth the cable costs to transmit its judgments." It seemed doubtful to many critics whether anything that the secretary might do could repair the damage. "Mr. Dulles has half-blinded our watchmen overseas at a moment when clear vision was never more needed."[72]

In a special letter to the *New York Times* published on January 17, 1954, five well-known and distinguished former members of the Foreign Service—Norman Armour, Robert Woods Bliss, Joseph Grew, William Phillips, and G. Howland Shaw—had warned the nation that the Foreign Service was being destroyed. They declared that with rare exceptions "the justification for these attacks has been so flimsy as to have no standing in a Court of Law." They were disturbed not only by the dismissal of many officers, who in the past had reported conscientiously only to have their loyalty and integrity suddenly challenged, but also by the ambiguous and cautious reporting of those who remained. "When any such tendency begins its insidious work," they added, "it is not long before accuracy and initiative have been sacrificed to acceptability and conformity. The ultimate result is a threat to national security. In this connection the history of the Nazi and Fascist Foreign Services before the Second World War is pertinent." These men wondered whether the Eisenhower security system, which attached undue consideration to political and economic views and casual associations, which opened easy avenues to anonymous informers, and which accepted the evaluations of persons inexperienced in affairs abroad, was not "laying the foundations for a Foreign Service competent to serve a totalitarian government rather than the Government of the United States as we have heretofore known it." It would be tragic, they agreed, if the emphasis on security "should lead us to cripple the Foreign Service, our first line of national defense, at the very time when its effectiveness is essential to our filling the place which History has assigned to us." Whether the security system had produced more protection against future subversion was doubtful, but it was certain that the system had done little for the competence, efficiency, and performance of the Foreign Service.

Eisenhower's unwillingness to defend public officials against charges of subversion posed a curious dilemma. In his administration's gesture at "unleashing" Jiang, its unwillingness to define policy for Asia in terms of Asian nationalism, its dogged pursuit of Foreign Service officers and dismissal of Davies, its refusal to defend the State Department, and its vigorous employment of Executive Order 10450, the president either believed that a few Americans were solely responsible

---

[72]Kennan, Krock, and Drummond quoted in ibid. 210 (January 1955): 20–21. Some former federal officials were troubled that Eisenhower refused to defend Davies.

for the collapse of the Guomindang and the Communist-led pressures on Asia, or he was willing to pay an exorbitantly high price for party unity. It was never clear how the administration could quiet the continuous new isolationist insinuations of past treason and protect U.S. policy from the effect of such attacks on both the country's understanding and its diplomacy unless it were willing to defend vigorously the premises that the United States had limited power to control events in Eastern Europe or to stem the tide of revolution in Asia. Although the president did little to contest the new isolationist notions regarding American needs abroad, he still refused to formulate actual policy on those assumptions.

Whatever the price to the country of the Eisenhower administration's acceptance of the neoisolationist assumptions of the decade, the price did not impinge on the American people generally or weaken the almost unprecedented foreign policy consensus that underwrote the Eisenhower-Dulles approach to foreign affairs. Eisenhower could assume the overwhelming support of liberal Republicans on foreign as well as domestic issues, but his foreign policy coalition required also a large Democratic element. Unfortunately, any purposeful move to solidify his Democratic support would have challenged his liaison with the Republican Old Guard and undermined the unity of the Republican party. In practice, therefore, the president discarded the machinery of bipartisanship, which did not injure his leadership because he received the support of Democratic leaders in Congress. This was especially true of the successive chairmen of the Senate Foreign Relations Committee following the Democratic sweep of 1954. It was the new isolationists whose favor he curried who remained rebellious at his leadership in foreign affairs because he could never fulfill their demands.

To Dulles fell the task of appeasing the Republican right wing. The specific problem of the administration was to prevent Knowland, Bridges, and Jenner from pushing the United States into war against mainland China and McCarthy from abusing the State Department. To quiet these new isolationists, Dulles breathed fire in defining American purposes abroad while he offered only negative policies. This maneuver seemed to work, for at heart the Republican right, bent on tax reduction, really wanted no more trouble than did the administration. Whereas Dulles's hard, intransigent stance looked to the Old Guard of his party, Eisenhower's persistent attitude of conciliation— his emphasis on peace and Western unity—looked to the world and to the American people in general. This cleavage was so obvious in the Eisenhower and Dulles speeches before the American Society of Newspaper Editors in April 1953 that it had produced a sharp reaction in

Europe. One Paris editor declared that the president's conciliatory words and generosity of tone were followed by "a harangue in which intransigence competed with mock innocence." The London *Times* found Dulles's remarks "strangely hard to reconcile with the spirit of the President's speech."

This concerted and successful effort to bridge the foreign policy gap within the Republican party ruled out any direct appeal to Democratic sentiment. If vocal opposition to Republican foreign policy was almost nonexistent among Democratic spokesmen, true bipartisanship, as Senator Vandenberg would have understood it, was absent from the Washington scene. Whatever hope Eisenhower had in January 1953 of creating a genuine bipartisan foreign policy that purpose lay buried by 1954 under the blanket charges of treason. The president had appointed no Democrats to important policymaking positions in his administration; those with long experience in foreign affairs were no longer consulted. Perhaps their attendance at high-level conferences would have made little difference. In Congress the Democrats gave Eisenhower the support he required, although he made little effort to cultivate it. Democratic leaders pointed out that their buildup of Chinese Nationalist forces on Taiwan during the two previous years had anticipated a move commensurate with the president's withdrawal of the Seventh Fleet. Many Democrats believed that the time had arrived to demand more purposeful defense activity from Western Europe as a condition to further aid. This Democratic cooperation, based largely on conviction, accounted for the smoothness of the administration's relations with Congress. The core of Eisenhower's political success lay in the fact that the Democrats defended his foreign policies in Congress without demanding in return that he defend them from Republican neoisolationist attacks.

American foreign policy evolved into a pattern far better than the administration's political and intellectual commitments to the new isolationism would suggest. It was the president's unwillingness to pursue the unlimited objectives of the new isolationism in practice that maintained the support of Democrats, liberal Republicans, and independents. His unwillingness to destroy the party symbols of 1952 nevertheless had limited his triumphs, extensive as they were, to areas of action which would not challenge the stereotypes of Yalta and Potsdam. The administration resisted those who would build fortress America on air and sea power alone and terminate aid to the Allies. It sought a truce in Korea rather than follow party demands for a renewal of war and a thorough conquest of the Chinese forces. It fought valiantly to maintain the strength and unity of NATO. These comprised in a sense the greatest foreign policy achievements of the Eisenhower administration. The president eschewed some tests which he could have carried with Democratic votes rather than antagonize the Republican right. Thus Republican unity demanded its price. No matter how successful its external relations might be, the administration would remain vulnerable to attack. No change in American leadership could alter Soviet or Chinese power and purpose, nor would new leadership in Washington reduce the force of nationalistic upheaval in Asia and Africa. Whatever external challenges the United States had faced in the postwar era would continue to exist, but men in power chose to act as if new and dynamic foreign policies were actually available that could achieve the goal of almost perfect security at reduced cost. Such official premises of invincibility, unfortunately, could never create the necessary foundation upon which to build an effective program that would bring the nation's commitments and its power into balance.

CHAPTER NINE

Vietnam: Challenge of the 1960s*

NEVER IN AMERICAN HISTORY did a single area of conflict dominate the nation's thought on foreign affairs as long and as divisively as did Vietnam during the decade that followed John F. Kennedy's accession to the presidency in January 1961. That this Asian country, recently established and lacking significant military power, could attain such importance suggests a profound dilemma. Why should the United States have concerned itself for so long and at such heavy cost with the internal affairs of a new Asian state, over 10,000 miles away, without a navy or air force and with exceedingly limited ground forces when contrasted to those which existed elsewhere even in Asia? On the other hand, why should a small, backward, jungle-ridden country embarrass the U.S. militarily when this country possessed more destructive power than any nation in history? Even a cursory examination of the 1950s is sufficient to answer the first question; the answers demanded by the second would become clear only with the passage of time.

Spokesmen of the Truman and Eisenhower administrations, by predicting disaster for the globe should South Vietnam fall, transformed that jungle nation after mid-century into a critical area in the struggle against world communism. President Eisenhower in April 1959, had stressed the military importance of Indochina in terms that had long been commonplace: "Strategically, South Viet-Nam's capture by the Communists would bring their power several hundred miles into a hitherto free region. The remaining countries of Southeast Asia would

---

*Published in *Cold War Diplomacy: American Foreign Policy, 1945–1975* (New York, 1977). Reprinted by permission.

be menaced by a great flanking movement. . . . The loss of South Viet-Nam would set in motion a crumbling process that could, as it progressed, have grave consequences for us and for freedom."[1] Such dramatic phraseology, leaving unexplained the process by which the collapse of South Vietnam would actually endanger the United States and freedom, rendered Washington powerless either to give up its commitments to South Vietnam's defense or to create the means required for victory against the demonstrated power and human resources of North Vietnam. Lacking clearly demonstrable interests in South Vietnam upon which they could build a national consensus, successive administrations in Washington attempted to sustain the war by avoiding all the fundamental issues that it raised. The United States drifted into the war, fought it, and left it without the benefit of a national decision. It is not strange that the involvement ended in disaster; it could hardly have been otherwise.

President Eisenhower bequeathed to Kennedy not only a deep commitment to the success of Ngo Dinh Diem's Saigon regime but also a dual program designed to gain that objective at a negligible cost to the American people. After 1954 Washington had assigned to Diem the major responsibility for containing the ambitions of Ho Chi Minh and the expansion of Communist influence and power into Southeast Asia. To assure Diem's success the administration embarked on a crash program of military and economic aid, including special funds for the resettlement of refugees from North Vietnam. As Diem, with lavish support, slowly brought some order to South Vietnam—in part at the price of sending his political opposition into exile—the enthusiasm of his American adherents exceeded the bounds of propriety. By 1957 Washington officials spoke freely of Diem's "miracle" in South Vietnam. When in May of that year the South Vietnamese president visited Washington, Eisenhower greeted him at the airport and hailed him as one of the truly outstanding leaders of the age. In their subsequent communiqué, the two presidents anticipated the peaceful unification of Vietnam under a freely elected government.[2] Such phrases were intellectually corrupting in both Washington and Saigon, for they created expectations of success that no reasonable expenditure of effort could achieve.

[1]Eisenhower's address at Gettysburg College, April 4, 1959, Department of State *Bulletin* 40 (April 27, 1959): 580–81. For a similar assessment of the danger see G. Frederick Reinhart's speech before the International Relations Club of the University of South Carolina, March 5, 1959, ibid. 40 (March 23, 1959): 398.

[2]Joint communiqué, May 11, 1957, ibid. 36 (May 27, 1957): 851. A typically optimistic view of Ngo Dinh Diem's leadership can be found in John Osborne, "The Tough Miracle Man of Vietnam," *Life* 42 (May 13, 1957): 156–76. Osborne declared that Diem had aroused his country and routed the Communists.

Even then the evidence of the miracle was largely nonexistent. Diem, concerned primarily with the security and well-being of his own regime, had made little effort to democratize his army or to satisfy the demands of the Vietnamese peasants. After 1957 Communist-led guerrillas began to organize the countryside, taking control of village after village until by 1960 they commanded most of the provinces of South Vietnam.[3] The miracle of Vietnam had been a miracle in public relations but little else. Still Eisenhower wrote to Diem in 1960 on the occasion of the Republic of Vietnam's fifth anniversary:

> During the years of your independence it has been refreshing for us to observe how clearly the Government and the citizens of Vietnam have faced the fact that the greatest danger to their independence was Communism. You and your countrymen have used your strength well in accepting the double challenge of building your country and resisting Communist imperialism. . . . Vietnam's ability to defend itself from the Communists has grown immeasurably since its successful struggle to become an independent Republic.[4]

Already terrorism and infiltration had begun to undermine the carefully constructed image of a stable and secure Vietnam. The insurgency spread even more rapidly with the formation in December 1960 of the National Liberation Front (NLF), the political arm of the Viet Cong dedicated to both the liberation of South Vietnam and the unification of the country. Diem continued to play down the Communist threat, for its existence reflected adversely on his leadership and the alleged triumphs of his government. When in 1961 he acknowledged his inability to counter the increasingly open and defiant guerrilla challenge to his regime, he reminded President Kennedy of the long-standing American commitment to South Vietnamese independence.

Washington had prepared meticulously for the possible failure of its political strategy, based on Diem's success in eliminating Ho Chi Minh's influence from South Vietnam, by developing a military strategy as well. After September 1954, SEATO had carried the military burden

---

[3]For superb analyses of Communist gains in Vietnam see Bernard B. Fall, *The Two Viet-Nams: A Political and Military Analysis* (New York, 1964), pp. 316–31; Fall, "The Theory and Practice of Insurgency and Counterinsurgency," *Naval War College Review* 17 (April 1965): 21–37; "Costly Victory in Vietnam," *Life* 49 (November 28, 1960): 30; Richard Goodwin, "Reflections on Vietnam," *New Yorker*, April 16, 1966, pp. 76–78; Robert Scheer, *How the United States Got Involved in Vietnam* (Santa Barbara, CA, 1965), pp. 54–60; and David Hotham, "South Vietnam—Shaky Bastion," *New Republic* 137 (November 25, 1957): 13–16.

[4]Eisenhower to Diem, October 22, 1960, Department of State *Bulletin* 43 (November 14, 1960): 758.

of containment in Southeast Asia. The efficacy of that alliance as a guarantor of Southeast Asian stability quickly moved beyond the realm of official doubt. Beginning with the first SEATO Council meeting at Karachi, Pakistan, in 1956, the organization had embarked on its program of self-adulation which continued with diminishing restraint into the 1960s.[5] As late as 1962, Secretary of Defense Robert McNamara assured a congressional committee that SEATO's evolution into a sound military organization had eliminated the need for U.S. ground forces in any foreseeable Asian conflict. On the occasion of SEATO's ninth anniversary in 1963, Prime Minister Sarit Thanarat of Thailand recounted the alliance's successes:

> At present it may be said that SEATO is an important fortress capable of making the Communists think carefully before committing any aggression against the area under the Treaty [which included South Vietnam]. Since this organization acts as an effective deterrent to potential aggressors, it has increasingly been attacked verbally by the Communists. This indicates how important SEATO is in resisting Communist aggression.[6]

Actually SEATO had never functioned as a unit because of internal disagreements over purpose. Nowhere in SEATO was there any force, other than the mobile striking power of the United States, that could resist the encroachments of Ho Chi Minh. The United States, however, had no greater commitment to action under SEATO than other members of the pact. As the chairman of the Senate Foreign Relations Committee declared on the occasion of the pact's approval, "the Treaty [SEATO] does not call for automatic action; it calls for consultation with other signatories. . . . I cannot emphasize too strongly that we have no obligations . . . to take positive measures of any kind. All we are obligated to do is to consult together about it."

Washington never contemplated a direct American military involvement in Southeast Asia. Still it continued to predict disaster if containment at the 17th parallel should falter. For the moment this chasm between the ends and means of policy mattered little. As long as Diem and SEATO guaranteed successful containment at minimal cost, the administration faced no need to prepare for action or explain

[5]First annual report of the SEATO Council, March 1, 1956, ibid. 34 (March 12, 1956): 403–08. For an optimistic evaluation of SEATO in 1956 see Arthur H. Dean, "Collective Defense in Southeast Asia," *Current History* 31 (July 1956): 7–14; and South-East Asia Treaty Organization, *SEATO: 1954–1964* (Bangkok, Thailand, 1965), pp. 5–9.

[6]Thanarat's statement, September 8, 1963, *SEATO Record* 2 (October 1963): 4.

what the United States was really containing. Eisenhower had accomplished none of his purposes in Asia. Diem's regime had not produced the political and economic miracle claimed for it, SEATO did not possess an effectiveness commensurate with the praise that Washington and others heaped upon it, and nonrecognition had not eliminated China's Beijing regime. When Eisenhower left office in January 1961, the Saigon government faced disaster everywhere and SEATO had demonstrated its profound ineffectiveness.

II

Neither President Kennedy nor his foreign policy advisers assumed office with any intention to review critically the policies which they inherited.[7] Anchoring his administration to past assumptions, the new president warned in his inaugural address that the United States would "pay any price, bear any burden, meet any hardship, support any friend, oppose any foe to assure the survival and success of liberty."[8] Still he reminded the nation that the instruments of war far outpaced the instruments of peace. If the Eisenhower policies had been popular and apparently peaceful, it was only because those policies held the assurance of success without reference to the price that the United States would pay to render them effective. Confronted with the rapidly deteriorating fortunes of Laos and South Vietnam, the Kennedy administration either had to give up the struggle against Ho Chi Minh or introduce ever larger increments of military and economic support to enable the nation's allies in Southeast Asia to resist more effectively the infiltration and insurgency.

In Laos the situation was explosive. The Eisenhower-backed pro-Western government had no chance against the pro-Communist Pathet Lao guerrilla forces. Still Eisenhower and Dulles refused to compromise the American goal of creating a strong anti-Communist regime in Vientiane. Kennedy recognized the American overcommitment to Laos, but was determined to avoid any humiliation. In March 1961 he warned Beijing, Moscow, and Hanoi via television that the United States would not tolerate a Communist conquest of Laos.[9] During April, however,

[7]See James C. Thomson, Jr., "How Could Vietnam Happen? *An Autopsy,*" *Atlantic Monthly* 221 (April 1968): 47–53. See also Leslie H. Gelb, "Vietnam: 'Nevertheless Our Presidents Persevered,' " *Milwaukee Journal,* June 20, 1971, p. V1–3.

[8]Kennedy's inaugural address, January 20, 1961, *Public Papers of the Presidents of the United States: John F. Kennedy, 1961* (Washington, 1962), p. 1.

[9]Kennedy's news conference of March 23, 1961, ibid., p. 214. Kennedy asserted in conversation with Arthur Schlesinger that month: "We cannot and will not accept any visible humiliation over Laos." See Arthur M. Schlesinger, Jr., *A Thousand Days: John F. Kennedy in the White House* (Boston, 1965), p. 310.

he followed the British and Soviet lead in calling a fourteen-nation conference in Geneva to resolve the Laotian question. The conference quickly agreed to a neutralized Laos and instructed Souvanna Phouma to form a coalition government that would include representatives of the right, center, and left in Laotian politics. The new government assumed office in June 1962, but within a year the Pathet Lao elements deserted, driving the neutral center toward the right and subjecting the country to a renewal of the civil war.[10]

Kennedy and his advisers agreed generally that the earlier perceptions of a Moscow-based monolith, which had motivated the initial opposition to Ho, had been inaccurate. However, the repeated assertion of an American interest in Vietnam, Kennedy's apologists argued, created a vital American interest which the new president could not ignore. Whether or not the domino theory was valid in 1954, wrote White House adviser Arthur M. Schlesinger, Jr., "it had acquired validity seven years after neighboring governments had staked their own security on the ability of the United States to live up to its pledges to Saigon."[11] In what had become standard phraseology, Vice-President Lyndon B. Johnson, upon his return from Saigon in June 1961, advised the president: "The battle against Communism must be joined in Southeast Asia with strength and determination to achieve success there—or the United States, inevitably, must surrender the Pacific and take up our defenses on our own shores." Vietnam had become symbolic of American trustworthiness and determination. Few Americans, the administration agreed, would accept any diminution of the country's prestige, especially in Vietnam where the perceptions of potential disaster were acute and the possibilities for success were still reassuring. Thus the Kennedy administration refused to question publicly the

---

[10]Bernard B. Fall, "Reappraisal in Laos," *Current History* 42 (January 1962): 8–14; Tillman Durdin and Robert Trumbull in *New York Times*, October 15, 1961, p. E4; Hans J. Morgenthau, "Asia: The American Algeria," *Commentary* 32 (July 1961): 43–47; Jacques Nevard in *New York Times*, June 10, 1962; text of the Fourteen Nation Declaration and Protocol on Neutrality in Laos, ibid., July 22, 1962; Denis Warner and S. L. A. Marshall, "The Front Lines of Asia," *Reporter* 26 (June 7, 1962): 21–29.

[11]Schlesinger, *A Thousand Days*, pp. 496–97. See also Schlesinger, *The Bitter Heritage: Vietnam and American Democracy, 1941–1966* (Boston, 1967), pp. 13, 31–32, 99. For a similar view that the United States had no choice after 1961 but to continue the war see Richard Goodwin, "Reflections on Vietnam," *New Yorker*, April 16, 1966, pp. 115–16; and Eugene V. Rostow, "L. B. J. Reconsidered," *Esquire* 75 (April 1971): 118. All seemed to accept the sense of obligation as expressed by Dean Rusk during a visit to Vietnam in 1966: "We are here because we made a promise. We have made other promises in other parts of the world. If Moscow and Peking ever discovered that the promises of the United States do not mean what they say, then this world goes up in smoke." Schlesinger, *The Bitter Heritage*, p. 49n.

assumptions and purpose upon which the two preceding administrations had based their commitments to the Saigon regime.

As Saigon's authority continued to deteriorate, Kennedy in October 1961 dispatched General Maxwell E. Taylor and State Department adviser Walt W. Rostow to Vietnam to gather information for a major reassessment of the American position in Southeast Asia.[12] Taylor, reporting to the president on November 4, accused North Vietnam of aggression and attributed Saigon's military failures to favoritism, inefficiency, and corruption. Nevertheless, to defend the frontier against infiltration, Taylor recommended an initial deployment of 10,000 American troops. His report offered the choice of defeat, reform, or a direct U.S. military involvement in South Vietnam. Kennedy rejected the first alternative without accepting the third. "Let me assure you again," he wrote Diem, "that the United States is determined to help Vietnam preserve its independence, protect its people against Communist assassins and build a better life through economic growth."[13]

With good reason Kennedy hoped to avoid a military solution in Vietnam. From the beginning, McNamara reminded him that no reasonable American involvement would tip the military scales in Southeast Asia; the United States might well become mired in a land war which it could not win. Kennedy shared that pessimism and wondered whether the United States would be more successful than the French in winning the support of the villagers, which was so essential for success against guerrilla forces. "No one knew," Theodore Sorensen recalled, "whether the South Vietnamese officers would be encouraged or resentful, or whether massive troop landings would provoke a massive Communist invasion—an invasion inevitably leading either to nuclear war, Western retreat or an endless and exhausting battle on the worst battleground he could choose."[14] Responding to Taylor's request for troops, Kennedy complained: "They want a force of American troops. . . . They say it's necessary in order to restore confidence and maintain morale.

---

[12]For the Taylor-Rostow mission see ibid., p. 22; and E. W. Kenworthy in *New York Times,* November 14, 16, 1961. John Kenneth Galbraith thought the Taylor-Rostow report was confusing because it advocated action but admitted that action would fail under the present government in Saigon. See Galbraith, *Ambassador's Journal: A Personal Account of the Kennedy Years* (Boston, 1969), pp. 211–12, 221.

[13]Kennedy to Ngo Dinh Diem, October 24, 1961, U.S. Department of State, *American Foreign Policy: Current Documents, 1961* (Washington, 1965), p. 1049. For Kennedy's oft-cited letter to Diem dated December 14, 1961 see Department of State *Bulletin* 46 (January 1, 1962): 13. Senator Mike Mansfield warned Kennedy in December 1962 that American policy in Vietnam would not succeed. See report on Southeast Asia, December 18, 1962, *Two Reports on Vietnam and Southeast Asia, April 1973,* 93d Cong., 1st sess., Senate Document No. 93–11 (Washington, 1973), pp. 3–14.

[14]Theodore C. Sorensen, *Kennedy* (London, 1965), p. 654.

But it will be just like Berlin. The troops will march in; the bands will play; the crowds will cheer; and in four days everyone will have forgotten. Then we will be told we have to send in more troops. It's like taking a drink. The effect wears off, and you take another."[15]

Determined to avoid a hard decision, Kennedy committed the nation to victory, but he did so with increments of military and economic aid sufficient only to sustain the administration's objectives and not large enough to require broad national approval. The president had genuine policy choices available; he chose not to exercise them. Politically, it was more feasible to entangle the United States gradually, promising with each increment the success that each preceding increment had assured by had failed to deliver. During 1962 the president increased the military aid to South Vietnam from 4,000 American advisers in January to 10,000 by October, while the secretary of defense assured the American people that the government had no policy for introducing combat forces into South Vietnam. Thus the Kennedy administration became trapped in a struggle which it dared not lose but could not win. Even such unpromising behavior seemed preferable to any clear alternative. Neither the acceptance of failure nor the pursuit of a decisive victory on Asian soil appeared politically and emotionally bearable. Half-way measures would not bring success, but they would buy time and keep Washington's options open. They would, over the short run, permit the administration to avoid painful decisions; over the long run they might permit some miraculous display of good fortune.

III

Kennedy required a strategy that would bridge the gap between the goal of victory in Vietnam and the reality of a limited U.S. involvement; he found it in the political-military program of counterinsurgency. During the spring of 1961 the president prepared to increase the effectiveness of the antiguerrilla activities in South Vietnam. On March 28 he reminded Congress that since 1945 the "most active and constant threat to Free World security" had been guerrilla warfare. To meet the challenge the United States, he warned, must organize "strong, highly mobile forces trained in this type of warfare, some of which must be deployed in forward areas."[16] The president accentuated the need for

[15]Schlesinger, *The Bitter Heritage*, p. 22.

[16]Kennedy's special message to Congress, March 28, 1961, *United States-Vietnam Relations, 1945–1967: Study Prepared by the Department of Defense* (Pentagon Papers), Book 7 (Washington, 1971), pp. C7-8; and *Public Papers of the Presidents: Kennedy, 1961*, pp. 231–32, 236. See also Rostow's recommendation for an antiguerrilla strategy in his address at the U.S. Army Special Warfare School, Fort Bragg, North Carolina, June 28, 1961,

responses that would be "suitable, selective, swift and effective." Once the challenge lay in general war; now the United States required forces that could deal successfully with small, externally equipped guerrilla bands. Reflecting the activist spirit of the New Frontier, counterinsurgency became fashionable, even faddish. Highly skilled and finely trained American units would be more than a match for any competing force, even in the jungles of Asia. Kennedy placed control of the counterinsurgency forces under a special group of high-ranking State and Defense officials in Washington. In Vietnam, however, the program achieved little; Washington refused to permit U.S. troops to move against the guerrillas. Despite intensive training the South Vietnamese acquired neither the skills nor the determination required for effective counterinsurgency operations. When American forces later assumed responsibility for South Vietnam's defense, they reverted to conventional modes of warfare.

Still Washington officials never questioned the capacity of U.S. conventional forces, with their superior equipment and firepower, to win the battle for the jungles or the cities. In Korea conventional forces had managed to stalemate the war and drive the enemy to the negotiating table. Such military advisers as Taylor never doubted their ability to repeat that success, for they assumed that Vietnam, as a battleground between two opposing forces in a divided country, ultimately would be a repetition of Korea, with the enemy succumbing in reasonable time to the power of American arms.[17]

Unfortunately, the struggles for power in Korea and Vietnam were scarcely identical at all. When the Eisenhower administration surfeited Saigon with equipment, advisers, and praise after 1954, it assumed that the known South Vietnamese enemies of that regime either would terminate their allegiance to Hanoi or at least, if they chose to resist, do so without any aid or encouragement from the North. At no time did the Eisenhower planning contemplate a war against the North Vietnamese, but the assumption of a limited struggle proved false. Perhaps it is true that Hanoi directed the South Vietnamese insurgency from the beginning. If true, the fact that the Viet Cong would accept the leadership of Ho Chi Minh, declared by Washington to be the enemy of self-determination in South Vietnam, suggested

---

Department of State *Bulletin* 45 (August 7, 1961): 237. Under the leadership of Kennedy, Rostow, and others, counterinsurgency became a fashionable idea in Washington. The administration never employed the concept in Vietnam, although in 1962 it adopted a program of strategic hamlets to curtail the enemy's guerrilla tactics.

[17]See, for example, memorandum, Taylor to Secretary of Defense Robert McNamara, January 22, 1964, *The Pentagon Papers as Published by The New York Times*, ed. Neil Sheehan (New York, 1971), pp. 282–85.

clearly that for them the assault on the Saigon government comprised the continuation of the old Nationalist-Communist revolution rather than an external aggression. It is not certain that the Viet Cong would court death and destruction in their homeland merely to serve the expansionist interests of another nation. To them North Vietnam was simply not a foreign power.

Thus in at least two important respects the war in Vietnam could not be a repetition of Korea. Unlike Ho Chi Minh, Syngman Rhee, the pro-Western South Korean spokesman for Korean independence and unity, had contributed little to the independence of the Korean people. Soviet and U.S. armies liberated Korea from Japanese control, and, following the postwar division of the peninsula at the 38th parallel, Washington handed the government of South Korea to Rhee. The fact that Ho Chi Minh's revolutionary forces liberated all of Vietnam, North and South, from French rule, dictated from 1954 onward that the 17th parallel could never equal the 38th parallel in significance as a boundary separating two nations, nor did the quality of war in Vietnam have much relationship to that in Korea. The Seoul government had the fanatical support of the South Korean populace, which permitted the United Nations allies in Korea to establish stable battle lines and to conduct the war as a conventional struggle in every respect. In South Vietnam, however, the enemies of Saigon moved freely through the entire countryside, striking everywhere and anywhere at will and reducing the actual warfare to a primarily civil struggle where success could be measured only by death and destruction, not by territory captured and held. It was not strange that those officials who anticipated a Korea-type war in Vietnam constantly underestimated the nature of the resistance and the difficulties in gaining clear, demonstrable battlefield successes.

Kennedy received repeated warnings that the burgeoning U.S. military involvement in Vietnam would ultimately fail. In July 1962, Nikita Khrushchev observed that the United States had stumbled into a bog in which it would be mired for a long time. Similarly, France's Charles de Gaulle, recalling the French disaster in Southeast Asia, warned Kennedy that Vietnam was totally unsuitable for Western tanks and politics.[18] John Kenneth Galbraith, then ambassador to India, argued against the dispatch of American forces to Vietnam or otherwise

---

[18]For Charles de Gaulle's warning of early 1961 see Anatole Shub in *Washington Post*, October 8, 1970, p. A21; telegram, Ball to Johnson and Rusk, June 5, 1964, in Gareth Porter, ed., *Vietnam: The Definitive Documentation of Human Decisions* (Stanfordville, NY, 1979), 2:279–81; and de Gaulle's address on Vietnam, September 1, 1966, in Russell Buhite, ed., *The Dynamics of World Power: A Documentary History of United States Foreign Policy, 1945–1973: Volume IV—The Far East* (New York, 1973), p. 507.

deepening the American involvement. The New Frontier—Kennedy's domestic program—would drown in the rice paddies of Southeast Asia, he predicted.[19] What encouraged Kennedy and his White House staff to ignore such advice was their common assumption that they could sustain the military operation in Vietnam indefinitely and thereby push a national decision into some unknown future.

Meanwhile, Washington exuded confidence, with the private optimism usually following, rather than preceding, each successive escalation of the American effort. When by 1962 Saigon's progress seemed substantial, official confidence knew no bounds. Following his first trip to Saigon that year, McNamara reported: "Every quantitative measure we have shows we're winning this war." The president summed up the year's success in his State of the Union message of January 1963: "The spearhead of aggression had been blunted in South Vietnam."[20] With the economic and military increments of 1963, the official optimism became even more pronounced. During March, Kennedy's Secretary of State Dean Rusk declared that "government forces clearly have the initiative in most areas of the country." Not long thereafter the Defense Department announced that "the corner has definitely been turned toward victory in Vietnam."[21] Long before the end of the year the war's end was officially in sight; apparently the long shot was paying off. What sustained this optimism was the army's reporting structure which encouraged every officer at every level to claim nothing but success for the operations under his command.

Still, in the absence of any direct U.S. military involvement in the war, the means for victory lay essentially in Saigon's capacity to organize, staff, and direct a successful counterinsurgency campaign across South Vietnam. However, it was clear long before 1963 that the Diem regime was the weakest component in the struggle. So determined was Diem's resistance to U.S. pressure for reform that his regime inspired attacks on the United States in the Saigon press. South Vietnamese leaders in exile warned Washington officials that only some alternative

[19]Galbraith, *Ambassador's Journal*, pp. 132–33, 231–34. On March 2, 1962, Galbraith wrote to Kennedy: "Incidentally, who is the man in your administration who decided what countries are strategic? I would like to have his name and address and ask him what is so important about this real estate in the space age. What strength do we gain from alliance with an incompetent government and a people who are so largely indifferent to their own salvation? Some of his decisions puzzle me." Ibid., p. 270.

[20]McNamara and other members of the administration quoted in Chalmers M. Roberts, "Our 25 Years in Vietnam," *Washington Post*, June 2, 1968, p. B5; and Stanley Karnow, "A Grim Notebook on Our Asian Tragedy," ibid., June 28, 1970, p. C2. Kennedy's statement in *Public Papers: Kennedy, 1963* (Washington, 1964), p. 11.

[21]Roberts in *Washington Post*, June 2, 1968, p. B5; Karnow in ibid., June 28, 1970, p. C2; Richard P. Stebbins, ed., *Documents on American Foreign Relations, 1963* (New York, 1964), p. 296.

South Vietnamese government, one that better represented the interests of the people, would command the power and respect to stabilize the politics of the country. Kennedy's continued quest for greater political awareness in Saigon received a critical blow when, in the summer of 1963, Diem's repression of the Buddhists threatened the very existence of his regime. In Washington the embarrassed Kennedy admitted: "[I]n the final analysis it is the people and the Government itself who have to win or lose this struggle. All we can do is help, and we are making it very clear. But I don't agree with those who say we should withdraw. That would be a great mistake."[22] In October, when Diem had alienated the administration in Washington, the Vietnamese generals struck, assassinating Diem and his brother Ngo Dinh Nhu. At that moment the United States had 16,000 troops in Vietnam, with a continuing commitment to victory and no plan of escape.

Whether Kennedy in time would have reversed his policy of escalation remains unclear. One account—that of Kenneth O'Donnell, a White House official—suggests that Senator Mike Mansfield's repeated warnings of disaster in Vietnam had created, by 1963, significant doubts in the mind of the president. According to O'Donnell, Kennedy called Mansfield to his office that spring and acknowledged his acceptance of Mansfield's argument for a complete American military withdrawal. "But I can't do it until 1965—after I'm reelected," Kennedy informed him. To desert Vietnam's cause early, the president feared, would create a right-wing uprising against his reelection. As he explained to O'Donnell, "in 1965, I'll be damned everywhere as a Communist appeaser. But I don't care. If I tried to pull out completely now, we would have another Joe McCarthy red scare on our hands, but I can do it after I'm reelected. So we had better make damned sure that I am reelected."[23]

IV

Johnson entered the presidency following the assassination of Kennedy in November 1963. Devoted to both the Kennedy staff and the drifting policies in Southeast Asia, Johnson, like his predecessors, had no interest in defeat. "Lyndon Johnson," he declared emphatically, "isn't going to be the first American President to lose a war." Maintaining a public

---

[22] Interview with Walter Cronkite, September 2, 1963, Department of State *Bulletin* 49 (September 30, 1963): 499.

[23] Kenneth O'Donnell, "LBJ and the Kennedys," *Life* 69 (August 7, 1970): 51–52. Kennedy was apparently impressed as well by General Douglas MacArthur's private warning that he avoid a land war on mainland Asia. See Hugh Sidey in *Time*, November 14, 1983, p. 69.

mood of caution, he warned the nation against any involvement that would tie the United States to a ground war in Asia. "I have not thought," he said, "that we were ready for American boys to do the fighting for Asian boys." Nothing would be more disastrous, he added, than to put American soldiers against 700 million Chinese on the Asian mainland. By 1964 those outside the administration who doubted the possibility of creating a successful program for Vietnam from such disparate and conflicting elements were legion. Inside Washington's power structure such voices were few.

Among the inside critics was Undersecretary of State George W. Ball who reminded the new president:

> The South Vietnamese are losing the war to the Vietcong. No one can assure you that we can beat the Vietcong or even force them to the conference table on our terms, no matter how many hundred thousand white, foreign troops we deploy. . . . The decision you face now, therefore, is crucial. Once large numbers of U.S. troops are committed to direct combat . . . we will have started a well-nigh irreversible process. Our involvement will be so great that we cannot—without national humiliation—stop short of achieving our complete objectives. *Of the two possibilities, I think humiliation would be more likely than the achievement of our objectives—even after we have paid terrible costs.*[24]

Johnson preferred the advice of those who argued that the United States had no choice but to pursue the goal of total victory in Southeast Asia. As Senator Russell explained to newsmen after a conversation with the president at the LBJ Ranch, "they [the Vietnamese] won't help themselves. We made a great mistake in going in there but I can't figure out any way to get out without scaring the rest of the world." With little hesitation the president determined that any adjustment in the American program would comprise the escalation of means and not the reduction of goals in Vietnam.

During August 1964, following a minor, even doubtful, North Vietnamese attack on American naval vessels in the Gulf of Tonkin, Congress, at the president's request, adopted a resolution which seemed to commit that body to any future executive action required to defend the Saigon government. The resolution declared that, inasmuch as the security of Southeast Asia was vital, the United States was "prepared, as the President determines, to take all necessary steps, including the

---

[24]*Pentagon Papers, New York Times,* pp. 459–60 (emphasis in original). Ball reminded the Johnson administration that the European allies all opposed U.S. policy in Vietnam. See Chalmers M. Roberts, "President Swatted Wrong Ball," *Washington Post,* July 5, 1970, p. D1.

use of armed forces, to assist any protocol state of the Southeast Asia Collective Defense Treaty requesting assistance in the defense of its freedom."[25] Johnson's still limited military commitments, no less than his policies in general, reaffirmed his leadership within the Democratic party and assured his nomination at Atlantic City's Convention Hall. Eventually they won for him and his vice-presidential running mate, Senator Hubert H. Humphrey, an easy victory at the polls in November. At the end of 1964 the administration had 23,000 troops in Vietnam.

Still reluctant to commit American forces to a jungle war, Johnson and his advisers, who included Taylor, now ambassador to Saigon, decided by late 1964 to await the proper occasion for launching an air war against North Vietnam. That moment arrived on February 7, 1965 when a Viet Cong attack on Pleiku, an outpost in the central highlands, killed eight Americans.[26] Even as the president announced that the United States would retaliate by air, he assured the nation that "we seek no wider war." The bombing, Washington assumed, would undermine the morale of the enemy, halt the infiltration from the North, and encourage resistance in the South. Victory would now be swift and inexpensive. According to official dogma in Washington, the bombing would bring Ho to the negotiating table in six weeks, at most ten.[27]

Fundamentally, Johnson had committed the United States to a course of military escalation which ultimately would employ American forces in combat. When the bombing failed to achieve any of its objectives, he responded by ordering the destruction of more targets. Still the tempo of war increased. It became clear during the spring of 1965 that the United States in order to terminate the war would be forced to destroy the enemy in the jungles. To this end the president discarded the "advisory" role of the 50,000 then under the command of General

[25]Johnson's request to Congress, August 5, 1964, in Buhite, *The Far East*, pp. 489–90. For the administration's defense of the resolution see *Joint Hearing . . . On a Joint Resolution to Promote the Maintenance of International Peace and Security in Southeast Asia, August 6, 1964* (Washington, 1966), pp. 2–33. A critical analysis of the Gulf of Tonkin episode can be found in Joseph C. Goulden, *Truth Is the First Casualty: The Gulf of Tonkin Affair* (Chicago, 1969).

[26]Telegram, Taylor to Rusk, February 7, 1965, in Porter, *Vietnam*, 2:348; McGeorge Bundy to Johnson, February 7, 1965, ibid., p. 358; William Bundy, statement of February 7, 1965, Department of State *Bulletin* 52 (March 8, 1965): 292.

[27]*Time*, February 26, 1965, p. 20; John W. Finney, "Vietnam: A Debate Over U.S. Role," *New York Times*, February 28, 1965, p. E3; comments on the wishful thinking in the Johnson administration in Thomson, "How Could Vietnam Happen," pp. 50–51. On February 27 the State Department issued a report, "Aggression from the North: The Record of North Viet-Nam's Campaign To Conquer South Viet-Nam," Department of State, *Foreign Policy Briefs* 14 (March 15, 1965): 1. Text of the North Vietnam White Paper in *New York Times*, February 28, 1965, pp. 30–32. Despite the general acceptance of the bombing decision, both James Reston and the *New York Times* issued words of caution. See especially *New York Times*, February 14, 1965.

William C. Westmoreland in South Vietnam. Finally, at his press conference of July 28, the president announced that the U.S. personnel in
South Vietnam would be increased from the 75,000 already there to
125,000. Should the United States be driven from the field in Vietnam,
he warned, no nation again could ever trust America's promises but,
he added, "we do not want an expanding struggle with consequences
that no one can perceive."[28] Johnson had again trapped the nation
between the need for victory and the abhorrence of fighting a jungle
people on the mainland of Asia.

Convinced that American prestige and security were at stake, the
president now prepared to escalate the U.S. military contribution to
any level required for victory. At the same time, the administration,
supported by the computers in the Department of Defense, reassured
the country that victory lay beyond each accretion of allied power in
Vietnam. The American troop buildup reached 200,000 in 1966 and
continued upward until it exceeded 500,000 in 1967. Meanwhile, the
bombing of North and South enemy targets mounted to astonishing
proportions. During 1968 the bomb tonnage dropped on Vietnam gradually surpassed by 50 percent that dropped on both Germany and
Japan during World War II, and the price of war reached 200,000
American casualties—30,000 dead—and $30 billion per year. What set
the limits to escalation even then was the president's informal bargain
with the American people that he would conduct the war without asking
for increased taxes.

Westmoreland, with little direction from Washington, formulated
a plan of operations in Vietnam designed first to avert defeat and then
to take the offensive with additional battalions. In its final phases, the
strategy anticipated victory sometime after 1968 as the United States
achieved total military predominance on the battlefield. To achieve
victory with reasonable speed, Westmoreland assigned the burden of
fighting to American forces. Except in the Delta he used the South
Vietnamese forces largely for pacification, the occupation and organization of regions presumably freed of Viet Cong control. Washington
accepted the notion that Westmoreland's war of attrition, based on air-
supported "search and destroy" operations, would break the enemy's
resistance. Without battle lines or territorial objectives, American officials resorted to body counts to measure the war's progress and to
demonstrate the success of allied military operations. Never before had
Washington relied so heavily on quantification to judge its battle effectiveness and the probabilities of victory. Still the war continued unabated,

[28]White House press conference, July 28, 1965, Department of State *Bulletin* 53
(August 16, 1965): 263–64.

with Hanoi, now fully committed to the struggle for the South, matching each new American increment with a continuing escalation of its own. As the war dragged on month after month, the freedom of the enemy, whether Viet Cong guerrillas or North Vietnamese regulars, to move through the countryside and strike anywhere and everywhere suggested that the struggle remained generally a civil war in which political, not military, effectiveness was the ultimate measure of success.

Somehow the death and destruction was no guarantee at all of an independent, non-Communist South Vietnam. For that reason McNamara argued for building an effective government in Saigon and for improving the pacification effort throughout the countryside. In 1967, Johnson gave Westmoreland responsibility for pacification, civil as well as military, and sent Robert Komar to Saigon as Westmoreland's deputy. Ellsworth Bunker, who replaced Taylor as ambassador in May 1967, refused to distinguish between military and civil pacification. "To me this is all one war," he declared. "Everything we do is an aspect of the total effort to achieve our objective here." At the same time, the president sent General Creighton Abrams to South Vietnam to improve the performance of its military forces, for victory demanded an effective military and political structure in South Vietnam as well as the elimination of all Viet Cong and North Vietnamese influence from the country.[29]

V

Even as the United States embarked on its massive escalation of the war in 1965, some Washington officials suspected that the effort would not succeed. Assistant Secretary of Defense John T. McNaughton began his famed memorandum of January 17, 1966: "We have in Vietnam the ingredients of an enormous miscalculation. . . . The ARVN is tired, passive and accommodation prone. . . . The bombing of the North may or may not be able effectively to interdict infiltration. . . . South Vietnam is near the edge of serious inflation and economic chaos. We are in an escalating military stalemate."[30] For McNaughton the only realistic purpose remaining in Vietnam was the avoidance of humiliation. The United States had remained in Vietnam to preserve its reputation as a guarantor and thus maintain its effectiveness elsewhere. To avoid

[29]On the pacification program see *Pentagon Papers: Senator Gravel Edition* (Boston, 1971), 2:515–623; report of meeting of U.S. and South Vietnamese leaders at Honolulu, February 6–8, 1966, Department of State *Bulletin* 54 (February 28, 1966): 302–07; Denis Warner, "Vietnam: The Ordeal of Pacification," *Reporter* 35 (December 1966): 25–28.
[30]McNaughton's memorandum, *Pentagon Papers, New York Times*, p. 502.

damage to its reputation the United States had escalated its involvement to a high level, but McNaughton understood clearly that, in the absence of a national decision, the United States would never bring enough power to bear on Vietnam to terminate the war with any measure of success. Since the issue at stake was the country's reputation, he warned the United States not to adopt obligations beyond those expected of the nation by those whose opinions comprised its reputation. That reputation required the prevention of Saigon's fall but not necessarily the prevention of a coalition government or a neutralized South Vietnam.[31]

For the more optimistic, or terrified, McNaughton's goal of reputation saving was scarcely adequate, although even that limited goal could become frightfully expensive. If Vietnam confronted the world with an incipient global aggression, the United States had no choice but to win totally. President Johnson summarized the basic objective of three previous administrations in his Baltimore address of April 7, 1965: "Our objective is the independence of South Viet-Nam and its freedom from attack. We want nothing for ourselves—only that the people of South Viet-Nam be allowed to guide their own country in their own way."[32] Such a goal, limited as it appeared, demanded no less than total victory over the Vietnamese enemy.

The United States, however, had a far more pervading objective: the creation at last of a world order free of aggression and all irrational uses of force. Dulles's doctrine of massive retaliation had been based on the premise that the United States, because of the destructive power that it wielded, could manage or eliminate change in the Afro-Asian world merely by threatening to employ force. Following the Korean truce of July 1953, no high Washington official had attached the country's global commitment to Communist containment to the necessity of fighting on the Asian continent. What rendered Dulles's concept of massive retaliation so acceptable to Americans was its guarantee of Afro-Asian stability without the danger of war.[33]

[31]Ibid., p. 503. In his testimony before the Senate Foreign Relations Committee in February 1966, George F. Kennan raised the question of the country's reputation: "I would submit there is more respect to be won in the opinion of the world by a resolute and courageous liquidation of unsound positions than in the most stubborn pursuit of extravagant or unpromising objectives." "Opinion at Home and Abroad," *New York Times*, February 13, 1966.

[32]President Johnson's Baltimore address, April 7, 1965, Department of State *Bulletin* 52 (April 26, 1965): 606–10.

[33]The growing U.S. involvement in Vietnam after mid-1961 raised the issue of military forces. Presidents Kennedy and Johnson remained reluctant to employ American military power in Southeast Asia, not because they shared Dulles's faith in massive retaliation but because they hoped that the political stabilization of South Vietnam would not require more than American military aid and advisers. See, for example, Rusk's

Before 1965 Kennedy and Johnson, no more than Eisenhower, anticipated the need to involve the U.S. militarily to preserve the Cold War lines of demarcation in Asia. Writing in June 1964, Rostow could claim victory for American policy in Laos and Vietnam because, he noted, Presidents Kennedy and Johnson had threatened military retaliation to any level necessary to punish those who sought to overthrow the status quo with force. Rostow described the triumph of containment in Southeast Asia:

> The military initiatives with respect to Laos and Vietnam, in pursuit of clearly-defined and limited political objectives, would have had no serious effect on the course of events unless the Communist leaders concerned were convinced that, echeloned behind these limited demonstrations of force, there had been both the capabilities and the will to deal with every form of escalation they might mount in response, up to and including all out nuclear war.[34]

Strangely the threat of retaliation to any level, including nuclear war, did not eliminate the subsequent decisions to dispatch over half a million soldiers to Vietnam. Obviously the military formula, based on massive retaliation, did not work.

Herein lay the military burden of Vietnam. Global containment, as it emerged during the 1950s, had never contemplated the destruction of the enemy in a series of wars; rather, it sought the prevention of unwanted change through the absolute assurance that any aggression would ultimately fail before the full might of the United States. In short, the objective was the maintenance of the status quo without fighting, but Ho Chi Minh exposed the hollowness of the nuclear deterrent as a controlling element in the politics of Asia. Still the military lessons of Vietnam in no way curtailed the global objectives of the Johnson administration; it merely confirmed the need for some form of victory in Vietnam. The decision to commit the nation's ground forces to Vietnam, thereby reducing the credibility of the nuclear threat, compelled the Johnson administration, if it wished to maintain the country's global posture, to establish the worldwide credibility of America's conventional power. A global commitment to the status quo required

---

testimony before the Senate Foreign Relations Committee, May 1961, in D. C. Watt, *Survey of International Affairs, 1961* (London, 1965), pp. 356–57. Throughout the years from 1961 to 1964 both Kennedy and Johnson had insisted that they would provide training and equipment but not fighting units for South Vietnam. See Tom Wicker in *New York Times*, November 27, 1966, p. E13.

[34]W. W. Rostow, "The Test: Are We the Tougher?" *New York Times Magazine*, June 7, 1964, p. 112.

either global wars or the maintenance of a recognizable threat of retaliation that would eliminate the necessity for demonstrating everywhere the existence of the national will. It was, finally, the administration's search for an effective non-nuclear deterrent that eventually overrode every argument for compromise in Vietnam.

To contain the global pressures of an expansive communism, ran the official argument, the United States would apply of necessity the so-called lessons of Munich. Rusk instructed the American Society of International Law in April 1965 that Western inaction in Manchuria and Ethiopia had demanded the terrible price of World War II. He asserted that "surely we have learned over the past decades that the acceptance of aggression leads only to a sure catastrophe. Surely, we have learned that the aggressor must face the consequences of his action and be saved from the frightful miscalculation that brings all to ruin."[35] "In Viet-Nam today," warned Senator Thomas J. Dodd of Connecticut, "we are confronted by an incorrigible aggressor, fanatically committed to the destruction of the free world, whose agreements are as worthless as Hitler's. . . . If we fail to draw the line in Viet-Nam, in short, we may find ourselves compelled to draw a defense line as far back as Seattle." Senator Henry M. Jackson reminded NATO officials in 1966 that "the world might have been spared enormous misfortunes if Japan had not been permitted to succeed in Manchuria, or Mussolini in Ethiopia, or Hitler in Czechoslovakia or in the Rhineland. And we think that our sacrifices in this dirty war in little Vietnam will make a dirtier and bigger war less likely."[36] President Johnson told a New Hampshire audience that men regrettably had to fight limited wars to avoid the need to fight larger ones.[37]

---

[35]Rusk's address to the American Society of International Law, April 13, 1965, Department of State *Bulletin* 52 (May 10, 1965): 697.

[36]The global dangers implied in these statements and the need to counter them seemed to culminate in Secretary Rusk's insistence before the Senate Foreign Relations Committee in February 1966 that the United States was obligated under the SEATO pact to fight in Vietnam and contain China even if it received the support of none of its allies. To this Walter Lippmann replied: "The Rusk doctrine, as expounded in the recent (Senate) hearings, is the reducto ad absurdum of the loose generalities of the Truman doctrine and the pactomania of Secretary Dulles." The *Milwaukee Journal* editorialized: "If [Rusk's] interpretation applies, then we are committed to fight alone almost all around the world, for we are tied to many pacts, largely due to the enthusiasm for such mechanisms by the late John Foster Dulles. And such an open end commitment is unthinkable—for we have neither the manpower, the wealth nor the national interest to take on everyone in the world with whom we disagree." For these editorial opinions see *Milwaukee Journal*, February 25, 1966.

[37]Johnson's address before the Navy League of Manchester, New Hampshire, August 20, 1966, Department of State *Bulletin* 55 (September 12, 1966): 368. It was not strange that the administration made unprecedented claims to executive primacy in the conduct of American foreign and military policy. See memorandum for the president

Similarly, a Freedom House statement of December 20, 1967, signed by fourteen Asian scholars, warned the nation against failure in Vietnam:

> To accept a Communist victory in Vietnam would serve as a major encouragement to those forces in the world opposing peaceful coexistence, to those elements committed to the thesis that violence is the best means of effecting change. It would gravely jeopardize the possibilities of a political equilibrium in Asia, seriously damage our credibility, deeply affect the morale—and the policies—of our Asian allies and the neutrals. These are not developments conducive to a long-range peace. They are more likely to prove precursors to larger, more costly wars.[38]

The concept of falling dominoes, placed in the context of Munich, became the most powerful of all governmental appeals for public support during the critical years of military escalation. Nevertheless, the enemy so defined and capable, if unrestrained, of bringing war to the world could not have been Hanoi; it could only have been the Soviet Union or China, or both. If the danger lay in Beijing or Moscow, the struggle in Vietnam could hardly resolve it. If, on the other hand, the problem lay in Hanoi, whose forces alone did the fighting and dying, what service the language of global disaster could render was equally unclear. Ho, victorious or not, was no Hitler; Hanoi was not another Berlin. How the Vietnamese enemy endangered the peace of the world no one bothered to explain.

Criticism of the war kept pace with official efforts to escalate both the costs and the importance of the struggle. The unleashing of such huge quantities of destructiveness against a jungle population 10,000 miles distant on the mainland of Asia injured the moral sensibilities of millions of Americans and gradually embittered much of the nation as

from Attorney General Nicholas D. Katzenbach, June 10, 1965, in Porter, *Vietnam*, 2:375–76. Katzenbach argued that the president had the constitutional and legal authority to use military forces in Southeast Asia without direct congressional approval. See also legal memorandum of Leonard C. Meeker, State Department legal adviser, Senate Committee on Foreign Relations, March 4, 1966, Department of State *Bulletin* 54 (March 28, 1966): 474–89.

[38] In his testimony before the Senate Foreign Relations Committee on January 31, 1967, Professor Edwin O. Reischauer of Harvard University, one of the statement's signers, presented a defense of the American involvement in Vietnam which was more comprehensive than the Freedom House statement. See U.S., Congress, Senate, Committee on Senate Foreign Relations, *Hearings on Asia, the Pacific, and the United States*, 90th Cong., 1st sess., January 31, 1967, pp. 14–15. Reischauer advocated deescalation of the American military effort only if the United States could do so without suffering a serious military defeat. Hans J. Morgenthau criticized Freedom House for its attacks on the war's critics in his article "Freedom, Freedom House, and Vietnam," *New Leader* 50 (January 2, 1967): 17–19.

had no previous external experience in its history. Most critics were not pacifists and agreed readily that the country had the right to kill those who threatened its welfare or existence. The domino theory and its variations had defined the enemies of Saigon as dangerous to the security of all Asia and thus of the United States. Those, however, who challenged U.S. military escalation in Southeast Asia agreed generally that the struggle for Vietnam was mainly an indigenous contest to be resolved by the Vietnamese people themselves. Such argumentation reduced the American effort to a largely illegitimate intervention in the internal affairs of another nation and an overcommitment of resources and manpower in an area where U.S. interests were secondary at best. The critics demanded a cessation of the bombing of the North, the segregation of all American forces to enclaves to reduce casualties, the imposition of a coalition government on Saigon which included all elements involved in that country's struggle for power, and, finally, a complete withdrawal of all U.S. forces from Vietnam, whatever its effect on that region's political future. Among the war's active critics after 1966 were not only many students, scholars, and writers but also retired generals of distinction and both Democratic and Republican members of Congress. Many of the critics in government and the press had supported the initial intervention; they entered the opposition only when it seemed clear that the United States could not win the war in any traditional sense.

VI

President Johnson, his advisers, and members of his cabinet defended the war in a massive national effort. Vice-President Humphrey, returning in late 1967 from a tour of the western Pacific, announced that U.S. policy was achieving gains on all fronts. Soon Ambassador Bunker, on a reporting trip to Washington, assured the nation that the allies were achieving steady progress in the war. General Westmoreland added confidently that, "whereas in 1965 the enemy was winning, today he is certainly losing." With American forces standing at a half million, he said, "we have reached the important point where the end begins to come into view."[39] This optimism mounted until late January 1968

[39]General Westmoreland appeared before Congress on April 28, 1967 as part of the administration's all-out effort to defend the war. See "The Week in Review," *New York Times*, April 30, 1967, p. E1. The attacks on this speech revealed the strength of congressional opposition to the war by 1967. Still, in September, Westmoreland assured Secretary McNamara that the United States could win the war with additional men. "Vietnam: How Much to Hold the Initiative?" *New York Times*, September 9, 1967. Such official optimism mounted through the final months of 1967 until Westmoreland addressed the National Press Club on November 21, 1967. See Department of State *Bulletin* 57 (December 11, 1967): 788.

when Rostow informed newsmen in his White House office that captured documents foretold the impending collapse of the enemy in Vietnam. Even as he spoke his staff relayed the news that the Viet Cong
had unleashed the Tet offensive, the most destructive enemy attack of
the war. Westmoreland requested an additional 200,000 men, while
the president's trusted advisers assured him that the Tet losses had
finally placed the enemy on the ropes. For Johnson the end had come.
Facing vigorous and determined opposition among Democratic leaders
as well as rank-and-file party members, he announced over television
on the evening of March 31, 1968 that he would order a partial halt
of the bombing, open negotiations with Hanoi, and withdraw from the
presidential race.[40] So thoroughly had been the repudiation of his policies that neither he nor Rusk dared any longer to travel freely and
openly around the country.

Late in April the president announced that talks with Hanoi
would soon open in Paris, with Averell Harriman acting as chief U.S.
negotiator. Washington heralded the forthcoming exchange as a major
breakthrough for peace, but its mood was not compromising. Those
who favored the continued escalation of the war in pursuit of victory
had not prevented a bombing halt, but they assured the president that
Tet had been an enemy disaster and that the improved allied military
situation in Vietnam would permit the United States to be demanding
in Paris. When the Paris talks opened on May 13, Xuan Thuy, the
North Vietnamese negotiator, made clear to Harriman that Hanoi
would be no less demanding. He accused the United States of intruding
into the affairs of the Vietnamese people and undermining the principle
of self-determination by placing its massive military power at the disposition of the Saigon minority. Xuan Thuy repeated Hanoi's insistence
that successful negotiations could proceed only after the United States

---

[40]For an optimistic view of the Vietnamese situation in early 1968 see Richard
Harwood and Laurence Stern in *Washington Post*, February 9, 1969; and Rostow's mem-
oranda for the president, February 5, 6, 14, 1968, in Porter, *Vietnam*, 2:494–97, 500–01.
On the shift in U.S. policy away from additional troops see the memorandum of the
"Clifford group" for the president, March 4, 1968, ibid., p. 505; Charles Roberts in
Newsweek, March 10, 1969, pp. 32–33; Clark M. Clifford, "Clifford's Conversion from
Hawk," *Washington Post*, June 22, 1969, pp. B1, B4–5; Richard Halloran in *New York
Times*, September 28, 1969; Robert K. Walker in *Daily Progress* (Charlottesville, VA),
February 7, 1970; and *Newsweek*, February 16, 1970, pp. 22–23. Theodore Sorensen dis-
cussed the evolution of the Vietnam issue in presidential politics in "Of Course the War
Will Be a Campaign Issue," *New York Times Magazine*, March 17, 1968; pp. 30–31. John-
son's radio and television speech of March 31, 1968, Department of State *Bulletin* 58
(April 15, 1968): 481–86. For the significance of the president's announcement, see Arthur
Schlesinger, Jr., "Vietnam and the End of the Age of Superpowers," *Harper's Magazine*
238 (March 1969): 41–49.

had halted the bombing of all North Vietnam. Clearly the search for peace had scarcely begun.[41]

Recognizing that any political settlement would endanger its existence, the Saigon regime anticipated the Paris talks with considerable anxiety. South Vietnamese Foreign Minister Tran Van Do declared in an interview on April 12: "I feel no qualms [about the future] as long as the fighting continues, [but] I look forward to negotiations with serious misgivings."[42] President Nguyen Van Thieu reminded Washington that he opposed any withdrawal of U.S. forces from Vietnam. Increasingly, Saigon made it clear that it would oppose both the recognition of the NLF as an independent political force and any halt in the bombing short of absolute guarantees from Hanoi. Washington reassured Thieu that the United States would never accept a political settlement for South Vietnam that defied the principle of self-determination. Clearly the answer to the country's dilemma still lay in Saigon on Thieu's success in building an effective military and political structure. Secretary of Defense Clark M. Clifford promised Thieu larger quantities of the best U.S. equipment. During July, Thieu announced that the United States could begin to phase out its forces in 1969, but few American commanders in Washington and Saigon were convinced.[43]

President Johnson's decision to limit the bombing scarcely slowed the pace of war in Vietnam, but it created a mood of euphoria in the United States that all but eliminated the war as a subject of political debate, especially after the Democratic convention at Chicago disposed of the war critics and nominated Humphrey for the presidency. Both Humphrey and Richard Nixon, the Republican nominee, promised

[41]Rowland Evans and Robert Novak in *Washington Post*, April 17, 1968; Joseph Kraft in ibid., May 19, 1968; *Newsweek*, April 22, 1968, pp. 40–45; Robert Stephens in *Milwaukee Journal*, May 12, 1968, p. VI; Hedrick Smith and Henry Tanner in *New York Times*, May 5, 1968; on Xuan Thuy's demands see Anthony Lewis in ibid., May 19, 1968. In the United States the president's offer of negotiations inaugurated a bitter debate between those who still believed that this country could win in Vietnam and those who thought it impossible. Some still hoped to achieve American goals in Vietnam at reduced cost and involvement. See, for example, Hans J. Morgenthau, "Bundy's Doctrine of War Without End," *New Republic* 159 (November 2, 1968): 18–20.

[42]Bernard Weinraub, "Saigon's Reaction," *New York Times*, May 5, 1968; A. J. Langguth, "Thieu and Ky Think About the Unthinkable," *New York Times Magazine*, April 14, 1968, p. 21; Don Tate in *Rocky Mountain News* (Denver), July 9, 1968.

[43]For an evaluation of the Paris talks see *Vietnam and the Paris Negotiations: Report of Senator Mike Mansfield to the Committee on Foreign Relations, September 1968*, 90th Cong., 2d sess. (Washington, 1968). Mansfield suggested that the United States modify the objectives of the Saigon regime to facilitate some agreement with the North Vietnamese. For the stalemate in Paris see also *Newsweek*, June 3, 1968, pp. 40–41; Joseph Kraft in *Washington Post*, July 14, 1968; and Ross Terrill, "A Report on the Paris Talks," *New Republic* 159 (July 13, 1968): 15–18.

peace, but both refused to dwell on the means for achieving that purpose. Meanwhile, the Paris talks, whatever the hopes they engendered,
did not move the war any closer to a solution. Hanoi refused to compromise its demands for a total bombing halt of the North. Washington,
in turn, required some promise from Hanoi of a de-escalation of its war
effort in exchange for a bombing halt.[44] Suddenly on November 1 the
president announced that new developments, which he failed to explain,
had permitted him to stop the bombing of North Vietnam. Simultaneously, he declared that within a week the conversations in Paris would
be broadened to include the Saigon government and the NLF.[45]

Washington quickly rediscovered that Saigon was no less a barrier
to settlement than Hanoi. Thieu announced that under no circumstances would his government send representatives to a meeting in
which the NLF sat as a separate and equal bargaining agent. As he
explained to Catholic leaders in Saigon, "[the NLF] will become the
winners. . . . Our existence is at stake." Xuan Thuy in Paris insisted
that the NLF was the only authentic voice of the South Vietnamese
people, but he welcomed a meeting, he informed the press, that included
a Saigon delegation. Mrs. Nguyen Thi Binh, heading the new Viet
Cong negotiating team, arrived in Paris on November 3, warning that
the "Vietnamese people will continue their struggle until final victory."[46] The central issue of the war remained unchanged: who would
control Saigon? For the moment, at least, Hanoi and the NLF would
accept a coalition government. To Saigon, however, acceptance of the
NLF as equals would lead to compromise, and compromise would
terminate in disaster.

This deadlock over purpose reduced the Paris negotiations to

[44]For the issues in the continuing disagreement in Paris see "Confusion over the
Bombing Issue," *New York Times*, August 4, 1968, p. E4; Tom Wicker in ibid., August 18,
1968, p. E15; Gene Roberts in ibid., October 20, 1968, p. 1; "The Week in Review,"
ibid., p. E1; "Hanoi Nibbles, But Has Not Yet Taken the Bait," ibid., October 27, 1968,
p. E3; and Murrey Marder, "Our Paris Foe is Courtly," *Washington Post*, September 8,
1968, p. B1. For the October negotiations over the bombing halt see Arthur L. Gavshon
in *Daily Progress*, November 13, 1968.

[45]For reaction to the president's announcement see Zalin B. Grant, "The Bombing
Halt," *New Republic* 159 (November 9, 1968): 13–15. One reason for Johnson's delay was
his failure to secure the approval of Saigon. See Gavshon in *Daily Progress*, November 13,
1968. President Thieu's bitter reaction in *Washington Post*, November 5, 1968, p. A19.

[46]On the impasse in Paris see "What Hanoi Wants at Paris," *New York Times*,
November 10, 1968, p. E3; Chalmers M. Roberts, "Vietnam's Bitter Kernel is Exposed,"
Washington Post, November 17, 1968, pp. B1–2; "Saigon Balks," *Newsweek*, November 11,
1968, p. 46; "Paris: A Long Way to Go," ibid., pp. 52–53; "Statements by Xuan Thuy,"
New York Times, November 3, 1968, p. 1; Mrs. Binh's arrival in Paris, *Washington Post*,
November 4, 1968.

matters of form, not of substance. American negotiators rejected Hanoi's suggestion of a single four-party conference around a single table, whether square, round, or doughnut-shaped. The United States countered with a seating arrangement that suggested a two-sided conference, proposing specifically a green baize barrier taped diametrically across a circular table. The order of speaking, once begun, would rotate around the table. Saigon accepted this proposal, but Hanoi, recognizing in the U.S. formula an effort to bury the NLF in a single Communist team, rejected it.[47] When late in November Saigon, under burgeoning American pressure, agreed to enter the Paris negotiations, one European journalist quipped that the decision would produce "one conference with two sides, three delegations, and four chairs." Vice-President Nguyen Cao Ky, heading Saigon's delegation, arrived in Paris only to make clear his refusal to compromise on procedure or protocol.[48]

Finally, in January 1969 the North Vietnamese and U.S. negotiators in Paris agreed on a seating arrangement for the conference. Their formula consisted of using an unmarked round table, flanked by two rectangular tables for secretaries; there would be no flags or other identifying symbols. The four delegations would sit as two opposing groups, each to be followed in speaking by the other on its side. This seating arrangement permitted Hanoi to claim the presence of four delegations, whereas the "AA, BB" speaking sequence permitted Saigon and Washington to claim a two-sided conference.[49]

Even as the Paris confrontation took form, neither side revealed the slightest intention to accept a compromise. The long and costly U.S. involvement had postponed the necessary political settlement for another half dozen years; it had in no manner created the occasion for an agreement by convincing either Saigon or Hanoi that it could not ultimately emerge victorious. Essentially it was the chasm between the ends and the means of policy that rendered the whole American effort ineffective. The ends of policy upheld the rights and expectations of Saigon, while the means, destructive as they were, failed to diminish

[47]For the debate on the shape of the table see William L. Ryan in *Daily Progress*, November 13, and December 14, 1968; *Washington Post*, December 8, 1968, p. A6.

[48]"The Peace Talks in Saigon," *Washington Post*, November 10, 1968, p. B6; on Ky see Murrey Marder in ibid., December 18, 1968. Clifford took the lead in advocating troop withdrawals and a compromise in Saigon's negotiating position. See George C. Wilson, "Clifford Controversy," ibid., December 29, 1968; *New York Times*, December 25, 1968, p. E3. Ky rebuked Clifford for accusing Saigon of intransigence. *Washington Post*, December 18, 1968, p. A20; "The Week in Review," *New York Times*, December 1, 1968, p. D1; *Newsweek*, December 9, 1968, pp. 27–28.

[49]Paul Hofmann in *New York Times*, January 5, 1969; "The Sudden Breakthrough," *Newsweek*, January 27, 1969, pp. 36–37.

the goals or expectations of Hanoi. "The Vietnam story," Adam B. Ulam concluded, "thus brings into full relief the immorality of unrealism in international politics. . . . Much could have been saved in human lives, in human freedom and contentment through the world, if only U.S. policies had been guided by less elevated and more practical goals."[50]

Within the United States the needed national consensus, favoring either compromise or victory, remained tantalizingly elusive. Ultimately, Johnson's Vietnam policies resulted in far more division at home than victory in Asia. The reason is clear: those policies were anchored to words and emotions, to high promises of success and dire warnings of the consequences of failure, and not to a body of easily recognizable circumstances, such as the power and ambitions of Hitler, which carried their own conviction and recommended their own responses. It was not strange that the country divided sharply between those who took the rhetoric and admonitions seriously and those who did not. To defend his direct military involvement in Vietnam with a half million men, the president was compelled to exaggerate the importance of that region to the United States and the rest of the world until he had expended more in cost and destruction than the results could justify. Even then the end of the struggle was nowhere in sight.

[50]Adam B. Ulam, *The Rivals: America and Russia Since World War II* (New York, 1971), p. 386. For a similar judgment see Lippmann in *Newsweek*, January 13, 1969, p. 11; and Robert L. Heilbroner, "Making a Rational Foreign Policy Now," *Harper's Magazine* 237 (September 1968): 64–71. For an analysis that predicted the failure in the Paris talks see Michael Goldsmith in *Daily Progress*, February 8, 1969.

Henry Kissinger: A Contemporary Appraisal*

BOTH KENNEDY AND JOHNSON accepted without question the assumptions and objectives of national action abroad which had been established earlier by Truman and continued, unchanged except in language and style, by Eisenhower. The uncritical acceptance of Soviet and Chinese aggressiveness determined the responses of the United States from mid-century through the Johnson years. Such assumptions underwrote the continued American commitment to NATO, the support of Asian allies in SEATO and elsewhere, the nonrecognition of the Beijing regime, and the war in Indochina. All of these policies partook of the single goal of containing Communist power in all its forms as the organized, determined enemy of the Western World. Acheson, Dulles, and their successors shared the assumption that in time successful containment would produce significant changes in the power and ambitions of the Communist world and create at last a new order of peace and stability. Somehow the Nixon-Kissinger policies of the 1970s bear no relationship to that vision at all.

Nothing illustrated better the collapse of the Acheson-Dulles assumptions of ultimate victory over Beijing and Moscow than the summits of 1972, for those meetings acknowledged the existing Communist world as a permanent element in international politics. The United States, whatever the validity of its perennial Cold War fears of Communist expansionism, had no apparent choice but to recognize the need for a more promising relationship with the two Communist powers. This tardy admission of the Soviet victory over Germany in 1945,

*Published as "Henry Kissinger and American Foreign Policy: A Contemporary Appraisal," *Australian Journal of Politics and History* 22 (April 1976): 7–22. Reprinted by permission.

an acknowledgment begun in 1969 by Willy Brandt's *Ostpolitik*, was in large measure the result of changing times. Still the Nixon adminis-tration, unlike its predecessors, was prepared to recognize and exploit the opportunities afforded by a changing world environment with pol-icies that might serve American interests and President Nixon's proper concern for his reputation as a diplomatist. Henry Kissinger, the dis-tinguished Harvard scholar who entered the Nixon administration as presidential assistant for National Security Affairs, explained the sit-uation that he faced in 1969:

> When I came into office with the Nixon Administration, we were really at the end of a period of American foreign policy in which a redesign would have been necessary to do no matter who took over. . . . First, Western Europe and Japan had regained economic vitality and some political constancy. Secondly, the simplicities of the cold war began to evaporate.
>
> The domestic pressures in all countries for putting an end to tension became greater and greater, and within the Communist world it was self-evident that we were no longer confronting a monolith. . . . So our problem was how to orient America in this world and how to do it in such a way that we could avoid these oscillations between excessive moralism and excessive pragmatism, with excessive concern with power and total rejection of power, which have been fairly characteristic of American policy. This was the basic goal we set ourselves.[1]

The Nixon-Kissinger approaches to China and the Soviet Union reflected a recognition of America's declining influence as well as an acknowledgment that new circumstances on the world scene, especially the Sino-Soviet conflict, created opportunities for improved East-West relationships. Nixon knew that the postwar Pax America was exhausted, and that the country had reached the outer limits of its power to influence the world of nations. He expressed this sense of limits in his address at the U.S. Naval Academy in June 1974. "America was no longer a giant," he reminded the nation, "towering over the rest of the world with seemingly inexhaustible resources and a nuclear monopoly"; the time had come for the country to reassess its responsibilities. Still any search for accommodation which reflected the new opportunities required greater pragmatism than Washington had displayed in the past. As the president explained, "we have to remember . . . that unreal-istic idealism could be impractical and potentially dangerous. It could

[1]Interview with Pierre Salinger of *L'Express* (France), news release, April 12, 1975, U.S. Department of State, Bureau of Public Affairs, Office of Media Services.

tempt us to forego results that were good because we insisted on results that were perfect."

For Nixon and Kissinger the dominant issue in world affairs was the conflict between the United States and the USSR, a conflict that extended to all parts of the world and thereby rendered the very nature of governments everywhere a matter of international security. Because the U.S.-Soviet conflict was global, the success or failure of American performance even in remote regions of the world could affect the world-wide equilibrium. Still Nixon and Kissinger agreed that the clear limitations which the world imposed on both the United States and the Soviet Union had created the foundations of a more promising East-West relationship. Kissinger's philosophical contribution to this notion sprang from his understanding of the nineteenth century's "stable structure of peace" which required above all a generally accepted legitimacy. Kissinger defined that necessary legitimacy in his book on Metternich:

> 'Legitimacy' . . . means no more than an international agreement about the nature of workable arrangements and about the permissible aims and methods of foreign policy. It implies the acceptance of the framework of the international order by all the major powers, at least to the extent that no state is so dissatisfied that . . . it expresses its dissatisfaction in a revolutionary foreign policy. A legitimate order does not make conflicts impossible but it limits their scope. . . . Diplomacy in the classic sense, the adjustment of differences through negotiation, is possible only in 'legitimate' international orders.[2]

Kissinger's necessary structure of peace for the 1970s required the stabilization of the Washington-Moscow rivalry through the establishment of new ground rules, hedging against sudden moves that might upset the global balance. Any new arrangement would require as well a code of behavior and a body of procedures that would discourage either side from endangering the perceived interests of the other. Kissinger's reliance on superior force and the will to use it assumed a progression of successful confrontations and the ultimate Soviet acceptance of agreements that would underwrite the necessary stabilization. Even as American power frustrated Soviet ambitions, shipments of grain and Western technology, needed credits, and relaxed tensions would reward the Soviets for their good behavior. Through a system of punishments and rewards, the United States would convince the Soviets that their interests lay in cooperation rather than confrontation.

President Nixon's experience at the Moscow Summit Conference

[2]Henry A. Kissinger, *A World Restored* (New York, 1964), pp. 1–2.

in May 1972, with its open displays of cordiality and its many agreements, created the impression that the Kremlin indeed had entered a new and more reassuring relationship with Washington. Kissinger's precise role in the diplomatic maneuvering, which culminated in the Beijing Summit of February 1972 and the Moscow Summit that followed, must await some future revelation. William Safire, writing in March 1975, asserted that Nixon was the creator and manager of U.S. policy in the critical years of 1971 and 1972.[3] He observed that the president used Kissinger artfully, sometimes thrusting him into the limelight, sometimes letting him down cruelly, but that Nixon was always the creative force. Kissinger's chief role was that of conducting the laborious preparations before the Beijing and Moscow summits. Thus his essential tasks, except for the nuclear disarmament negotiations, were completed before the summits occurred.[4] Still it seems clear that the underlying precepts of national policy belonged to Kissinger as well as to Nixon.

Kissinger's assumption that the Soviets threatened Western security on many interrelated fronts underwrote his concept of linkage. Both Nixon and Kissinger doubted that the issues between the United States and the USSR could be approached satisfactorily and profitably in isolation from one another; success on one front depended on Soviet attitudes and behavior elsewhere. The global balance demanded that the United States maintain its commitments to those nations of Asia, the Middle East, Africa, and Latin America that had declared their opposition to Communist-led revolution. It was essential, therefore, that Washington not permit the Soviets to exploit their special gains in Europe by extending their operations in the Third World. Détente required guarantees of legitimate Soviet behavior everywhere. Coexistence, as Kissinger explained in his *Pacem in Terris* address of October 8, 1973, entailed precise guidelines for U.S. policy: "We will oppose the attempt by any country to achieve a position of predominance either globally or regionally. We will resist any attempt to exploit a policy of détente to weaken our alliance. We will react if relaxation of tensions is used as a cover to exacerbate conflict in international trouble spots."[5]

[3]William Safire, "Puppet as Prince," *Harper's Magazine* 250 (March 1975): 12–17. Safire believed that Kissinger became the dominant force in the conduct of American foreign policy after February 1973. Henry Brandon suggested that from the beginning Kissinger had major influence on Nixon. See Brandon, *The Retreat of American Power* (New York, 1974), pp. 33–34.

[4]Kissinger at the time of the Moscow summit acknowledged that the basic decisions in foreign affairs belonged to Nixon. See Marvin Kalb and Bernard Kalb, *Kissinger* (Boston, 1974), p. 314. In an interview of November 1975, Nixon insisted that he was at least "half of Henry Kissinger." *Washington Post*, November 18, 1975.

[5]Department of State *Bulletin* 69 (October 29, 1973): 528.

The Soviet Union, he added, could not ignore these principles in any area of the world without imperiling its entire relationship with the United States.

Kissinger's ultimate purpose was to terminate unwanted Soviet pressures against the global balance of power. He left no doubt that he favored the prompt and effective use of force to counter possible Soviet gains. Unfortunately, the American defense of the status quo outside Europe, often binding the United States to unpromising regimes, had become expensive and divisive. Therefore, he hoped that his system of incentives would encourage the Kremlin to terminate its political and military assistance to revolutionary movements and thereby resolve the uniquely troublesome American problem of dealing with Third World upheavals. Kissinger would eliminate the sources of global instability through Soviet self-containment.

For Kissinger other world issues—relations with Beijing, the European allies, Japan, and the non-Communist Third World, along with the status of minorities and dissidents within the Soviet Union itself—were secondary to the overarching U.S.-Soviet relationship. China remained relatively weak and was obviously not as aggressive as two decades of apocalyptic American pronouncements had insisted. The European allies and Japan scarcely endangered any basic American interests. The underdeveloped countries were numerous but relatively unimportant in the realm of power politics. The Soviet Union alone had the power, the reach, and the policy choices to challenge America's primary interests. Thus the United States, despite the gains of détente, maintained its commitments of the past; it sustained its alliances and military relationships under the continuing assumption that the world had not been totally freed of the danger of aggression. Changes in U.S.-Soviet attitudes and policies were real, if limited. Fundamentally, the Nixon-Kissinger approach to the Communist-led powers attempted to multilateralize the burden of maintaining world stability without compromising any established American objective in areas of U.S.-Soviet competition.

Measured by the assumptions of détente—that is, that China and the USSR were essentially status quo powers—the continuing Nixon involvement in Vietnam after 1969 had appeared illogical. The American commitment to Saigon, based on the concept of falling dominoes, assumed that South and Southeast Asia and even more would fall to some Communist monolith, centering in Moscow, should the United States falter in its defense of South Vietnam. Détente, however, had meaning only if the aggressive Communist monolith of the past no longer existed. Nixon's Vietnamization of the war was designed to stabilize the administration's relations with Congress and the American people. So successful were the president's efforts to reduce American casualties in Vietnam that by 1972 he had neutralized the Vietnam issue in U.S. politics. Meanwhile, Nixon's military initiatives in that country itself—the invasion of Cambodia in 1970, the move into Laos in 1971, the mining of Haiphong harbor, the acceleration of the offensive that culminated in the Christmas bombing of 1972—were designed not only to win the war but also to impress the Soviets. Nixon was convinced, wrote Safire, that negotiations with the Kremlin would achieve little unless the United States could convince the world that it was willing to use power to gain its objectives. Thus the president explained his decision to mine Haiphong harbor: "If . . . when I went to Moscow, late in May, at that time we had had Soviet tanks run by North Vietnamese rumbling through the streets of Hue, and Saigon being shelled, we would not have been able to deal with the Soviets on the basis of equal respect. We wouldn't have been worth talking to . . . in a sense, and they would have known it."[6] Nixon wanted a "reputation for fierceness" which required the exercise of will. It was Kissinger's role in Moscow to convince Soviet leaders that the president's reputation for fierceness was thoroughly merited.

Kissinger's preferences in Vietnam differed little from those of Nixon. No less than the president he favored a hard line on Vietnam, again in part to assure the success of détente.[7] For Kissinger the essence of the nation's capacity to limit and ultimately to eliminate international conflict lay in the credibility of its power. If American credibility alone permitted the considerable security the world enjoyed, it was essential that the United States protect its credibility by employing force around the globe, interfering if necessary in the affairs of other countries and demonstrating a willingness to elevate local and secondary conflicts into global tests of strength and will. It was to protect this credibility everywhere that Kissinger and Nixon argued against any precipitous withdrawal from Vietnam. Kissinger supported Nixon's thrusts into Cambodia and Laos under the shared assumption that any show of force in Southeast Asia would increase the possibilities for success at the summit.

To maintain the nation's credibility, Kissinger favored the bombing of North Vietnam which after 1970 had grown into the most massive

---

[6]Safire, "Puppet as Prince," p. 12. In explaining his decision to bomb Haiphong in May 1972, Nixon declared that the United States was "faced with the specter of defeat, and I had to make a choice, a choice of accepting that defeat and going to Moscow hat in hand, or of acting to prevent it. I acted." See Kalb and Kalb, *Kissinger*, p. 306.

[7]Ibid., pp. 120–72. Kalb and Kalb recount Kissinger's association with Vietnam from early 1969 through the Cambodian venture of 1970. They reveal Kissinger's general support for the Nixon approach to Vietnam and his tendency to accept all assumptions regarding the need for American success to uphold the global position of the United States.

air war in history. If, in his public statements, he seemed to regret the destruction, it was not because he opposed the bombing but because he wanted to soften the effect of what he knew was a hard and demanding policy. Still the United States could not maintain its global credibility by fighting in Vietnam forever. Ultimately, in January 1973, Kissinger achieved an agreement with North Vietnamese negotiator Le Duc Tho in Paris which provided for the withdrawal within sixty days of all U.S. forces from South Vietnam in exchange for the return of all American prisoners. Nixon heralded the agreement as "peace with honor," and Kissinger received the Nobel Peace Prize for his efforts. This agreement brought no peace; whether it brought any honor to the United States or to the Nixon administration was questionable.[8]

Kissinger's design established the foundations for U.S.-Soviet cooperation in areas of tension but always under the imperative that the USSR not alter any situation to its advantage. In his manipulation of rewards and punishments to restrain Soviet behavior, Kissinger forever seemed to pursue some international order in which all nations, but especially the USSR, would live by American rules. In every circumstance, he would preserve American primacy. His purposes never allowed for the inevitability of assaults on the treaty structure which the United States could not and would not control. That détente scored any victories at all measured the willingness of the Soviet Union to accept some conditions favorable to the West as the price of transforming U.S.-Soviet relations toward increased cooperation and trade in Europe. Outside Europe, however, the rules of détente imposed far more restraints on Soviet than on American behavior, forcing the Kremlin to consider whether Soviet gains were sufficient to render the arrangement worthwhile. Washington's power to influence Soviet policies to its advantage everywhere never existed. Ultimately, the United States discovered that it could not control Soviet activities in Africa, the Middle East, or Southeast Asia. For those who took linkage seriously détente had merely permitted the Soviets to improve their military defenses and extend their activities in the Afro-Asian world. For its critics détente was dead by 1973.

II

Many analysts anticipated, with considerable pleasure, Kissinger's appointment as secretary of state in August 1973. His professional competence, they believed, would enhance the nation's opportunities for world leadership. His appointment would make him more accessible

---

[8]Le Duc Tho refused to accept his Nobel prize because he believed that the Paris agreement had not achieved peace.

to Congress and the people, thereby subjecting his views to the country's democratic processes.[9] Moreover, it would encourage the administration to rebuild and revitalize the State Department by restoring it to its traditional role in the creation of foreign policy. For too long successive administrations had ignored the talents of that agency. Kissinger's nomination faced little opposition in the Senate. The response abroad, noted Joseph Kraft, was "positively lyrical."[10]

Still many feared that Kissinger, as secretary, could not sustain his past record which had brought such effusive praise. His move to the State Department might well increase his influence there, but his departure from the White House could reduce his influence within the departments of Defense, Treasury, Commerce, and Agriculture. These departments had strong constituencies and, whereas they were subject to the National Security Council (still chaired by Kissinger), there was no coordinating machinery to bring them under State Department control.[11] It required no more than the Yom Kippur War of October 1973 in the Middle East for Kissinger to establish his predominance in the Nixon administration. When the new secretary of state argued that the Israelis required additional equipment to establish a stronger base from which to negotiate a cease-fire, he faced determined opposition in the Pentagon. Secretary of Defense James R. Schlesinger feared that the Arabs, if pressed by Israel, would cut off oil from the Western nations. When Kissinger accused the Pentagon of defying the president's orders, it retorted that the secretary was attempting to run the war without the cooperation of the military. With Nixon's backing he finally won the argument, and the huge airlift of supplies which Kissinger advocated was soon on its way to Israel.[12]

It was Kissinger's diplomatic agility in his search for a Middle Eastern peace, however, that sent his prestige skyrocketing toward its zenith in 1974. Already the American policy of evenhandedness toward the Middle East provided the Nixon administration with a maximum of credibility in its search for a settlement of the Arab-Israeli conflict. Early in December 1973, Kissinger had set out on a fifteen-day diplomatic venture that carried him to thirteen countries in Europe and the Middle East. By late December, for the first time in twenty-five years of conflict, he had brought Israel and the Arabs, except for the Syrians, to the peace table at Geneva. Then in May 1974 he capped

[9]See George W. Ball in *Newsweek*, November 20, 1972, p. 21.
[10]Kraft in *Washington Post*, September 9, 1973.
[11]For Kissinger's special challenges as secretary of state see Joseph Kraft, "Secretary Henry," *New York Times Magazine*, October 28, 1973, p. 21.
[12]For Kissinger's successful effort to control Middle Eastern policy see Kalb and Kalb, *Kissinger*, pp. 450–78.

one of the greatest displays of personal diplomacy on record by securing an agreement between Israel and Syria over the disputed Golan Heights. For twenty-eight days he flew back and forth between Jerusalem and Damascus to arrange the Israeli withdrawal from Syrian territory and the return of Israeli prisoners of war. The breakthrough came late in the month when Israel dropped its insistence on a Syrian guarantee against Arab guerrilla infiltration. The United States, Kissinger promised, would support Israel politically should it be compelled to retaliate against Arab attacks. During June the United States reopened its embassy in Damascus, previously closed for seven years, and signed a wide-ranging economic and military pact with Saudi Arabia. Kissinger not only had brought at least a momentary peace to the Middle East but also had elevated the Arab world's estimation of the United States. President Nixon ratified this new relationship with a triumphal tour of Egypt, Saudi Arabia, Syria, Israel, and Jordan; millions of Arabs turned out to cheer the American president. Kissinger's Middle Eastern triumphs resulted from good timing, momentum, and a remarkable display of fairness.

Even as Nixon's reputation disintegrated during 1974 under the impact of Watergate, Kissinger's popularity reached an almost unchallengeable position. Miss Universe named him "the greatest person in the world today"; polls made him overwhelmingly the most popular personality in the United States; and even the noted Vietnam critic, Richard A. Falk of Princeton University, admitted that "Kissinger has realized the dream of every political figure—to become so valuable a public servant that it seems irresponsible to criticize him." Kissinger was brilliant in maintaining his base of support. During the very months in which Nixon and his White House staff termed the press the enemy, he maintained a remarkably good relationship with reporters, largely because he regarded that relationship essential. His handling of the press was elegant; he nurtured the necessary contacts within the Washington press corps. In turn, the press courted him as Washington's most engaging personality.

Even in Congress his power seemed complete. Few members cared to challenge him and, when members of Congress and the press threatened to make an issue of the knowledge that the secretary had requested FBI surveillance of several associates, Kissinger set the price that his detractors would pay for the luxury of attacking him. At the time of his Senate confirmation, Kissinger had denied that he had initiated any wiretap program in his office, but at Salzburg, Austria, in June he admitted that, "in submitting these names, we knew that an investigation was certain." The government, he declared, had a right to defend itself against leaks. Then the secretary, knowing that the Senate Foreign Relations Committee would succumb to pressure, threatened to resign if Congress did not resolve the charges against him. During August the committee agreed unanimously that the secretary had not misled it.[13] Eventually Kissinger was the only high-ranking member of the Nixon team to survive Watergate.

III

Still the Kissinger leadership was flawed; by the autumn of 1974 it had come under serious attack. Some insisted, indeed, that neither the secretary's approaches nor his methods served the country's best interests. In part, critics condemned Kissinger for his style, noting his preference for secrecy and surprise in the formulation of policy. George E. Reedy, press secretary under Lyndon Johnson, recognized both the advantages and dangers of secrecy: "The arguments for the tactics of strategic surprise seem to be overwhelming when a nation faces an enemy or what it perceives as an enemy. The advantages of an open society—which are very real indeed—seem trivial in a struggle for survival. Unfortunately, secrecy can become habit-forming, and persist even after the excuses for it have disappeared."[14] Decisions arrived at alone or with a few trusted assistants lack the infusion of fresh ideas or warnings of potential failure that can come only from direct challenge. Such an approach to decision making assumes a monopoly of wisdom which does not exist. American foreign policy has suffered repeatedly from the narrowness of views within government that comes from the elimination of all from the advisory process who are not already committed to established policy assumptions and goals. Too often the government has ignored outside analyses far superior to its own.

Some State Department officials had anticipated Kissinger's appointment as secretary of state with "restrained euphoria," convinced that he would integrate the department into the policymaking process. At the time of his appointment he had noted: "Durability in foreign policy is achieved in the final analysis through the deep and continuing involvement of the dedicated professionals of the State Department . . . who will manage our foreign affairs long after this Administration has ended."[15] Still the fear persisted that he would isolate himself on the

[13]John M. Crewdson in *New York Times*, September 29, 1974. For Kissinger's troubles over the tapes see "The Week in Review," *New York Times*, June 16, 1974; and *Newsweek*, June 24, 1974, pp. 25–28. For a criticism of Kissinger's behavior in June see Anthony Lewis in *Daily Progress* (Charlottesville, VA), June 14, 1974.

[14]George E. Reedy in *Washington Post*, September 15, 1974.

[15]Leslie H. Gelb in *New York Times*, September 23, 1974.

seventh floor and surround himself with his old White House confidants. Kissinger's distrust of the bureaucracy was well known. As he once wrote, "it is no accident that most great statemen were opposed by the 'experts' in their Foreign Offices, for the very greatness of the statesman's conception tends to make it inaccessible to those whose primary concern is with safety and minimum risk." Under Kissinger the State Department suffered not only from disuse and drift but also from the suspicion that characterized the Nixon White House. There was the same fear of leaks, the same demand for loyalty. State Department morale made little recovery from the collapse it experienced under Kissinger's predecessor, William P. Rogers.

During his White House years, Kissinger's personal diplomacy scarcely concerned the State Department; by late 1974 its demoralizing impact on the department had become clear. In undertaking so much himself, he had become the sole instrument of U.S. foreign policy. Other governments refused to believe that they were dealing with the United States unless they were dealing with him. Only his presence could assure other countries that Washington was not actually ignoring them. Officials in the State Department complained that the secretary never bothered to explain American policy to them; there was no one with authority to deal with questions outside the scope of his immediate concern. James Reston had observed as early as February 1974 that "[Kissinger] is trying to toss too many continents around. He is not organizing the State Department to handle all the problems that need to be handled at the same time, but is almost replacing the State Department with his personal concentration on crisis situations."[16] State Department critics noted that Kissinger's successes were often tentative, evaporating quickly when basically unresolved tensions began to reassert themselves.

Nixon had used Kissinger's personal prestige to control Congress on matters of foreign policy. In general the technique worked, especially since Kissinger had the full support of J. William Fulbright, chairman of the Senate Foreign Relations Committee. Kissinger, at the time of his appointment to the State Department, reassured the nation that the necessary institutionalization of American foreign policy, in order that it could be passed on to succeeding administrations, would require not only a greater use of the professionals in the State Department but also a closer partnership with Congress in the planning and execution of future policy. "[W]e know," he declared, "that we will be able to work out such an arrangement with the members of the Congressional committees, all of whom I know personally and have worked with in

[16]Reston in ibid., February 17, 1974.

the past."[17] Thereafter, he told Congress what it wanted to hear: that he planned to broaden the base of decision making. Senators wanted to believe him but suspected quite correctly that nothing would change.

After a year of growing frustration, Congress found the occasion to defy Kissinger in October 1974 when it moved to cut off military aid to Turkey which the secretary regarded essential for the achievement of American purpose in Cyprus. Congress had long forbidden the use of American weapons for aggressive purposes, and Turkey had employed such weapons in its successful invasion of Cyprus following the Greek coup of July 1974. What mattered to Congress, however, was not Turkish policy, which in large measure was justifiable, but rather the growing disillusionment with Kissinger's operating style. Among the congressional frustrations was his approval of the Central Intelligence Agency's operation against the duly elected Salvador Allende government in Chile. The congressional assault on Kissinger, when it came, was bitter. Members accused him of abusing the powers of government. Congressman Benjamin S. Rosenthal, Democrat of New York, declared: "There is a two-tiered Kissinger. The one who is public and eloquent and says the right things, and the one who deals from within the corridors of power." Similarly, Senator Thomas F. Eagleton of Missouri accused Kissinger of double-talk: "Our distinguished Secretary of State is famous for his tilts. He tilts toward the junta in Chile. He tilts toward Thieu in Vietnam. . . . His current tilt, his pro-Turkey tilt, is no wiser than the others." Kissinger's troubles were not unexpected. What disturbed his supporters was the vehemence of the congressional attack. As one State Department spokesman expressed it, "I'm not surprised that Congress is beginning to assert itself more. The only thing that troubles me is that it has gotten off to such a raucous beginning—which has such a vindictive air about it."[18]

Kissinger's most bitter critics accused him of employing public relations, deviousness, and outright dishonesty to sustain his popularity and control of foreign policy. One Nixon administration official observed in private that "Henry's problems arise from the fact that he is a constitutional liar. As long as he remembers what he says to whom, he's all right. If he forgets, he's in trouble."[19] One congressional critic complained of Kissinger's lack of forthrightness: "It's the same old thing. We say give us treaties, and Kissinger gives us executive agreements. We say no military advisers in Cambodia, and Kissinger says

[17]Press conference, western White House, news release, August 23, 1973, U.S. Department of State, Bureau of Public Affairs, Office of Media Services.
[18]Murrey Marder and Marilyn Berger in *Washington Post*, October 6, 1974.
[19]Peter Lisagor in *Daily Progress*, September 23, 1974.

we only have weapons delivery systems there. It's still government by Roget's Thesaurus."[20] By 1975 all leading candidates for the Democratic presidential nomination had taken a public stand against Kissinger. Senator Lloyd M. Bentsen, Jr., of Texas accused Kissinger of running a "dangerously constricted and convoluted [foreign policy] with an . . . emphasis on secret diplomacy, personal negotiations, and one-man authoritarianism."[21] Even earlier Senator Jackson succeeded in preventing congressional approval of the most-favored-nation principle, as embodied in the administration's commercial agreement with the Kremlin, until the Soviets adopted a more liberal Jewish emigration policy. Predictably, they rejected the congressional offer.

Criticizing Congress for meddling, Kissinger admitted, in an interview with Reston, that "there is an almost instinctive rebellion in America against the pragmatic aspect of diplomacy . . . that seeks to settle for the best attainable, rather than for the best."[22] At Los Angeles on January 24, 1975, the secretary called for a "new national partnership" to avoid further domestic confrontation over foreign policy. He insisted that the administration would explore new approaches in its relations with Congress and seek the advice and consent of that body in the broadest sense.[23] Such promises mattered little; Congress continued to assert its independence. In December 1974 it had voted to discontinue all military aid to Turkey unless the negotiations between Greece and Turkey over the future of Cyprus made substantial progress. Kissinger reminded congressional spokesmen that military aid to Turkey served essential Western security interests, and that the aid cutoff would be a "disaster" for American policy. Nevertheless, when early in February 1975 State Department officials could not verify the necessary progress, the congressional cutoff went into effect. Clearly Kissinger had not resolved the need for consensus. As G. Warren Nutter, former assistant secretary of defense, complained, "confusion reigns in Congress and the public, and it cannot be dispelled by consensus because diplomacy has become personalized. There is no way for the legitimate organs of government to guide the direction of American foreign policy as long as it conforms to Kissinger's grand design."[24]

[20]Gelb in *New York Times,* June 16, 1974.
[21]Reston in ibid., February 9, 1975.
[22]See Stephen S. Rosenfeld in the Cleveland *Plain Dealer,* October 25, 1974; and Meg Greenfield in *Newsweek,* November 11, 1974, p. 46.
[23]News release, January 24, 1975, U.S. Department of State, Bureau of Public Affairs, Office of Media Services; Gelb in *New York Times,* January 26, 1975.
[24]Marder in *Philadelphia Inquirer,* October 12, 1975. Frances R. Hill complained that Kissinger, as secretary of state, seemed destined, like Bismarck, to leave what Kissinger called "a heritage of unassimilated greatness." See *Worldview* 17 (October 1974): 33.

IV

Critics noted that Kissinger's successes responded to several unique circumstances that made them appear more innovative and pervasive than they actually were. First, in large measure the initiatives for détente came from Beijing and Moscow. Building on the clearly expressed desire of both the USSR and China to improve their relations with the United States, Kissinger had merely to convince them that their interests were limited. Second, in both China and the Soviet Union he dealt with regimes run from the top down, permitting him to engage in secret negotiations that could bind those governments more readily than his own. Third, the previous relations between the United States and the two Communist-led giants were so thin or nonexistent that it required no more than the summits of 1972 to create what seemed to be a massive diplomatic achievement. Thus there was always a chasm between the appearance and the reality of success. Kissinger, moreover, focused on immediate arrangements, not long-term goals. His openings toward Beijing and Moscow, and even his cease-fire agreement with Hanoi, emphasized tactics and not strategy.[25] The initial summits established the foundations for additional agreements, but succeeding meetings could never again match the first in drama, significance, or genuine gains. Somehow Kissinger's policies, despite their heralded triumphs, remained no less expensive and demanding than those of previous administrations.

Kissinger sought essentially to negotiate a formal diplomatic settlement of the war, a process begun by Brandt. More than his predecessors he was willing to accept the changes wrought by the Soviet victories of 1944 and 1945. He refused to criticize the Kremlin for its repression of Eastern Europe and its refusal to liberalize the Soviet political system. Much of his success, therefore, hinged on his lack of public concern for human rights inside the Soviet bloc, although it was his conviction, often expressed, that he could serve those rights more effectively with policies aimed at relaxation rather than tension. Countless Americans, tired of Washington's former Cold War posture, which seemed to achieve so little, agreed. For them Kissinger's diplomacy was credible and praiseworthy. Some, however, charged that in order to defend détente he had created a false alternative between international tranquility and constant crises. "Tension is, after all," wrote Nutter, "the natural reaction to a perceived threat, and it alerts and

---

[25]Kraft in *Washington Post*, November 5, 1974. For a critical examination of Kissinger's diplomacy see Simon Head, "The Hot Deals and Cold Wars of Henry Kissinger," *New York Times Magazine*, October 26, 1975, p. 13.

stimulates the will to resist." What the country required was the restoration of "a healthy state of alert based on appreciation of the external dangers threatening the Western way of life, and a sense of confidence that they can be overcome."[26]

Whatever the achievements of détente, and they were considerable, U.S. relations with Western Europe and Japan would always assure a lesser return. Here the links were strong, the existing arrangements voluminous. Among the NATO allies the secret negotiations that Kissinger preferred would achieve little. The unresolved issues, largely economic, were too complex and unpromising to permit any startling diplomatic triumphs.[27] For Kissinger, moreover, détente with the Soviet Union was vastly more important than satisfactory communications with Britain or France. His personal style, enhanced by a trace of arrogance in his relations with those who could not injure him or his policies, permitted Kissinger alternately to ignore and imperil traditional American ties with Western Europe and Japan. European leaders complained that the secretary did not consult them on issues that affected their region. Peter Jenkins of the *Manchester Guardian* wrote that Kissinger "regards Europe as he regards the State Department—as an adjunct to his personal diplomacy, to be seen and not heard." If Europeans praised his efforts in the Middle East, they often wondered what he was doing.

After 1973 Kissinger had demanded that Europe act as a unit on matters of trade with the United States, and that it carry a heavier burden for its defense. However, he criticized Europe's leaders publicly when they acted without consulting Washington in advance.[28] Europe demonstrated its divergent interests and independence when it refused to cooperate with the American effort to supply Israel during the Yom Kippur War. Kissinger attributed the need for speed and secrecy to the seriousness of the international crisis, yet it seemed illogical that the United States would insist on operating secretly and unilaterally in a situation, proclaimed dangerous, without consulting its most important allies. Kenneth Thompson condemned these unilateral tendencies in official U.S. behavior toward Europe. "The Administration," he wrote in July 1974, "understands national power but not national prestige. . . . It has used its power without magnanimity or grace. . . . [Nixon and Kissinger have] been so relentless and cold-blooded [in their pragmatism] that they have not inspired trust, especially among those who might be expected to feel most trusting of Americans, namely

[26]Nutter quoted by Marder in *Philadelphia Inquirer*, October 12, 1975.
[27]See Kraft in *Washington Post*, May 27, 1973; and Chalmers M. Roberts in ibid., August 26, 1973.
[28]Reston in *New York Times*, February 28, 1974.

Europeans."[29] Kissinger's shocks to Japan were notorious. He failed to inform Tokyo of either the new approaches to China or basic American commercial and monetary decisions that affected Japan.

In undertaking the classical tasks of diplomacy, Kissinger was in some degree overtaken by events beyond his control. Just as he came to grips with the fundamental Cold War issues of the previous quarter century, he faced a full spectrum of new problems far more complex and dangerous: resource scarcities, energy, inflation, food, markets, land-tenure, hunger, reform, and the harsh disparities of wealth and technology. These new issues threatened to tear apart the new international order of the 1970s, for they could impinge on the lives of more people than the Cold War ever did. At the same time, these issues were too varied and pervading to respond effectively to private diplomacy. Basically internal they were really not subject to traditional forms of foreign policy at all. Obviously, Kissinger preferred to deal with questions that seemed amenable to international diplomacy.[30] He admitted early in 1975 that "as you know, I'm not accustomed to publicly conceding my own weaknesses. So when I acknowledge that international economics are not particularly my own forte, you've just got to believe me."[31]

Still Kissinger was mindful of the relationship between economic and political stability in international life. In August 1975 he reminded a Birmingham, Alabama, audience: "A look at our contemporary agenda leaves no doubt that peace for us is inseparable from global tranquility and that our well-being is intimately bound up with the prosperity of the rest of the world." Therefore, he assigned to State Department officials the burden of framing approaches to the new global challenges. Clearly any program, to be effective, required the support of American productivity and that of other industrial countries. Thus the initial challenge to matters of economic welfare lay in the performance of the Western economies themselves. Indeed, this caused great concern in Europe for the status of the American economy.

Hunger posed a more immediate challenge. Despite its amazing food production, the United States alone could not feed the hungry nations. In search of global cooperation, Washington had called the World Food Conference which convened in Rome during November 1974. Acting on American proposals, the conference designed an international program to stimulate food production and improve the storage

[29]Thompson in *Worldview* 17 (July 1974): 61.
[30]Roger Morris in *New York Times*, February 23, 1975.
[31]*Newsweek*, February 17, 1975, p. 25.

and distribution of future supplies.[32] Subsequent negotiations on wheat and other grains attempted to build world food reserves, but the world was not heading for any substantial change. For Americans, energy, not food and raw materials, was the issue that mattered.

Oil became a special problem for both the Western and the underdeveloped world when the producing countries, largely Arab, discovered amid the Yom Kippur War that the world demand for oil would permit both higher prices and profits. The fivefold price increase that followed produced a $40 billion payments deficit among the industrial nations, a $20 billion yearly deficit among the nations of the developing world. At the Washington Energy Conference of early 1974, the Western consumer nations had agreed on collective action, and in November they formed the International Energy Agency. Unwilling to threaten economic reprisal or create policies designed to curtail demand, the Western consuming nations were powerless to act.

In February 1975, Kissinger unveiled a new energy proposal that favored the support of high oil prices to encourage alternate sources of energy production. In the long run, he believed, this policy would permit the West to escape the clutches of the oil cartel. Many in Congress and elsewhere opposed the plan because of its acceptance of high prices. Europeans complained that high minimum oil prices favored the energy position of the United States to the disadvantage of other consuming nations. What stalled all agreements was the insistence of the oil-producing countries that the agency members discuss the price not only of oil but also of all commodities, but the United States refused. In May the State Department agreed to three parallel conferences, one each on oil, other commodities, and the needs of the poor countries. At the economic summit, which met in Paris during November, the industrial nations agreed to stimulate world recovery with increased trade, energy conservation, and greater efforts at economic cooperation.[33]

In such matters as food, energy, and general productivity, the offer of programs did not assure satisfactory progress toward a higher level of economic welfare, for the realities of economic life throughout the world reflected historic and environmental limitations not readily responsive to even the most dire necessities. On September 1, 1975, Kissinger warned the United Nations:

[32]Kissinger's address at Birmingham, Alabama, news release, August 14, 1975, U.S. Department of State, Bureau of Public Affairs, Office of Media Services. See also Edwin L. Dale, Jr., in *New York Times*, June 8, 1975; and John M. Goshko in *Washington Post*, April 13, 1975.

[33]*Newsweek*, February 17, 1975, p. 25; *Washington Post*, May 30, 1975; Bernard Kaplan in ibid., June 29, 1975; Hobart Rowen in ibid., November 18, 1975.

These economic issues have already become the subject of mounting confrontations—embargoes, cartels, seizures, countermeasures, and bitter rhetoric. Over the remainder of this century, should this trend continue, the division of the planet between North and South, between rich and poor, could become as grim as the darkest days of the cold war. We would enter an age of festering resentment, of increased resort to economic warfare, a hardening of new blocs, the undermining of cooperation, the erosion of international institutions—and failed development.

Still such challenges to courage and imagination in no way diminished the need for a continuing American effort.

V

Any change in the favorable conditions which existed between 1971 and 1974 would undermine Kissinger's authority to effect any notable gains at all. When by 1975 the interests of other states seemed to transcend the preferences of the United States, there was little that he could do to hold American policy together. The failure of the United States and Britain to react to the 1974 Greek coup in Cyprus had invited the Turkish invasion of the island. Thereafter, Turkish officials, no less than Kissinger, accused Congress of acting irresponsibly in cutting off military aid. Turkey threatened to close all U.S. bases, but it made no move to withdraw from the NATO alliance. If Washington antagonized Turkey, it failed equally to establish better relations with Greece.

Unfortunately, the alliance was faltering along the entire Mediterranean basin. Italy's rapid economic disintegration presaged the collapse of that country's active role in the European alliance. As one Western diplomat commented early in 1975, "we used to say that Italy was our first step toward the Middle East. Now we say it's our last stop on the road to South America." Meanwhile, in April 1974 Portugal had experienced a revolution that toppled a dictatorship which had lasted fifty years. The prestigious General Antonio de Spinola became the country's head as leader of the Junta of National Salvation, but soon he faced a frenzy of left-wing agitation. The Communists, the country's strongest political force, were influential in the armed forces, labor unions, press, schools, and public administration. Finally, the left-wing pressure drove Spinola into semiseclusion, and by January 1975 the Communists had established a single labor confederation under their control. Then in March the radicals triumphed again with the formation of the High Revolutionary Council of the Armed Forces to run the country. With Communists in positions of authority in the Portuguese government, NATO's relations with Lisbon, especially those of a confidential nature, were no longer open. These developments offered no clear advantages to the USSR, and, to the extent that they lay outside American control, Kissinger faced little criticism either in Europe or in the United States for this erosion of NATO's southern flank.[34]

Kissinger's Middle Eastern diplomacy, despite its outward brilliance, did not resolve any basic issue. By November 1974 the Arabs had compelled him to accept their decision to recognize the Palestine Liberation Organization as the legitimate agency for "liberating" the Israeli-occupied West Bank. Undoubtedly, the failure of Kissinger's sixteen-day effort in March 1975 to secure an Egyptian-Israeli agreement over the Sinai weakened U.S. influence in the Middle East. Upon his return to Washington the secretary admitted that American purpose faced disintegration everywhere, especially in the region of the Mediterranean.[35]

Where Kissinger's diplomacy failed in March to obtain an Egyptian-Israeli agreement on the strategic Mitla and Gidi passes, it succeeded in August but at a potentially heavy price for the United States. The new agreement, heralded as another major diplomatic triumph, served to separate the armies and extend the period of peace, but, by assigning 200 American civilian technicians to surveillance stations along the vital passes, the agreement made the United States the keeper of the peace. The agreement, along with its secret protocols which Kissinger termed binding, provided also for military aid to Egypt and Israel which could amount to $15 billion over the first five years.[36] The agreement satisfied Egypt's concern for peace and security, but other Arab states regarded it a sellout of their interests as it ignored such substantial issues as the Golan Heights, the Palestinians, and Jerusalem.[37] Mike Mansfield opposed congressional approval and reminded the Senate that "the sending of American technicians to the Sinai changes the nature of our involvement in the Middle East. By placing the American flag in the middle of the conflict the chances of our

---

[34]Still there were many who attributed the failures of Western policy in Greece and Turkey to Kissinger for refusing to use the counsel of "the best minds and spirits available." For a vigorous critique of Kissinger for his less than successful policies see Ted Caplow in *Daily Progress*, April 24, 1975; Laurence Stern in *Washington Post*, June 15, 1975; and "Once Again, an Agonizing Reappraisal," *Time*, April 7, 1975, pp. 10–36.

[35]See Kraft in *Washington Post*, November 11, 1974. For a good review of Kissinger's failure of March see ibid., March 23, 1975. Earlier Henry Kamm had criticized Kissinger's approach to the Middle East in *New York Times*, March 9, 1975.

[36]*New York Times*, September 7, 1975.

[37]See *Newsweek*, September 15, 1975, p. 33.

involvement in the next round of fighting, should it occur, will be greatly increased, as will the danger of confrontation with the Soviet Union."[38] Still early in October 1975 the Senate and House overwhelmingly approved the arrangement, largely because they had no alternative to offer.

VI

Much of the criticism of Kissinger's pragmatism centered less on his dealings with major powers and regions, where U.S. interests in peace and security loomed large, than on those with minor and more remote states where the acceptance of undemocratic and inhumane conditions without any show of displeasure seemed both cynical and unnecessary. Even as Washington boasted of the gains of détente in achieving a higher degree of international stability, it continued, with extensive programs of economic and military aid, to underwrite its allegiance to a wide variety of repressive governments, some of which used torture to eliminate their opponents. Under the assumption that U.S. security still demanded the support of all avowedly anti-Communist regimes, the United States continued to furnish military aid to countries whose armies had no useful purpose except to keep the recipients in power.[39] Kissinger remained silent on the abuses perpetrated by such governments. He had explained in July 1974 that the United States continued to authorize economic and military assistance for the South Korean government, despite its declining reputation for humaneness and justice, because "where we believe the national interest is at stake, we proceed even when we do not approve." Having authorized the Central Intelligence Agency $8 million to "destabilize" the Allende government of Chile, the United States supported the new military regime of Augusto Pinochet Ugarte, regarded one of the most repressive in the world, with by far the largest American aid program in South America.[40] The vast bulk of food aid went not to the desperately needy countries but to a few military-political clients of the United States such as South Vietnam, Thailand, Iran, Israel, and Jordan.[41] Despite the Nixon Doctrine's promise of retrenchment everywhere, the United States, because

[38] *Philadelphia Inquirer*, October 12, 1975.

[39] See Lorrin Rosenbaum, "Government by Torture," *Worldview* 18 (April 1975): 21–27. Assistant Secretary Philip C. Habib insisted in June 1975 that the U.S. government was concerned with human rights. See news release, June 24, 1975, U.S. Department of State, Bureau of Public Affairs, Office of Media Services.

[40] Jack Anderson in *Centre Daily Times* (State College, PA), October 11, 1975; *Washington Post*, May 18, 1975.

[41] Anthony Lewis in *Daily Progress*, January 26, 1975. See also Kissinger's interview with Bill Moyers in *Worldview* 18 (March 1975): 37–45.

of its lingering globalism, remained a hostage to weak governments that could not sustain themselves without American aid.

Even after the cease-fire agreement of January 1973, the Nixon-Kissinger leadership had preserved the U.S. commitment to Saigon under the continuing assumption that the perpetuation of that regime would guarantee the peace of Asia, and that its collapse would bring disaster wherever international relations remained fluid, especially in the Middle East, Berlin, and Latin America. Kissinger admitted that the United States had no formal commitment to South Vietnam, but he informed Congress that the Paris agreement and the long involvement in Vietnam bound the country politically and morally. For that reason, he said, the United States must continue its support of Saigon as long as it was needed. During May 1974 the Senate had reduced the Vietnam appropriation from $2.4 billion to $1.1 billion; the administration reacted bitterly.

Throughout the spring of 1975 the inexorable disasters in South Vietnam created a profound moral and intellectual crisis in Washington. In its retreat from Hue the South Vietnamese army abandoned or destroyed hundreds of millions of dollars worth of supplies and equipment. In robbing and killing their own people, these forces revealed a lack of will and discipline scarcely matched in modern times. A decade of official U.S. policy was reaching the end long predicted. Still Kissinger and the Ford administration battled Congress into March and April for military aid appropriations to save the South Vietnamese and Cambodian regimes. Vice-President Nelson A. Rockefeller predicted the extermination of one million Vietnamese in a Communist takeover.[42] Still, if that were true, only a genuine, permanent victory for Saigon would prevent it, something no one contemplated any longer.

Kissinger led the attack on Congress for its refusal to appropriate the requested $722 million in military aid for Cambodia and South Vietnam. What kind of people, he asked, would deliberately destroy an ally? Arguing against the principle of "selective reliability," he warned that peace was indivisible. Any break in the circle would cause the whole international order to collapse.[43] As late as April, Kissinger reminded the Senate that the United States had moral obligations to the South Vietnamese which it could not set aside. "[O]ur failure to act in accordance with that obligation," he said, "would inevitably influence other nations' perceptions of our constancy and our determination. American credibility would not collapse, and American honor

[42]Tom Wicker in *New York Times*, March 16, 1975.
[43]See Gary Wills in *Washington Post*, March 31, 1975. On President Gerald Ford's warning of falling dominoes, issued at the University of Notre Dame in March, see Reston in *New York Times*, March 20, 1975.

would not be destroyed. But both would be weakened, to the detriment of this Nation and of the peaceful world order we have sought to build."[44] When it was finally clear that Congress would not act, Kissinger conceded that "the Vietnam debate has now run its course. Let all now abide by the verdict of Congress—without recrimination or vindictiveness."[45] Throughout the crisis it was clear that the administration hoped less to save Saigon than to effect a graceful escape from its self-imposed dilemma. The overriding task in 1975 was that of assuring the world that whatever the outcome of the Indochina struggle, it would not be the fault of the United States. As one American official in Cambodia explained, "sometimes you have to go through the motions. Sometimes the motions are more important than the substance."[46]

If U.S. interests demanded no less than a graceful withdrawal from Southeast Asia under conditions of political stability, it is not clear why Kissinger failed to encourage the Saigon and Phnom Penh regimes to seek a political settlement with their insurgent enemies while they still possessed some bargaining power. If the military and political resiliency of these two pro-American governments was essential to the satisfactory solution of the Southeast Asia problem, the United States might have insisted on a higher level of honesty and efficiency in those governments. Certainly the Lon Nol government could not escape responsibility for its collapse any more than could the government in Saigon. To attach this nation's global standing to regimes at once weak and inflexible could lead only to disaster. Still the United States allegedly entrusted its whole international posture to governments and military forces that had little chance of success. Kissinger, in defending an always questionable and ultimately disastrous policy to the end, in a sense became its final victim. For many his claims to statesmanship would never survive that performance.

VII

Even as Saigon's fall threatened to sweep Kissinger from power, White House Press Secretary Ronald Nessen announced that the secretary of state would remain at least until the end of President Gerald Ford's current term, ending January 1977. A loyalist of the new president, Kissinger had supported him since his inauguration in August 1974; no one, it seemed, could better lace together a post-Vietnam foreign policy. Whatever the decline in his national popularity, Kissinger, with President Ford's full backing, wielded more authority in Washington

[44]News release, April 15, 1975, U.S. Department of State, Bureau of Public Affairs, Office of Media Services.
[45]*Newsweek*, April 28, 1975, p. 16.
[46]Quoted in ibid., March 24, 1975, p. 92.

than ever before.[47] Kissinger, moreover, had no desire to resign. As he confided to NBC's Barbara Walters, "to leave in a period of turmoil, when people are looking for a sense of direction and when foreign nations are watching us—I think it would not be a service to the country."[48] His determination to remain at his post was made clear by reaffirming his desire to establish a closer rapport with Congress, by occasionally criticizing dictatorial regimes, by admitting error in U.S. actions toward Vietnam and Japan, and by revealing greater concern for the economic issues in international relations.[49]

Few of Kissinger's critics, except some in the State Department, would quarrel with the president's judgment, and many foreign policy analysts and Kissinger watchers named him the "most remarkable Secretary of State in American history."[50] His outstanding record on the Chinese, Soviet, and perhaps even the Middle Eastern fronts established his primacy among the secretaries of the twentieth century. Some thought that if Kissinger stayed on he would step down as national security adviser. An executive-congressional commission, even while praising him for his performance in both roles, recommended in June 1975 that in the future the office of secretary of state should be removed from that of presidential assistant for National Security Affairs; staff functions appeared incompatible with the responsibilities of a cabinet office. As late as October the American people appeared generally satisfied with both Kissinger and his diplomacy.[51]

In many major respects Kissinger's contribution was unique. He was the first secretary of state in three generations to think and act in political rather than judicial terms. Unlike his predecessors reaching back to William Jennings Bryan, he did not search for the rightness and wrongness in the policies of other countries. Even after his disappointing failure in the Middle East during March 1975, he implored the American people not to pass judgment on either contestant. He judged countries and dealt with them on the basis of interests and power. It was precisely this political approach to diplomacy and the arrangements which it permitted that brought such widespread approval of his role. What was astonishing in this acceptance of Kissinger's

[47]*Washington Star*, March 31, 1975; *Chicago Tribune*, May 3, 1975; *Daily Progress*, June 12, 1975; Rowland Evans and Robert Novak in ibid., January 16, 1975.

[48]*Time*, May 19, 1975, p. 69.

[49]Kraft in *Washington Post*, June 22, 1975. During 1975, Kissinger spoke increasingly on economic matters and attempted to satisfy his critics that he was concerned over his relations with Congress, and that he favored principle as well as pragmatism in foreign relations. Still the hostility on Capitol Hill continued and, indeed, increased. Some complained that Kissinger came to Congress only when his policies required money. See Dana Adams Schmidt in *Christian Science Monitor*, October 17, 1975.

[50]See Cyrus L. Sulzberger in *New York Times*, March 24, 1974.

[51]*Washington Post*, June 29, 1975; *U.S. News and World Report*, October 6, 1975, p. 12.

basically pragmatic, amoral approach was the fact that it won the plaudits in the same population which had lauded the largely moralistic and legalistic policies of his predecessors such as Hull, Acheson, Dulles, and Rusk.

Perhaps the American people had developed some appreciation of the cost of policies that produced moral judgments and little else. They were ready for some measurable diplomatic accomplishments and were prepared to praise them whether they were based on pragmatism or not. Tragically, even Kissinger's failures seemed unnecessary. There was no need for him to neglect the institutionalization of his personal policies by denying a policymaking role to Congress and the State Department. Nothing compelled him to antagonize Europe and Japan, or generally ignore the plight of the Afro-Asian world. Kissinger continued with some success to counter the charges that détente gave too much to the Soviets. Whether he could respond adequately to the post-Cold War issues was still to be seen. His chief critics remained those of the Center and Left who believed that his policies lacked humaneness, and those of the Right who believed that they failed to maintain the necessary tensions in U.S.-Soviet relations.

By late autumn 1975 the pressures on Kissinger began to mount. One congressional committee cited him for contempt because of his refusal to deliver subpoenaed State Department documents, and another embarrassed him with questions about his role in covert U.S. operations in Chile. Clearly Kissinger's influence in the White House had declined and with it his image as Washington's dominant personality. No longer did American achievements abroad, both real and imagined, sustain his standing as a diplomat. President Ford's trip to China in late November achieved little, the peace campaign in the Middle East was stalled, and negotiations with the USSR over strategic arms limitation made little progress and clouded the future of U.S.-Soviet summitry. Conscious of his growing vulnerability, Kissinger confided to a friend: "I received perhaps excessive praise at one stage—I may receive excessive criticism now."[52] Whatever his shortcomings, however, Kissinger still stood above the Washington crowd. Even as the criticism became more strident, only a small minority of Americans cared to ponder the choice of a successor.

[52]Kissinger survived the cabinet shake-up of early November 1975, which included the firing of his rival, Secretary of Defense James R. Schlesinger. The firing of Schlesinger, however, unleashed new criticism of Kissinger's policies of détente. In December, President Ford sustained Daniel Patrick Moynihan at the United Nations despite Kissinger's open criticism of Moynihan's flamboyant style. For a review of Kissinger's declining prestige see *Wall Street Journal*, November 5, 1975; and *Newsweek*, December 8, 1975, pp. 36–37.

CHAPTER ELEVEN

The Decline of America: A Countering Appraisal*

FOR MANY AMERICANS the world of 1982 had become singularly dangerous. Through much of the 1970s the prevailing view of the Soviet Union, despite its burgeoning lead in conventional and nuclear power, had been reassuring. Facing potential enemies in Western Europe and China, Soviet leaders had argued effectively that the USSR's military obligations were unique, but the Soviet invasion of Afghanistan in late December 1979 demolished the nation's complacency. That action persuaded American leaders and journalists alike that the Soviets were now prepared to project their mushrooming power far beyond their borders. President Jimmy Carter addressed the country on January 4, 1980: "A Soviet-occupied Afghanistan threatens both Iran and Pakistan and is a stepping stone to possible control over much of the world's oil supplies." Any Soviet moves into adjacent countries, the president warned, would endanger "the strategic and peaceful balance of the entire world."[1] Several days later the president told a White House gathering that the "Soviet invasion of Afghanistan is the greatest threat to world peace since the Second World War."[2] Ronald Reagan caught the post-Afghanistan alarms at full tide, embellished them, and rode them to victory. He entered office in January 1981, proclaiming the coming decade as one of supreme danger to Western civilization. Alexander M. Haig shared Reagan's somber view of the world. At his

---

*Published as "The Decline of America: A Countering Appraisal," *Virginia Quarterly Review* 58 (Summer 1982): 369–91. Reprinted by permission.

[1]Carter's address to the nation, January 4, 1980, Department of State *Bulletin* 80 (January 1980): A–B. Carter declared that no longer could any nation committed to peace continue "to do business as usual with the Soviet Union."

[2]Report of meeting with members of Congress at the White House, *Newsweek*, January 21, 1980, p. 22.

confirmation hearing as secretary of state in January, Haig reminded members of the Senate Foreign Relations Committee that "the years immediately ahead will be unusually dangerous. Evidence of that danger is everywhere."[3] That mood of anxiety seemed to permeate American society. In an NBC-Associated Press survey of November 1981, 76 percent of Americans polled expected nuclear war within the decade. Armageddon, it seemed, was just around the corner.

What rendered Soviet aggressiveness especially threatening was the apparent weakening of the American commitment to international order. For writers such as Norman Podhoretz, it was the conjunction of the country's decline and the Soviet Union's ascendance that exposed the world of the 1980s to a frightened and dangerous antagonist. Beset with a loss of purpose, the nation seemed unable to define its interests, much less defend them. Its repeated acceptance of humiliation, without even an expression of outrage, appeared to symbolize its moral and physical deterioration. Aleksandr Solzhenitsyn had reminded his Harvard audience in June 1978 that the consequences of the nation's failure to choose victory over defeat in Vietnam would endure in the tragedy of the Vietnamese people and the aggravated appetites of the Communist aggressors.[4] In his book *The Real War*, former President Nixon pointed to two disturbing realities. "The first of these," he wrote, "is that if a war were to come we might lose. The second is that we might be defeated without war. The second prospect is more likely than the first, and almost as grim." Reagan adviser William R. Van Cleave concluded an interview with the assertion that "the United States is almost irrelevant."[5] Despite its high levels of defense spending, the country, to such observers, seemed to be headed toward national extinction.

Such widespread assumptions of national failure assumed that the United States once dominated international life and needlessly permitted its vaunted position to crumble through faltering leadership and military inadequacy. This view of history is not without merit. Emerging from war unscathed in 1945, the United States had inherited the earth. Its undamaged industrial capacity exceeded that of the rest of the industrialized world. It possessed an atomic monopoly and two-thirds of the world's capital wealth. Its technological supremacy was

[3] For Haig's views see "The Week in Review," *New York Times*, January 11, 1981. As secretary of state, Haig continued to accuse the Soviets of fomenting terrorism. See Philip Taubman in ibid., May 3, 1981.

[4] Solzhenitsyn's speech of June 8, 1978, quoted in *Newsweek*, June 19, 1978, p. 43; *New York Times*, June 9, 1978, p. A8. For critiques of Solzhenitsyn's views see James Reston in ibid., June 11, 1978, p. E21; and editorial, ibid., June 13, 1978, p. A18.

[5] Richard M. Nixon, *The Real War* (New York, 1980), pp. 2–3; Van Cleave quoted in "The Week in Review," *New York Times*, October 12, 1980.

so obvious that the world assumed its existence and set out to use or copy American products. During the late 1940s the United States had reached the highest point of world power achieved by any nation in modern times. British writer Harold J. Laski wrote in November 1947:

> America bestrides the world like a colossus; neither Rome at the height of its power nor Great Britain in the period of its economic supremacy enjoyed an influence so direct, so profound, or so pervasive. It has half the wealth of the world today in its hands, it has rather more than half of the world's productive capacity, and it exports more than twice as much as it imports. Today literally hundreds of millions of Europeans and Asiatics know that both the quality and the rhythm of their lives depend upon decisions made in Washington. On the wisdom of those decisions hangs the fate of the next generation.[6]

So excessive was American power that the country did not require allies to protect its clear and vital interests. Europeans scarcely questioned the capacity or the intention of the United States to maintain world peace against any discernible aggression, assuring them security at little cost or obligation.

What projected that great power across the world was not its mere existence but perceptions of danger that sanctioned nothing less. The country's ever-widening commitments flowed from the assumption that the threat to Western security lay in international communism as well as Soviet armed might. As early as mid-century the notion that the Kremlin, as the center of world communism, would extend its dominance through the techniques of subversion and revolution posed dangers to world security in events that occurred far outside the reach of Soviet military power. The decision to define the Soviet challenge in ideological rather than historic terms set deceptive standards of policy and created objectives that no country could achieve. Like its predecessors, the National Security Council's noted policy recommendation of April 1950, known by its serial number NSC 68, explained why the burdens of containment had no visible limit. It concluded that the USSR, "unlike previous aspirants to hegemony, is animated by a new fanatic faith, antithetical to our own, and seeks to impose its absolute authority over the rest of the world."[7] Through its alleged

---

[6]Harold J. Laski, "America—1947," *Nation* 165 (December 13, 1947): 641. Article dated at London, November 30, 1947.

[7]For the statement in NSC 68 see Thomas H. Etzold and John Lewis Gaddis, eds., *Containment: Documents on American Policy and Strategy, 1945–1950* (New York, 1978), p. 385.

control of China's Communist government, the Kremlin now endangered the independence of all South and Southeast Asia. The Soviet assault on free institutions, warned NSC 68, was worldwide and, "in the context of the present polarization of power, a defeat of free institutions anywhere is a defeat everywhere."[8] To meet the danger of Soviet expansionism, the United States would establish a defense line around the perimeter of the Communist-controlled Eurasian land mass. NSC 68 assumed that the United States, with increased military power, could win the struggle against communism everywhere.

As late as the mid-1960s the American anti-Communist consensus held firm. Years earlier the Hungarian revolution had relegated the liberation of peoples inside the Soviet empire to the realm of lost causes. In Western Europe, however, the NATO shield, backed by the nuclear arsenal of the United States, continued to underwrite that region's remarkable stability and economic progress. If the nation's security and self-image as world leader demanded that it hold the line against Communist-led encroachments outside Europe as well, the means for achieving that goal seemed no less promising. Throughout the Third World, but especially in South Korea, Taiwan, the Philippines, Thailand, Pakistan, Iran, Turkey, Israel, and Saudi Arabia, pro-Western governments appeared willing, even anxious, to join the United States in bilateral or multilateral defense pacts, provide military bases, or accept American economic and military aid. Unfortunately, the defense lines that marked the periphery of the Communist world had moved far beyond the borders of the Soviet Union into regions where Communist-directed sabotage, insurgency, and guerrilla warfare rendered interests and the means to defend them ambiguous. President Kennedy, in a speech he prepared just before his assassination in Dallas on November 22, 1963, recognized the special burden that such threats to pro-Western regimes outside Europe placed on the United States. "We in this country, in this generation," ran his admonition, "are—by destiny rather than by choice—the watchmen on the walls of world freedom. We ask, therefore, that we may be worthy of our power and responsibility."[9] Soon the American struggle for Vietnam would carry the full burden of that responsibility.

II

That the position of the United States in world affairs deteriorated in the 1970s is not a matter of serious contention. However, did the decline from the previous decade reflect some form of national failure or simply

---

[8]Ibid., p. 389.
[9]Kennedy's speech prepared for delivery in Dallas, November 22, 1963, *Public Papers of the Presidents: Kennedy, 1963* (Washington, 1964), p. 894.

predictable changes in world relations over which the United States had little control? Some writers have pointed to America's failure in Vietnam as the "hidden ulcer" in the country's decline.[10] Actually, America's special place among the nations of the world slipped in the 1970s for reasons far more fundamental than the loss of a limited Asian war. Every statistical measure revealed the relative decline of the United States, both economically and militarily. At mid-century the United States accounted for 50 percent of the world's military expenditures, in 1975 only 25 percent. In 1950 it had produced 60 percent of the world's manufactured goods, with only half that percentage accounted for in 1975. Six European countries—Switzerland, Denmark, Sweden, West Germany, Belgium, and Norway—claimed per capita incomes higher than those of the United States. In many areas of modern economic life the United States no longer led the other industrial democracies. Three basic American industries—steel, automobile, and tire—could scarcely compete with the better engineered and better made products of Western Europe and Japan. Half the new cars on California's crowded highways were Japanese. No longer could the United States protect its vital interests in oil against the power of the Middle Eastern oil barons. Without the capacity to project its power and influence to many parts of the globe, the United States seemed scarcely a superpower.[11] In large measure, however, America's relative economic decline reflected less a national failure than the remarkable success of the nation's postwar policies in rebuilding war-torn Europe and Japan. Thus the decline of America as an economic giant was inevitable, given the artificially predominant status that it had enjoyed amid the ruins of 1945.

At the policy level the nation's retreat was even more predictable. Washington's postwar neglect of the historic limitations on American foreign policy would eventually demand retrenchment. In areas or on issues of potential dispute, no nation has ever operated successfully outside the realm of its generally recognized national interests. The Founding Fathers had defined those interests almost two hundred years

---

[10]This is the theme of Oscar Handlin's chapter on Vietnam in his book *The Distortion of America* (Boston, 1981), p. 92.

[11]Certainly the United States remained by far the richest and most productive country in the world, but thirty years after the end of World War II it no longer moved in a world of ruined economies and disintegrating empires. Other Western economies, as well as that of Japan, if much smaller in total production and consumption, possessed the power to manufacture and sell certain key products competitively, even in the American market. Economic power in such countries encouraged feelings of security and a determination to resist American leadership, both politically and diplomatically. The Third World, freed of its colonial restraints, offered its own forms of resistance to American will. On the growing power of the Middle Eastern oil-producing countries to defy Western interests see Anthony J. Parisi, "OPEC Learns to Supply Less and Demand More," *New York Times*, December 16, 1979; and editorial, ibid., October 7, 1979.

ago. For Alexander Hamilton, writing in *The Federalist*, it seemed essential that first the United States maintain its political and military dominance of the Western Hemisphere. In practice this objective emphasized the concept of the two spheres, with the United States playing the leadership role in the Western Hemisphere. Second, the United States in order to maximize its security would support the European balance of power, taking a stand against any country that through its dominance of Europe might endanger the Western Hemisphere. Similarly, the United States would seek to prevent the rise of a dominant power in the Orient. Finally, Hamilton understood, the United States would maintain a worldwide commercial empire. Because commerce, itself a peaceful pursuit, might lead to conflict, Hamilton had urged America to maintain the necessary engines of coercion to protect its outlying interests.[12] These varied concerns, historic and easily stated, guided the country through much of its history. When the United States pursued its limited interests with accuracy and diligence, the triumphs in diplomacy and war were often spectacular. When it failed to judge its interests with precision, the costs were invariably excessive.

Those early Cold War successes, which measured the genuine triumphs of American postwar diplomacy, conformed to the nation's historic interests. In Europe the conditions had changed, demanding American efforts to rebuild the Continent's political and military equilibrium. Washington gained its objectives readily and quickly because Europe's specific challenges gave the economic and military supremacy of the United States a special relevance. The marvelous triumphs of American policy coincided largely with what the nation's power would buy at a time when that power was excessive: the economic rehabilitation of Western Europe and Japan, the promotion of international trade and investment, and the maintenance of a massive defense structure which underwrote the containment effort and played an essential role in Europe's postwar political evolution. Even as American military power reinforced the division of Europe, its economic strength, working through international agencies for trade and monetary stabilization, contributed to the world's unprecedented prosperity. The ease whereby the United States gained its postwar position of unchallenged leadership in Europe and elsewhere exaggerated the notion that its new global posture reflected a permanent rearrangement of power in the world—that American might had indeed become global.

What contributed to this illusion of permanent U.S. supremacy, even in Asia, was the wartime destruction of all the imperial structures

---

[12]Alexander Hamilton, "The Federalist No. 11," in Edward Mead Earle, ed., *The Federalist: A Commentary on the Constitution of the United States* (New York, n.d.), pp. 62–69.

that had established the traditional boundaries of American influence. The war not only destroyed the power of Germany and Japan but also presaged the final collapse of the British and French empires. Indeed, the United States after mid-century had expanded into a worldwide power vacuum. As a result, Walter Lippmann observed: "We flowed forward beyond our natural limits. . . . The miscalculation . . . falsified all our other calculations—what our power was, what we could afford to do, what influence we had to exert in the world."[13]

This overextension of American commitments beyond Europe, at least momentarily, received encouragement from the absence of indigenous pressures against the country's varied commitments and the assumption that threats of massive retaliation, if necessary, would protect these commitments from external aggression. Secretary of State Dulles had assured the nation in January 1956 that the calm of East and Southeast Asia was simply a triumph of his strategy of massive retaliation.[14] Soon the American involvement in Vietnam demonstrated that the threat of massive retaliation was not the controlling element in Asia at all. No external force could prevent the increasing politicization of Third World societies and the creation of governments more anti-Western, nationalistic, self-centered, and resistant to external influence than the former pro-Western, often aristocratic, regimes which they replaced. The 1970s brought anti-Western political upheavals to Iran, Ethiopia, Pakistan, South Vietnam, Cambodia, Nicaragua, Angola, Mozambique, Rhodesia, and Nigeria. The world of Asia and Africa, in large measure, moved outside the realm of great power control.

That simple Cold War environment, in which the possession of power was the key to success, disappeared sometime in the mid-1960s. For a decade thereafter the U.S. government had perpetuated the illusion of effective global power, based on the will to use it, by fighting in Vietnam. In that struggle the American commitment to resist communism in all its forms reached a dead end. After Saigon's fall in 1975, the United States remained the world's leading power, but by then the troublesome issues that captured the headlines challenged few traditional American interests and thus defied the exertion of will or even the creation of genuine policy. How could the United States curtail the violence, terrorism, infringements on human rights, international traffic in arms, and undeclared conflicts that threatened world stability? How could it relieve the problems of poverty or slow an arms race that was

[13]Lippmann quoted by Henry Brandon, "A Talk with Walter Lippmann, at 80, About This 'Minor Dark Age,' " *New York Times Magazine*, September 14, 1969, pp. 25–26.

[14]James Shepley, "How Dulles Averted War," *Life* 40 (January 16, 1956): 71–72.

costing the world $1 billion per day? Meg Greenfield, writing in February 1978, saw the dilemma facing the country and asked:

> So what *are* we going to do about it if the rulers of Cambodia embark on a policy of national genocide, if the Cubans take up (Soviet) arms in Africa, if the Saudis lower production or increase the price of oil, if Southern Africa moves toward all-out racial war, if the Indians continue to build nuclear explosives, if the Western Europeans vote Communists into office? Is there anything we can do in an era in which we have even been admonished for expressing the hope that Italy remain a democracy? If that is regarded as an act of aggression, it tells you something about our role as a 'superpower' in the post-Vietnam world.[15]

The United States had approached the stage where it neither could admit that what happened abroad was not its concern nor act effectively when it did.

III

Already the central challenge to American policy was clear: how would it adjust to the reality of Third World assertiveness and the country's limited interest and influence in opposing it? President Carter met the challenge by acknowledging America's declining world role and, with that recognition, a diminution of the strategic importance of Asia, Africa, and Latin America. His assumption that the Third World countries had interests of their own and the will to pursue them reinforced his determination to avoid simple anti-Soviet postures to perpetuate the status quo. In his University of Notre Dame speech of May 1977, he rejected the traditional Cold War assumption that American interests were global. "Being confident of our own future," he said, "we are now free of that inordinate fear of communism which once led us to embrace any dictator who joined us in that fear."[16] For Carter the political, economic, and ideological potential of the Third World was sufficient to eliminate any serious Soviet threat. In a world of triumphant nationalism, American power had no legitimate or necessary use. In deserting the old commitment to global containment, the Carter administration accepted the growing Soviet presence in Africa, the Middle East, and Asia with general unconcern, if only to the dismay

---

[15]Greenfield in *Newsweek*, February 13, 1978, p. 100.
[16]President Carter's University of Notre Dame speech, May 22, 1977, "A Foreign Policy Based on America's Essential Character," Department of State *Bulletin* 76 (June 13, 1977): 622.

of those who accused the administration of assigning world primacy to the Soviet Union. If Soviet policy in Africa and the Arabian peninsula was regrettable, it did not, for Carter, endanger American security. Zbigniew Brzezinski, Carter's assistant for national security affairs, attributed the public's widespread acceptance of the Carter policies to the fact that "the country, as a whole, fatigued by the Vietnam War," was not prepared to confront the Soviet Union.[17]

Third World assertiveness could not eliminate the worldwide Soviet-American competition for power and influence; it could only compel the two powers to alter their methods. Ultimately, the Carter administration faced the choice of declaring Asia and Africa irrelevant to the world's balance of power—a necessity which the Nixon-Kissinger leadership hoped to avoid by securing Soviet compliance with the rules of détente—or framing a confrontationist response. Amid domestic ruminations about the administration's failure of nerve, the expanding Soviet-Cuban presence in Africa could only embarrass the president. During the spring of 1978, State Department officials charged the Kremlin with maintaining 37,000 Cuban military personnel in twenty African countries. Unwilling to counter this Soviet-Cuban presence in Africa with a direct economic or military involvement, the administration searched in vain for some means to multiply the costs to the Kremlin. Finally, the president, in his Annapolis address of June 1978, accused Soviet leaders of waging an "aggressive struggle for political advantage" in Africa. His challenge was blunt: "The Soviet Union can choose either confrontation or cooperation. The United States is adequately prepared to meet either choice."[18] Many in Washington scarcely concealed their satisfaction with Carter's new toughness.

[17]On July 1, 1977, Secretary of State Cyrus Vance explained U.S. policy in Africa when he declared that "the most effective politics toward Africa are affirmative policies. . . . A negative, reactive American policy that seeks only to oppose Soviet and Cuban involvement in Africa would be both dangerous and futile. Our best course is to help resolve the problems which create opportunities for external intervention." Quoted in Anthony Lake's lecture at the Johns Hopkins University School of Advanced International Studies, October 27, 1977, Department of State, Bureau of Public Affairs, speech, October 27, 1977, p. 2. Lake outlined a program for Africa designed to support self-determination, minimize military involvements, and avoid confrontation with Cuba and the Soviet Union. On the Carter approach to Africa see also Vance's statement before the Senate Subcommittee on African Affairs, May 12, 1978, secretary of state, Bureau of Public Affairs, statement, May 12, 1978, pp. i, 5.

[18]For Carter's Annapolis address see *New York Times*, June 9, 1978, p. A3; *Newsweek*, June 19, 1978, pp. 41–44; and *Time*, June 19, 1978, pp. 32–33. On the Cuban presence in Africa and the administration's concern see ibid., March 13, 1978, pp. 36–45. The toughening of opinion in Washington is analyzed in ibid., May 29, 1978, pp. 20–21; and *Newsweek*, June 12, 1978, pp. 26–41. Robert W. Tucker discusses the efforts of the Carter administration to adapt to Third World pressures in "America in Decline: The Foreign Policy of 'Maturity,'" *Foreign Affairs* 58, no. 3 (1980): 451–84.

Critics challenged the fears that underwrote the administration's changing mood. They reminded the country that Britain, France, Portugal, Belgium, Italy, and Spain had abandoned their respective possessions in Africa because they found them economically unprofitable and impossible to govern. How others could succeed where the Europeans had failed was not clear. It seemed incredible that African countries, which had sought independence for so long, would willingly become puppets of Cuba or the Soviet Union. Most Africans could detect nothing objectionable in Soviet behavior, for the Soviets and Cubans had gone only where they were invited. Nowhere had they broken international law. When New York Senator Daniel Patrick Moynihan and former Secretary Kissinger charged that the United States should not have permitted the Cubans to enter Ethiopia, the *New York Times* editorialized:

> One man says threaten anything, no matter what the chances of making good on the threat. The other says never mind the particular stakes or possibilities, in geopolitics everything is tied to everything else. . . . There, we submit, walks the ghost of Vietnam. . . . Whatever the stakes on the ground, or the possibilities, for geopolitical reasons Hanoi had to be stopped. . . . To resurrect that logic against a President who seeks new techniques for applying American influence around the world is a dangerous game indeed.[19]

Far better, said the *Times*, to portray the risks and costs to Moscow. Experience suggested that the Kremlin would be no more successful than Washington had been in converting Ethiopia into a bulwark against anything. Despite the accusations of weakness, Carter held to his policies of inaction. Following the Democratic defeat in 1980, Brzezinski asserted that the fatigue of Vietnam had prevented U.S. counteraction to ward off Soviet and Cuban assistance to Ethiopia; he never specified the nature of that counteraction. Perhaps Carter's mistake lay less in his rejection of force than in his neglect of a confrontationist posture which might have maintained the illusion of power and will while

[19]"The Ghosts of Vietnam," *New York Times*, June 4, 1978. Soviet expert Robert Legvold argued similarly that "by and large, as the Soviet leaders know, change in Africa unfolds at its own pace and its own fashion. There is change that the Soviet Union would be delighted to abet and, at the margin, it doubtless sees a role for itself. This role, however, is essentially as benefactor not instigator." Legvold, "The Soviet Union's Strategic Stake in Africa," in Jennifer Seymour Whitaker, ed., *Africa and the United States: Vital Interests* (New York, 1978), p. 165. The Carter administration's determination to avoid military involvements in Africa pleased many members of Congress and such newspapers as the *New York Times*.

cloaking the reality of limited intent. If any of his critics really wanted an American war in Africa, they never revealed it.

IV

Strategically, the Middle East loomed more important than Africa, made so by its gigantic stores of oil, its central location astride the major routes to the Orient, and its proximity to the Soviet Union. After the Suez crisis of 1956, the United States had displaced the British and French to become the protector of Middle Eastern stability. To limit Soviet influence in the region, it offered aid to pro-Western regimes under the Eisenhower Doctrine of 1957, supported Israel against the Arab world in an otherwise evenhanded policy, and sought to transform Iran into a bastion of Middle Eastern security with heavy sales of sophisticated military equipment to Shah Mohammed Reza Pahlevi. Washington's policy faced its initial test in early 1979 when a Moslem revolution overthrew the shah, an event which dramatized the vulnerability of American power in the Middle East. The Carter administration responded with a reassertion of America's global interests. "The United States," declared Defense Secretary Harold Brown in late February, "is prepared to defend its vital interests with whatever means are appropriate, including military force where necessary, whether that's in the Middle East or elsewhere." Energy Secretary James Schlesinger added that "the United States has vital interests in the Persian Gulf. The United States must move in such a way that it protects those interests, even if that increases the use of military strength."[20] The president advocated additional arms sales to Egypt, Saudi Arabia, and Israel; otherwise he continued his policy of inaction. With the seizure of the U.S. embassy in November 1979, Iran challenged American sensibilities but not American security. For Carter this again eliminated any resort to force. Some charged the president with softness, suggesting that other undisclosed actions would have secured the immediate release of the embassy personnel. Overwhelmingly, the American people recognized the limits of national policy in Iran and lauded the president's moderation.[21]

Already facing open challenges to its will and prestige in the

[20]Brown and Schlesinger quoted in Donald E. Nuechterlein, "Persian Gulf Region Vital for National Interests," *Daily Progress* (Charlottesville, VA), November 25, 1979.

[21]Carter defended his Iranian policy in his news conference on November 28, 1979, U.S. Department of State, Bureau of Public Affairs, *Current Policy No. 115*. Polls indicated that the American people generally accepted the president's policy as the best available. See *Newsweek*, December 10, 1979, p. 53, and December 17, 1979, pp. 28–29; *Daily Progress*, December 12, 1979; and Tom Wicker in ibid.

Middle East, the United States reacted to the Soviet invasion of Afghanistan in December with bewilderment and rage. Afghanistan was not a Western interest, nor did Soviet occupation alter the world's strategic balance. For the first time since 1945, however, the Soviets had used force outside Eastern Europe. The president admitted bitterly that the Soviets had taken him in. Unable to ignore the Soviet action, Carter faced an unfortunate decision. He either could inform the American people that the Soviet invasion, while irresponsible, did not touch any vital American interest, or declare Soviet behavior dangerous to all Southwest Asia, thus demanding some form of retaliation. The administration could assume greater public approval for the latter choice. Brzezinski argued that the Soviet Union threatened American interests from the Mediterranean to the Sea of Japan, especially Pakistan and the states bordering the Persian Gulf. On NBC's "Meet the Press" on January 20, 1980, the president repeated the warning: "This in my opinion is the most serious threat to world peace since the Second World War. . . . It's a threat to an area of the world where the interests of our country and those interests of our allies are deeply embedded."[22] The president then set forth his Carter Doctrine. "An attempt by an outside force to gain control of the Persian Gulf region," he declared in his State of the Union message, "will be regarded as an assault on the vital interests of the United States." He continued with the assurance that such an assault "will be repelled by any means necessary, including military force."[23] Nevertheless, Carter scarcely took his own warning seriously. If he suspected that the Soviets had embarked on a program to control the oil and sea lanes of the Persian Gulf, he would have called not for embargoes on grain, technology, and the Olympics but for national mobilization.

Afghanistan vindicated those who had long charged American policy with weakness. For them, the USSR's imperialistic behavior revealed a decline in the essential cautiousness of Soviet leaders and a diminishing respect for American power. The widespread assumption that the Soviet invasion exposed all Southwest Asia to further Soviet encroachment pushed American hawkishness to a new high. What mattered was not the reasons why the Soviets had entered Afghanistan

[22]Interview on NBC's "Meet the Press," January 20, 1980, U.S. Department of State, Bureau of Public Affairs, *Current Policy No. 130.*

[23]*Newsweek*, February 4, 1980, p. 22. Among those who warned against an American military overcommitment in Southwest Asia were Drew Middleton in *New York Times*, January 6, and February 3, 1980; Reston in ibid., January 30, 1980; Reston in *Daily Progress*, February 4, 13, 1980; *New York Times*, February 17, 1980; and Jack Anderson in *Daily Progress*, April 10, 1980. On Carter's search for the necessary means to make his new posture of firmness in the Middle East effective see *Newsweek*, February 11, 1980, pp. 42–43; and Roger Fisher in *New York Times*, March 30, 1980, p. E21.

but the fact that they had gained a strategic position from which they could more easily threaten Pakistan, Iran, and the Persian Gulf states. When asked in a *New York Times* interview what evidence he had that the Soviets would go further, Richard E. Pipes of Harvard University replied:

> No evidence except that it would make no sense to occupy Afghanistan for any other purpose. Afghanistan has no natural resources of importance, and the risk of antagonizing the West is very high for a bit of mountainous territory with a primitive economy, with a population that has never been subdued by any colonial power. To run all these risks for the sake of occupying this territory seems to make little sense—unless you have some ultimate, higher strategic objectives.[24]

Many American and European observers rejected such assumptions of danger to South and Southwest Asia. The Kremlin had long understood the limited possibilities of its strategic position in Hungary or East Germany. Similarly, the occupation of Afghanistan, some argued, was no measure of Soviet intentions toward the regions beyond.[25]

Few questioned the importance of the Persian Gulf region to the Western world. Still, the widespread addiction to Arab oil failed to eliminate doubts regarding the appropriateness of the American response to the Afghan crisis. The administration made no effort to explain what had happened in Afghanistan and why the Soviet invasion endangered all of Southwest Asia, much less how the United States intended to defend the region. State and Defense department officials agreed that the United States could not confront the Soviets successfully along their southern flank. Some analysts wondered, moreover, how the United States could fashion an effective containment strategy for the Middle East when the dangers to regional stability lay less in Soviet expansionism than in the local and national animosities that existed within the region itself. For the first time in its history, the United States had created a vital interest beyond its control. Any regional war that involved

---

[24]See interview with Pipes in *New York Times*, February 10, 1980, p. E4. For similar reactions to the Afghan invasion see Dave Gergen, "Toughening of America Detected by the Pollsters," *Washington Star*, April 6, 1980, p. C4; William K. Stevens in *New York Times*, February 3, 1980; and Joseph J. Collins, "The Soviet Invasion of Afghanistan: Methods, Motives, and Ramifications," *Naval War College Review* 33 (November–December 1980): 59–60. Gergen and Stevens discovered an ambivalence in the American reaction: growing assumptions of danger but no inclination to use armed force.

[25]For the more moderate analysis of Soviet motives in the Afghan invasion see Bernard Gwertzman in "The Week in Review," *New York Times*, December 30, 1979; Selig S. Harrison, "Did Moscow Fear an Afghan Tito?" ibid., January 13, 1980; and editorials, ibid., January 27, and February 3, 1980.

the big powers would begin with the oil's destruction, either by the United States or by the Soviet Union. For some the only answer to American vulnerability in the Middle East was the reduction of energy use. "If the Persian Gulf is really vital to our security," observed George Kennan, "it is surely we who, by our unrestrained greed for oil, have made it so. Would it not be better to set about to eliminate, by a really serious and determined effort, a dependence that ought never have been allowed to arise, than to try to shore up by military means, in a highly unfavorable region, the unsound position into which the dependence has led us?"[26]

Determined to halt the retreat of the Carter years, the Reagan administration committed itself to the reassertion of the country's global leadership. Apprising the Soviets that their days of military dominance were numbered, the new president pressed Congress for larger military expenditures, with apparently little concern for where the money would go. The needed message to the world would emerge from the expenditures themselves. Even earlier the Reagan team had sought to exorcise the memories of Vietnam and the limitations they imposed on American will.[27] The new globalism, freed of its recent restraints, required that the United States again confront Soviet expansionism wherever it occurred in Africa, the Middle East, or Central America. Reagan resurrected the domino theory to explain his decision to take a stand in El Salvador. "What we're doing," he said, "is to try to halt the infiltration into the Americas, by terrorists and by outside interference, and those who aren't just aiming at El Salvador but, I think, are aiming at the whole of Central and possibly later South America and, I'm sure, eventually North America."[28]

Reagan's critics predicted that his administration would never close the gap between its fears and its actions. Indeed, the new leadership, despite its confrontational mood, framed no policies that conformed to its self-proclaimed global obligations. The foreign policy phrases honed in the early days of the administration were not the determinants of policy at all. Reagan's continuing anti-Soviet crusade in El Salvador brought neither security to the cities nor peace to the countryside. He, no less than Carter, coexisted with the Soviet presence in Afghanistan, Africa, and the Arabian peninsula. In late April 1981, Reagan undermined his policy of toughness completely by ending President Carter's embargo on grain shipments to the Soviet Union. So

[26]Kennan criticized the Carter response to the Afghan crisis in *New York Times*, February 1, 1980, p. A27.

[27]George C. Herring, "The 'Vietnam Syndrome' and American Foreign Policy," *Virginia Quarterly Review* 57 (Autumn 1981): 594–612.

[28]Reagan quoted in Alexander Cockburn, *Wall Street Journal*, March 12, 1981.

casual, inconsistent, and cautious were the Reagan policies toward the Soviet Union that analysts accused the administration of having no strategy at all. Columnist George Will condemned Secretary Haig's pronounced tendency to preach toughness and to act otherwise. "In Carter's State Department," he wrote in mid-January 1982, "rhetoric and policy were both bad, but at least they meshed. Haig's rhetoric does not fit the policies that give an appearance of action without real action. The mismatch is confusing the country."[29] In his disenchantment with the Reagan administration's apparent failures, the columnist seldom advised Washington how it might square its words and actions. Ultimately, the world would impose its will on the Reagan administration precisely as it had on Carter's.

V

If the United States cannot deter Soviet advances everywhere, it has no choice but to determine with some precision what it must defend. At issue is the protection of those minimum conditions which will enable the country to survive and prosper. Never before in written history has the potential price of miscalculation in projecting interests been so high. "The more clearly the superpowers define their vital interests—the kind they'd fight to protect," editorialized the *New York Times* on September 28, 1980, "the greater the chances that they will respect them and avoid a fight." The great powers defined those interests in Europe long ago; that definition, in large measure, has accounted for Europe's persisting peace. The task of defining ends with such precision elsewhere is exceedingly difficult; no wartime conquests have delineated the spheres of influence. What has prevented any direct U.S.-Soviet confrontation outside Europe has been less the existence of well-defined and heavily armed frontiers than Third World resistance to external pressure and the absence of major interests in conflict. Still, if the USSR is to be deterred in the future, it must know from what. The need to prevent miscalculation requires a serious effort at communication, the breakdown of which invariably increases suspicion and tension. The former ambassador to the Soviet Union, Malcolm Toon, warned the American people in the wake of Afghanistan:

> I am a hard-liner in the sense that I think we should deal with the Soviets as they are, not as we'd like them to be, that is, without

[29]George Will quoted in *Times Herald Record* (Middletown, NY), January 14, 1982. For a broader criticism of the Reagan foreign policies see Norman Podhoretz, "The Neo-Conservative Anguish Over Reagan's Foreign Policy," *New York Times Magazine*, May 2, 1982, pp. 96–97.

any illusions as to what they are up to, what their long-range goals are and what their real attitude is toward the United States. But despite Afghanistan, despite the banishment of Sakharov to Gorky, despite, in a word, bestial Soviet behavior both at home and abroad, despite all of this, we must deal with the Soviets. We cannot ignore them. We cannot refuse to talk with them. The nuclear world, in my view, is just too dangerous a place for such an approach.

Perhaps the most troublesome challenge to American policy is that of defining and defending interests in areas where the Soviet Union enjoys a clear strategic advantage. In its commitment to the important Persian Gulf region, where the United States could not win a conventional war, the problem confronting the United States is not unlike that which faced British Prime Minister Neville Chamberlain in Eastern Europe after 1938. Britain did not have the power, scarcely the interest, to save Austria or the Sudetenland from Nazi aggression. When Hitler seized Czechoslovakia and threatened Poland in March 1939, Chamberlain had warned Berlin that a move into Poland would inaugurate not a British defense of the region but a general war.[30] Beyond the threat of a wider war, Britain's lone possibility for a short-term deterrent against Hitler was a coalition of powers which would include the Soviet Union. It was London's failure to come to terms with the Kremlin in 1939 that had enabled Hitler to attack Poland without even facing an effective and restraining coalition. If the USSR's threat to regions around its periphery is indeed serious, the experience of the late 1930s suggests the only promising formula for future policy: the assurance of a wider war. Whether the simple threat of nuclear retaliation would defend the Middle East from Soviet attack is uncertain. What undermines the credibility of massive retaliatory power in that distant region is the knowledge that any nuclear war fought to protect the oil would endanger the United States and Europe as well. To court such disaster in defense of the Persian Gulf appears dangerous, even irresponsible. It denies above all the power and interests of other nations.

In any genuine defense of the international equilibrium, the potential sources of deterrent power far transcend the American nuclear arsenal; nearly every nation on the globe opposes Soviet aggression. Amid the world's general concern for stability, the possibilities of coalition diplomacy should be promising enough. Alliances enable their members not only to maximize the means of policy at their disposal but also to create essential opportunities for mutual instruction. Coalition diplomacy rests primarily on agreements concerning interests and objectives. No country will entrust its defense to another unless the policies they pursue

---

[30]See Alan Alexandroff and Richard Rosecrance, "Deterrence in 1939," *World Politics* 29 (1977): 404–24.

and the ends they seek reflect common perceptions of the dangers they face. It is at the level of ends, not of means, that coalitions break down. Obviously, the United States and its European allies have failed to sustain the vital relationships and the common assumptions of danger that once gave NATO its relevance. Britain, the least critical among European countries of Washington's leadership, never regained its pre-war status as a major military-political European power. France, recovered but fiercely independent, has scarcely followed the American lead. West Germany's dissatisfaction with America's European role has been even more confounding, inasmuch as that steadfast country was central to Europe's defense structure, and former Chancellor Helmut Schmidt made no effort to conceal his disenchantment with Washington. Indeed, U.S. policies outside Europe have produced little or no support within NATO. In some measure the problem of declining good faith in American leadership lies within Europe itself. Europeans have not always been constructive in presenting their views or in coming to terms with America's contribution to Europe's defense and its special role as world leader.[31]

Reagan's confrontationist approach to the Soviet Union did nothing to reverse the steady vitiation of the alliance. Europeans understood, if some members of the administration did not, that tough language, massive increases in defense spending, and symbolic sanctions would not compel the world to conform to Washington's designs. Neither, for them, did Europe's security demand such conformity. They had long rejected the perceptions of danger that generated the global policies of the United States. To Europeans, détente was no failure; moreover, they could discover no genuine alternative. On Third World issues they rejected the Reagan administration's hard-line phraseology, not because they opposed the stated objectives but because they feared that the administration had not considered the consequences of its pronouncements. Europe's peace had been the core of international stability, and Western Europe had no interest in becoming the battleground of a war begun elsewhere over issues that concerned it remotely, if at all.[32] In a world declared dangerous because of Soviet policies in Africa

[31]Peter Jay, "Europe and America: Europe's Ostrich and America's Eagle," *Atlantic Community Quarterly* 18 (Summer 1980): 151; Jay, "Regionalism as Geopolitics," *Foreign Affairs* 58, no. 3 (1980): 491–93.

[32]See *New York Times*, October 25, 1981: "Europeans are drifting emotionally out of superpower custody. The prosperous and democratic West Europeans in particular want to control their destiny and avoid the superpower quarrels elsewhere. They do not wish to risk their livelihoods, let alone their lives, for Afghanistan. Merely harping on Soviet perfidy is the worst possible American response. No European believes that Russians intend to march to the North Sea. What Europe's politicians are now hard put to explain is how *European* interests depend on the division of the continent into Soviet and American spheres of influence."

or the Middle East, NATO members were admittedly reluctant to play host to cruise and Pershing II missiles or to neutron bombs; the massive antinuclear demonstrations of 1981 merely reinforced that reluctance. Reagan's first major foreign policy initiative—his proposal to eliminate U.S. and Soviet medium-range missiles from Europe—demonstrated his administration's tardy recognition of the rising anti-American neutralist sentiment in Western Europe.[33] If the allies occasionally shared the administration's sense of outrage at Soviet behavior, they questioned the administration's power to improve the situation with verbal threats and limited sanctions, which would only irritate Kremlin leaders without intimidating them or altering their policies.

What limited Western cohesion from the beginning was the persistent unilateralism in American foreign policy. With the attitude of the rich and powerful, the United States remained careless in its relations with its allies, seldom troubling itself with the assets and liabilities which they represented. As long as the power of the United States assuaged Europe's fears and underwrote its prosperity, the allies accepted a master-servant relationship with Washington. With the recovery of its productivity and confidence, Europe became less tolerant of American Cold War attitudes and corresponding distractions in other regions of the world. Facing profound disagreements on basic approaches to the Soviet problem, the United States less and less sought or received European support for its global reactions. In confronting the Afghan crisis, the Carter administration, even as it proclaimed the unprecedented danger of Soviet aggression, neither acknowledged any defense arrangements with Europe nor made any reference to European interests or commitments. To announce policies for the Middle East, where European interests in oil exceeded those of the United States, in the absence of coalition diplomacy suggested again that the administration did not regard the Soviet invasion of Afghanistan as a very serious matter. Much to Europe's annoyance, President Carter neglected to notify NATO about his decision to postpone the development of the neutron bomb; in 1981 European leaders had complained that the Reagan administration refused to coordinate on its plans to produce and stockpile the neutron bomb. During his visit to Washington early in 1982, Chancellor Schmidt expressed dissatisfaction that Washington, following the imposition of martial law in Poland, embarked on its program of limited economic sanctions without consulting its European

---

[33] For Reagan's peace offensive of November 18, 1981 see *Newsweek,* November 30, 1981, pp. 30–33; Anthony Barbieri, Jr., in Baltimore *Sun,* November 20, 1981; George F. Will in *Sunday Record* (Middletown, NY), November 22, 1981; Hedrick Smith, "How Reagan Rode Out 1981," *New York Times Magazine,* January 10, 1982, pp. 44–45.

allies.[34] Such unilateralism assumed either that American power was too dominant, the Soviet danger too remote, or the interests too negligible to require the attendance of an effective Western coalition.

Fortunately, the decline of the United States, both as a military superpower and as spokesman of the Western world, was no demonstration of national failure. American power was not the only source of stability in the non-Soviet world; neither did the elements of stability exist only as the United States gave them unity and purpose. Instead, they lay essentially in the sovereignty of nations. Amid such advantages the United States succeeded where it mattered. It protected its essential interests in the world's balance of power by promoting the independence of those areas whose independence comprised the international equilibrium. It discouraged attacks on its own soil and on the territories of the world's non-Soviet industrial centers. The Soviet invasion of Afghanistan in no measure threatened the integrity of Britain, Western Europe, Japan, China, or even the oil regions of the Middle East. Kennan, acknowledging the world's fundamental stability, urged Americans not to exaggerate Moscow's military capabilities or the expansiveness of its intentions. "If we insist," he warned, "on viewing [Soviet leaders] as total and incorrigible enemies, consumed only with their fears and hatred of us and dedicated to nothing other than our destruction—that, in the end, is the way we shall assuredly have them, if for no other reason than that our view of them allows for nothing else, either for us or for them."[35]

The emphasis on being strong does not communicate very much about what the country can or should do with that strength in confronting Soviet influence in the Third World. The Soviets gained nothing militarily and little politically from the continuing revolutions that swept the Asian and African continents. The events of the 1970s had shattered the myth of the Communist monolith as the vehicle of Soviet expansionism. For the Kremlin no Third World gain could conceivably counterbalance China's bitter defection from the Soviet camp. Indeed, two-thirds of the Communist-led peoples of the world look to the United States, not to the USSR, for support. If the limited Soviet military presence outside the Soviet bloc remained troublesome, countering policy could have efficacy only in regions where interests were clear

[34]For a critique of American unilateralism see Flora Lewis in *New York Times*, March 23, 1980. The Polish sanctions troubled Helmut Schmidt especially because of his good relations with the Kremlin. See Lewis in "The Week in Review," *New York Times*, January 3, 1982, p. E1. On Schmidt's views of the United States and its anti-Soviet policies see John Vinocur in ibid., March 2, 1980; and Vinocur, "The Schmidt Factor," *New York Times Magazine*, September 21, 1980, pp. 108–15.

[35]Kennan quoted in *New York Times*, November 18, 1981.

and strategic advantages unmistakable. Officials achieve nothing by declaring interests that no other country will take seriously, or that the American people will not sustain with a full national response. The record has demonstrated repeatedly that the interests which will elicit the necessary public support over time are exceedingly limited. However, the restraints, great as they are, have never eliminated the opportunities for sound leadership to define and to protect those interests which historically have underwritten the security and welfare of all Americans.

Articles and Essays by Norman A. Graebner

"Thomas Corwin and the Election of 1848: A Study in Conservative Politics," *Journal of Southern History* 17 (May 1951): 162–79.

"United States Gulf Commerce with Mexico 1822–1848," *Inter-American Economic Affairs* 5 (Summer 1951): 36–51.

"Maritime Factors in the Oregon Compromise," *Pacific Historical Review* 20 (November 1951): 331–45.

"James K. Polk's Wartime Expansionist Policy," East Tennessee Historical Society's *Publications* 23 (1951): 1–14.

"James K. Polk: A Study in Federal Patronage," *Mississippi Valley Historical Review* 38 (March 1952): 613–32.

"Depression and Urban Votes," *Current History* 23 (October 1952): 234–38.

"Polk, Politics, and Oregon," East Tennessee Historical Society's *Publications* 24 (1952): 11–25.

"American Interest in California, 1845," *Pacific Historical Review* 22 (February 1953): 13–27.

"Party Politics and the Trist Mission," *Journal of Southern History* 19 (May 1953): 137–56.

"A Bipartisan Foreign Policy," *Current History* 24 (June 1953): 327–32.

"Political Parties and the Presidency," *Current History* 25 (September 1953): 138–43.

"The American Presidential Tradition," in *Selecting the President: The Twenty-Seventh Discussion and Debate Manual* (1953). Prepared by the National University Extension Association.

"Farm Welfare, 1954," *Current History* 26 (January 1954): 111–16.

"The Farm Issue," *Current History* 27 (October 1954): 249–55.

"Politics in Foreign Policy," *Current History* 28 (January 1955): 7–14.

"Consequences of the China Debate," *World Affairs Quarterly* 26 (October 1955): 255–74.

"The Roots of Our Immigration Policies," *Current History* 29 (November 1955): 285–92.

"New Books on American Foreign Policy," *Current History* 30 (March 1956): 172–75.

"Foreign Policy in '52," *World Affairs Quarterly* 27 (April 1956): 3–26.

"The Changing Nature of the Democratic Party," *Current History* 31 (August 1956): 70–76.

"Foreign Aid and American Policy," *Current History* 31 (October 1956): 212–17.

"The Truman Administration and the Cold War," *Current History* 35 (October 1958): 223–28.

"The West and the Soviet Satellites," *Current History* 36 (April 1959): 193–99.

"The China Illusion," *Current History* 37 (October 1959): 222–27.

"United States: Foreign Relations," *Collier's Year Book, 1960*, for the year 1959. These surveys continued each year until 1975.

"The Cold War: An American View," *International Journal* 15 (Spring 1960): 95–112.

"Alliances and Free World Security," *Current History* 38 (April 1960): 214–19.

"Eisenhower's Popular Leadership," *Current History* 39 (October 1960): 230–36.

"Lincoln and the National Interest," in O. Fritiof Ander, ed., *Lincoln Images: Augustana College Centennial Essays*. Rock Island, IL: Augustana College Library, 1960.

"Northern Diplomacy and European Neutrality," in David Donald, ed., *Why the North Won the Civil War*. Baton Rouge: Louisiana State University Press, 1960.

"Lincoln's Humility," in Ralph G. Newman, ed., *Lincoln for the Ages*. Garden City, NJ: Doubleday and Company, 1960.

"Politics and the Oregon Compromise," *Pacific Northwest Quarterly* 52 (January 1961): 7–14.

"China and Asian Security: An American Dilemma," *International Journal* 16 (Summer 1961): 213–30.

"Nebraska's Missouri River Frontier, 1854–1860," *Nebraska History* 42 (December 1961): 213–35.

"World Report," in *Contemporary Civilization 2*. Chicago: Scott, Foresman and Company, 1961.

"James K. Polk," in Morton Borden, ed., *America's Ten Greatest Presidents*. Chicago: Rand McNally and Company, 1961.

"China: Unanswered Challenge," *Current History* 42 (January 1962): 36–42.

"1848: Southern Politics at the Crossroads," *The Historian* 25 (November 1962): 14–35.

"The United States and the Indochina Crisis: 1954," *World Review* 2 (July 1963): 12–22.

"Can a Nuclear World War Be Avoided?" *The Annals of the American Academy of Political and Social Science* 351 (January 1964): 132–39.

"The United States and European Unity," in Jack D. Dowell, ed., *The Unity of Western Europe*. Pullman: Washington State University Press, 1964.

"U.S. Foreign Policy and Presidential Politics: 1964," *World Review* 4 (March 1965): 14–29.

"Obligation v. Interest in American Foreign Policy," *Australian Journal of Politics and History* 11 (August 1965): 137–49.

"The Limits of Military Aid," *Current History* 50 (June 1966): 353–57.

"United States: Civil War and Reconstruction," in *Encyclopaedia Britannica* (1967).

"American Nominating Politics and the Failure of Consensus: 1968," *Australian Journal of Politics and History* 14 (December 1968): 393–408.

"The University Student and Political Action," *Proceedings of the Fourth Annual Faculty Assembly*. Faculty Senate, State University of New York, 1968, pp. 89–111.

"History and Politics," in Malcolm B. Parsons, ed., *Perspectives in the Study of Politics*. Chicago: Rand McNally and Company, 1968.

"The Uses of Diplomatic History," in Mary B. Humphreys, ed., *Approaches to the Study of International and Intercultural Relations*. Chicago: North Central Association of Colleges and Secondary Schools, 1968.

"Cold War Origins and the Continuing Debate: A Review of Recent Literature," *Journal of Conflict Resolution* 13 (March 1969): 123–32.

"Whither Containment?" *International Journal* 24 (Spring 1969): 246–63.

"Global Containment: The Truman Years," *Current History* 57 (August 1969): 77–83.

"NATO: An Uneasy Alliance," *Current History* 58 (May 1970): 298–303.

"The United States and the Evolution of NATO, 1949–1951," *Teaching History* 4 (May 1970): 15–28.

"The United States and the Soviet Union: The Elusive Peace," *Current History* 59 (October 1970): 193–98.

"The Vitality of Libraries," *Illinois Libraries* 52 (November 1970): 885–90.

"Vietnam and the Intellectual Crisis," *Virginia Journal of International Law* 11 (March 1971): 281–89.

"Germany Between East and West," *Current History* 62 (May 1972): 225–28.

"Diplomacy from the Outside: American Intervention in Vietnam," in Robin Higham, ed., *Civil Wars in the Twentieth Century*. Lexington: University of Kentucky Press, 1972.

"Presidential Politics in a Divided America: 1972," *Australian Journal of Politics and History* 19 (April 1973): 28–47.

"Europe and the Superpowers," *Current History* 64 (April 1973): 145–49.

"World Politics in the New Age," *World Review* 12 (July 1973): 8–21.

"Hoover, Roosevelt, and the Japanese," in Dorothy Borg and Shumpei Okamoto, eds., *Pearl Harbor as History: Japanese-American Relations 1931–1941*. New York: Columbia University Press, 1973.

"How Isolationism Was Nineteenth-Century American Foreign Policy?" In Milton O. Gustafson, ed., *The National Archives and Foreign Relations Research*. Athens: Ohio University Press, 1974.

"Introduction," in Richard Dean Burns and Edward M. Bennett, eds., *Diplomats in Crisis: United States-Chinese-Japanese Relations, 1919–1941*. Santa Barbara, CA: ABC-Clio Press, 1974.

"Japan: Unanswered Challenge, 1931–1941," in Margaret F. Morris and Sandra L. Myres, eds., *Essays on American Foreign Policy*. Austin: University of Texas Press, 1974.

"United States Policy and NATO's Southern Flank," *The Globe* 13 (August 1975): 1–4.

"History, Society, and the Right to Privacy," *Proceedings of the First Rockefeller Archive Center Conference*, 1975, pp. 20–24.

"The Manchurian Crisis, 1931–1932," in Robin Higham, ed., *Intervention or Abstention: The Dilemma of American Foreign Policy*. Lexington: University of Kentucky Press, 1975.

"Presidential Power and Foreign Affairs," in Charles W. Dunn, ed., *The Future of the American Presidency*. Morristown, NJ: General Learning Press, 1975.

An Essay on Freedom. University Park: Pennsylvania State University, 1975.

The Records of Public Officials. New York: American Assembly, 1975.

"European Interventionism and the Crisis of 1862," *Journal of the Illinois State Historical Society* 69 (February 1976): 35–45.

"Henry Kissinger and American Foreign Policy: A Contemporary Appraisal," *Australian Journal of Politics and History* 22 (April 1976): 7–22.

"America's Search for World Order," *Virginia Quarterly Review* 52 (Spring 1976): 161–82.

"Christianity and Democracy: Tocqueville's Views of Religion in America," *Journal of Religion* 56 (July 1976): 263–73.

"America in the World," in William T. Alderson, ed., *American Issues: Understanding Who We Are*. Nashville: American Association for State and Local History, 1976.

"The Spirit of Expansion: 'Fifty-four Forty or Fight,' " in Henry Steele Commager, ed., *The American Destiny: An Illustrated Bicentennial History of the United States*. London: Danbury Press, 1976.

"Thomas Corwin and the Sectional Crisis," *Ohio History* 86 (Autumn 1977): 229–47.

"The Limits of Victory," *Studies in Modern European History and Culture* 3 (1977): 75–93.

"Morgenthau as Historian," in Kenneth Thompson and Robert J. Myers, eds., *Truth and Tragedy: A Tribute to Hans Morgenthau*. Washington, DC: New Republic Book Company, 1977.

"Changing Perceptions of China Since Midcentury," in John Chay, ed., *The Problems and Prospects of American-East Asian Relations*. Boulder, CO: Westview Press, 1977.

"Lessons of the Mexican War," *Pacific Historical Review* 47 (August 1978): 325–42.

"Government Without Consensus," *Virginia Quarterly Review* 54 (Autumn 1978): 648–64.

"The Apostle of Progress," in Cullom Davis, Charles B. Strozier, and Rebecca Monroe Veach, eds., *The Public and the Private Lincoln*. Carbondale: Southern Illinois University Press, 1979.

"Lutherans and Politics," in John E. Groh and Robert H. Smith, eds., *The Lutheran Church in North American Life*. St. Louis: Clayton Publishing House, 1979.

"Teaching and Learning at Oxford," *British Association of American Studies Newsletter*, no. 41 (January 1980): 2–3.

"The Mexican War: A Study in Causation," *Pacific Historical Review* 49 (August 1980): 405–26.

"Moralism and American Foreign Relations," in Kenneth W. Thompson, ed., *Herbert Butterfield: The Ethics of History and Politics*. Washington, DC: University Press of America, 1980.

"Human Rights and Foreign Policy: The Historic Connection," in Kenneth W. Thompson, ed., *The Moral Imperatives of Human Rights: A World Survey*. Washington, DC: University Press of America, 1980.

Roosevelt and the Search for a European Policy 1937–1939. Oxford: Clarendon Press, 1980. (Harmsworth Lecture)

"From Carter to Reagan: An Uneasy Transition," *Australian Journal of Politics and History* 27, no. 3 (1981): 304–29.

"The United States and NATO, 1953–69," in Lawrence S. Kaplan and Robert W. Clawson, eds., *NATO After Thirty Years*. Wilmington, DE: Scholarly Resources, 1981.

"Between the Wars: The Intellectual Climate of American Foreign Relations," in John N. Schacht, ed., *Three Faces of Midwestern Isolationism*. Iowa City: Center for the Study of the Recent History of the United States, 1981.

"America's Limited Power in the Contemporary World," Phi Beta Kappa, *Key Reporter* 47 (Spring 1982): 2–5.

"The Decline of America: A Countering Appraisal," *Virginia Quarterly Review* 58 (Summer 1982): 369–91.

"Coming to Terms with Reality," *Naval War College Review* 36 (September–October 1983): 91–113.

"Public Opinion and Foreign Policy: A Pragmatic View," in Don C. Piper and Ronald J. Terchek, eds., *Interactions: Foreign Policy and Public Policy*. Washington, DC: American Enterprise Institute for Public Policy Research, 1983.

"Divided America in Search of Security." Reynolds Lecture delivered at Davidson College, October 18, 1982. Published by Davidson College, 1983.

"Western Disunity: Its Challenge to America." Reynolds Lecture delivered at Davidson College, October 19, 1982. Published by Davidson College, 1983.

Adams and Jefferson in Europe, 1783–1789. Three essays. The 1982 Carroll Lectures, Mary Baldwin College. Published by Mary Baldwin College, 1984.

Index